ON THE EDGE OF THE WORLD

ON THE EDGE

Richard Longstreth

OF THE WORLD

four architects in San Francisco

at the turn of the century

UNIVERSITY OF CALIFORNIA PRESS

Berkeley · Los Angeles · London

This book is a print-on-demand volume. It is manufactured using toner in place of ink. Type and images may be less sharp than the same material seen in traditionally printed University of California Press editions.

University of California Press
Berkeley and Los Angeles, California

University of California Press, Ltd.
London, England

© 1983 by the Architectural History Foundation and
The Massachusetts Institute of Technology

First California Paperback Printing 1998

Library of Congress Cataloging-in-Publication Data

Longstreth, Richard W.
    On the edge of the world : four architects in San Francisco at the
turn of the century / Richard W. Longstreth.
        p.   cm.
    Originally published: New York : Architectural History Foundation ;
Cambridge, Mass. : MIT Press, c1983, in series: American monograph
series.
    Includes bibliographical references and index.
    ISBN 0-520-21415-3 (alk. paper)
    1. Eclecticism in architecture—California—San Francisco.
    2. Architecture, Modern—19th century—California—San Francisco.
    3. San Francisco (Calif.)—Buildings, structures, etc.   I. Title.
NA735.S35L66   1998
720′.9794′61—dc21   97-36898
                                                          CIP

Designed by Gilbert Etheredge

Printed in the United States of America

The paper used in this publication meets the minimum
requirements of ANSI/NISO Z39.48-1992 (R 1997)
(Permanence of paper)

CONTENTS

ACKNOWLEDGMENTS

This study began as a dissertation on the work of Ernest Coxhead and Willis Polk under the direction of Norma Evenson, David Gebhard, Robert Judson Clark, and Stephen Tobriner (University of California at Berkeley, 1977). Their advice and encouragement was of enormous benefit in realizing the project and in pursuing the topic further. William Jordy and Harold Kirker kindly read the text and offered many valuable suggestions. Others have been most helpful in scrutinizing this manuscript: David Bell and William Miller read preliminary drafts of the first chapter; Esther McCoy reviewed the material on Maybeck, as did Rosemarie Bletter on Gottfried Semper. Robert Judson Clark, Thomas Hines, Loren Partridge, Kevin Starr, and David Streatfield read the entire manuscript. Their comments generated many necessary improvements in both its form and content.

Numerous people have been generous with information during the course of my research. John Beach, who has been investigating Coxhead's career for over a decade, gave me free access to his extensive collection of material. All students of California architecture owe a special debt to David Gebhard, whose pioneering work has opened many doors and laid an essential foundation for further work. Kenneth Cardwell graciously shared his notes on Maybeck with me. Kevin Starr provided an abundance of citations on important but obscure material pertaining to the region's cultural development. J. Mordaunt Crook, Mark Girouard, and Alastair Service gave valuable insights on Coxhead's work in relation to that of his English contemporaries.

Descendants of Coxhead, Maybeck, Polk, Schweinfurth, and other San Francisco architects and artists supplied information otherwise unobtainable. They include: Helen Coxhead Strong (Coxhead's granddaughter), Jacomena Maybeck (Maybeck's daughter-in-law), Frederick Barreda Sherman (Polk's nephew), Sheila and Harold Mack (Polk's and Page Brown's great-grandchildren), the late Mrs. Pembroke Woods (Schweinfurth's niece), Gladys Tilden (Douglas Tilden's daughter), Catherine Porter Short (Bruce Porter's daughter), and the late Merodine Keeler McIntyre (Charles Keeler's daughter). Descendants of clients have also been of great assistance: the late Mrs. Robert Bowie, Loy Chamberlin, Marion Gorrill, F. Bourn Hayne, Elizabeth Knight Smith, Mr. and Mrs. Scott Knight Smith, George Livermore, Mrs. Robert Morrow, Marguerite Murdock, the late Britton Rey, the late Mrs. Leon Roos, and Jane van Keulen.

Chesley Bonestell and the late Walter Steilberg deserve special thanks. Bonestell, who worked for Polk during the 1910s, spent many hours answering questions and offering a detailed account of the architect's personality and practice. Steilberg, who knew Maybeck and many others of his generation, was likewise generous with his time and instructive in his comments. The late Edward Hussey, who worked for Maybeck in the 1930s, provided additional insights, as did several former Polk employees: Michael Goodman, Emily Michaels, Lefler Miller, and John O'Shea. Together, these people provided a picture of the Bay Area during the early twentieth century that no written account could supply.

Others have helped in ways too numerous to mention: Joseph Baird, Gunther Barth, Anthony Bruce, Edward Clarke, Jennifer and Robert Clements, Michael Corbett, Richard Crook, Mrs. Lockwood de Forest, Joan Draper, Mrs. George Eastham, Sturla Einarsson, Joseph Esherick, Elliott Evans, Willis Forbes, Frederick Gleason, Wheaton Holden, John Jacobus, Mrs. Walter Jennings, Steven Levin, Frank Littleford, Donald McLaughlin, Charles Moore, Skip Norfolk, Francis Rapp, Dimitri Shipounoff, Mrs. Max Stern, Allan Temko, Elizabeth Thompson, Mrs. Othmar Tobisch, Paul Turner, and Helen van Cleve Park. I am further indebted to the people who kindly allowed me to study, photograph, and measure their houses.

My gratitude also goes to the staffs of the following institutions: Bancroft Library and College of Environmental Design Library, U.C. Berkeley; California Historical Society; California Room, San Francisco Public Library; Society of California Pioneers; History Room, Wells Fargo Bank; California State Library; California Division of Mines and Geology; California Room, Oakland Public Library; San Mateo County Historical Association; Episcopal Diocese of Northern California; Belvedere Land Company; Los Angeles Public Library; Henry Huntington Memorial Library; State Historical Society of Wisconsin; Missouri Valley Room, Kansas City Public Library; Missouri Historical Society; Library of the Art Institute of Chicago; Cayuga County Historical Society; Adirondack Museum; Princeton University Archives; Avery Architectural and Fine Arts Library, Columbia

University; Royal Academy Library; and Royal Institute of British Architects Library.

Portions of my work were supported by two faculty research awards from Kansas State University and a grant from the Ludwig Vogelstein Foundation. Kim Spurgeon Fly made superb measured drawings from my often sketchy field notes. Gene Guerrant at K.S.U. and the Camera Corner and Herrington-Olson in Oakland deserve credit for the meticulous printing of photographs. Carol Knepper and Dorothy Klein did the expert typing, often at a moment's notice.

Enough appreciation cannot be given to Robert Stern, who supported the project, and provided criticism and guidance. The staff of the Architectural History Foundation—Victoria Newhouse, Julianne Griffin, and Karen Banks—have helped in every way to make an arduous task a pleasure. One could not ask for a more sympathetic and efficient publisher. Finally, I am, as always, grateful to my wife for her interest, enthusiasm, and enduring patience while my thoughts were preoccupied with things in San Francisco.

A note on the floor plans

Measurements of buildings in their current state provided the basis for many of the plans illustrated in the text. Measurements for Figs. 86, 99, 103, 121, and 137 were made by the author with the assistance of John Beach, Floyd Campbell, and Steven Levin. Those for Figs. 66, 115, 122, and 244 were made by students in the College of Environmental Design, U.C., Berkeley; those for Fig. 145 by Skip Norfolk. Figures 107, 172, and 249 were made from working drawings, the first in possession of John Beach, the latter two in the CED Documents Collection. Measurements for Figs. 81, 108, and 131 were taken from other archival sources. Old photographs and examination of the building fabric provided the basis for the reconstructions. In addition, Marguerite Murdock, Edward Clarke, and the late Merodine Keeler McIntyre provided invaluable assistance for the reconstructions shown in Figs. 81, 131, and 244, respectively.

FOREWORD

This book presents the work of four very talented architects who brought the sense of a great moment to California, to what seemed then the Edge of the World. It now seems more the midst of the world, but issues faced by the architects described in this book are very much of the moment. How are we to respond to a place and a time that are not matched? (What time, or for that matter what place, have been matched?) We are forever destined to suppose at once that we are unique and that if only we would look closely enough there would be a precedent that would set the world in order. The balance shifts, experience tempers, society oscillates in its role, and architects become *agents provocateurs* of the society's intentions.

Polk, Coxhead, Schweinfurth, and Maybeck arrived in California at the tail end of one of the most optimistic moments in the history of American architecture. It was a moment still illuminated by reflections from the vigor and inventiveness, the explorative certainty of Richardson's work, yet newly lit from within by a quest for cultivation, for recognizable guides to propriety. Though the propriety sought was of a grander, more far-reaching scope than any that stems from mere neighborly conventions.

These men, this generation, our predecessors sought at first to explore, to reach beyond the confines of common expectations, and to create buildings that would suit their place especially—not by inventing *de novo,* but by studying, absorbing, adapting, modifying, bringing into new relationships, distorting as pragmatics required, and giving alternative vision to all they had learned and experienced in buildings of the past. It is this explorative work that captures our eye, that rekindles the flame in those of us who hope still to fuse the improvisational and the precisely guided.

Polk, Coxhead, and Schweinfurth ended their careers victimized by tradition. Maybeck, the latest to bloom, stands as the embodier *par excellence* of freewheeling invention, an adventurer in foreign lands who made the familiar seem magical by superimposing the features of exotic places on the precise realities of simple buildings and present acts.

Longstreth's sympathetic rendering of the times, of the related but independent inquiries conducted by these four men, and of the practical realities of their quest for professional opportunities puts before us the dynamic tension between precedence and adaptability, confidence and acquiescence, loony inventiveness and stifling decorum.

Some will side with the forces of rectitude and welcome the retreat from naive exuberance, others will pine for the golden age of experimentation and hope that our century holds yet another just around the corner. Still others will simply take heed that within even fairly short lifetimes the balance between their impulses shifts and that the most tightly balanced works are the ones that sustain our attention most, that neither bore nor befuddle. Such works most often serve, as well, to fit the problem at hand and to convey that the human spirit both invents and replicates for good purposes.

Right now we are experiencing the play all over again. Parallels to the present moment are almost too evident; we must step back from supposing that the parallels may lead us to predict the outcome of present stylistic explorations, or confirm that they are apt. Some may be, but the moments we face are very different. It is after all the midst of the world, not any longer the edge, and the wilderness we face is shaped like a mushroom, not like a horizon.

Donlyn Lyndon

ON THE EDGE OF THE WORLD

INTRODUCTION

California "is in many respects the most striking [state] in the whole Union, and has more than any other the character of a great country, capable of standing alone in the world." That observation, made by James Bryce in *The American Commonwealth* (1888), reflected a widespread attitude toward the Golden State that had existed since the mid-nineteenth century.[1] The notion of California's distinctiveness was fostered by visitor and resident alike. Isolated, wild, abundant in natural beauty and resources, unbound by tradition, California was seen as the land of infinite potential, a land that engendered independence of spirit and action. The California dream was in fact the American dream intensified, and it became an incantation that left its imprint on every aspect of the state's culture.

The vision of California as a new Eden was matched by the stigma of its isolation. Californians were proud of, but also sensitive about, their location in the West—the Far West—far removed from other, well-settled regions. In the late nineteenth century, after most vestiges of frontier culture had disappeared, California's frontier reputation lingered while the populace yearned to be in the mainstream. Boosterish claims proliferated because many people, like Bryce, believed that California was destined for greatness. But the sheer extravagance of these pronouncements also connoted an underlying insecurity. Californians were immigrants, and, as in all such societies, customs and standards were imported. Most fields of endeavor were characterized by emulation of practices elsewhere. The self-conscious pursuit of distinction coexisted with the self-conscious desire to be equated with recognized centers of culture.

This dilemma was summarized by San Francisco writer Gelett Burgess in a 1902 essay, "On the Edge of the World." He began with an oblique analogy between California and outposts of the British Empire.

The colonial who realizes his poverty of artistic and intellectual resources . . . must in self-defense and to compensate for his isolation, make friends with the world at large. . . . To avoid the reproach of provincialism he studies the vagrom hints from the great centers of thought and watches eagerly for the first signs of new growth in fads, fashions, art and politics. . . . The British colonial is more British than the Englishman at home.

1

Burgess considered this pattern foolish: "It is best to follow the style of one's locality." Then he reminded his audience that catering to the latest fashion was not limited to the provinces. Residents of major cities were scarcely less fickle, according to Burgess. In fact, living in an outpost carried certain advantages: "Waste not pity upon him at the edge of the world." Pioneer society was virile: "The reddest blood has flowed in the veins of the pioneer ever since the first migration. He does things rather than talks of things others have done—he knows life, even if he knows not Ibsen." Besides being uninhibited, these people now enjoyed rapid communication with other parts of the globe. In the modern era, "distance is swept away and no land is really isolate." He concluded that these conditions afforded great promise: "The pioneer lives . . . above all distinctions of time, at once in the past, the present and the future."[2]

Burgess was neither calling for a return to California's frontier days nor adding his voice to the chorus of local boosters, but he did recognize the state's potential. California might not be a new Eden,

1. Coxhead, Polk, and friends at "Stagden," Polk's apartment in Oakland, ca. 1890. (CED Documents Collection)

but it could partake of what the world had to offer while cultivating its own presence. Events that had occurred in San Francisco over the previous decade gave rise to this optimism. The city was now attracting talented young artists, architects, and writers, including Burgess himself. For the first time, local residents sustained, and even encouraged, these artists' creative efforts. Culturally, the region was beginning to come of age.

Among the most dramatic and conspicuous evidence of this maturation lay in the field of architecture. Until the turn of the century, design practices tended to adhere to norms established elsewhere as closely as resources and abilities permitted.[3] Burgess's generation loathed this legacy of the recent past because to them it represented the hallmark of ostentatious provincialism. A new course for local work was established during the 1890s, in large part by four architects of this generation: Ernest Coxhead, Willis Polk, A. C. Schweinfurth, and Bernard Maybeck (Figs. 1–5). Energetic and eager to experiment, they looked to "the world at large" for ideas, drawing from a wide

2. Polk (second from right) with Karl Bitter and Ernest Peixotto to his right at the Bohemian Grove, ca. 1912. (California Historical Society)

range of historical and contemporary precedents and interpreting them in new ways. Local factors, such as topography, cultural interests, and vernacular building traditions, also left an imprint on their designs, imparting a specificity evident in few earlier buildings.

Their work no doubt would have been quite different had it been designed in the East or Midwest; however, it did not constitute a new style or regional mode, as popular thought has maintained in recent years.[4] The distinctiveness of their contributions stemmed from the strength and individuality of each architect's talent. Their inclusive, urbane, and often unorthodox approach became an important model for subsequent work in the region. San Francisco has never generated fundamentally new ideas in art. But since the 1890s, a number of its designers have given such new and significant forms to ideas that the city may be considered a center of innovative architectural activity in the United States.[5] This work has not been the product of a separate culture any more than it was in Boston, Philadelphia, or Chicago. Rather, the work of San Francisco architects stands on its

3. Coxhead with his daughter in the garden of their San Francisco house, ca. 1900. (Courtesy John Beach)

4

4. Schweinfurth and unidentified draftsman in A. Page Brown's office, San Francisco, ca. 1893. (Northeastern University, courtesy Wheaton Holden)

own merits as a vital part of American architecture. Burgess's hope has seen fruition.

Several introductory texts have been written on the turn-of-the-century architecture of the San Francisco Bay Area.[6] Rather than following the pattern of these studies, I have concentrated on the work of Coxhead, Polk, Schweinfurth, and Maybeck during the 1890s so that a seminal period of creative endeavor may be explored in depth. Beyond a basic documentary objective, the book seeks to investigate broader topics: the nature of eclecticism as it was practiced around the turn of the century, the diffusion of ideas from the East and from Europe to San Francisco, and the impact the Bay Area had on design. Coverage of the architects' work is selective, focusing on examples that give the most insight into these topics.

The four architects moved to San Francisco in 1889–1890, bringing with them the benefits of training in Europe's foremost professional schools and prominent East Coast offices. They were

5. Maybeck and his family in front of their Grove Street house in Berkeley, photographed in the early 1900s. (Courtesy Jacomena Maybeck)

taught academic principles that had long governed design in France and that were beginning to have a consequential effect on practice in the United States and England. They sought to implant these principles on western soil, and once settled on the West Coast they never waivered in their commitment. Yet they arrived at the onset of their independent careers without sufficient experience to have developed fixed ways. Since they were geographically removed from the architectural mainstream, they felt a sense of freedom, more freedom perhaps than they would have exercised in older cities. San Francisco provided both independence and receptive patrons to sustain their efforts.

Coxhead and Polk were the key figures in setting the tone for change during the early 1890s. Foremost among their concerns was to demonstrate that remote San Francisco was capable of matching the architectural standards of great cultural centers. But in pursuing this aim, they avoided following the example of any one person or place. Diverse in vocabulary and character, their buildings resist easy categorization. Coxhead and Polk experimented with vernacular and high-style precedents, rustic and urban imagery, cheap and costly materials, picturesque and formal compositions, and intimate and grand spaces.

6

Yet their oeuvre was not an encyclopedic register of current modes. Each architect possessed the confidence and ability to assimilate ideas and mine diverse sources in developing a manner uniquely his own.

Schweinfurth held the same basic allegiances, and likewise nurtured a broad-based, personal style. However, his primary interest lay in creating work that would be considered distinctly Californian, an interest stimulated by the recognition of the state's Hispanic heritage. His approach was far from parochial, as he drew from a spectrum of building traditions, few of which had direct ties to California or even to the United States. He practiced independently for only about four years, his career cut short by an early death. His work had little influence in the region; his legacy is a collection of unique buildings, not the inception of a new mode.

Struggling to give his ideas focus and direction, Maybeck designed very little on his own until the late 1890s. In the process he learned much from his San Francisco colleagues. Like Coxhead and Polk, he gave no evidence of striving for distinctly regional architecture, but his work was so unique that it came to be seen as a regional phenomenon. As such, it has influenced many architects in San Francisco up to the present day. Maybeck remains the figure with whom Bay Area design is most often identified. However, of the four architects, his oeuvre is the most diverse and his designs the most cosmopolitan and sophisticated in their theoretical base. His buildings offer a rich synopsis of the multifaceted complexion that distinguished efforts of this period. He was "at once in the past, the present and the future." Of the four architects, Maybeck has received by far the most scholarly attention; hence, this study focuses on important aspects of his career's formative stage that have heretofore received little attention.

San Francisco attracted other talented designers during the 1890s, but their buildings tended to be more derivative and conventional. Only A. Page Brown is singled out from among these architects, since both Polk and Schweinfurth were important figures in his office. For a brief period Brown led the reorientation of San Francisco architecture from the Victorian to the academic sphere.

Primary source material on the four architects before the twentieth century is scarce. Their office records and personal papers have mostly been destroyed.[7] Polk was the only one to commit his thoughts to writing on more than a few occasions, and then it was never about his own designs. Associates and friends have not left many records either. Thus, the work itself must serve as the major document. To broaden the perspective, I have relied on contemporary literature and related archival material. Collectively, these data shed light on the circumstances surrounding many projects and on the professional and cultural contexts in which the architects worked.

The region is an important focus of this book, as are the relationships between San Francisco architecture and comparable work in the East and in Europe. Coxhead, Polk, Schweinfurth, and Maybeck were key figures in introducing a new movement to the West Coast, one that flourished there under their aegis. Since the movement has only begun to be assessed from a historical perspective, the first chapter outlines some of its major characteristics, offering a broad introduction to the chapters that follow.

I

ACADEMIC ECLECTICISM:
The Question of Style

The American architect is passing into his incipient Renaissance, copying less from the masters he has studied and reveres, and dropping the word style from his practice.

Bruce Price, *Scribner's Magazine*, July 1890

It is probable that we shall never again have a distinctive style, but what I hope and believe we shall someday possess is something akin to a style—so flexible that it can be made to meet every practical and constructive need, so beautiful and complete as to harmonize the heretofore discordant notes of Art and Science, and to challenge comparison with the wonders of past ages, yet malleable enough to be moulded at the designer's will.

Bertram Goodhue, *Craftsman*, June 1905

To get a style by avoiding a style—that is the paradox of American architecture.

Robert Andrews, Boston Architectural Club. *Catalogue*, 1904

ECLECTIC ARCHITECTURE created in the United States between the 1880s and 1930s was characterized by a new degree of inclusiveness that represented a major shift in the way Americans approached design. Architects of that period sought to foster a gradual evolution in their art by drawing from a wide range of historical precedents, modifying and combining them according to contemporary needs. In the process, they rejected the nineteenth-century conception of style. They believed in an all-encompassing order, unconfined by traditional stylistic parameters and based on broad, abstract principles. Proponents of this approach were adamant about forging links to the creative spirit of past eras. Neither their ideas nor their methods were revolutionary; however, their liberal perspective of the past and their flexibility in adapting its lessons resulted in a substantive departure from earlier phases of eclecticism. The paradox identified by Boston architect Robert Andrews was thus generated by embracing historicity and innovation in more or less equal measure and by expressing these dual values in numerous ways.

9

This approach to design is perhaps best described as "academic eclecticism" and the resultant tendency as "the academic movement."[1] The aim was academic in encouraging architectural development through a scholarly knowledge of the past. The method was academic in the importance given to formal education as a means of acquiring that knowledge. The movement's origins were academic in having emerged from a system of instruction and practice that had been cultivated in France since the seventeenth century.

Academic eclecticism was introduced to San Francisco by young architects who came to the remote metropolis around 1890, among whom Ernest Coxhead, Willis Polk, A. C. Schweinfurth, and Bernard Maybeck were the most talented. All four men received their training in the East and abroad during the 1880s, when the movement was in its formative stage. Thereafter, they became key agents in the movement's diffusion, being among the first designers to champion its cause on the West Coast. The fact that they were far removed from New York and other cities, where academic eclecticism was strongest, seems to have deepened their commitment. With missionary zeal, they hoped to eradicate the city's retardataire architectural milieu by introducing a new sense of order and purpose.

But isolation also encouraged independence. The four architects considered California to be a special place, filled with energy and promise. Their work offers ingenious responses to the local landscape and culture. Rather than creating a new mode, a Bay Region style, each experimented with myriad forms of expression, looking to the world at large for ideas. Collectively, their designs embody the paradox of academic eclecticism to a degree seldom matched elsewhere at the turn of the century. Coxhead, Polk, Schweinfurth, and Maybeck created buildings that are of intrinsic merit, formative products of the region's maturing culture, and spirited interpretations of the academic movement's ideals. Examination of those ideals and of some of the seminal ways in which they were manifested provides an essential perspective for understanding the endeavors of these architects.

Many proponents of academic eclecticism believed that the future would bring a significant change in architectural expression and that they were laying the groundwork for this transformation. Yet they were also certain that such developments must be evolutionary; that is, external circumstances would establish the general framework of growth and change in design. Proponents asserted that these changes had always occurred gradually. They considered attempts to accelerate this process counterproductive, and felt that the result was a chaotic spectrum of individual gestures. Thus, the academic movement's champions expressed disdain for most previous nineteenth-century architecture. They regarded both the romantic pursuit of reviving past styles and the High Victorian quest for a new (and in the United States, an American) style to have interrupted the natural course of evolution, denying architecture any progress. The "fundamental blunder" of revivalism, insisted A.D.F. Hamlin, one of the movement's leading protagonists, lay in its attempt to restore "the architecture of a bygone age." He believed that revivalist architects' aims were "accomplished if the details . . . used could each claim an exact historic precedent . . . no matter how incongruous with the spirit and methods of that age might be the plan and construction of the building."[2] The search for a new style was considered even worse. In imitating past forms, revivalists might produce tasteful design; however, when the principles of the past were discarded, the results lacked cultural meaning. The inclinations of each individual were the only guide, and the self-consciousness that characterized their work condemned design to the realm of fashion, discarded as quickly as initiated.

Victorian architects had also relied on the concept of evolution to support their call for a nineteenth-century style. Because conditions of modern society were changing so radically and with such speed, they believed it was imperative to develop new forms. Using a similar argument, proponents of an American style asserted that circumstances in the United States were sufficiently different from those in Europe to warrant new and distinctly national modes of expression.[3] Advocates of academic eclecticism, however, rejected such deterministic notions. As others had manipulated evolutionary thought to justify the search for a new style, so now proponents of this movement employed it to help substantiate the desire for order and stability.

Academic eclecticism sought to reestablish a continuity with the past, forging a new link, after the "natural" development of architecture had been broken by Victorian "excesses." The interaction between the forces of continuity and change was seen to constitute the essence of the evolutionary process and to provide the basis for innovative work. The drive for continuity with the past was not intended as a retreat to established formulas, but rather to set standards that would guide creative endeavor. Ralph Adams Cram phrased this belief in his typically messianic way: "We are building for *now*. . . . It is art, not archaeology, that drives us. *From* the past, not *in* the past. We must return for the fire of life to other centuries, since a night [i. e., the nineteenth century] has intervened. . . . We must return, but we may not remain. It is the present that demands us. . . ."[4]

Hamlin, Cram, and many others recognized that current conditions were not wholly analogous to those of earlier periods. They considered innovation in the past to have been an unconscious process, with change in large part resulting from external factors. Given the enormous amount of historical information that had been uncovered during the last hundred years, that state of innocence was admittedly lost forever. They regarded simple determinism as impossible because the new awareness of history offered myriad choices to the designer. Proponents of the academic movement felt that their immediate predecessors had been overwhelmed by the discovery of the past and had drawn from precedent indiscriminately. Choice should not be a "license," but a privilege. In developing this faculty, an architect must acquire a thorough understanding of history. The architect must become a scholar, investigating both the buildings and their sociocultural context in detail.

The notion of scholarly training for architects had gained increasing stature in Europe during the nineteenth century, and was used to advance both revivalist and determinist causes. By the 1880s, however, the emphasis had shifted to gaining a detailed knowledge of all major periods in order to make a wide range of critical choices. Lacking this perspective, it was argued, the architect's use of history was limited to pastiches from the past, selected for appearance or association without regard to either original or contemporary contexts. Sufficient quantities of scholarly material, drawn from publications and travel abroad, had only recently come within the reach of enough American architects for such an objective to be realistic.

Interest in a number of historical periods had been a basic component of eclecticism since the early nineteenth century, but both the great range of precedent studied and the emphasis given to impartiality were part of the new academic approach. Most architects, at least in England and the United States, had regarded work of the distant past as the only precedent worthy of emulation, and had considered the cinquecento as the endpoint of historical legitimacy.[5] By the 1880s, however, all periods up to the beginning of the nineteenth century were respected. Greater interest was expressed in the buildings of countries out of the mainstream of architectural development, in minor monuments, and in vernacular architecture. Proponents of academic eclecticism became more concerned with the enormous diversity found in historic precedent. Hamlin advised, "Let us be

12

catholic in our criticism and study of architecture, and we shall find our resources of design wonderfully enlarged and enriched."[6] Architects were tired of hearing the arguments about the superiority of one period over another that had raged in Europe, and to a certain degree in the United States, during the previous decades. No consensus had been reached in these debates, as both Gothicists and classicists had constructed convincing rationales. The episode was felt to have obscured the essential point: the principles of good design are universal, irrespective of the ways in which they are applied at a particular time. "Gone are the days of the 'Battle of the Styles,' " declared Cram. "Architecture is much bigger than its forms . . . the fundamental laws are the same for all good styles."[7]

Veneration of the "principles" or "laws" of design appears throughout the literature of the period, but neither architects nor critics ever delineated them precisely.[8] The judgmental criteria for good architecture were considered to be subjective, measured through experienced intuition rather than theoretical constructs. Learning the principles required a sensitivity developed through study of numerous examples from all major historical periods. Although these principles were deemed universal, they had been applied in a variety of ways in different times and places. Obtaining a comprehensive view of the past supposedly could increase the architect's faculty for critical analysis of abstract qualities, which could then be applied to new work regardless of changes in requirements and taste. The aim of the movement was academic in a liberal sense of the term: developing a broad base of knowledge founded on precedent in order to formulate solutions for contemporary problems in a rational manner. Far from constituting a theory of design, these principles were a series of loosely defined attributes, based on interpretations of the past, that could lend authority to architecture without inhibiting its growth and change.

Among the qualities most frequently cited by the proponents of academic eclecticism as essential for good design was "unity." In contrast to the visual bombast of Victorian architecture, in which the parts often received emphasis at the expense of the whole, it was believed that all elements should act in concert to form a logical and coherent statement. Herbert Croly, editor of the *Architectural Record* from 1900 to 1906, was one of many critics who stressed that "the most important point is not that certain forms be used, but that the strictly architectural merit of complete form should be resident . . . dominating expression, materials, proportion and style."[9] Through a carefully ordered composition, each component, regardless of size or

13

importance, could contribute to and be a logical outgrowth of the overall conception. It was equally important that this sense of unity encompass the decorative program and grounds of a building and govern the organization of urban schemes.[10] Not surprisingly, classical models were most often cited to illustrate these points; however, other precedents were no less relevant. Witness Cram's declaration that: "In good Gothic [architecture] the relation of all the parts to each other and to the whole, the subservience of every feature to the total effect is imperative."[11]

The attribute of "simplicity" also received frequent mention. The term did not imply abstinence from complex uses of form and space or from rich embellishments. Rather, it denoted those attributes that made a unified composition appear to have been designed effortlessly.[12] Simplicity also was used to differentiate the restrained character of new work relative to the "theatrical posturing" of Victorian architecture with its profusion of novel forms and ornamental motifs. Similarly, "dignity" rather than ostentation should distinguish architecture. "Refinement" of elements entailed eloquence of expression, as opposed to the allegedly "crude" detailing of earlier nineteenth-century design. "Repose" was essential for the whole and for its parts, in contrast to the Victorian tendency toward agitation.[13]

The ultimate aim of the architect, many proponents believed, should be "beauty." Defending this stand in the early stage of the movement, Mariana van Rensselaer offered an explanation:

Architectural beauty is not an extrinsic, superficial thing, depending . . . on ornamental features, but is . . . bound up with the very attainment of "firmness" and "commoditie." The really vital beauty of an architectural work consists in its clear expression of these two qualities, and of the material way in which the parts are framed; for architecture is, like every other art, *first of all a means of expression.*

She rebuked Ruskin's theory that beauty is synonymous with ornament, and also the notion of structural determinism advanced by Viollet-le-Duc:

Some critics go much too far. They demand that a building should not only be truthfully expressive, but should be this in a precise, particular, and complete way, even to the possible detriment of beauty.[14]

Once again, the strategy entailed achieving a balance between divergent forces. Hamlin was quite specific on the matter:

14

The demands of use and beauty not infrequently pull in opposite directions. . . . [They] are independent of each other . . . however . . . when they coexist in one design, so that the perfect structure serves at once the ends of use and beauty, each enhances the other. . . . the true purpose of architecture . . . is *to harmonize the independent and oft-conflicting claims of use and beauty,* so that the very forms devised to meet practical needs in the most perfect manner shall also satisfy the human craving for beauty, grace, refinement.[15]

This marriage of opposites was seen as the art of architectural design and helps explain why the architect was considered an artist first, above other professional responsibilities. Fulfilling utilitarian needs required technical expertise; expressing those needs cogently and imbuing them with vitality was viewed as an art.

Beyond creating beautiful objects, the artist was seen as a civilizing agent whose work mitigated the effects of a materialistic society. Croly explained that art "will enrich and refine this poor coarse, sensuous life. . . . Under its influence you will gain an eager, searching, selective, correct eyesight . . . the whole world will become expressive . . . instead of being merely arid and blank. Sensation will begin to have meaning." At the same time, this art could not be elusive, "the patented possession of a cultured few."[16] The champions of beauty felt that no matter how sophisticated a design might be, it must also be understandable by the public.

These ideas were based upon the instructional philosophy of the Ecole des Beaux Arts and the approach to design practiced by many French architects. The notions of maintaining continuity with the past; of balancing tradition and innovation; of studying the best historical examples from all periods in order to learn the principles of good design; of achieving unity, order, and simplicity through careful, rigorous compositional techniques; of striving for a rational synthesis of beauty and utility; and of the architect's role as an artist were all prevalent French attitudes during the later part of the nineteenth century. The Ecole was largely responsible for the belief in America that academic instruction provided the best means for the initial study of the past, for understanding its "principles," and for learning how these lessons might be applied to contemporary situations. The Ecole gave impetus to the establishment of architectural schools in the United States and provided the primary model for developing their curricula. The basic concepts of good design advanced by the Ecole were accepted; however, by the 1890s, considerable debate arose over the degree to which this Franco-American bond was productive.

The harshest criticism directed at the Ecole charged that its methods were too far removed from the conditions under which actual buildings were designed. Others felt that the system fostered undue conservatism among its students. Even some of the Ecole's staunchest supporters expressed dismay over the trend to employ current French mannerisms in American designs. The substance of its ideology, not the exposure to current French modes, was generally felt to constitute the essential value of the institution.[17] An underlying concern was that design should respond to national conditions rather than simply imitate European precedent. In 1908, Hamlin went so far as to suggest that attending the Ecole was no longer necessary. American schools, he asserted, now offered training of equal caliber: "They have adopted from the French school all that has been found in its methods to be best fitted for American conditions . . . [and] must in the future become increasingly well adapted to the special needs . . . of American practice." He concluded that American architecture must become independent of French dominance and develop its own expression.[18]

Hamlin was not reviving the call for an American style; he was concerned primarily with how the lessons of European precedent could best be adapted to American conditions. Numerous architects on this side of the Atlantic were now more interested in judging their work on its own merits, not by comparison with contemporary European achievements. This attitude stemmed from the awareness that the programmatic requirements of numerous American building types—from skyscrapers to suburban houses—differed substantially from those in Europe. But many people also believed that the United States lacked long-standing architectural traditions and that, therefore, its designers could work with a freedom unknown to their European colleagues. Just as the movement sought a balance between the establishment of strong links with the past and a creative response to the present, so it strove to find a balance between the reflection of European traditions and the response to American needs. The work of Coxhead, Polk, Schweinfurth, and Maybeck expressed this phenomenon. Its conceptual framework was international, drawing from myriad precedents at home and abroad. At the same time it was consciously tailored to what each architect saw as the Bay Area's special qualities.

A spirit of independence was engendered at the movement's inception by the example of Henry Hobson Richardson. His mature work embodied a marriage of order and diversity, vigor and restraint, individuality and sensitive interpretation of precedent that provided a foundation for subsequent endeavors. Richardson was not so much the

16

initiator of the movement as he was the principal figure to effect the transition between the Victorian world and the academic one. Not long after his death, his Romanesque mode became passé, yet his contribution continued to be seen as pivotal. That feeling was well expressed by van Rensselaer several years after writing Richardson's biography:

We thought that he had shown us the virtue of the Romanesque style when what he had really shown us was the difference between weak, confused, commonplace, trivial buildings and buildings with instinct and vigor, individuality, and beauty. We are not likely to forget his teaching with regard to the essentials of good architecture: in a greater degree than any one can estimate it has affected and will affect the work of the whole profession.[19]

As Louis Kahn did in the 1960s, Richardson ended the old order, but even while he was at the height of his career, young disciples were turning the lessons of his work in new directions that were very much their own.

The beginnings of academic eclecticism were not entirely obvious at first. Richardson's work was so different from the norm in the late 1870s that it seemed to constitute a movement all by itself. During that decade related concerns, such as scholarly study of the past and the reestablishment of a sense of unity between architecture and the allied arts, were rapidly gaining favor, and many sensed that they were on the threshold of a new era. However, these changes did not coalesce into a coherent approach to design until the first half of the 1880s.[20] Only then were the departures from prevalent Victorian modes and Richardsonian Romanesque able to clarify the nature of this new movement. Instead of amalgamating into a strong, individual style comparable to Richardson's, the new movement assumed a heterogeneous composition. This was the start of a period of eclectic diversity that was more intense than at any previous time.

The central figures during the formative stage of academic eclecticism were McKim, Mead, and White. No other architects did so much so early to create the framework within which the movement developed.[21] Their work owed an enormous debt to Richardson. But in contrast to the narrow scope of historical references used by Richardson, the firm of McKim, Mead & White turned to a multitude of sources, encompassing buildings of numerous periods, regions, and types. It interpreted and combined these sources in a variety of ways. The result was a design vocabulary of unusual breadth that became a major influence in establishing the parameters of expression over the

17

next several decades. The firm's well-known Shingle Style buildings represent the most important initial thrust of what would rapidly become a multifaceted approach.

Many aspects of McKim, Mead & White's contribution to the Shingle Style have been examined by Vincent Scully in his classic study.[22] However, that analysis and subsequent accounts overlook a characteristic of the firm's designs that significantly altered the mode's complexion. During the late 1870s, Charles McKim and others had experimented in a bold, simple manner, abstracting and combining features of recent English and early American domestic architecture. Then, at a crucial point in the formative period of the Shingle Style, the firm introduced a new method of using historical precedent that was far more cosmopolitan in nature than previous efforts. The change came in 1879 after Stanford White joined the firm, having returned from a fifteen-month tour of Europe. A substantial portion of his time abroad was spent studying the postmedieval vernacular architecture of northern Europe, especially buildings in the French provinces of Normandy and Brittany.[23] The lessons White learned from this expe-

6. Manoir d'Ango, Varengeville-sur-Mer, Normandy. (Raymond Quenedey, *La Normandie; Recueil de documents d'architecture civile* II:25)

rience had a decisive impact on the firm's subsequent work. Critics at the time noted that the favored Anglo-American precedents fell short of meeting the requirements of new suburban and resort architecture in the United States.[24] The continental vernacular buildings that so interested White offered possibilities for exterior treatment which helped resolve the situation. The size and scale of Norman manor houses in particular were comparable to those of English examples and appropriate for the new American dwellings, while their simplicity was similar to that of the admired "old Colonial." The elemental forms of their turrets suggested means of augmenting picturesqueness without disrupting the overall composition, and the porches provided examples of integrating such appendages with the main block of the building. The massive forms of the manor houses, with great expanses of rough yet evenly textured masonry wall surfaces, could easily be translated into shingles. They demonstrated how strength and cohesiveness might be given to sizable buildings while valued unpretentious and informal qualities were retained (Figs. 6,7). McKim, Mead & White's designs could no longer be labeled "Colonial," "English," or, for that matter,

7. McKim, Mead & White. Casino, Newport, Rhode Island, 1879–1881.
(*Monograph of the Works of McKim, Mead and White*, plate 1)

"French." By drawing from a variety of sources and synthesizing them into decisively new designs, the architects removed their work from ties to a single period or place. Associational references remained important, but they were so modified that the buildings appeared style-less at that time.

Equally important was the underlying sense of unity and order that Charles McKim brought to the Shingle Style. For the first time in domestic architecture, Beaux Arts principles, developed for major public buildings, were effectively fused with characteristics of the picturesque tradition.[25] In so doing, the Shingle Style bridged a gap between two formerly divergent strains in eclecticism. This synthesis had a great impact on American residential design, demonstrating that it was possible to maintain rustic, informal qualities while expressing the new taste for restraint and cohesiveness. From another perspective, the Shingle Style gave academic practice a new dimension, broadening its vocabulary and application in a manner that was for the time being distinct to this country. While American house design assumed new forms of expression over the next several decades, much of it was inextricably tied to this new inclusive attitude toward precedent. Coxhead, Polk, Schweinfurth, and Maybeck created some of the most adventurous work done in this vein around the turn of the century.

Such free interpretation of the past was not identified in contemporary accounts as an attempt to create a new style or distinct national architecture, but rather as an imaginative response to new and particular conditions in this country. Van Rensselaer, whose writings appear to reflect the ideas of McKim, Mead & White rather closely, offered a detailed explanation of these factors. She noted that American country houses were for seasonal use, yet, unlike European resort villas, were centers of social intercourse and required more expansive accommodations. American clients placed greater emphasis on physical comfort and on the individuality of each design; however, lot sizes were often relatively small, necessitating a degree of unobtrusiveness. Hot summers required porches, making large banks of unsheltered windows impractical. The low cost of wood assured its predominance as a building material. Bruce Price also cited the need for ample cross-ventilation in summer as a principal reason for the open plan, and the need to retain heat in cold weather as justification for low ceilings.[26] The scope and extent of these circumstances suggested substantive departures from convention and thus challenged architects to develop appropriate new forms of expression.

The Shingle Style was not a singular phenomenon—a new

8. McKim, Mead & White. Henry Villard houses, New York, 1882–1885;
altered. (Courtesy Robert Judson Clark)

manner of design used for a great range of building types—as was
Richardsonian Romanesque. By the mid-1880s, when the shingled
mode reached maturity, it represented only one portion of a highly
eclectic package. The rational commitment to expression that is evident
in the Shingle Style offers a partial explanation for this broad vocabulary, in whose development McKim, Mead & White was so instrumental.

The Villard houses in New York (1882–1885) suggest the breadth
of the firm's approach (Fig. 8). The design was radically different
from most other large urban buildings in the United States at that time
in both selection and interpretation of classical precedent. McKim,
Mead & White sought to capture the spirit of the late quattrocento
palace in form, mass, scale, and composition, as well as in detail.
Few statements could be more dissimilar from the firm's contemporaneous Shingle Style houses, yet these differences were not antagonistic
in direction.[27] The Villard scheme was complementary in that it
responded to the fundamentally different practical and symbolic needs
of an enormous urban residential compound. Its historical references
were more specific and complete than those of the Shingle Style because
the prototypes and the new building were viewed as being far more

21

analogous. Like the Italian Renaissance palace, these houses were designed as sumptuous accommodations for rich businessmen and were intended to present an image of monumental dignity that would give focus to the dense, heterogeneous urban landscape.

This method of developing expression according to the degree of functional and symbolic correspondence between a new building and historic precedent was a method McKim, Mead, and White employed in most, if not all, of their designs during this period. Their moderate-sized city houses display abstract, classical qualities of order and formality, which they regarded as essential in the urban context; however, reference to the palazzo, considered inappropriate for buildings of this scale, was avoided. Instead, considerable liberties were often taken with historical sources, as is evident in the New York residence of Philip and Lloyd Phoenix (1882) (Fig. 9). Drawing from a variety of urban prototypes, the design is classical in feeling yet

9. McKim, Mead & White. Phillip and Lloyd Phoenix house, New York, 1882; demolished. (*Architectural Record*, Great American Architects Series, May 1895, p. 63)

10. McKim, Mead & White. St. Paul's Church, Stockbridge, Massachusetts, 1883–1885. (Stockbridge Public Library)

evokes no specific period or place. The situation paralleled that of Shingle Style houses, which also had requirements that significantly differed from most classical precedent. Here was a single building with narrow street frontage—as opposed to a unit in a row—that needed an individual composition which was not disruptive to its neighborhood.[28]

Office buildings presented an even greater array of new problems, and the firm handled them with comparable freedom. On the other hand, McKim, Mead & White's ecclesiastical work is much more historicizing. Episcopal churches, such as St. Paul's in Stockbridge, Massachusetts (1883–1885), set a new standard for a direct interpretation of village parish churches in England and northern France, reflecting the importance of tradition and the absence of pronounced change in the liturgy (Fig. 10). Buildings for newer denominations, where the service departed from Anglican and Roman Catholic practices, were less bound to specific models but retained some distinct historical references that conveyed a common heritage.[29]

Programmatic conditions played an important role in McKim, Mead & White's development of diverse architectural expression. Nevertheless, the firm avoided a deterministic approach. Its work

23

11. McKim, Mead & White. H.A.C. Taylor house, Newport, Rhode Island, 1884–1886; demolished. (Newport Historical Society)

demonstrates how a variety of solutions could be created in response to similar circumstances. The H.A.C. Taylor house in Newport (1884–1886), for instance, makes a pronounced departure from Shingle Style residences designed during the same period, in the same region, and for the same purposes (Fig. 11). By using late eighteenth- and early nineteenth-century New England houses as their primary models, the architects created a scheme fundamentally different in its massing, composition, organization of space, and use of imagery, with overt historical references in the details. In other ways, the New York residence of Charles L. Tiffany (1882–1884) is worlds apart from the slightly later Villard group (Fig. 12). In the Tiffany house, allusions are to postmedieval urban dwellings in northern Germany and are kept discrete and vague.

Client preferences may well have contributed to the development of such diverse solutions, yet this factor alone cannot explain the intensely varied nature of McKim, Mead & White's oeuvre. The firm's clientele was perhaps less conservative and less intellectual than was Richardson's; otherwise the two groups did not substantially differ. The increasing taste for refined elegance and for association with venerated traditions that their patrons displayed was a less pronounced shift than the change in approach to design from Richardson to McKim, Mead & White. The broadening discovery of historic precedents and the urge to experiment with their vast array of characteristics appear to have been the central factors in this transformation. Greater concern for the conditions of each project as generators of expression afforded a means by which the urge could be logically and sensitively mani-

24

12. McKim, Mead & White. Charles L. Tiffany house, New York, 1882–1884; demolished. (Byron Collection, Museum of the City of New York)

13. Richard Morris Hunt. William K. Vanderbilt house, New York, 1879–1882; demolished. (Museum of the City of New York)

fested. Van Rensselaer voiced the enthusiasm many young architects must have felt for the possibilities availed by such diversity. Comparing the Tiffany house with Richard Morris Hunt's residence for William K. Vanderbilt (Fig. 13), she remarked that "No two houses . . . could be more unlike in idea, in material, in treatment, or in degree of ornamentation." Yet she considered both designs excellent in their own way:

They prove how wide are the limits that bound architectural excellence even in one branch of city domestic work; how foolish it is to try and fetter effort with narrow artistic creeds, with rigid dogmas as to style and treatment and amount of decoration.[30]

Van Rensselaer was one of the first critics to recognize that this diversity was tantamount to rejecting the nineteenth-century notion of style: " 'Style' is not the question at all, only the rational or irrational use of whatever style may be selected."[31] Rather than being a collection of divergent "styles," the academic movement was a single thrust, unified in principle, but encompassing a spectrum of forms to realize its objectives. This catholic attitude rapidly gained acceptance after the mid-1880s.

Hamlin identified eclectic diversity as being a logical and natural reflection of the age. He emphasized that no single form of expression was possible when so much investigation of the past was occurring and when conditions were changing so rapidly:

We are in the presence of a somewhat novel phenomenon in the history of style—the development on eclectic principles of a number of quite distinct forms of architectural expression for distinct types of buildings.

And:

The freedom with which our architects handle, modify, and adapt the historic styles to the varied problems they have to solve is the despair of the purist, but it is the pledge of sincerity and progress. . . . it may perhaps never again happen that a single system of forms and details, constituting a style . . . will be applied alike to all . . . buildings.

Finally:

The "style" of the twentieth century will be recognized not by the use of any one set of details, nor any one type of plan or system of construction,

26

but by certain broad and fundamental characteristics which will be recognized by our descendants whether we recognize them or not, and quite without reference to historic labels that may be applied to their details.[32]

Eclectic diversity provided ways to expand the possibilities of creative design without abandoning ties to tradition. It offered a vehicle for achieving an eventual synthesis, but one that would never possess the characteristics of a historical style. Diverse expression was seen as not only the way of the present, but also that of the future.

By the early 1890s, eclectic diversity had become a widespread phenomenon, and McKim, Mead, and White were regarded as being both its leading exponents and among the country's foremost architects. Their example had great influence on established firms, as well as on a younger generation just beginning independent practice. The concept of eclectic diversity was fundamental to the four San Francisco architects' attitude toward design. Polk, Schweinfurth, and Maybeck all had contact with McKim, Mead, and White in the late 1880s, when the concept had reached maturity. Polk and Maybeck, especially, varied the character of their designs to a degree matched by few of their contemporaries.

Diverse expression remained a significant aspect of the movement for its duration. However, new attitudes toward historic precedent emerged during the 1890s. One of them advocated regional expression, the other focused on what might be called academic specialization. They helped confirm the legitimacy of drawing from a wide range of historical sources, and they even contributed to broadening that range. But these ideas also raised arguments that challenged the practice of eclectic diversity as developed by McKim, Mead, and White, asserting that external conditions and the architect's own abilities imposed limitations on the forms of expression used in any one place by any single person.

Some of the initial concern for regional architecture stemmed from mounting popular interest in America's past, a pursuit that reached significant proportions during the 1870s. Among designers, this interest focused on the study of early New England buildings, and it had a decisive effect on the development of the Shingle Style. Yet the fact that this precedent was Colonial and hence American appears to have been the important factor, not its regional characteristics. Contemporary literature neither emphasized local qualities nor suggested that the Shingle Style was a regional mode. Most accounts indicate that archi-

27

14. McKim, Mead & White. Ramona School, Santa Fe, New Mexico,
ca. 1886, project. (Courtesy Leland Roth)

tects considered it applicable to many parts of the country.[33] A similar
attitude was reflected in the first phase of the Colonial Revival that
McKim, Mead & White helped launch with the H.A.C. Taylor house
in Newport. Largely inspired by late eighteenth- and early nineteenth-
century New England buildings, the mode rapidly gained favor with
architects in that region. But the Colonial Revival gained popularity in
other portions of the United States as well, and contemporary writings
give no indication that it was intended to be a localized phenomenon.

Concern for developing regional forms of expression emerged
in the mid–1880s, fueled by the pursuit of eclectic diversity. As an
increasingly wide range of historical sources abroad had become the
subject of study, interest often focused on the national and even local
characteristics of old buildings as well as on regional differences in
early American architecture. The vast territory now encompassed by
the United States and the ever greater ease with which the country
could be traversed generated a new appreciation for the varied character of the American landscape. The emphasis now placed on expressing the conditions of a given project resulted in a more pronounced
influence of local character on design. Early manifestations of this
new regional consciousness came from prominent New York and Boston
firms working in sections of the country that were radically different

28

from the Northeast. The unusual, sometimes exotic, nature of these projects no doubt reflected the novelty the architects saw in each locale. However, they turned to European precedents that seemed appropriate to the perceived ambience of the region, making little or no reference to local building traditions.

Among the earliest examples of this regional approach is Stanford White's proposal for the Ramona School in Santa Fe, designed not long after he toured New Mexico in 1882 (Fig. 14). Although White purportedly sought to embody his "conceptions of the typical style of architecture suited to the history, climate and surroundings of the state," the predominant references are to Italian buildings.[34] A similar approach was used in the design for Stanford University in Palo Alto, California, begun in 1887 (Fig. 15). Leland Stanford played a major role, insisting that the campus be "distinctly Californian" in character in order to embody the state's Spanish heritage and the special qualities of the landscape. The designers, Shepley, Rutan & Coolidge and Frederick Law Olmsted, shared their client's interest, yet the plan appears to have been primarily inspired by monumental urban schemes and palatial compounds in Europe, and many of the buildings were patterned after Richardson's work.[35]

15. Shepley, Rutan & Coolidge and Frederick Law Olmsted. Leland Stanford, Jr., University, Palo Alto, 1887–1891. (Stanford University Archives, courtesy Paul Turner)

One of the most significant and influential examples of this form of regionalism was the resort complex Carrère & Hastings designed for Henry Flagler in St. Augustine, Florida. Both architects had worked for McKim, Mead & White, and this, their first independent project, exhibits the discipline and the highly imaginative use of precedent that distinguished the best work of the parent firm. Among the Flagler buildings, the Ponce de Leon Hotel (1885–1887) is an especially brilliant synthesis of diverse sources that summarizes much of McKim, Mead & White's oeuvre up to that point without being derivative in the slightest way (Fig. 16). A balance is achieved between abstracting and combining references into something wholly new, as in the Shingle Style, and making very specific references to individual periods and buildings, as in the Villard houses. Images drawn from Italian Romanesque; Moorish; and Italian, Spanish, and even French Renaissance architecture are ordered by a rigorously formal parti inspired by Beaux Arts models. Signification of the region's special qualities, including

16. Carrère & Hastings. Ponce de Leon Hotel, St. Augustine, Florida, 1885–1887. (*American Architect,* June 13, 1896)

30

its Spanish heritage, figured prominently in descriptions of the scheme; however, the only local influence was tabby construction that inspired the architects' then novel use of concrete.[36] The design of the Flagler buildings was as persuasive as any built before the turn of the century in demonstrating how foreign sources could be employed to provide regional associations. This approach to regional expression became widely used in the 1890s. Schweinfurth introduced it to California, developing a vocabulary that evoked the state's Spanish Colonial heritage and yet had no direct connections to its early architecture.

Increasingly, some proponents of regional design argued that local conditions not only made certain forms of expression more suitable than others, but were actually determinants for developing a design mode that would be distinct to a given region. They asserted that the heterogeneity of American architecture should arise from the differences of its regions. The early architecture of several areas came to be seen as exemplifying the sensitive adjustment of design to local conditions and as a model for new work. Among the places where this concern first exerted a strong influence on design was Philadelphia.

Regional expression in Philadelphia was nurtured by the area's unusually rich heritage of Georgian architecture. The historical associations of this legacy had been revered for some time, but not until the 1880s was serious attention paid to its physical qualities. During the next decade, references to the area's colonial architecture became an increasingly important means of reflecting Philadelphians' long-standing pride in their city and its traditions. The most prominent figure in the initial stages of this effort was Walter Cope, who, together with his partner John Stewardson, played a key role in introducing the academic movement's ideals to Philadelphia. Cope studied the region's Georgian buildings in detail and set new standards of accuracy in their restoration. The Leamy Home (ca. 1898–1899) illustrates how he sought to create very precise allusions to early architecture in the region through massing, proportion, materials, and details (Fig. 17). Cope limited his use of this imagery to projects that were at least somewhat comparable in scale and function to their prototypes. When conditions were not analogous, he drew from other sources and, indeed, was best known for adaptations of Tudor and Jacobean architecture in his collegiate buildings.[37] Nevertheless, Cope's great interest in regional expression had a decisive influence on younger Philadelphia architects, many of whom concentrated on residential design conceived in this manner. In contrast to the New England-inspired Colonial Revival, few examples of work derived from early Philadelphia architecture

17. Cope & Stewardson. Leamy Home, Philadelphia, ca. 1898–1899. (*Brickbuilder*, November 1902, p. 30)

were built outside the area. By the 1910s, the city became widely recognized for the distinct regional qualities evident in much of its suburban architecture.[38]

Whether drawing from foreign or local sources, the pursuit of regional expression differed markedly from earlier practices that led to regional vernacular idioms. Rather than embodying a limited range of forms passed down from one generation to the next, regional expression was broad-based and fluid. Reference to local work was a matter of choice, exercised by architects who had a knowledge of many historical precedents. New designs were seldom based on a single source. In most instances other models were incorporated into a scheme, and the product was as much a reflection of contemporary tastes and conditions as it was those of an earlier period. Regionalism assumed entirely new dimensions.

Concurrently, other architects were concerned with creating a sense of identity in a region without developing a regional mode. H. Langford Warren was one of several prominent Boston designers who sought this form of "distinctive local character."[39] Warren explained that numerous buildings in one area could be readily distinguished from those of another: recent work in his own locale was characterized by its allegiance to traditional English design, and New York architecture was becoming identified with the showy, elegant classicism derived from student projects at the Ecole des Beaux Arts and from recent Parisian buildings. Frank Chouteau Brown elaborated on the idea, stating that regional qualities comprised a general manner of design that was produced in greater quantity and with better results in one area than in others. He noted, "Often . . . what seems to be a distinctive local type is not so much the . . . expression of that locality—historically—as it is the product of a particular office or group of offices."[40] Brown intimated that the architect should embody the generalized sentiments and characteristics of the community—in the case of Boston, using "conservative English precedent"—and that when this objective was followed consistently, regional distinction could be attained. Walter Cook, a New York architect, expressed similar ideas. He believed that regional qualities seldom had much to do with local traditions: "The style and character of a building often proceeds directly from the individuality, the traditions, and the education of the architect."[41] That such regional distinction had been nonexistent in preceding decades was a questionable assertion. The significant fact was that many architects now recognized the phenomenon and were eager to exploit its potential. Among the practitioners committed to this urbane attitude toward regional identity were Coxhead, Polk, and Maybeck. They generally turned to sources that they felt were suitable for, but not specific to, the region. "Distinctive local character" was imparted by affinities in each man's approach to design and by the strong personal qualities present in their work.

The other tendency, toward academic specialization, grew out of the emphasis that proponents of the movement placed on scholarly investigation of the past. Hamlin was the first to argue that in-depth study of precedents demanded limitation in the scope of material investigated. In 1892 he insisted that no one could achieve a comprehensive understanding of more than two broad historical periods ("styles") in a lifetime. The architect must specialize in both research and design, departing from his chosen path only when the circumstances of a commission required.[42]

Hamlin was not calling for an end to eclectic diversity. He reasoned that the rapid development of new building types, new methods of construction, and the broad spectrum of individual taste precluded uniform applicability of any single mode of expression. The selection of an area of specialization was left to the architect. True to Hamlin's prediction, eclectic diversity continued to characterize American architecture as a whole. However, some proponents of specialization challenged the notion of diversity. Their intense study of a single period led to increasingly narrow forms of expression, and their strong allegiance to a limited range of precedent nurtured the hope that the future would witness a new unity of style.

33

18. Cram & Wentworth. Project for a country church, Berkshire County, Massachusetts, ca. 1890. (*American Architect*, November 29, 1890)

19. Bertram Goodhue. St. Matthew's Cathedral, Dallas, Texas, 1891, project. Drawing by Bertram Goodhue. (*Architectural Review*, August 1, 1892, plate LIV)

Many of the architects who first made a commitment to academic specialization were almost a generation removed from McKim and others who had laid the movement's foundations. These young designers came to feel that the practice of eclectic diversity had been a necessary form of experimentation during the movement's initial stage. Now design needed greater focus and discipline acquired through concentration on the work of individual periods. Among the first architects to pursue this course were Ralph Adams Cram and his associate (as of 1891), Bertram Goodhue. For both men, expression was closely related to building type. After they decided that the firm would concentrate on ecclesiastical design, the partners turned to early English Gothic and, later, French High Gothic architecture, which they believed best represented the spirit of tradition-oriented denominations in a predominantly Anglo-Saxon culture. They were soon filling the pages of architectural periodicals with designs that expressed the nature of academic specialization as clearly as any essay. These projects exhibited considerable differences in treatment, many of which were a result of specific conditions such as size, function, and location. Country chapels, therefore, were not simply small versions of moderate-sized urban churches; nor were the latter given the appearance of major cathedrals (Figs. 18,19). Each was inspired by analogous medieval examples, yet all were unified by reference to precedents that were clearly limited in type, period, and place. Cram and Goodhue also introduced into their churches a new consistency in the precision with which the work of a past period was interpreted. At the same time, they were adamant about capturing the spirit of the past rather than reviving its forms. Their buildings could never be confused with those in England or France. They were not so much derived from individual models as they were masterful representations of qualities that denoted specific design traditions. The architects by no means limited their practice to churches or to interpretation of medieval sources. Both men had a serious interest in other periods and, beginning in the early stage of their practice, experimented with a wide variety of sources.[43] Nonetheless, the creation of a new Gothic architecture remained their foremost concern, and it was largely through such work that the firm gained its reputation and influence.

Another aspect of specialization is illustrated by the work of Charles Platt, who rose to national prominence shortly after the turn of the century. He approached the design of country houses in much the same way that Cram and Goodhue did churches. Platt selected a limited range of sources that he considered most suitable for express-

20. Charles Platt. High Court, Annie Lazarus house, Cornish, New Hampshire, 1890–1891; burned and rebuilt according to a different design. (*Monograph of the Work of Charles A. Platt,* plate 11)

21. Charles Platt. Blendon Hall, Anna Osgood (F. S. Culver) house, Hadlyme, Connecticut, 1902. (*Monograph of the Work of Charles A. Platt,* plate 129)

ing the type: sixteenth-century villas in northern Italy and their eighteenth-century descendants in England and America. Platt, too, developed historical analogies according to function. His large country houses rely mostly on European examples of comparable size and use, while smaller residences tend toward a synthesis of high style and vernacular work from both continents (Figs. 20,21). Paralleling Cram and Goodhue, Platt strove to capture the spirit of the Anglo-Palladian tradition rather than follow specific models. But, until later in his career, he had little concern for either most other building types or for other historical periods. Seldom venturing outside his chosen realm, Platt became the consummate specialist. Lauding Platt's approach, Herbert Croly argued that "style" could be achieved only through consistent use of a limited number of prototypes. Although Croly avoided stating a preference for one source or another, his emphasis on consistency indicated the desire for a new unity of expression at some future date.[44]

Such consistency also became an important objective for the firm of Carrère & Hastings, which assumed a leading role in the drive for academic specialization during the 1890s. Not long after their St. Augustine commission, the partners began to develop a personal style, primarily derived from French classical sources. Unlike Cram, Goodhue, or Platt, they studied work that spanned some four centuries and utilized this range of precedents—from the early Renaissance to the age of Louis XVI, as well as recent French interpretations of these periods—to achieve a wide variety of expression while remaining within clearly defined historical and geographical boundaries. Moreover, these sources were not confined to any single building type. Carrère & Hastings sought to create an architectural vocabulary that would be applicable to the fundamentally different requirements of country houses, civic buildings, churches, and office towers (Figs. 22,23). Hastings thought that "the irrational idiosyncracy of modern times is the assumption that each kind of problem demands a particular style of architecture"; he urged designers to strive for "the consistency of style which has existed in all times until the present."[45] The classical tradition must continue. Here, again, the undercurrent of a drive for stylistic unity can be detected. The effort to achieve that unity was influenced by practices at the Ecole, where reliance on French classical precedent found in the projects could readily be interpreted as the basis for a superior architectural vocabulary. Despite persistent claims that the school's methods fostered no style, some of its strongest American advocates argued that it was "laying the foundations for a true style."[46]

37

Most American architects, however, were leary of insisting on a single method to attain the commonly held aims of order and consistency in design. After the turn of the century, some designers did begin to limit the historical sources with which they worked. Yet they failed to reach a new unity of expression, due in part to individual preferences for a given period, which many architects maintained, and to the reticence that most of them had for advocating one form of expression above all others.

Academic eclecticism was thus characterized by differing views which enlivened the dynamics of the movement but which also tended to balance one another. Proponents of stylistic unity were met by others who insisted that modern conditions precluded such a synthesis. Some architects believed that expression must be related to type or region, while others took a more inclusive approach. For all those individuals who became confirmed specialists, there were many who preferred the freedom of diversity. Increasing numbers of designers

22. Carrère & Hastings. Walter Jennings house, Cold Spring Harbor, New York, 1897. (*American Architect,* December 1, 1900)

23. Carrère & Hastings. First Church of Christ, Scientist, New York, 1898. (*Architectural Record*, February 1904, p. 158)

became devoted to classical precedents, yet architects such as Cram persuasively reminded people that their ties to the Middle Ages were far from dead. Such differences in attitude were ultimately less consequential than the ideals that these architects held in common. The differences, however, serve to illustrate that this movement, like most others, did not possess the simple complexion that has often been assumed.

II

TRAINING: London, New York, Paris

Appropriate . . . expression in architecture can only be secured by . . . a learned profession . . . thoroughly versed in the history of art, familiar with precedent, unprejudiced, free, catholic, without national bias.

Henry Van Brunt, American Institute of Architects,
27th Annual Convention, *Journal
of the Proceedings,* 1893

We cannot hope to attain any full appreciation of fundamental aesthetic principles unless we study sympathetically, however, critically, all things that men have called beautiful.

Henry Rutgers Marshall, *Architectural
Record,* July–September 1895

THE CATHOLIC attitude toward precedent, so basic to the academic movement's perspective, entailed a reorientation in the way designers studied the past. Examining the work of previous eras had been important for American architects since the early nineteenth century, but the process was at first limited to sources that could be directly applied to current work. The scope of historical investigation began to broaden by the 1860s, following the example of formally trained architects such as Richard Morris Hunt. The learning process was ever more valued for its own sake; the material studied did not have to have a direct correlation with work on the boards. The principal objective became to develop a way of thinking, not just to expand one's vocabulary.[1]

Coxhead, Polk, Schweinfurth, and Maybeck received their training during the 1880s and were deeply affected by this new perspective on the past. Coxhead and Maybeck benefited from a formal education at the Royal Academy and the Ecole des Beaux Arts, respectively. Polk and Schweinfurth took the more traditional course, learning in offices. The attitudes all four men acquired in the process left a lasting imprint on their work.

40

The details of each man's experience vary, yet important parallels exist in their backgrounds and in the steps they took to acquire expertise. All four architects came from families of moderate means and all, with the exception of Maybeck, were raised in provincial communities. Polk, Schweinfurth, and Maybeck were initially exposed to design by their fathers. Coxhead, Polk, and Schweinfurth started professional training before they reached fifteen. By the time each man had turned twenty-one, he had moved to a major urban center— London, New York, or Paris. While in those cities, they came into contact with leaders in the profession, acquired a more worldly attitude toward design, and became committed to academic precepts. They moved to California soon afterward, fresh with ideas but not set in their ways.

Ernest Albert Coxhead was raised in a lackluster English environment. From an early age he nurtured ambitions to become an architect and constantly sought the means to improve his preparation for the field. His father, William Palmer Coxhead, had been a schoolmaster in Hampstead, but his career abruptly ended around the time he turned forty. Thereafter he worked as a lodging-house keeper in the Sussex coastal town of Eastbourne. Ernest, the fourth of six children, was born in 1863, shortly after the family moved to this seaside resort. For about a decade, the Coxheads lived in one boarding house after another, and by 1871 they were able to purchase a modest dwelling across from the railroad station.[2]

At fifteen, Ernest was articled to a local civil engineer, George Wallis, who was engaged in numerous public works that were instrumental in Eastbourne's resort development. In 1878, when Coxhead entered the office, Wallis also listed himself as an architect and was designing villas for the town's burgeoning summer population. Over the next five years, the young apprentice worked on both engineering projects and residential commissions, receiving a thorough introduction to the technical aspects of his future calling.[3] Concurrently, he sought to develop a knowledge in other areas, devoting spare time to the study of English Gothic architecture. In 1880, Coxhead entered a draftsman's competition for a school chapel with a scheme that reveals the influence of Pugin and other Gothic revivalists (Fig. 24). Pugin's *True Principles* no doubt had been studied with great care. This scheme, along with several other self-initiated designs from the early 1880s and a set of measured drawings documenting St. Mary's, Eastbourne, the finest local example of thirteenth-century design, suggests that the scholarly concerns of the Gothic Revival were of greater interest to

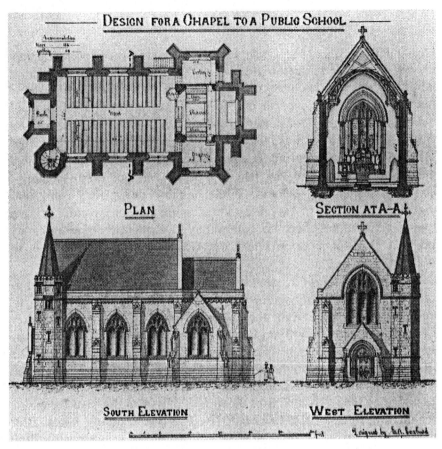

PLAN

SECTION AT A-A.

SOUTH ELEVATION

WEST ELEVATION

24. Ernest Coxhead. "Design for a Chapel to a Public School," 1880, *Building News* Designing Club competition entry. (Courtesy John Beach)

Coxhead than the prevailing High Victorian taste for stylistic agglomeration.[4]

Coxhead left Eastbourne for London in 1883, where he worked for Frederic Chancellor, supervising construction of several buildings and preparing working drawings. Chancellor was an unexceptional designer, but he possessed a keen interest in old churches, restoring almost sixty of them during his career. Perhaps the most valuable part of Coxhead's responsibilities was to assist in recording church tombs. The project resulted in a thick tome, *The Ancient Sepulchral Monuments of Essex* (1890), for which Ernest drew fifteen of the plates (Fig. 25). Such monuments were then receiving recognition as some of the earliest examples of pure classical design in England.[5] Through his work, Coxhead could study firsthand an entirely different language from the one he had been learning. He also began to respect the accouterments and character that a building might acquire through

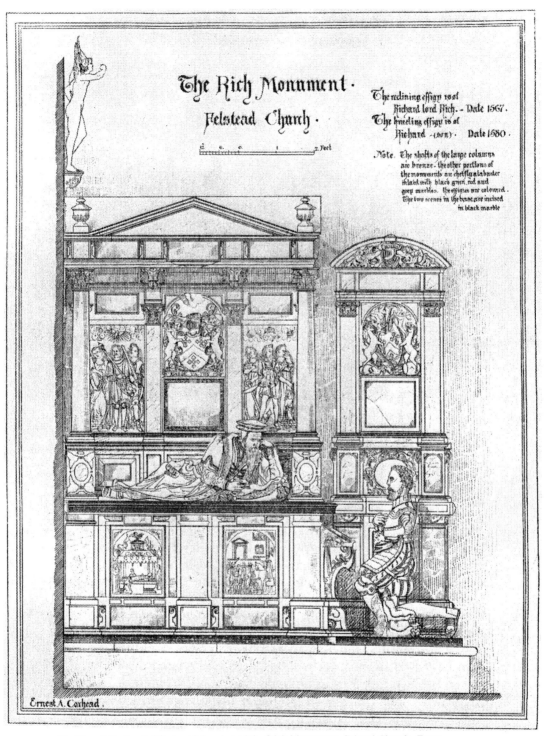

The Rich Monument.
Felstead Church.

The reclining effigy is of
Richard lord Rich. - Date 1567.
The kneeling effigy is of
Richard -son. - Date 1580.

Note. The shafts of the large columns
are bronze- the other portions of
the monuments are chiefly alabaster
inlaid with black green red and
grey marbles. The effigies are coloured.
The two scenes in the base are incised
in black marble

Ernest A. Coxhead.

25. Ernest Coxhead. Measured drawing of the Rich Monument, Felsted Church, Essex,
ca. 1883–1885. (Frederic Chancellor, *Ancient Sepulchral Monuments of Essex*, plate XLIII)

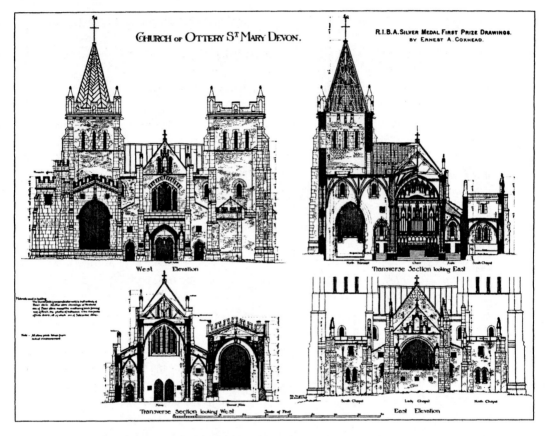

26. Ernest Coxhead. Measured drawings of the Church of Ottery St. Mary, Devon, 1885, RIBA Silver Medal First Prize drawings. (*Building News,* June 12, 1885)

time. Although neither man was a member of William Morris's anti-restorationist Society for the Protection of Ancient Buildings (1877), they appear to have been sympathetic to its aims. Little is known about Chancellor's own work with old churches, but his views were probably those of an antiquarian. He was an early supporter of the Essex Archaeological Society (1852) and active in similar organizations. His book on sepulchral monuments records precisely the kind of fixtures then destroyed in most restorations. Coxhead shared these concerns, as can be seen in his measured drawings of the Church of Ottery St. Mary in Devon, which won the Royal Institute of British Architects Silver Medal in 1885 (Fig. 26). The product of three major construction campaigns from the late thirteenth to the early sixteenth centuries, the church is permeated by the accumulative character that Morris and his followers staunchly defended.[6] Coxhead did not select Ottery St. Mary out of hand, for it lies in a hamlet far removed from the region he frequented. His drawings offer careful documentation of how the fabric had grown and changed over time. Some years later, this interest in conveying a sense of age in architecture became an important factor in his own designs.

Soon after joining the office, Coxhead was proposed as a student at the Royal Academy of Fine Arts by his employer. He was admitted in July 1883 and remained for about three years. He also attended the Architectural Association's evening classes, which were to prepare draftsmen for admittance to the Royal Institute of British Architects. Coxhead was elected an associate of the Institute in November 1886.[7] This tutelage helped him to develop a strong sense of discipline, greatly expanded his knowledge of history, and afforded him exposure to some of the profession's most eminent figures. Numerous dignitaries were invited to lecture at the Architectural Association. The time Coxhead spent at the Academy was even more important. For decades it had been the only school in the country to offer an extensive curriculum emphasizing the practice of architecture as an art. The program was held in high esteem; it gave the most thorough preparation in the field then available in England.[8] However, unlike many of its counterparts on the continent, the Academy was not yet regarded as an essential steppingstone to professional prominence. Relatively few architectural students enrolled. Those who did may have sought training in abstract design principles that they could not receive in most offices.

Through his formal studies Coxhead became committed to the tenets of the academic movement, then emerging as a major force in English as well as American architecture. The Master of the Architectural School at the Academy, Richard Phené Spiers, led the drive. One of the few men in the country to have attended the Ecole des Beaux Arts, Spiers vigorously promoted the adoption of its methods. He believed that buildings should rationally express their function and materials; that careful study of precedent afforded the only means of developing this expression; and that academic instruction provided the best means of acquiring the necessary expertise. Above all, Spiers was a classicist and among the most knowledgeable Britons in antique architecture. He regarded the classical language as a primary vehicle for restoring order and unity to design, and he advocated abandoning the prevalent English approach of composing in an additive, picturesque manner in favor of French methods that emphasized overall cohesiveness. Spiers had a decisive influence on members of Coxhead's generation, who would lead the resurgence of classicism in England during the 1890s.[9]

Spiers's ideas were reinforced and broadened by the Visitors, who were responsible for lectures and design projects given at the Academy. George Aitchison was an authority on Imperial Roman architecture and had many concerns that paralleled Spiers's. George

27. Ernest Coxhead. "Design for an Entrance Hall and Staircase of a National Gallery," 1885. (Courtesy John Beach)

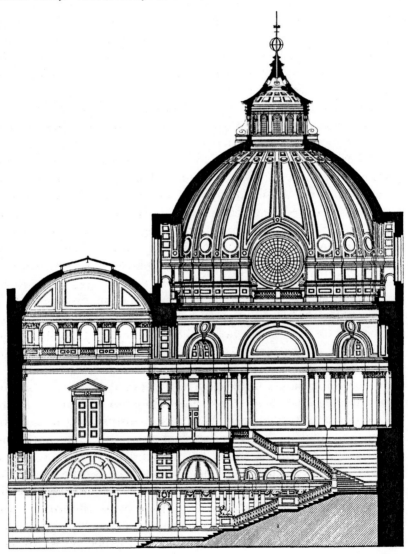

Bodley, one of Britain's finest designers of churches during the late nineteenth century, championed the return to a scholarly use of Gothic precedent. Most famous of this group was Richard Norman Shaw, who was beginning to use classical sources with the same imagination and skill that he displayed with postmedieval vernacular architecture.

Some of the initial effect this training had on Coxhead's work is evident in an 1885 project for an entrance hall, almost certainly done at the Academy (Fig. 27). The study has epic proportions, commensurate with the period's expansive tastes, and is typical of advanced academic work. It reflects the new interest in the monumental classicism of Wren and his followers, which many English students regarded as consummate representations of order and unity on a grand scale. For the present, these ideas were largely confined to paper, but they would characterize a substantial portion of Britain's civic architecture by the turn of the century.[10]

Thus Coxhead proved to be an able expositor of English Baroque, just as he had demonstrated an understanding of *True Principles,* a combination unthinkable to earlier generations. At the same time, he appeared to have had little interest in the postmedieval vernacular sources that preoccupied the attention of so many of his contemporaries. His compositions were carefully ordered, if sometimes dull, and were utterly devoid of the apparent casualness then in vogue. Surviving sketchbooks are filled with notes and dimensioned building details, but contain only a few, stiffly rendered freehand drawings.[11] Then, a few months prior to embarking for America, Coxhead began to draw quick, impressionistic studies of vernacular subjects. One explanation for this change is the possibility that he came into contact with young colleagues who were spearheading the Arts and Crafts Movement in London. Whether he had any direct association with this circle or not, Coxhead would assimilate much of the spirit of English arts-and-crafts work by the early 1890s.

Having concluded his studies, won the RIBA's Silver Medal, and been elected to the ranks of that organization, Coxhead left England for the United States. The move was probably not long contemplated, yet it was a decisive step. By January 1887 he had opened an office in Los Angeles, assisted by his older brother Almeric, who took charge of the firm's business affairs.[12] The only clues to Coxhead's motivation for moving to so distant and provincial a place are circumstantial. The most likely factor was a promise of work from the Episcopal diocese. Between 1887 and 1889, Coxhead designed the great majority of southern California's new Episcopal churches. Chancellor, or perhaps even Bodley, may have provided an introduction to the Bishop of California, William Ingraham Kip, an urbane and scholarly New Yorker whose sympathies lay with High Church Anglicanism. Whether they were secured through prior arrangement or not, Kip no doubt welcomed the services of an architect who had a thorough knowledge of English church design, as few Americans then did, to instill the spirit of tradition in his frontier demesne.[13] The Episcopal church, with its rapidly expanding operations in California, gave Coxhead far greater opportunity to do ecclesiastical work than he would have had in England, where the demand for new parish churches was slight and the ties between the clergy and established practitioners strong.

Coxhead's move to California may have been prompted by other factors as well. Ample promotional literature was circulated in England portraying southern California as a new Eden, a land of unlimited promise. A well-publicized building boom began in Los Angeles in 1886. Concurrently, there was an upsurge of interest in American design among English architects. While Coxhead was still in London, the RIBA mounted an exhibition entirely devoted to recent American work and the prestigious journal *British Architect* included numerous illustrations of Shingle Style houses. The praise accorded to one example is typical: the building's "simple character" had great virtue, the editors commented, and they "would rather be the author of this design than of all the rank and file 'Queen Anne' revivals here."[14]

Once in southern California, Coxhead responded quickly to contemporary American modes, using them with confidence and imagination. While the Gothic churches he had studied so carefully continued to influence his work, Richardsonian Romanesque and Shingle Style buildings were now his primary sources. The most significant impact these modes had on him was the freedom with which he interpreted a variety of medieval precedents. Through the late 1880s, this aspect of American design provided Coxhead with a substitute for analogous qualities in English arts-and-crafts work, few examples of which were then published. All Saints' Church, Pasadena (1888–1889), is a good example of his development (Fig. 28). Resting on a rugged stone base, the main block is treated like an impressionistic diagram of the timberwork framing in a late medieval English hall. To one side, the composite tower seems to be woven out of shingles, exhibiting the same fantastic presence found in recently published drawings by Harvey Ellis. At the same time, the design possesses an underlying order that controls and strengthens its picturesque qualities.

48

28. Ernest Coxhead. All Saints' Church, Pasadena, 1888–1889; demolished 1923.
Drawing by Henry L. Merritt. (*American Architect*, March 30, 1889)

Coxhead's most accomplished work in southern California is
the Church of the Angels (1889), erected as a memorial to Alexander
Campbell-Johnston, a rich Englishman who had died while visiting
the ranch he owned near Pasadena (Fig. 29). The building had to
accommodate High Church services, but only for a tiny congregation
of local gentry, so that the chancel was made larger than the nave.[15]
Coxhead accentuated the dichotomy between the large liturgical space
and the small congregational area by treating the two parts as if they
were different buildings. The chancel is housed ceremoniously, bearing overt references to several Romanesque and Gothic sources, while
the broad, low-slung mass and simple details of the nave recall the
Richardsonian Romanesque work in Boston's suburbs. The contrasts

49

29. Ernest Coxhead. Church of the Angels, Los Angeles, 1889; altered.
(Los Angeles Public Library)

in scale, imagery, and character enrich the scheme without fragment-
ing it. After first studying architecture as a scholar and then developing
his intuitive faculties, Coxhead was now able to balance these concerns
skillfully. The Church of the Angels is a telling prelude to his work in
the Bay Area.

Coxhead's assimilation of recent American precedents is the
more remarkable because he had no chance to study significant examples firsthand, except perhaps during his trip from England. Most
contemporary architecture in Los Angeles employed High Victorian
modes. The isolation of southern California probably forced Coxhead
to rely on secondary sources. Yet his designs impart an understanding
of some of the best contemporary American work that imagination
and published illustrations alone could not provide. The person who
was no doubt instrumental in Coxhead's acquiring this facility, Willis
Polk, had worked in both the East and the Midwest. Polk stayed in

50

Coxhead's office for only a few months, as the two men had different temperaments and thus had a stormy working relationship. However, they became close friends and eventually influenced each other's work when they both moved to San Francisco in 1889.

Polk's youth was itinerant. His father, Willis Webb Polk, traveled throughout the Midwest and the South as a carpenter, holding other jobs when business was slow. Willis Jefferson Polk was the third of seven children, born in October 1867 while the family was living in Jacksonville, Illinois.[16] About six years later they moved to St. Louis, where Polk's father came to enjoy a stable and prosperous practice, offering both design and construction services. He achieved prominence in local trade organizations and was a well-known advocate of temperance. Willis was raised, apparently without formal education, in this sober, hardworking environment. At the age of eight, he started work with a local contractor, and within five years he graduated to the rank of office boy in the architectural firm of Jerome B. Legg. Shortly thereafter he began to assist his father.[17]

By 1885, the family had moved to Kansas City, Missouri, where the partnership of W. W. Polk & Son was established. Most of the firm's commissions were for moderate-sized suburban dwellings and speculative row houses. Responsibility for designing at least some of these projects was delegated to Willis. An early example of his work, the David McMechan house (1885), suggests the enthusiasm with which he approached design, but also the limitations of his architectural knowledge (Fig. 30). As with so many architect-builders' products of the period, an array of ornate elements is grafted onto a standard house form. The principal sources for Polk's vocabulary were no doubt plan books, trade journals, and manufacturers' catalogues.

Soon Polk grew dissatisfied with his provincial milieu. A pivotal point in his career occurred in the early months of 1887 when he dissolved the partnership with his father to work as a draftsman for Van Brunt & Howe, the eminent Boston architects, who were then in the process of moving their practice to Kansas City. The change could hardly have been more pronounced for Polk, who found himself leaving the tradesman's world for that of the artist and professional. During the 1880s, few American architects could match Henry Van Brunt's concern for examining design precepts or his prolific writings on the subject. These years were also a period of ideological transition for Van Brunt, as he abandoned the structuralist notions of Viollet-le-Duc and embraced classicism, which he believed more fully embodied

51

human values with a "variety of expression hitherto unknown in art." Its methods, he argued, were based on "authority and discipline" that could also accommodate differences in program and national temperament. Van Brunt was an ideal tutor; he considered the education of young draftsmen to be very important and may well have run the office

30. W. W. Polk & Son. David McMechan house, Kansas City, Missouri, 1885; no longer standing. Drawing by Polk. (*Inland Architect*, May 1886)

·PROPOSED·MVNICIPAL·BVILDINGS·
·WASHINGTON·D·C··
·ARCHITECT·:WILLIS·POLK··

31. Willis Polk. City Hall, Washington, D.C., 1887, project. Drawing by Polk.
(*American Architect*, February 23, 1889)

as an atelier, fashioned after that of his mentor, Richard Morris Hunt.[18]
    While working for Van Brunt, Polk began to realize that design
represented more than the resolution of practical requirements and the
display of decorative embellishments. Polk never shared Van Brunt's
intellectual interests, but he became strongly committed to the academic
movement. Van Brunt's immediate effect on Polk's work is evident in
an 1887 project for a new City Hall in Washington, D.C. (Fig. 31).
Inspiration for the scheme came more from Van Brunt's ideas than
from his buildings. The previous year he had written an article identifying clarity in order and expression as the qualities that placed Richardson at the top of his profession. Polk's design had a picturesque
composition that related to several large commissions then in the office,
but the vocabulary and the character are taken directly from Richard-

53

son. Thus, Polk demonstrated that he could absorb this lesson and use it effectively in a short period of time. After less than a year in Van Brunt's employ, he created a design that rivaled the best work in the office.[19]

Polk's budding talent was matched by his restlessness. He remained with Van Brunt only about six months. During the next two years, he crossed the continent three and a half times, working for at least five architects.[20] Polk was eager to broaden his horizons and impatient with gaining the means necessary to do so. He craved recognition, sending measured drawings, ideal schemes, and other projects to the *American Architect* every step of the way.[21] But his work habits were erratic. John Galen Howard, who knew Polk in Los Angeles, described his attitude:

Polk is clever, brilliant, facile—but with so little depth, so little appreciation for the meaning of real art that it is more encouraging to think of another fifty years of silence in our art than to anticipate it falling into such light hands.

Howard's assessment is unduly critical, yet it sheds light on an aspect of Polk's personality. It was probably Polk to whom Howard was referring when he wrote that "[Coxhead is] very desirous to engage me. There has been some dissatisfaction between him and his head man who wishes to come and go as he pleases—has 'fits of work.' "[22] Polk's natural ability was not as yet balanced by restraint. In New York he found both the authority and the inspiration for that control.

Polk's move to New York was as beneficial to his education as London had been for Coxhead. He was now in the center of American artistic activity, surrounded by the leaders of the academic movement, and he sought to assimilate as much of that world as possible. He secured permission to attend classes in architecture at Columbia College given by William Robert Ware, Van Brunt's former partner. Ware was as influential a figure in the development of architectural education in the United States as Spiers was in England. He founded the country's first school of architecture at the Massachusetts Institute of Technology and was later asked to establish a similar program at Columbia. His lectures offered one of the most thorough investigations of architectural history then to be found in an American institution. Polk remained in the city only long enough to audit a portion of the curriculum; however, he later recalled that it was among the most valuable experiences of his youth.[23]

·HOVSE·AT·PLYMOVTH·MASS·
·FOR·MISS·KITTIE·BEARDSLEY·
·WILLIS·POLK·ARCHITECT·N·Y·C·

32. Willis Polk. Kittie Beardsley house, Plymouth, Massachusetts, 1889, probably a project. Drawing by Polk. (*American Architect*, July 17, 1889)

In New York Polk first gained employment with Charles Atwood, who subsequently became chief designer for D. H. Burnham & Company.[24] Several months later, Polk was hired as a draftsman by A. Page Brown, an ambitious architect with excellent connections who was only a few years his elder. Trained in the office of McKim, Mead & White, Brown had started his own practice in 1884 under the patronage of Mrs. Cyrus McCormick. Most of his early designs were for institutional buildings commissioned by the Chicago heiress as part of her extensive philanthropic activities. The majority of Brown's projects when Polk entered the office came directly or indirectly from Mrs. McCormick's East Coast friends.[25]

Brown was not so much a creative designer as he was a skillful expositor of McKim, Mead & White's urbane style. His practice was still modest, yet he delegated a substantial portion of both design and supervisory tasks to assistants. Through his employer, Polk gained some familiarity with McKim, Mead & White's work and met the partners themselves. Both offices were located in the same building,

55

at 57 Broadway, and close ties were maintained between parent and offspring firms. McKim, Mead & White's quarters were much more than a place of business; they had become an unofficial center of the academic movement and, according to White's biographer, "a council chamber where men could meet and discuss the renaissance of American Art." Besides the staff and young protégés, such as Carrère and Hastings, a host of leading painters and sculptors—Frank Millet, John La Farge, Augustus Saint-Gaudens, William Chase, John Singer Sargent—came to these gatherings. Polk got to know many of these men and maintained contact with them for a number of years.[26]

The time spent at 57 Broadway consummated Polk's training. To a greater extent than the intellectual perspectives afforded by Van Brunt and Ware, Polk was affected by McKim, Mead & White's commitment to beauty as the architect's ultimate aim. Polk worked on intuition, and he appears to have learned more by example than by theoretical analysis. By studying McKim, Mead & White's work, he realized a crucial synthesis between theory and practice. From Charles McKim, he learned the clear, logical ordering of form and space; and from Stanford White, the spirited manipulation of historical references and decorative details. An independent project for a summer house, designed while Polk was in Brown's office, shows his debt to McKim, Mead & White and also his ability to apply lessons learned in a creative fashion (Fig. 32). Brown no doubt recognized this talent, and when he moved his office to San Francisco he asked Polk to come with him.

Employment at 57 Broadway also played a formative role in the training of Albert Cicero Schweinfurth, who worked for Brown during the mid-1880s and whose departure from the office appears to have opened the position for Polk. Schweinfurth was born in January 1864 in the central New York manufacturing city of Auburn. His father, Charles J. Schweinfurth, was trained as an engineer in Germany. Forced to flee the country after the Revolution of 1848–1849, Charles came to the United States and moved to Auburn in 1852, where he began work as a woodcarver. Within a decade, he opened his own shop, specializing in the design and crafting of architectural ornament. The business prospered, and Charles Schweinfurth rose to a position of some prominence in the community.[27]

Schweinfurth and his three brothers received their introduction to design through their father's trade. All of them became architects; the two eldest gained national reputations. Charles Frederick established a practice in Cleveland in 1883 and was soon lauded as the city's finest architect. Julius Adolphe went to work for Peabody & Stearns in 1879; in 1887 he was appointed chief designer, and nine years later he embarked on a distinguished career of his own.[28]

Albert's youthful ambitions no doubt were influenced by his brothers' example. At age sixteen he left high school, moving to Boston where he shared an apartment with Julius. Initially, he clerked for J. R. Osgood & Company, printers of the *American Architect,* and in 1882 he joined Peabody & Stearns as a draftsman. By that time, the firm had earned a national reputation. Major commissions were received from many parts of the country, yet the office remained small and the staff closely knit. Albert stayed for about three years, long enough to learn the partners' methods well, particularly since Julius was now assisting Peabody in design. Peabody was among the first architects to make a serious study of early New England buildings and to advocate the use of this precedent in contemporary work. He

33. A. Page Brown. Museum of Historic Art, Princeton University, Princeton, New Jersey, 1887–1892; demolished 1964. (*Building,* September 8, 1888)

placed special value on the associational qualities of colonial architecture, which never seemed to be as important to McKim or White.[29] Peabody's nostalgia for this allegedly indigenous vernacular tradition left a lasting impression on Schweinfurth that would be of great consequence to his work in California.

Equally influential on the young draftsman was the transformation then taking place in the firm's approach to design. The last vestiges of High Victorian agglomerative composition were being replaced by a strong sense of Richardsonian order. Peabody maintained his own distinct style; nevertheless, his work during the first half of the 1880s represented some of the most sensitive variations on Richardson's manner.[30] Schweinfurth came in the midst of this change and was also able to study its sources firsthand. In Richardson, Schweinfurth found a hero. He never forgot the bold, elemental simplicity that gave the master's work such power and sense of purpose.

By February 1885 Schweinfurth had moved to New York and was working for Brown, who had opened his office only a few months previously. Schweinfurth had almost as much experience as his employer and was entrusted with major design responsibilities from the start of their association. The imprint of his hand was soon evident in the office's designs, reflecting the influences of Peabody, Richardson, and now of McKim, Mead & White. The mark of these influences is apparent in the Museum of Historic Art at Princeton, New Jersey (1887–1892) (Fig. 33). The parti is the same as that of Peabody's Museum of Fine Arts in St. Louis (1879–1881), and the entrance zone is a direct adaptation of his Memorial Hall at the nearby Lawrenceville School (1884–1885).[31] The details, on the other hand, are rendered with a delicacy and refinement that emulates White's manner.

Schweinfurth's borrowings were overt, but he progressively broadened his vocabulary. McKim, Mead & White drew from a much wider range of precedent than did Peabody & Stearns at that time, and they used a spectrum of foreign sources to develop an imagery tailored to a particular locale. The New York firm's early experiments with regional expression had a decisive influence on Schweinfurth, while Peabody's interest in New England Colonial architecture was not directed toward developing a distinct regional mode. White's Ramona School was no doubt in Schweinfurth's mind when he created the Mediterranean allusions in the Princeton Museum, and the school's regional overtures would provide a paradigm for his California work. The Ponce de Leon Hotel, then being designed by Carrère & Hastings, had even

34. A. C. Schweinfurth. Charles Dennison house, Denver, 1890;
no longer standing. (*Brickbuilder*, July 1894, p. 129)

more influence on Schweinfurth, who would eventually synthesize the
massive, elemental forms of Richardson and the diverse eclecticism of
McKim, Mead & White with a concern for regional expression.

Schweinfurth yearned for independence despite the responsibilities Brown gave him. Depressed over complications that threatened
cancellation of a favorite project, he left Brown in June 1886 to join
his brother Charles. However, the association failed, and Schweinfurth
returned to Brown within the year. He quit again in the fall of 1888 to
start his own office in New York. This venture was unsuccessful also,
and by that time Brown had left for the West Coast. Exhausted and
sick, Schweinfurth moved to Denver to recuperate. He soon found
employment in the branch office of a prominent Boston firm, Andrews
& Jacques.[32] By the latter months of 1889, he was again in business
for himself, having secured commissions for several residences. One
of these, designed for Charles Dennison (1890), gives an indication of
the architect's progress (Fig. 34). It is both a strong, simple gesture
and an intricate, even slightly exotic one, incorporating overt and
abstracted historical references. The scheme is less derivative than

59

those he did for Brown, yet its contrasting characteristics appear unresolved. Schweinfurth was still groping for a means to express the ideas he had acquired over the past decade.

There was tension in Schweinfurth's professional life as well. He found Denver's cultural climate stifling. In February 1890 he wrote an acerbic letter to the locally based *Western Architect and Building News,* complaining that the city's clientele were provincial and uninformed in their architectural tastes. Irritated by this assault on the booster spirit, the magazine's editor carped that Schweinfurth was "an extremist of the more virulent type."[33] The exchange was only symptomatic of his difficulties. Within a matter of weeks after the letter was printed, Schweinfurth left Denver for San Francisco, even though his projects were just beginning construction. Once again, Brown's office offered the stability that he could not find on his own.

While Schweinfurth and then Polk worked for Brown in New York, Bernard Maybeck held a comparable position with Carrère & Hastings. Maybeck probably met both draftsmen during this period. Later, he became acquainted with other members of the Polk clan and married the sister of one of Polk's friends in Kansas City. His move to San Francisco appears to have been encouraged by Polk.[34] Maybeck's early career is paradoxical compared to those of the other three architects. He was the only one to grow up in a major cultural center, to be raised by a family with intellectual interests, and to develop a serious concern for theory. He was the eldest, and he received the most intensive and highly esteemed training by attending the Ecole des Beaux Arts. Upon his return to the United States, he worked on projects of greater consequence than did the others. Yet Maybeck was the last to become a significant figure in his own right.

From an early age, Maybeck came into contact with people who were concerned with the dualities that existed in nineteenth-century design—craft and art, structure and composition, rationalist deduction and intuitive response—which he would seek to reconcile as an architect. His grandfather was a prominent master builder in Olde, Westphalia, and his father, Bernhardt Maybeck, studied sculpture before leaving Germany for New York as a result of the Revolution of 1848–1849. In New York, he applied his artistic talents to making ornamental cabinetry, giving his son both a respect for craft done by hand and a broad exposure to cultural and political subjects. The Maybeck household was a center for the city's German-American intellectuals, where discussions of art, music, and philosophy were a part of daily life. Bernard Maybeck became fluent in French as well as German. He was encouraged to pursue his interest in drawing and, later, to study design in Paris.[35]

Perhaps even before Maybeck left for Europe, he was introduced to the ideas of Gottfried Semper. Unlike most nineteenth-century theorists, Semper believed that the principles governing art and craft were synonymous, and he sought to formulate a rational methodology for analyzing them. Deviating from then current evolutionary thought, Semper maintained that all architecture consisted of four irreducible elements: hearth, floor, roof, and enclosure. He offered these archetypes to explain the complexities of present forms, rather than as an argument for returning to an elemental vocabulary. He was fascinated by the primitive hut and enamored with the cinquecento. For all his rationalist concerns, Semper felt that these archetypes could never be fully manifested; the work of art must remain a thing of mystery. Semper's magnum opus was *Der Stil* (1860, 1863), an unfinished treatise ponderously written and generally ignored by the English-speaking world. But for Maybeck, the book's message had great importance. He planned to translate at least portions of the text for Polk's *Architectural News* in the early 1890s. The project never materialized, yet the impact of Semper was evident in the architect's work a few years later.[36]

From 1882 to 1886, Maybeck attended the Ecole, working in the atelier of Jules André. A former pupil of Henri Labrouste's, André admired his mentor's attempt to cleanse architecture of excesses and to begin anew with the essentials of classical order as a basis for expression. Equally important to André was Labrouste's frank and lyrical use of cast-iron construction to articulate space and to satisfy contemporary needs. At the same time, André championed the academic predilection for intuitive design, where composition, not structure, was the primary ordering device. When Maybeck entered the atelier, it exemplified the elegant, urbane classicism of Charles Garnier. From the start, Maybeck learned Beaux Arts principles from the inner sanctum. André's buildings enriched the picture. His most important commission at that time, the Museum of Natural History in Paris (1872–1885), draws from both Garnier's exquisite compositional order and from Labrouste's bold structural expression.[37] The integral relationship André espoused between these two aspects of design had an enduring influence on Maybeck's work.

Maybeck's interest in structure was further stimulated by the writings of Viollet-le-Duc, which he probably studied while he was in

Paris. Viollet's tempestuous episode at the Ecole some two decades earlier may still have been discussed among students. One of André's star pupils, Julien Guadet, had led the popular revolt against the theorist. Maybeck held Guadet in high esteem, but he was no less fascinated by Viollet's ideas.[38] Maybeck was perhaps initially attracted to these writings out of a love of French medieval architecture. The *Dictionnaire raisonné* (1854–1868) and *Entretiens sur l'architecture* (1863, 1872) not only afforded an encyclopedic register of medieval building elements, but also gave them life and meaning. Viollet's commitment to freedom in design, based on his rationalist interpretation of past periods, also had a great effect on Maybeck's thinking. The lucid analysis of the creative spirit that permeates the *Entretiens* gave a very different perspective to design than that emphasized at the Ecole. The independence of Viollet's thoughts would be paralleled in Maybeck's career; at an early date he nurtured an inclusive attitude toward ideas and historic precedent.

Upon returning to New York, Maybeck joined the office of Carrère & Hastings. Hastings was a friend and former colleague in André's atelier; he and Maybeck now worked closely together on design.[39] Hastings had more experience, and his position as a partner suggests that he played the dominant role. However, Maybeck was only two years his junior and had much the same training. Their influence on one another was no doubt considerable. Hastings set the tone for the firm's work with the Ponce de Leon Hotel, designed shortly before Maybeck entered the office. Adapting André's structural interests to local conditions, the complex is built of reinforced concrete, left exposed yet kept subordinate to a rigorous composition. The hotel was also the largest and among the most imaginative examples of French planning techniques then to be found in the United States. This discipline is matched by the fanciful aura of its exotic embellishments and dramatic gesture. Maybeck's contribution came later and was probably focused on the interior.[40] The details in many of the principal rooms appear to have been taken right out of a handbook on ornament, suggesting the work of a novice, yet the motifs are combined in a most spirited way (Fig. 35). Large in scale and lavishly applied, they give the spaces a decorative exuberance all their own. The effect is quite different from the restrained ambience found in contemporary work by McKim, Mead & White, yet bears affinity to that of interior schemes Maybeck would design in the Bay Area during the next two decades.

Maybeck probably played a more consequential role in design-

35. Carrère & Hastings. Ponce de Leon Hotel main parlor.
(*American Architect*, June 13, 1896)

ing the Alcazar Hotel (1886–1888), across the street from the Ponce de Leon.[41] Reflecting the tight budget, its concrete walls are unadorned. Composition is paramount. Then, on the towers and an unexecuted shopping arcade, the surfaces erupt into ornament derived from antiquity and the Italian Renaissance, but Churrigueresque in its effect (Fig. 36). The lesson in abstract form becomes a magnificent decorative indulgence.

The élan that distinguishes these buildings was not just a result of their location and pleasure-oriented use, however. The most extraordinary early design by the firm is a competition entry for the Cathedral of St. John the Divine in New York (1889) (Fig. 37). The scheme surpasses the most chimerical essays prepared for the Prix de Rome, rising like a vision in an extravagant dream. Yet here, too, the underlying order is implicit in the orchestration of both form and space. The remarkable manner in which such elaborate designs are controlled is almost certainly due to Hastings, but some of their fantasy may have

36. Carrère & Hastings. Alcazar Hotel, St. Augustine, Florida,
1886–1888. Detail of tower. (Author)

come from Maybeck.[42] Whatever his responsibilities with the firm,
Maybeck owed it a lasting debt for demonstrating how creative and
varied were the possibilities of putting French theory into practice on
American soil.

64

Maybeck's imagination was fertile, his enthusiasm unabashed, and his desire for independence paramount. By the latter months of 1889 he moved to Kansas City. No work was forthcoming, but he did join two local architects to enter a national competition for the St. Louis City Hall. Illustrations of the scheme have yet to be found; however, remarks by the competition's advisor, William Robert Ware, offer important clues about its appearance. He condemned the design for its lack of cohesiveness:

The separation into three parallel structures is vicious from the point of view of both plan and elevations, requiring an extravagant amount of staircases and corridors, and destroying the simplicity and unity of the exterior.

37. Carrère & Hastings. Cathedral of St. John the Divine, New York, 1889, competition entry. (*American Architect*, October 5, 1889)

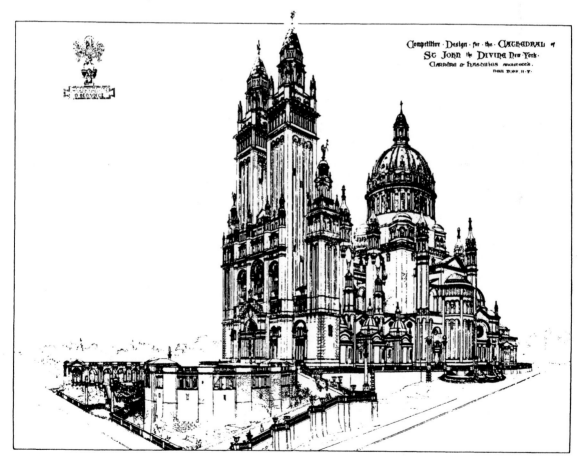

But:

The architectural treatment, especially the rotunda, is so imposing, and the central feature of the dome, with its four flanking turrets, is so praiseworthy for elegance and dignity of line, that it appears only fair to award this design, in spite of its grave and fundamental defects, a special honorable mention.[43]

Without the discipline provided by Hastings, Maybeck floundered.

Immediately after the competition, Maybeck left for San Francisco, where he joined Polk and Schweinfurth in Brown's office. He did not remain there, or with any other firm, for long. His first independent commission was not until 1895, and another seven years elapsed before he opened an office. His struggle stemmed partly from the search for the means to channel his imagination toward resolving the divergent concerns that so intrigued him.

III

SAN FRANCISCO: The Modern Cosmopolis

California is positive, it is individual, it is great in opportunity, and when the ages have lent it dignity, it will go down in history with Egypt, with Greece, with Rome and with France. It will be the inheritor of all their greatness, but the projector of its own!

Willis Polk, *Wave*, April 15, 1898

SAN FRANCISCO was an ideal place for Coxhead, Polk, Schweinfurth, and Maybeck to establish themselves as architects. Each man had completed his training in a major metropolis and would never lose his taste for the cultural stimulus such cities provided. At the same time, all four men restlessly sought independence and recognition. They left London and New York in search of places not bound by tradition, where they could make their reputations without catering to an established professional hierarchy. They had worked in smaller communities—Los Angeles, Kansas City, and Denver—only to leave a short time later. San Francisco provided the right balance between promise for the future and the resources to exploit that potential creatively. It was both urbane and provincial, boasting a sophisticated populace but as yet unable to manifest its energies in enduring forms of cultural expression.

Through their designs, Coxhead, Polk, Schweinfurth, and Maybeck strove to give San Francisco that expression. They emphatically rejected the prevalent tendencies in local architecture. Among their primary concerns was firmly to implant the academic movement on western soil. Yet they also shared the feeling that California would not only inherit the greatness of other places, but would be "the projector of its own." The architects drew inspiration from San Francisco's special character and from the region's spectacular landscape, found support and stimulus from local intellectuals and artists, and gained the patronage of prominent businessmen and philanthropists. These circumstances not only encouraged productivity, but also had a substantial influence on all four architects' work.

67

The identity that California had acquired as a unique place was partially a result of the vast distances that lay between it and other, well-settled regions. James Bryce observed:

Cut off from the more populous parts of the Mississippi Valley by an almost continuous desert of twelve hundred miles, across which two daily trains move like ships across the ocean, separated from Oregon on the north by a wilderness of sparsely settled mountain and forest, it has grown up in its own way and acquired a sort of consciousness of separate existence.[1]

Most of the West, Bryce remarked, was populated by persons from neighboring regions to the east, but California attracted immigrants from all over the world. Intense development had occurred in less than half a century, yet it seemed much older. California's perceived distinctness arose not so much from any single quality as from the great spectrum of qualities and their intensity. It was a land of contrasts, a land of extremes.

If California was seen as an empire, San Francisco was the undisputed capital. Bryce asserted that it "dwarfs the other cities [in the state; it] is a commercial and intellectual centre, the source of influence for the surrounding regions, more powerful over them than is any eastern city over its neighborhood. It is a New York which has got no Boston on one side of it and no shrewd and orderly rural populace on the other."[2] The city had seemed extraordinary from the start. More sensational than the gold rush that ignited the stampede of settlers was the ensuing transformation of San Francisco from village to metropolis within a decade. And unlike other western centers, this instant city was also an international city. Between 1870 and 1890, the percentage of foreign-born residents exceeded that of either New York or Chicago. There were sizable colonies of European and Oriental immigrants.[3] As the city seemed isolated from all places, so it was considered to be the center of many places. Being in San Francisco, wrote William Henry Bishop, was equivalent to a journey around the world. The metropolis's astonishing ascendency and international character were considered to be prophetic of its future greatness:

San Francisco has come to be the dividing-ridge between the Old World and the New—the point which separates the Past from the Present—the pivot upon which the world's trade and exchange now turn. . . . She dares everything, and attempts everything—[San Francisco is] the most audacious city in the world.[4]

No other American metropolis so electrified the imagination.

Among the most appealing attributes of San Francisco and its environs was the physical setting. David Starr Jordan, president of Stanford University, was one of many people who considered the region's landscape as important in attracting new residents as its mild climate and reputation for independence. Most of the city's established architects appear to have had scant interest in the matter; however, Coxhead and other members of his generation were captivated by the variety of terrain. They looked at this landscape as artists, with a romantic fascination for its great scale and multitude of images. These men were probably the first architects who felt that San Francisco's setting demanded special responses in design. Shortly after his arrival, Polk reflected this enthusiasm: "Perhaps there isn't a city in the world as picturesque and as beautiful . . . or where greater opportunities are presented to the architect."[5]

Much of San Francisco's charm was identified with the overall visual effect of the city rather than individual landmarks. The scale of building was small, and the settlement dense. Little focus existed, only the panoply of edifices clinging to the dramatic terrain, creating an ever-changing sequence of views (Fig. 38). Many visitors remarked that it was unique among American cities. It was described as being "more cosmopolitan than New York and more sensuous than New Orleans." Its character seemed to come from another land. An eastern journalist, who had been told that San Francisco in many respects resembled New York, was taken by complete surprise:

. . . you can scarcely imagine the foreignness of the effect looking down on the city from one of its hills. Over a very great district the entire hill-studded view is covered with brown-painted wooden houses, mainly very small and low, and built in rows to the tops of many of the hills. As each house is seen with photographic distinctness in that clear air, the whole is . . . like a great painting of some place in a foreign land as if you visited it from within the enclosure of a cyclorama.

San Francisco was compared to Rome, Corinth, Naples, Geneva, London, Florence, Bombay, and Constantinople, but its essence was difficult to pinpoint. Robert Louis Stevenson offered an apt summary of the "modern cosmopolis":

One brief sensation follows and obliterates another . . . the city leaves upon the mind no general and stable picture, but a profusion of airy and incon-

38. San Francisco, California Street looking west toward Nob Hill,
ca. 1888. (San Francisco Public Library)

gruous images of sea and shore, the east and west, the summer and winter.[6]

San Francisco's specialness resulted in part from this quality of eluding precise description. Gelett Burgess would later reminisce:

Black-leg and fanatic, boulevardier and scholar, light-of-love and philanthropist, crank and cynic, straggler and businessman . . . all touch elbows in the crowded life of the town. It is a little cosmos, bizarre, isolate, remote, all things to all men, wrapped in a variegated mantle of chance and change . . . where every street climbs a half-dozen hills, changing its character at every lamp post.[7]

San Francisco's streets also conveyed a sense of age, despite the fact that the city had existed for only a few decades. One observer even felt that the mid-nineteenth-century business district looked much

70

older than comparable sections in New York and Philadelphia. Around the city's center lay ample vestiges of early settlement. The jerry-built structures were aging rapidly, and many of them had begun to decay, creating an effect that, combined with their Gold Rush-era associations, created a romantic appeal. Clusters of these buildings existed on hillsides too steep to be reached by the otherwise ubiquitous grid. A favorite haunt of artists, the old houses clinging to the slopes appeared somewhat comparable to the configuration of Mediterranean villages.[8]

As San Francisco seemed to embody many worlds, so the surrounding area seemed to be a microcosm of California's multifaceted landscape. The enormous bay brought these diverse settings into a single focus, at once conveying a sense of expansiveness and reducing the perceived scale of the whole. The scene was likened to "a noble amphitheatre . . . Grecian in form and contour, exquisitely varied in play of light and shadow."[9] To the east lay the flatlands of Oakland and neighboring towns, now rapidly developing as suburban enclaves. Framing them were grassy hills, extending far to the south and providing a welcome shield from the hot, dry inland valleys. Northward, the mountains of Marin County rose precipitously from the water, sheltering small fishing towns and resort communities in their midst. South on the San Francisco peninsula stretched a pastoral landscape of rolling fields and live oak trees, interspersed with the cultivated grounds of large country houses. And beyond lay the Santa Cruz Mountains, the orchards of the Santa Clara Valley, the deltas above San Pablo Bay, the lush vineyards of the Napa and Sonoma valleys, and the redwood groves along the Russian River, terminating at the Pacific Ocean.

Cosmopolitan urbanity, picturesque rusticity, and topographical diversity—all would be reflected in the young architects' work. The means by which these qualities were imparted to their buildings varied. Coxhead, Polk, and Maybeck envisioned the terrain as a great classical landscape and developed monumental schemes on an expansive scale that echoed its sublime dimensions. Schweinfurth was enticed by other analogies to the Mediterranean and sought an architecture that embodied the legacies of more primitive southern cultures. All four men also cultivated a rustic imagery inherited from the postmedieval vernacular traditions of northern Europe, employing it in city and suburbs alike. Coxhead, Polk, and Maybeck often used a rich assortment of elements set at a tiny scale and compacted them into small buildings, reflecting the many worlds that were present in the region. Schweinfurth gave massive forms an elemental simplicity that he felt embodied the strength and promise of the nascent land.

71

San Francisco's promise was sustained by more than enthu-siastic descriptions and a beautiful setting. In 1890, it ranked seventh in population, fourth in foreign trade, and eighth in manufacturing among American cities. No city west of St. Louis came close to rivaling its stature or the fervency with which promoters predicted its future preeminence. San Francisco had both the resources and ambi-tions to produce great works; however, that potential was far from being realized.

Culturally, San Francisco remained a provincial outpost. In 1892, sculptor Douglas Tilden offered harsh criticism of its citizens' indifference to art. There was little enthusiasm, he complained, for concerts or exhibitions; no museum existed; and the region's few artists received even fewer commissions.[10] The city had amassed great wealth, yet this very phenomenon contributed to an absence of matu-rity in some other aspects of urban life. San Franciscans were charac-terized as a people bent on pleasure, the ultimate materialists in a materialistic age. Most of their riches were channeled into business and gaudy display. Elegant hostelries, sumptuous cuisine, lavish parties, and ostentatious houses were the primary cultural symbols.

Ironically, within the first decade of settlement, the city's afflu-ence and vivacious character attracted an array of creative talent that was unmatched in the early history of the West. However, the local populace was for the most part indifferent to such endeavors. The flourish of literary activity that began in the 1850s was dissipated in little more than a decade for want of support.[11] The best writers, Mark Twain and Bret Harte, moved east in pursuit of more rewarding careers. Their migration became an established pattern over the ensuing years; dozens of young men who sought distinction in the liberal and fine arts saw little hope of realizing their ambitions in San Francisco. Others persisted. Several painters, most of them European or trained in Europe, settled in the city during the 1860s and formed a small Bohemian colony. Much of their work went unsold. Rich collectors traveled east to make their purchases, buying canvases by foreign painters of recognized stature. Yet sufficient interest existed in local efforts to establish the San Francisco Art Association in 1871. Two years later, the California School of Design was organized under the Association's auspices. Both institutions were the first of their kind in the West. They helped coalesce the artistic community and provided a training ground for local talents.[12]

The city's size, wealth, and geographic isolation created a demand for other institutions at an early date, fostering the growth of intellectual activity. Three substantial libraries were founded in the 1850s, as were St. Ignatius College and the California Academy of Sciences. In nearby Berkeley, the state university was established during the next decade, and by the late 1880s it had emerged as the major institution of higher learning west of the Mississippi. The adjacent town became a center for scholars and many others with shared interests. The intellectual communities of San Francisco and Berkeley alike were still relatively small, parochial, and boosterish, yet they were increasingly influential and provided a cultural stimulus surpassed by only the largest American cities. Coxhead, Polk, Schweinfurth, and Maybeck found both friendship and support from these people. All four men believed that architecture practiced as an art could not flourish as an isolated phenomenon; it must be part of a broad cultural impulse. The region's artists and intellectuals provided an essential part of that context, as well as a large segment of the young architects' clientele. Many of them were easterners who had cultivated tastes and wanted simple, inexpensive, yet uncommon houses. They welcomed the arrival of designers who could respond to their needs creatively. Without such clients, none of the four architects could have maintained independent practice for long.

The steady growth of artistic and intellectual pursuits led to a significant change in attitude toward the century's close. Increasing numbers of prominent San Franciscans sought to have their city become a great cultural center. This drive was fueled by the omnipresent desire to emulate larger, more established cities. Despite San Francisco's reputation for independent thought and judgment, its citizens continually looked to the accomplishments of East Coast metropolises as a yardstick by which to measure their own. In declaring its progress, the city, like others in the West, was intensely promotional. This boosterism fostered self-consciousness, for it depended upon the assessment of outsiders as much as that of residents. San Franciscans grew ever more vulnerable to criticism by visitors about their city's lingering reputation as a crass, gaudy town that lacked cultural refinement.

Efforts to improve the situation were not entirely reactionary. Motivation also stemmed from the uninhibited optimism that had made San Francisco a leading entrepôt and was encouraged by members of a younger generation who were well educated, financially secure, and devoted to the betterment of their city. Although the self-made railroad and bonanza kings captured headlines for their lavish demeanor, a large segment of San Francisco society was composed of people who came from distinguished East Coast families and were more refined in their cultural predilections.[13] The latter group set the tone for the emerging civic leaders and philanthropists of the 1880s and 1890s. These rich San Franciscans also became important patrons for Coxhead, Polk, Schweinfurth, and Maybeck. A less sophisticated class of prominent citizens might well have been indifferent to the special talent each architect had to offer. The opportunities afforded by this clientele and the promise of cultural transformation that they nurtured were perhaps the most appealing aspects of all to the four architects.

An indication of the improving cultural climate lay in the number of young artists and writers who began to work in San Francisco during the early 1890s. Even as Douglas Tilden bemoaned local conditions, he was aware of the prospects for change. Tilden, along with painters Charles Rollo Peters and Ernest Peixotto, had attended the California School of Design. Like so many of their colleagues, they continued their education in Paris; however, they broke the usual pattern by returning to San Francisco. Bruce Porter was also a native son, but received no formal training. After several years of self-guided study in Europe, he came back in 1891 to embark on a career that included stained-glass and garden design, mural painting, house decoration, and writing. Gelett Burgess arrived the same year, fresh from MIT's School of Engineering. In 1894, he began to design furniture, but soon became known for his novels and satirical essays. The most talented figure of this period was Frank Norris, who began his career as a journalist in 1894 after graduating from Berkeley.[14]

These men and others like them soon discovered kindred spirits in the architects who had arrived a year or so earlier. This youthful band hardly constituted a close-knit group; not all of them were even friends. No one person was the acknowledged leader, even though two members of an older generation, painter William Keith and Swedenborgian minister Joseph Worcester, were held in particular esteem.[15] Fin-de-siècle San Francisco failed to become a spawning ground for a community of great artists. Only Burgess and Norris gained national reputations, and they too eventually made the migration eastward. Yet during the 1890s, the presence of gifted artists working in a variety of creative disciplines provided an atmosphere of convivality, exchange, and mutual reinforcement that was of great benefit to the four architects' work.[16]

Coxhead, Polk, Schweinfurth, and Maybeck found little of comparable value in the region's architecture. However appealing the overall physical ambience of San Francisco and its environs, few individual buildings gained their respect. The dearth of venerated precedent fostered a sense of freedom as well as urgency in the four architects' cause. Their role was seen as being analogous to that of McKim, Mead & White and others in the East a decade earlier, without the example of Richardson to prepare the way. They admired the Franciscan missions and other remnants of Hispanic rule. However, only Schweinfurth felt that such buildings constituted a major source for new work, and in practice he drew much more from European models.[17] The few products of American settlement to elicit praise from this generation dated from the mid-nineteenth century.

During the 1850s, San Francisco had attracted several professionally trained architects whose abilities far exceeded those normally found in the initial years of a city's development. Their finest buildings compared favorably with the advanced contemporary work in New York, Philadelphia, and Boston. Gordon Cummings's Montgomery Block (1853), erected less than six years after the city was founded,

39. Kenitzer & Farquharson. Lick House, San Francisco, ca. 1862; burned 1906. Dining room. (Author's collection)

40. S. C. Bugbee & Sons. David Colton house, San Francisco, 1871–1872;
burned 1906 (*left*). Augustus Laver. James Flood house, 1886; remodeled
by Polk for Pacific Union Club, 1908–1910. (Bancroft Library)

was among the largest and best-constructed office buildings in the
country at that time. The John Parrott house (1854) possessed an
elegance and restraint that would have made it noteworthy in the most
fashionable eastern suburb. Peter Portois's West End Hotel (1863)
exhibited the new French taste for a complex yet tightly ordered layering of wall planes and ornament associated with Parisian work of the
Second Empire—work that would have a major impact on American
architecture only after the Civil War. One of the most remarkable
products of the era was the dining room in the Lick House (ca. 1862),
designed by Henry Kenitzer and David Farquharson (Fig. 39). Few
large public spaces in the country were more opulent, and the pervasive order and unity given this room would not be matched until large
academic schemes began to be designed almost three decades later.[18]

Buildings of this era were largely forgotten until Polk and his
contemporaries praised them in the early 1890s. Polk cited the David
Colton house (1871–1872) as being "the most artistic . . . dwelling
in the . . . city," adding that no other residence approached it "in
modesty, dignity, and simple grandeur" (Fig. 40). Subsequently, he
admonished the lack of deference to such work.

76

There are a lot of houses belonging to the early period of San Francisco that stand in silent, solemn, and dignified protest against the horrors of [later years]. . . . They were built by men . . . who regarded architecture as an art, and who declined to look upon it as a speculative trade.

Others agreed. Looked at through academic glasses, these buildings were marred by "coarse" details; yet seldom was any collection of Victorian architecture singled out for such favorable comment at the turn of the century.[19]

During the 1870s and 1880s, architecture in the region lost its precociousness. Local examples of High Victorian modes closely followed established patterns, suggesting that plan books were a primary source of ideas. Contemporary accounts never ceased to comment on practitioners' desire to be up to date in their work; however, currency was based on widely disseminated information. In its aim and content, San Francisco's High Victorian architecture was thoroughly provincial.

One characteristic set these buildings apart: the persistent use of wood. Stevenson remarked that "the whole city is . . . a woodyard of unusual extent and complication." Two decades later, Charles Fletcher Lummis reiterated that "woodenness so willful and so expansive probably marks no other city."[20] Redwood and pine were readily available and so were prevalent during the Gold Rush era when expedient construction was essential, skilled labor scarce, and permanency undesirable. A series of devastating fires in the 1850s resulted in the erection of masonry and iron-front buildings in the commercial district, but the trend proved to be short-lived. For most of the city, no fire codes were implemented to prohibit the use of wood construction. The material continued to be used because it was cheap. Sufficient deposits of stone and clay did not exist close by, and later, when regional quarries and brickyards began to operate on a large scale, their products were more expensive than those in many other parts of the country. Moreover, a local superstition regarding the unhealthfulness of masonry buildings was fed by ignorance of proper insulating methods. There was also a widespread fear that masonry construction would collapse in a major earthquake, so the resiliency of wood framing was generally preferred even when other materials could be afforded.[21]

The omnipresence of wood for structure and finish affected the design of local buildings in two ways. Wood frames were conducive to complicated, picturesque massing, and wooden sheathing allowed for a proliferation of surface patterns and other decorative details at relatively small cost. Given the High Victorian taste for picturesqueness and ornament, it is understandable why the region's architecture

77

was so profusely adorned. Furthermore, by the 1870s, the simplicity of earlier buildings came to be viewed as an unfortunate vestige of the all too recent pioneer past. In their efforts to be fashionable and to demonstrate that the city possessed "beautiful" architecture, San Franciscans employed wooden embellishments with an intensity, and sometimes an exaggeration, unsurpassed in other parts of the country.

By the mid-1880s, there was a growing dissatisfaction with the qualities of these ornate wooden buildings. The normally complacent *California Architect and Building News* lamented that few travelers came to the city without ridiculing its wooden houses.[22] Yet the initial rumblings of discontent were dwarfed by the vehement attacks that came from the young architects and their contemporaries during the next decade. The newcomers were not offended by the prevalence of wood, but by the fact that it was so often treated in ways traditionally associated with masonry. Burgess saw this absence of "truth" in materials as embodying the philistine qualities San Franciscans were trying so hard to eradicate: "As the women seek to counterfeit the charms denied them by the use of rouge and enamel, so the men daub and spatter deceptions of concrete and cement to indecent limits." Equally objectionable was the prevailing High Victorian ostentatiousness. These critics regarded the work of the past two decades as grotesque and undisciplined, violating every principle of design that they had been taught. Page Brown caustically remarked that the city would be blessed were a great fire to sweep it away. Peixotto described recent Queen Anne houses as "absurdities . . . piled up without rhyme or reason—restless, turreted, gabled, loaded with meaningless detail, defaced with fantastic windows and hideous chimneys." He lamented that "the more 'features' a house has, the more 'artistic' it is considered," scorning the ignorance of a public that "craves display and wants something new and fashionable."[23]

No one was more acerbic than Polk. He branded the Western Addition, the site of some of the newest residential development, as "an architectural nightmare conceived in a reign of terror and produced by artistic anarchists." He denounced the untrained architects whom he held responsible for such work and whose methods he remembered all too well from his youth: "The real estate speculators, speculative contractors, and disappointed carpenters who have passed themselves off . . . as architects all over the country, seem to have found their last refuge in San Francisco" (Fig. 41). Polk mocked the High Victorian pursuit of newness, saying: "The proudest boast of our modern householder is that . . . his gables, turrets, bay-windows, and filigree

41. "San Francisco's Architectural Monstrosities." (*Wave*, March 20, 1897, p. 6)

CHAOS AVENUE: AN ARCHTECT'S NIGHTMARE

An honest failure

The chef d'œuvre of a pioneer contractor. The porch and belfry executed by an intelligent but misguided foreman during a fit of melancholia.

The ubiquitous corner tower

STUDIES IN FANTASTIC "SKY LINES"

...wing how the beauty of the most picturesque and romantic spot on the Pacific Coast has been heightened by the erection of a wooden bird cage and a half-gross assortment of triangles

A gingerbread palace (white marble and redwood)

Details of typical "A," "B" and "C" flat entrance with "columns" and porch decorated in the highest style of planing mill art; imitation stained glass a specialty

work are entirely original . . . no one else has anything like them; no imitation of old-fashioned ideas for him, *if* you please." These claims were dismissed as phoney: "While San Francisco . . . really discriminates between fake articles and genuine merit, it usually accepts the fake."[24]

However different Polk's assessment of this Victorian legacy is from those today, the provincialism he ridiculed did exist. Harold Kirker has argued that California's remote location and the inherent conservatism of its "colonial" populace were the reasons for such retardataire work.[25] Yet this rationale fails to explain the unusually fine products of the 1850s and early 1860s. The transfer of ideas to the West Coast could have been impeded by the vast distances separating the two ends of the continent, but San Francisco's architectural sophistication experienced a pronounced decline *after* completion of the transcontinental railroad, which greatly improved communications with the East. Furthermore, the architecture in many American communities close to metropolitan centers was scarcely less provincial than that of the city by the Golden Gate.

Perhaps the major factor contributing to the provincialism of High Victorian buildings in San Francisco was the lack of talented designers settling in the region for more than two decades after the Civil War. An influx of architects during the early 1870s may well have undermined the stature of the older generation, but none of the newcomers possessed comparable abilities. A few of them had impressive credentials: Albert Pissis had attended the Ecole des Beaux Arts; F. F. Hamilton had worked in the offices of both Gridley Bryant and Peabody & Stearns in Boston. However, those architects were the exception. Many of the new arrivals, such as William Curlett, Henry Geilfuss, and Julius Krafft, were trained in technical schools. Others, including William Mooser, Clinton Day, and the Newsom brothers, immigrated as youths and were apprenticed in local offices of little distinction. Once established in San Francisco, most of these architects seem to have had little direct contact with new developments in the field, and the atmosphere became stagnant.[26] By 1889, the professional establishment consisted primarily of men who had been removed from the architectural mainstream and who continued to work in ways they had learned early in their careers.

The disdain Coxhead, Polk, Schweinfurth, and Maybeck had for their elder colleagues must have made them feel all the more isolated, but it may also have freed them from many local influences. Had they located in a city such as Chicago, where a number of revered architects were in practice, where professional organizations flourished, and where a provocative journal was being issued monthly, their work would surely have been affected, perhaps dominated, by these forces. Moving to San Francisco before they had developed fixed ways no doubt reinforced each man's independent inclinations.

By 1889, the mood was ripe for change. For the first time, San Franciscans were seeking the services of prominent architects from the East and Midwest. The prestige of commissioning a famous designer from hundreds of miles afield may have influenced their choices, but there was a growing sentiment that local architects were incapable of creating the desired quality of work. The trend was initiated by Leland Stanford. Seeking the best designers in the country to prepare the master plan of his new university, he hired Frederick Law Olmsted in 1885 and Shepley, Rutan & Coolidge the following year.[27] In 1887, newspaperman Michael de Young turned to the Chicago firm of Burnham & Root for the design of the Chronicle Building, the city's first skyscraper. Not long after it was completed, a reporter exclaimed that at last the era of diminutive architecture was drawing to a close, adding that to date San Francisco had been outclassed by such "third grade" cities as Denver and Omaha with respect to its major buildings. Other businessmen followed de Young's example. His archrival, William Randolph Hearst, had Burnham & Root make preliminary studies for the headquarters of the *San Francisco Examiner* in 1890, and Darius Ogden Mills secured the firm's services for the plans of an office building considerably larger than the Chronicle.[28]

The run on outside talent did not last long. By 1890 several new firms were established in San Francisco and were capturing many of the prize commissions. Even before Brown and Polk arrived in July 1889, Chicagoan John M. Wood had moved to San Francisco and was completing plans for a major hotel. James and Merritt Reid, who would enjoy a long career designing commercial and residential buildings, came at about the same time. The beginnings of a significant departure in the work of Pissis & Moore were visible in the firm's winning design for the Hibernia Savings and Loan Society in March 1889, suggesting it may have acquired a new designer fresh from New York or even Paris.[29] But the architect who had the most significant impact on San Francisco at this time was Page Brown. With Polk, and soon Schweinfurth and Maybeck, in his employ, he was considered the leader of the new "renaissance" in the Bay Area.

IV

TRANSITION: A Few Young Men

A few young men . . . have begun to think while they work, with a result that inspires every citizen of San Francisco with the enthusiasm of a promise . . . .
San Francisco Call, August 9, 1896

DURING THE early 1890s, many San Franciscans became aware that a significant change was occurring in their architecture. These years were no less pivotal for the men who inaugurated that change—in establishing themselves in practice, in coalescing their ideas, and in translating them into coherent forms of expression. By 1893, Page Brown gained recognition as one of the foremost designers and the leading advocate of academic eclecticism in the region. His office served as a center for others who were committed to the movement, including Polk, Schweinfurth, and Maybeck. As Brown's chief draftsman, Schweinfurth began to resolve the divergent tendencies in his work, developing a clear, bold approach to the use of form. Polk started to work on his own. Although he received few substantial commissions, he became more independent in thought and practice. Coxhead gained a solid reputation, with major projects for the Episcopal church rendered in a strong, personal style.

The extent to which San Franciscans were eager for change is evident in the phenomenal success of Brown's career from the moment he arrived in the city. Less than two years elapsed before the volume of his work was equal to, if not greater than, that of established firms. While in New York, Brown had confided in his mentor, Mrs. Cyrus McCormick, about the difficulties of sustaining a practice where so many architects were vying for commissions, and expressed an interest in relocating where the opportunities were greater. That chance came when he was commissioned to design several projects for the widow of railroad magnate Charles Crocker. Brown opened a San Francisco office in July 1889 on a trial basis. He did not take long in deciding to remain permanently. Construction began on the Crocker

42. A. Page Brown. Crocker Old People's Home, San Francisco, 1889–1890; altered. Drawing by Polk. (*Building*, July 27, 1889)

family tomb in Oakland and the Crocker Old People's Home in San Francisco (Fig. 42) a few weeks after he arrived.[1] Soon Crocker's son, William, who headed the family's extensive banking interests, became a steady client. In October, Brown started work on additions to Grace Episcopal Church, one of the city's most fashionable parishes, where William was a leading force on the building committee. By January 1890 preliminary plans were accepted for the Crocker Building, among the largest office towers at that time in the West (Fig. 43). The following year, Brown designed San Francisco's new YMCA, of which William was the treasurer.[2] Both James Donohue, president of the Donohue-Kelly Banking Company, and Frederick W. Sharon, who controlled some of the most extensive real estate holdings in the region, also commissioned large office buildings. Among Brown's numerous residential projects were houses for Alban Towne, second vice-president and general manager of the Southern Pacific Railroad; Alexander Hawes, manager of the New York Life Insurance Company's local branch; Robert McLean, a leading physician; and Frederick Ginn, cofounder of Ginn and Company, publishers.

Brown came to San Francisco with the right credentials. His association with McKim, Mead & White and a portfolio of work

43. A. Page Brown. Crocker Building, San Francisco, 1890–1892;
demolished ca. 1960. (Courtesy Sheila Mack)

designed for prominent East Coast families quickly made him the
favored architect of local society, purveying the latest, most fashionable ideas from New York—something for which San Franciscans had
a particular weakness. His friendship with Mrs. McCormick and now
the Crockers gave him a social and professional entrée. He thrived in
this setting, joining the best men's clubs and becoming a conspicuous
figure among the sporting set. He could charm grand dames, young
Turks, pragmatic businessmen, and Bohemian intellectuals. Brown
was the cultivated gentleman, polite and discreet about his affairs,
self-effacing in public, yet hard-working and always conscious of
advancing his position. He had come to know well the ways of his

clients and proved to be facile as a creator of settings that made them feel at home.

Brown's interests focused on developing a large, prestigious practice. The volume of his work and the efforts necessary to attain more commissions meant that he had less time to spend on the projects themselves. After moving to San Francisco, he lamented that his tutelage under McKim, Mead & White had been too short. A more thorough training would have been beneficial, for now he had "too much work to 'digest.' " He longed for "two or three years to simply carry out one idea at a time." Yet the prestige and financial rewards of a large practice were even more enticing. One account noted that he "directed, supervised, suggested"; however, "it was out of the question that he should attempt his own designing, [for he employed] excellent men to execute his conceptions on their own."[3]

The consistency evident in Brown's work indicates that he influenced its composition, form, and details. At the same time, the personalities of his head draftsmen, Polk and Schweinfurth, are also evident. Polk appears to have been the dominant force until he left the office around August 1890. Then Schweinfurth held control for the next four years; once he departed in 1895, there was a pronounced decline in the quality of Brown's work.[4] Brown's death the following January, after injuries suffered in a carriage accident, was considered a great loss to the cause of good architecture; however, much of his reputation was due to the designers on his staff. Yet Polk and Schweinfurth derived no less benefit from their association with Brown. He induced both men, and perhaps Maybeck, to settle on the West Coast. He provided the benefits of steady employment, and he gave them the opportunity to work on projects larger and more complex than they could have secured independently.

For several years, Brown's office was the local center for young proponents of the academic movement, echoing the role of 57 Broadway in New York. Alexander Oakey, who had worked for both Richard Morris Hunt and Richard Norman Shaw, moved to San Francisco with Brown and Polk. Charles Rousseau, a former employee of McKim, Mead & White, joined the firm shortly thereafter. Maybeck came in the early months of 1890 and was associated with Brown on at least two other occasions during the next five years. Another promising designer was Joachim Mathisen, a Norwegian trained as a civil engineer at Hanover's Technische Hochschule. Several Californians who worked in the office—William Knowles, Sylvain Schnaittacher, Frank Van Trees, and James R. Miller—became prominent figures in the region after the turn of the century.[5] Only Schweinfurth remained with Brown for long, but the steady influx of able assistants provided a lively, productive working atmosphere. Under Brown's leadership the academic movement quickly gained acceptance in the region. He gave the new movement the necessary initial momentum and offered a climate where his draftsmen could acquire a footing before setting out on their own.

Brown's work was regarded as heralding a new era for San Francisco's architecture.[6] Radically different from the local norm, his buildings possessed a reserved character, scholarly allusions to the past, and elegant details. But no matter how new this work seemed on the West Coast, it was essentially a polished replication of McKim, Mead & White's style. Now that Brown was far removed from New York, the influence of his mentors became more pronounced. The Crocker Building (1890–1892), for instance, incorporates an arcaded base patterned directly after McKim, Mead & White's Goelet Building in New York (1886–1887); the delicate terra-cotta banding is modeled on that of their Yo-semite Apartments, also in New York (1889); and the dropped cornice and treatment of the attic stories are slight variations on an unexecuted project for the Exchange Building in Boston (1888). Brown's house for Alban Towne (1890–1891) is a reiteration of the firm's Colonial Revival work, especially of the details of the Appleton house in Lenox (1883–1884) (Fig. 44). Likewise, the Crocker Old People's Home is derived from McKim, Mead & White's Union Pacific Railroad Employees' Hospital in Brainerd, Minnesota (1883).[7] Even though Brown was much more familiar with advanced tendencies in design than were his elder colleagues in San Francisco, his reliance on and adaptation of East Coast precedent reflected the same importation process that had determined the nature of California architecture for most of the nineteenth century.

Polk's role in Brown's designs remains unclear. Brown may have held the upper hand by specifying modes of expression and perhaps even suggesting the models he wanted used. But Polk may have sought, or at least welcomed, the opportunity to master McKim, Mead & White's vocabulary. Whatever the circumstances, a marked change occurred in Brown's work following Polk's departure, when Schweinfurth became the principal figure in the office. Placed in charge of designing major commissions, Schweinfurth was probably given more freedom to develop these schemes in his own way. He was allowed to concentrate on design without worrying about the other aspects of practice. Throughout his tenure with Brown in San Francisco, he listed himself as an "architect," not as a draftsman. In essence, he served as a silent partner. He appears to have had a somewhat nervous, brittle disposition, and he could be frank to the point of rudeness. Having firm convictions, he viewed his work with the utmost seriousness; however, he also continued to search for ways to imbue design with fresh, vital forms of expression.[8]

The winning entry in the competition for Trinity Church, San Francisco (1891–1894) gives an indication of Schweinfurth's interest in working with massive, elemental forms, expressed more forcefully here than in any of his previous designs (Fig. 45).[9] Contrasting with contemporary churches by Ralph Adams Cram and others who sought to design fully in the spirit of medieval architecture, Trinity supports historical references that seem almost incidental to its effect. The play between abstract geometry and Gothic details remains tenuous, imparting a character that is no doubt unintentionally crude. If the design is less refined than earlier work, it is also less conventional.

Schweinfurth released the firm from its dependence on McKim,

44. A. Page Brown. Alban Towne house, San Francisco, 1890–1891; burned 1906. (Courtesy Sheila Mack)

45. A. Page Brown. Trinity Church, San Francisco, 1891–1894. (Author)

Mead & White's example. He was also discovering sources more suited to his tastes. An initial step was taken in the lemon warehouse designed for William Crocker's Rancho Las Fuentes in Montecito (1891) (Fig. 46). The building owes an obvious debt to Richardson and the Shingle Style; however, its repetitive simplicity also conveys much of the spirit found in the long, arcaded blocks of the Franciscan missions. California's Hispanic legacy, and a number of analogous sources, provided a primary foundation from which Brown and Schweinfurth sought to develop new and distinctly regional forms of expression during the next six years.

Unlike Schweinfurth, Maybeck played a minor role in Brown's office, probably involving the design of decorative details. His tenure in 1890 was brief, with perhaps equally short periods spent there in 1892 and 1894. He held several other jobs during this same period—as a supervisor of construction for Wright & Sanders, as a draftsman

88

for Julius Krafft (both firms of little distinction), and as a designer for the popular interior decorating firm of Charles Plum & Company. Maybeck also seems to have assisted Coxhead, formed a short-lived partnership with Mathisen and George Howard, and entered at least one competition on his own. The only known visual record of these years is the interior scheme of Francis Marion Smith's house in Oakland (ca. 1891), produced while he was with Plum (Fig. 47). The rooms possess the exuberance of Carrère & Hastings's Ponce de Leon Hotel but still lack the discipline of a mature designer. Maybeck devoted much of his time to teaching. In 1891 he attempted to form a local school of architecture, and several years later was appointed director of the newly organized architectural section of San Francisco's Mark Hopkins Institute of Art. Maybeck gave up a well-paying job in Brown's office to become an instructor in descriptive geometry at the University of California in September 1894.[10] He maintained a Bohemian appearance and a European air. In 1892 he moved to a remote part of Berkeley, where he began to construct a rustic *Bauerhütte* in the spirit of the dwellings of his German ancestors. Few people took him seriously as an architect; Schweinfurth remarked that "those of our profession who know Mr. Maybeck will not dispute the fact that he is a freak." Nevertheless he won increasing respect for his ideas and his commitment to art.[11] Only later would he realize those ideas in concrete form.

Polk's initial years of independent practice were difficult. He struggled to develop a personal style, becoming self-conscious about

46. A. Page Brown. Crocker and Company lemon curer and warehouse, Rancho Las Fuentes, Montecito, 1891; altered. Drawing by Schweinfurth. (*Architecture and Building,* December 5, 1891)

47. Walter Mathews. Francis Marion Smith house, Oakland, ca. 1891;
demolished. Hall. Interiors by Charles Plum & Company;
Bernard Maybeck, designer. (Oakland Public Library)

the derivative designs he did for Brown. Few of his projects left the
drafting board during this period; those that did were mostly for modest
residences. Yet Polk already considered himself the leading proponent
of academic eclecticism in the region. He never hesitated to criticize
his colleagues' work, alienating many of them in the process. His
arrogance and flamboyant personality made his practice all the more
tempestuous.

Polk's professional methods were the antithesis of Brown's.
His energies were consumed in design, and he was a poor businessman and manager. He formed partnerships to ameliorate the situation;
however, he could be demanding and intolerant; formal arrangements
did not survive long. Polk joined forces with Fritz Maurice Gamble
around 1890. Gamble seems to have had neither professional training
nor experience, but he had excellent social connections, and his father
had been a partner in one of Oakland's largest real estate firms.
Gamble was no doubt instrumental in securing commissions and may

90

have attended to office affairs, but the partnership was dissolved after little more than a year.[12]

In the meantime, Willis Polk's family had settled in San Francisco. Family relations were stormy, and the clan became notorious for its quarreling. Willis lured a client away from his father, but the elder Polk had financial resources that his son needed, so in October 1892, Willis, his father, and his brother Daniel launched a new partnership, Polk & Polk. Willis controlled the design of projects. Daniel was a gifted draftsman who soon took charge of several minor commissions. Their father concentrated on technical matters and ostensibly directed field operations on work where the firm functioned as both architect and general contractor.[13] The office enjoyed moderate prosperity, but it collapsed when the elder Polk retired in 1896. Daniel had already left to play the banjo in vaudeville. Willis began to work out of the family's house on Russian Hill, paying rent to the family. Incoming work steadily diminished, until July 1897, when he filed for bankruptcy.[14] During the next two years, Polk managed to secure enough commissions to remain in practice, but both his reputation and his ego had suffered a severe blow.

Polk's volatile personality did not help his professional standing. Ebullient and gregarious, he became well known as a bon vivant, raconteur, and reckless gambler, always seeking to be the center of attention. The *Wave,* an irreverent weekly review of regional events, filled its gossip columns with his escapades: Polk the performer— insulting a German baron at the fashionable Hotel Rafael with the ensuing challenge to a duel, only to appear at the specified time with boxing gloves as his "weapon"; Polk the nonconformist—attending a formal reception dressed in loud tweeds; Polk the practical joker— pulling the chair out from under an elderly gentleman at a lavish dinner party; Polk the carefree Bohemian—delighting gathered artists with duets at restaurants in the Latin Quarter; Polk the dandy—forming coteries with social lions and artists, one of which chartered a yacht as its headquarters. His taste for high living left little for essentials. Addison Mizner, who worked briefly in the office during the mid-1890s, later recalled that Polk was "a genius, only spoiled by having read Whistler's 'Gentle Art of Making Enemies'. . . . [and] became a genius at this as well."[15] With childish glee, Polk hurled insults at colleagues, public officials, and anyone else with whom he disagreed. Adored by some, despised by others, he gained widespread recognition for his talent, but many people refused to consider him a responsible architect.

Despite the unstable nature of his practice, Polk was untiring in his efforts to advance the cause of good design. He started a monthly journal, the *Architectural News,* which was inaugurated in November 1890 as an alternative to the pedestrian *California Architect and Building News.* Dedicated to academic ideals, the *News* was a mouthpiece for the young architects who had come to San Francisco. The majority of designs in the journal were by Polk and Coxhead, but draftsmen such as Robert Turner (employed by the Reid Brothers), W. Redmore Ray (employed by John Wood), and Charles Mitchell and Henry Merritt (both employed by Polk) contributed sketches of historical buildings at home and abroad. A schism may already have occurred between Polk and Brown, for the latter's work was conspicuously absent.

The *News* revealed an interest in local precedent by publishing the first article devoted to California's mission churches to appear in an architectural magazine. However, its principal aim was to address broad design issues and to inform the readership of recent developments outside the region. Polk hoped to strengthen ties with colleagues in other major cities and to demonstrate that a new generation of San Francisco architects was concerned with more than technical and trade matters. Articles that appeared in the *News* included: a short history of church planning by Coxhead; a lead article on proportion by Ray; reprints of essays by Henry Van Brunt and Royal Cortissoz; and contributions by John Galen Howard from Paris, Bertram Goodhue from New York, and Schweinfurth from Denver. Maybeck began to prepare a translation of Gottfried Semper's *Der Stil,* which regrettably never came to fruition. The *News* made an impressive start; however, financial difficulties caused it to cease publication in January 1891, after only three issues.[16]

During the 1890s, Polk also wrote critiques of San Francisco architecture for the *Examiner* and the *Wave* that shed considerable light on his maturing approach to design. While defending simplicity, refinement, and the scholarly use of precedent, he also singled out imitation as an underlying cause of poor architecture. To a certain extent, Polk was reiterating a common academic conviction that the designer must understand the past, not copy its motifs. Yet the term "imitation" was frequently posited as a beneficial trait when it denoted an approach in which precedent was used with understanding and purpose in design. From this liberal perspective, imitation was considered essential to correct the vagaries of the recent past and to establish a solid foundation for creative development in the future. Thus, while a growing number of Polk's East Coast colleagues believed that academic principles required the use of historically consistent forms of expression, Polk increasingly emphasized change. In 1892, he admonished: "Standards in art are set by the best work of [the] ages, but no age has the power to impose its beauty on succeeding ages; no age is compelled to take its beauty from preceding epochs . . . we must neither depreciate nor imitate, but we should understand and originate."[17] The difference in atittude was not great, but it does suggest that Polk was no longer always willing to conform to East Coast preferences.

Polk's initial attacks on imitation were directed at local architects who had begun to emulate Brown's work. J. Cather Newsom, aggressive in purveying what he believed to be the latest mode, was the subject of particularly harsh treatment:

Mr. Gruesome, an "architect," said that he couldn't build his own house without "extras" because so many new ideas kept appearing in books and magazines that his ideals of Art underwent many changes. He was simply imitating poor ideas from poor periodicals.

Polk considered Newsom's approach to design superficial, reducing ideas to appliqué, where one series of details could easily supplant another in response to the newest trend, making architecture little more than a passing fashion. Polk cited the Colonial Revival, then rapidly becoming popular in San Francisco, as a primary example. He maintained that "these disciples" of McKim, Mead & White, "without knowing the reasons, without at all understanding the *motifs*" of early American architecture, "have multiplied countless weak and absurd imitations of the new and proudly dubbed it 'Old Colonial.' " The mode had been taken over by "the Smythes, Jones and Newsoms of the profession."[18]

Even Brown was not safe from Polk's pen. About a year after he left the office, Polk wrote that the Towne house was far better than those designed by Newsom, but still fell "much below a good standard." The architect, he taunted, was no doubt "unconsciously . . . influenced by some of McKim, Mead & White's work." Two years later, the attack grew more pointed. Brown's work had generated a new fad no better than the preceding High Victorian modes:

The old colonial poison, innoculated with the advent of the Towne house, has now permeated all parts of our municipal system. . . .

Colonial is the fad . . . people in the east set the fashion, so, people in the west . . . must be in style too.

Polk did not decry the use of classical precedent; rather he objected to subservience, where San Francisco architecture followed every development that occurred in the East, even when certain forms of expression were not particularly appropriate. Local architects, he concluded, "must intelligently study [the classical tradition] and create [the necessary] modifications. They must cease imitating."[19]

Polk also lashed out at work by his contemporaries that he felt lacked unity and purpose. An unexecuted proposal for the City Hall tower "threatens to perpetuate a bastard combination of a Spanish clerestory crowned by an English cupola resting on a Franco-Roman base." The preliminary design prepared by the Supervising Architect of the Treasury, William Martin Aiken, for San Francisco's Post Office was damned as monotonous and without unity. Its mélange of references failed to offer appropriate allusions to historical precedent or to express present conditions; its parts gave no suggestion of the building's purpose: "Its faculties are imitative, not creative." It was no more than "an affectation of the Spinach Reminiscence [i.e., Spanish Renaissance] . . . Madison Square Garden, a few apartment houses

48. Polk & Polk. Casino and beach house for the Hotel Arcadia, Santa Monica. 1893, project. Drawing by Polk. (CED Documents Collection)

and any old thing." The gesture was futile, belonging only to "the Ironical Order of Architecture."[20]

Polk's contemptuous remarks indirectly repudiated his own efforts. He had contributed to the Towne house design and thereafter had done similar work independently.[21] His subsequent attempts to develop more original schemes were not easily achieved and, at first, not always successful. There is evidence of his struggle in an 1893 project for a bathhouse and casino adjacent to the recently completed Hotel Arcadia in Santa Monica (Fig. 48). The scheme is both more derivative and discordant than Aiken's Post Office, with one section bracketed by two outrageous miniatures of the Campanile di San Marco and the other terminated by a cartoon of McKim, Mead & White's casino at Narragansett Pier, Rhode Island.

The criticism Polk gave to others was, in a sense, autobiographical, focusing on weaknesses in his own work that he had identified and struggled to overcome. He attacked San Francisco's carpenter-architects, whose approach to design he had learned and subsequently rejected; he opposed overt importation of East Coast modes once he had become less dependent upon such models; and he criticized incongruities in form and allusions in local architecture after he had learned to combine diverse sources in a manner that expressed the project's conditions. But if his essays reflect a growing maturity and confidence, Polk's repeated emphasis on the fallacies of imitation and on the provincialism he felt it represented suggests a self-conscious apprehension that he could still fall victim to echoing the work of others. He seems to have remained insecure about being removed from the mainstream of architectural developments and about how his work would be perceived by East Coast colleagues. This nervous sensitivity, in turn, may have reinforced his creative instincts.

The extent to which Polk came to value a personal approach to expression is revealed in an unpublished article written around the mid-1890s. As always he deferred to the supposed universality of artistic principles: all design must subscribe to "a common standard, a common alphabet, common rules"; however, the individual's creative faculties are what ultimately determine the merit of a work. In the final analysis, architecture "is an art as free as the wind."[22] Polk's defiance of conformity indicates that his approach to design was essentially intuitive. He no doubt scanned contemporary journals and architectural monographs for inspiration, but he seldom, if ever, engaged in prolonged study. His response to the world around him was emotional, and design was a vehicle to convey his emotions. Since he learned best from experience, the work of his friend Coxhead, who had developed a strong personal style by the early 1890s, was of immense value to him.

Several factors probably convinced Coxhead to move from Los Angeles to San Francisco. He had received commissions from the Episcopal church, his principal client, for three large parish churches in San Francisco, Alameda, and Stockton prior to his move in November 1889.[23] The building boom in southern California ended that same year. Also, the Bay Area had a much larger, richer, and more urbane populace than did Los Angeles, affording greater cultural stimulus and a clientele more receptive to a well-trained architect's services.

Once he had settled in San Francisco, Coxhead prospered and gained recognition as one of the city's most promising designers. The office remained small, with probably no more than two or three draftsmen at any given time. Coxhead's principal assistant, his brother Almeric, was made a partner around 1890. Almeric managed the office and did some construction supervision. He may also have offered valuable support, giving criticism and suggestions about designs in progress.[24] In contrast to Polk's fluctuating office structure, the two Coxheads maintained a close association until Almeric died in 1928. But like Polk, Coxhead's foremost concern was design, which he considered to be a strictly personal act. Commenting on Aiken's proposal for the Post Office, Coxhead indicated that an architect should design no more than one major project at a time, so that all energies could be devoted to its development.[25] He maintained that a building, no less than a painting or a piece of sculpture, required the artist's undivided attention. His own methods were no doubt meticulous. He knew architectural history far better than did Polk and may well have scrutinized specific examples very carefully when developing a scheme.[26] Surviving preliminary studies of his buildings are more conservative and bear greater fidelity to historic precedent than the final designs, suggesting that some of his most inventive work was conceived at a late stage when intuition gained the upper hand.

Coxhead was also more disciplined than Polk and appears to have let few activities interfere with his job. By nature he was a very private person, judging from the paucity of contemporary accounts about him. Several acquaintances from later years recall that he was taciturn and reserved, rarely socialized, and had few close friends. He was inclined to dismiss criticism from many of his colleagues, and when a client disputed his judgment, his normally agreeable disposi-

49. Ernest Coxhead. Church of St. John the Evangelist, San Francisco,
1890–1891; destroyed 1906. (Courtesy John Beach)

tion could turn sour.[27] But what may have been difficult for him to
express verbally was lucidly conveyed within the secluded confines of
the drafting room. Beneath his demure temperament he was somewhat
of an eccentric who, in spite of himself, created buildings that taunted
bourgeois pretensions.

Coxhead's first project in San Francisco, the Church of St.
John the Evangelist (1889–1891), is a harbinger of his mature style.

The initial proposal, which he did while still in Los Angeles, uses Romanesque and early Gothic forms in a restrained, confident manner, reflecting academic practices in ecclesiastical design that were well accepted in England and soon to become popular in the United States.[28] Apparently, the scheme was too expensive, and the conception was radically altered, eliminating all references to traditional Anglican imagery. In these revised plans, a centralized mass is dominated by an enormous tower and spire that hover above discretely articulated masses (Fig. 49). The portal and flanking stair towers, together with the adjacent chapel and baptistry, recall details of Burgundian Romanesque and Ottonian churches. Around the corner a Byzantine apse protrudes, flanked by stepped "minarets"—the whole composed as if it was a Carolingian *Westwerk*—and topped by a Tuscan colonnade positioned like the arcade on the facade of a French High Gothic cathedral. Such seemingly incongruous references may have been inspired by Phené Spiers's speculations on the ties between Near Eastern architecture and that of early medieval Europe, yet these forms are abstracted, simplified, and given unity in a manner quite American.[29]

Above this encyclopedic assemblage looms a cross-gable roof that is half swallowed by the tower, a composition derived from late medieval churches in Normandy and Brittany. The whole upper section is accentuated by its monstrous size, yet softened by an all-encompassing coat of shingles that lap around windows and roll over corners. The whole effect denies a sense of substantive mass and stands in sharp contrast to the taut masonry forms of the lower zone. The dichotomy between these sections is reaffirmed by allusions and scale. References in the lower zone are to monumental urban churches, while those above are to vernacular examples in villages and rural settings. Miniaturized below and magnified above, the building appears to be much larger than its actual size. Only when measured against neighboring structures do the church's dimensions begin to become apparent.

The prominence of St. John's within its urban context is reinforced through another series of allusions as well. The squat mass, Greek-cross configuration of the main block, and overscaled tower are found on numerous American parish churches of the period, all of which owe a debt to Richardson's Trinity Church in Boston (1873–1877). But the general impression conveyed here is more akin to that of sketches by American and English architects of Mont-Saint-Michel and other medieval towns, depicted as a pyramid of clustered roofs crowned by the soaring mass of a church. Such picturesque visions of the city sometimes provided inspiration for composing large ecclesiastical buildings. Here the compactness renders the effect bolder and tougher. The church stands as a defiant citadel amid its tawdry surroundings.

Coxhead's unconventional design was no mere flight of fantasy. St. John's was among the oldest and most distinguished parishes in the state, even though it suffered from a dwindling congregation and lack of resources. Located in the heart of San Francisco's Mission District, it had been bypassed by fashionable new residential developments. Constructing a conspicuous edifice appears to have been part of a campaign by the rector to restore the church to its former prominence. A landmark was needed, but on a meager budget. The building cost approximately $45,000, far below the sum required for a masonry structure with the appropriate decorations.[30] By using simple brick walls surmounted by a wood frame and relying on a rich diet of allusions and exaggerated scale, Coxhead designed an imposing symbol for a poor parish striving for regeneration.

For all its ingenuity, the scheme failed to achieve a complete resolution between its symbolic and utilitarian needs. The side arches

50. St. John the Evangelist, sanctuary. (Courtesy John Beach)

of the main portal are too low for passage and are awkwardly isolated from the steps. Inside, the confrontation between illusion and reality is the most pronounced. In creating a sanctuary that would seem grand but could be simply and inexpensively executed, Coxhead turned to Byzantine sources (Fig. 50). These Eastern references are fused with the English tradition of arched plaster ceilings suspended from a wooden frame and treated as a billowy membrane to enhance a sense of expansiveness. Yet no interplay is established between this grand spatial gesture and the church's actual size. The resulting confinement caused Peixotto to regret that the sanctuary makes one feel "so like Gulliver in the land of the Lilliputians."[31] Furthermore, the view of the altar is blocked from many of the seats. Symmetry, both inside and out, prevails at the expense of circulation. Location of the main entrance at the center of the north transept, for example, inhibits direct access to more than half the pews.

Coxhead was miffed by such criticism. In his article on church planning written for Polk's *Architectural News,* he condescendingly defended his position:

The medieval church builders were not called upon to sacrifice everything to obtain in the nave an unbroken view for every worshiper. Had it been considered . . . necessary that each . . . member of the church be seated luxuriously within easy earshot and in full view of the preacher, we might safely say that . . . those sublime achievements in architecture—the cathedrals and great churches of Europe—would not have been possible.[32]

The architect repeatedly emphasized the importance of continuity in, and a scholarly approach to, design. At the expense of some practical requirements, Coxhead looked to a variety of ecclesiastical traditions to create a vigorous image of the church, but soon the discord between beauty and utility that he discussed in the *News* would be reconciled.

During the early 1890s, Coxhead's work became increasingly versatile, and he developed different forms of expression in response to programmatic conditions. This agility is indicated by his design for the Church of the Advent in San Francisco (1891–1892) (Fig. 51). Like St. John's, the parish had a notable history, was experiencing decline, and now sought to restore its former prominence. The site was equally lackluster, and it was situated in the middle of a block. The budget was only about $30,000, while the seating capacity needed to be greater than St. John's, 900 compared to 750. The sanctuary also had to accommodate cathedral services, necessitating side aisles

51. Coxhead & Coxhead. Church of the Advent, San Francisco, 1891–1892; burned 1906. Drawing probably by Coxhead. (*Pacific Churchman*, October 15, 1891, p. 12)

and a large chancel. Coxhead's solution, as at St. John's, was to manipulate form, scale, and imagery to create a conspicuous building that appears to be very large. Here the similarities end.

The church's main block is an unadorned, bulky mass draped in dark red brick and slate. Like a train shed, it is largely obscured by

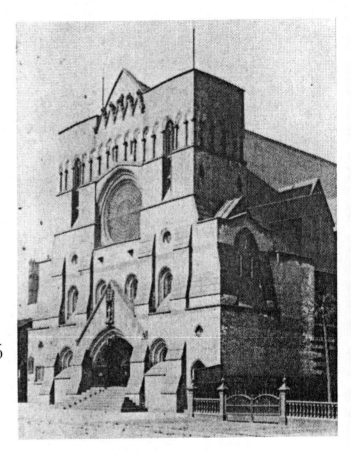

52. Church of the Advent as built. (California Historical Society)

a massive twin-towered facade that is accentuated by a buff-colored brick and terra-cotta facing. The elevation recalls those of northern French cathedrals from the thirteenth century, but because of the tight budget, it is rendered with mural wall surfaces and little applied ornament in the manner of southern French medieval churches. This Mediterranean character was more pronounced without the spires, which were to be built at some later date—a provision that Coxhead took into account when developing the scheme (Fig. 52).[33] The decorative details are largely derived from English medieval sources, but the robust, plastic handling of form bears some affinity to the most inventive mid-nineteenth-century work of Butterfield and Burges, which parallels several more or less contemporary English arts-and-crafts schemes.[34]

The interior is a surprise, but in this case the dichotomy between interior and exterior is controlled through a spatial sequence. Func-

102

tional considerations led to an arrangement, then often used in moderate-sized urban churches, where the sanctuary rests on the second story with subsidiary rooms placed below. The principal space is reached by a broad flight of steps that squeeze through the squat portal into a low, groin-vaulted porch, ascend at right angles and then turn again to reach twin vestibules, with several more steps connecting to the sanctuary. The sensation must have been similar to that of coming up from a crypt; but the sequence is reversed so that one leaves the street to enter a dim, cryptlike nave (Fig. 53). The space is at once grand and confined, a duality that now seems purposeful. Nave and chancel are bordered by a massive arcade with thick, composite moldings, patterned after early thirteenth-century English work, which bulge over the piers. Stuccoed arches loom above, encasing timber trusswork and cross bracing—a treatment that suggests they were part of another construction campaign. These haunting, expressionistic forms effectively reduce the perceived spatial volume. As at St. John's, the furnishings seem too big, but here they accentuate the emphatic compression of space. Derived from both Gothic and Renaissance sources, they also enhance

53. Church of the Advent, sanctuary. (California Historical Society)

the feeling of age—a ruined abbey hastily reroofed and gradually fitted with rich embellishments over several centuries.

Coxhead also exhibited a new flexibility in dealing with buildings of different size. Many of his commissions from the early 1890s were for small parish churches and chapels, where he avoided the complexities of form, space, and historical allusion present in bigger work. The finest example of the modest projects is the Chapel of St. John the Evangelist near Monterey (1890–1891) (Fig. 54). Originally located on the grounds of the Del Monte Hotel, one of the West Coast's most fashionable resorts, the building was erected at the initiative of the rector of St. John's, San Francisco, as part of his drive to regain the parish's former stature. In form, the chapel is little more

54. Coxhead & Coxhead. Chapel of St. John the Evangelist, Del Monte (Monterey), 1890–1891; altered. Drawing probably by Coxhead. (*Pacific Churchman*, July 1, 1891, p. 9)

55. Chapel of St. John the Evangelist, nave. (Author)

than a barn, and the tower and facade treatment are the principal indicators of its function. Contributing to this simplicity is the coat of shingles draped over the mass like rolled thatch. This treatment, combined with the miniature scale of the elements, introduces a sense of fantasy that is more pronounced than in most ecclesiastical designs of the period. Like Coxhead's quick sketches of English hamlets, the church is an idealized depiction of pastoral innocence—imagery quite appropriate to the carefree atmosphere of an exclusive watering place. The interior is equally simple and consistent in its allusions, creating an effect at once straightforward and slightly unreal (Fig. 55). Here is a storybook vision of the archetypal English country church, an interpretation strikingly similar to that of the English cottage then emerging in the work of Charles Voysey.

The facile manner in which Coxhead combined seemingly disparate qualities through opposition and contrast, his unconventional

105

use of space and scale, and the versatility of his expression all had a great influence on Polk. And, as Polk's own work matured, his sophisticated manipulation of spatial sequences, the seemingly casual order and playful juxtaposition of formal and informal qualities found in his designs became important lessons for Coxhead. Moreover, the Englishman benefited from Polk's experience in residential work, particularly after 1892, when he ceased to receive commissions from the Episcopal church.[35] Most of Coxhead's subsequent efforts were devoted to designing houses, for which he had shown little interest in previous years. Neither man had a dominant influence on the other; their exchange was mutual. Each man retained a distinct artistic personality. Nevertheless, the designs of one are the more understandable when compared with those of the other.

V

COXHEAD AND POLK: The Rustic City House

We think of an architect as an interpreter of the greatest of all arts—that which gives intelligent expression to the joys of life. But we feel that his achievements are the most incomplete as relating to the production of houses of moderate cost.
[Willis Polk], *Architectural News*, November 1890

POLK'S CONCERN for inexpensive house design stemmed from the reality of his practice. At first, most of his commissions were for modest, middle-class residences. Coxhead found himself in the same position after 1891. Both architects treated these circumstances as an opportunity. They were fortunate in attracting clients who shared their artistic interests and who were not content with commonplace surroundings. Coxhead and Polk became accomplished at compacting a variety of spaces and allusions into restricted areas, creating houses that were sheltering and expansive, humble and grand, worldly in their character yet attuned to the special qualities of the regional landscape. Among the finest results were the rustic houses they designed in San Francisco.

For all their unconventional qualities, these rustic city houses were an outgrowth of what was considered to be a "complete revolution" in the concept of the moderate-sized urban residence. During the 1880s, major changes occurred in the internal configuration and external appearance of the type, reflecting the academic movement's notion that a project's conditions should serve as a generator of its expression. Proponents of this viewpoint stressed that while size and cost should help determine a solution, such factors should not affect its artistic integrity. The modest house should be no less a work of art than a palace. Polk reaffirmed this belief in an editorial written for the *Architectural News:*

The fact that a dwelling-house should express, without affectation, the simplest object of its being, that of furnishing a comfortable shelter to the home-life, avoiding everything tending to display, and without imitating the pretentious houses of men of wealth, of which few are models of anything but poor taste, is the real basis for the proper conception of an ideal home of moderate cost.[1]

To a degree, these concerns had been voiced since the 1840s, when attention had been focused mostly on suburban and rural residences. The interest in moderate-sized city houses was new, as was the belief that they should be of individual rather than formulaic design. Critics had no kind words to describe Victorian practices, which they considered to have produced merely "a mechanical accumulation of spaces and openings unbeautiful in themselves and uncombined with one another."[2] The largest city houses were regarded as being great only in their dimensions, while smaller ones differed by being less spacious and ornate. For too long, observers charged, the narrow, deep configuration of urban lots had been cited to excuse mediocre design. They contended that such problems were not insurmountable, but rather should be a basis for innovative solutions.

In resolving the constraints of moderate-sized urban houses, functional requirements were accommodated while a sense of confinement was mitigated with a new freedom in the arrangement of space. Rooms used for formal occasions or for circulation were reduced, thus providing larger areas for daily domestic activities. A key device was the central stair hall, which had already been employed in suburban and country houses. This circulation core became an extension of the living spaces and permitted greater variety in the room arrangements around it. On the exterior, a primary objective was to give a sense of individuality while contributing to a dignified, cohesive urban context. Reacting to what was seen as the dull monotony of mid-nineteenth-century houses and the rampant discord of their High Victorian successors, architects now sought to develop facades that were singular yet restrained and unobtrusive components of a larger urban whole. Contemporary accounts maintained that such a balance could be achieved by keeping compositions simple, accentuating only a few selected elements. Individuality would result from indications of interior arrangement and from the use of historical references. Proponents of this approach believed that adjacent houses could be given quite different forms of expression and still enhance an overall urban order.[3]

No trace of this new attitude could be found in San Francisco when Coxhead and Polk arrived in 1889. Most new houses adhered to the standard Victorian arrangement: a long hall, often reached by a

56. San Francisco, Pacific Avenue looking west from Franklin Street.
(*San Francisco News Letter,* August 29, 1896)

stoop, and a linear sequence of rooms on one or both sides. Other residences, particularly those in the new, affluent districts of the Western Addition, were compact villas with characteristic High Victorian suburban house plans. Such dwellings were common to cities in the Middle and Far West; however, houses in San Francisco tended to be on smaller lots; even the largest freestanding houses were often placed close to the street with meager yard space to either side (Fig. 56). Areas with less elaborate houses followed the same pattern, regardless of how much property the building actually occupied.

The suburban atmosphere that typified many residential districts in western cities was further denied in San Francisco by the scarcity of landscaping. Thick summer fogs made exposure to sunlight desirable, and thus shade trees were seldom planted. San Francisco possessed residential quarters that were both denser and more urban in feeling than those of many cities, yet far less compressed and ordered than comparable East Coast metropolises. Local architects do not appear to have questioned the paradox of designing suburban house types for a quasi-urban setting. Even Page Brown, after a decade of experience in New York, used suburban models for the Towne house and most of his other San Francisco residences.

Coxhead and Polk soon rejected this rural imagery, turning to specifically urban sources. Neither architect had experience in designing city houses, but they were familiar with recent examples of the type. Polk no doubt knew of urban designs by McKim, Mead & White, who had been instrumental in changing the form of moderate-sized urban residences. Coxhead was aware of equally innovative work by Norman Shaw and others in London, perhaps from his student days, and from English periodicals.[4] However, the character of San Francisco's residential districts, combined with the irregular topography that prevailed in most areas, suggested a less formal treatment than that used in major Eastern or English cities. The fact that wood construction was still permitted allowed a freer arrangement of space and mass on a low budget than was possible with masonry. Coxhead and Polk took advantage of this situation to develop a wooden architecture that was responsive to the compact, picturesque fabric of the city.[5] They also sought to reflect the growing veneration among Bay Area residents for the rustic aspects of their local heritage and landscape.

Until the late nineteenth century, many Californians, like other Americans in the West, regarded the natural landscape as a hostile place or as a recreational resource to be experienced from the comfort of a resort hotel. But almost from the beginning of statehood, a small, conspicuous segment of the West Coast populace took pleasure in the isolation and beauty of the foothill and mountain regions. By the late 1860s, well-to-do Bay Area residents made a regular pastime of camping trips along the Coastal Range and Russian River. Later, the scope of such excursions was expanded to include the Sierra and other remote areas. The ruggedness of these ventures was relished, as indicated by journalist Albert Evans's declaration: "Better one month of camp life in the California mountains than years on years of life at the fashionable 'watering-places' and 'summer resorts' of the East and Europe." Supplementing the campsite were small inns where outdoor life in the wilderness remained the focus of daily activities. Both the intentionally unassuming character of these hostelries and the unstructured routines they fostered were in marked contrast to the elaborate resort hotels of the period. Some people sought equally informal vacations in less rugged terrain, renting unpretentious farm houses in Napa,

110

Sonoma, Mendocino, and other northern counties. The primitive dwellings that dotted these regions were now viewed as picturesque components of the pastoral landscape.[6]

The efforts of artists, writers, naturalists, and others who venerated California's wilderness were also beginning to gain widespread acceptance by the early 1890s. Novels and short stories celebrating the state's frontier legacy were at last becoming popular on the home front. William Keith was now considered a patriarch among local artists because of his romantic portrayals of the natural landscape. John Muir's long-standing crusade to save the Yosemite Valley became an organized effort in 1892 with the founding of the Sierra Club, for which Polk designed the shield. Among the most remarkable manifestations of the growing interest in rusticity was the annual encampment of the Bohemian Club, where the celebration of the wilderness developed into a spectacular ritual. Founded in 1872 as a coterie of writers, the organization grew to include many of the region's leading artists, educators, and businessmen. By the late 1880s, the club's outings had become lavish dramatic productions, staged amid redwood groves, blending hedonistic revelry with a quasi-religious reverence for nature.[7]

Infatuation with the wilderness was by no means limited to the Bay Area, but the degree to which its residents came to identify with the rustic landscape was probably not matched in other metropolitan regions. To San Franciscans, the East Coast landscape seemed domesticated compared to their own situation, where, beyond the metropolis, lay expanses of rugged topography. Once the terrain that had long astounded visitors came to be widely appreciated among residents, it was embraced with a passion.

Coxhead and Polk were very much a part of this emerging veneration of a rustic ideal. From the time they moved to the Bay Area they had been partial to the setting and believed that their work should reflect its special qualities. Their concerns were reinforced by friends who were active in fostering a greater sensitivity toward the natural environment. Joseph Worcester appears to have had a particularly strong influence on Coxhead and Polk. A Swedenborgian minister, Worcester had considered becoming an architect in his youth and maintained a strong interest in the subject throughout his life. Few people took stock in Worcester's advocacy of a simple, harmonious relationship between nature and design before the 1890s, but soon thereafter he became a spiritual leader to many of the young artists and intellectuals working in the region.[8]

111

In 1876 Worcester designed a cottage for himself in the East Bay suburb of Piedmont that was perhaps the first dwelling in California to cultivate rustic qualities (Fig. 57). Its long, low rectangular mass, capped by a shallow hipped roof that extends to form a porch in the front, was a relatively common form for small Victorian houses. But the absence of decoration and the use of shingles to sheathe the exterior were unusual for any part of the country at that time. Worcester was not drawing from local building traditions. Except for roofing, shingles remained an anomaly in the West. Raised in eastern Massachusetts, Worcester probably sought to recall that region's early architecture, where shingles had been used as an inexpensive substitute for clapboards since the eighteenth century. The design not only harks back to this tradition, but the concept of the design evokes the ideals of Emerson and Thoreau, whose writings so pervaded the society in which Worcester grew up. Worcester never lost the innocence of their perceptions, even after moving permanently to California in 1868. He nurtured a transcendental communication with and contemplation of nature in this cottage that sat in lofty isolation above the Bay. Worcester was also aware of the newly emerging interest in early American buildings from East Coast architectural magazines. In character and to a certain degree in form, his cottage bears greater affinity to the picturesque renderings then being made of this work than to the buildings themselves.[9]

Worcester also introduced the idea of the rustic house to San Francisco. In 1887 he persuaded a member of his congregation, Mrs.

57. Joseph Worcester house, Piedmont, 1876–1877; altered.
(Courtesy Sturla Einarsson)

58. Speculative houses for Mrs. David Marshall, San Francisco, ca. 1888–1889
(center); Joseph Worcester house, completed 1890 *(right)*;
both buildings on right demolished. (Courtesy George Livermore)

David Marshall, to invest in land atop Russian Hill. Like Telegraph
Hill nearby, this promontory remained a picturesque, quaint backwa-
ter, with steep slopes that resisted dense settlement and even construction of several platted streets. Only a few old houses could be found
on its heights, most of them dating from the 1850s and 1860s. Worcester encouraged Mrs. Marshall to develop her property in a manner
sympathetic to Russian Hill's unspoiled appearance. She erected three
small speculative houses, which may have been the first in the city
consciously designed to enhance such a rustic setting. Worcester was
delighted and was allowed to erect a new house for himself on part of
the land. (Fig. 58).[10]

Finally, Worcester has been credited with initiating the use of
unstained redwood for interior paneling, but this practice was well
known to Coxhead and Polk before they settled in San Francisco. In
the 1870s Worcester's appreciation for the material's natural qualities
was unusual. Abundant and inexpensive, redwood had been favored
in local construction since the mid-nineteenth century. The absence of
resin in its fiber made it less susceptible to rot and fire than pine or fir.
But redwood usually was painted or, by the 1880s, cut into small
pieces and stained to imitate exotic woods.[11] If Californians remained

113

59. McKim, Mead & White. Samuel Tilton house, Newport, Rhode Island, 1881–1882.
Entrance hall. (Photo Robert Meservy, Preservation Society of Newport County)

indifferent to redwood's inherent properties, a growing contingent of
easterners welcomed the material. Untreated, it offered rich, vibrant
tones in broad yet subtle patterns that were appropriate for a variety of
interior settings. McKim, Mead & White often used redwood for the
intricately detailed rooms in their summer houses (Fig. 59).[12] In other
instances, it was handled with the same primitive simplicity that
Worcester admired (Fig. 60). From publications and the time he spent
in New York, Polk was probably aware of the material's possibilities,
and Coxhead had already employed it in his southern California
churches.[13] Through the work of both architects, untreated redwood
paneling became one of the most prevalent and distinctive forms of

114

60. W. S. Hoyt house, Pelham, New York, before 1883; no longer standing.
Living hall. ([George Sheldon], *Artistic Houses* II:142)

interior finish in the region.

Worcester's enthusiasm for design should not be confused with
leadership as a designer. His houses were thoroughly amateurish in the
handling of form and space. The ideas they represented, rather than
their design, influenced Coxhead and Polk. After the arrival of Brown,
Polk, and others in San Francisco, he relied on their services. Even his
anonymous-looking cottage on Russian Hill shows some professional
assistance on the interior; the refined proportions and delicate details
of the paneling around the living room fireplace are not likely the work
of a lay person (Fig. 61). Worcester may well have received some
assistance from his good friend Brown, and the style is unmistakably

115

Polk's.[14] Worcester finally met architects who not only shared his interests but were capable of translating his ideas into three-dimensional form.

Worcester's primary contribution to their work was his commitment to the correspondence between nature and extremely simple expression in art. His spiritualism accommodated a love of physical beauty guided by the ideals of the English Arts and Crafts Movement. He believed that art was a conditioner of life. Artistic value was embodied in plain, functional objects. By revealing their purpose and expressing their materials simply, these objects were true to nature and hence beautiful. The notion of "truth" in design was not new to Coxhead or Polk, yet neither architect had previously known so fervent an advocate of this idea. Worcester was a catalyst who offered a

61. Worcester house, San Francisco, living room. (Courtesy Sturla Einarsson)

conceptual premise for the rustic simplicity that infused much of their work.

Inspired by Worcester, Coxhead and Polk turned to contemporary English residential design for ways to manifest arts-and-crafts ideals. Bringing a new vitality to interpretations of vernacular precedent, English arts-and-crafts houses offered a far more engaging model than recent American rustic design, the development of which had languished since the Shingle Style had reached maturity in the mid-1880s.[15] At the same time, scant precedent for wooden buildings that were distinctly urban in character could be found in modern work on either side of the Atlantic. Most nineteenth-century rustic design had been tailored to suburban or rural settings and derived from historic examples in villages or in the country.

To resolve this dilemma, Coxhead and Polk scrutinized post-medieval vernacular dwellings in northern French and English towns, a long-admired but seldom-used source for urban work. This example was well suited to the special conditions of varied topography and to San Francisco's new taste for rustic ambience. Furthermore, its adaptation was untinged by the importation of popular forms from another American locale. Coxhead and Polk drew from classical sources as well, imbuing many of their rustic designs with a sense of order and with high-style embellishments that reflect their academic predilections. The rustic city house was thus a hybrid of aspects of the picturesque and classical traditions and was inspired by both foreign precedent and local conditions, paralleling the synthesis McKim, Mead & White had given to the Shingle Style a decade earlier. These dwellings can, in fact, be considered urban counterparts to Shingle Style villas. While the San Francisco work has its own lineage, it embodies many of the ideas and intentions found in its East Coast predecessors.

An integration of these influences was first achieved by Polk in a double house on Russian Hill (1892) directly across from Worcester's cottage. The commission initially came from Mrs. Virgil Williams, a painter, whose husband had founded the California Institute of Design and who was herself a prominent figure in the local artistic community. Her property, which contained a change in elevation approximately equal to its width of 44 feet, had long been considered an impossible site for a building. Polk accepted the challenge, convincing his client that a party-wall house with two units could be erected on the premises, and reputedly waived payment to secure the eastern 20-foot frontage for his family. Polk's parents purchased the property, financed

62. Willis Polk. Double house for Mrs. Virgil Williams and W. W. Polk,
San Francisco, 1892. (Author)

the work, and may well have taken charge of building the entire
complex.[16]

The front elevation of the Williams-Polk house is treated as a
single residence (Fig. 62). The Williams (west) side is dominant; the
Polks' unit has fewer and smaller elements, and a front door that is
tucked beneath an understated secondary entrance. Bands of simple
casement windows stretch across both sections at a uniform height,
concealing the actual difference in floor levels of about 3 feet between
the two apartments. With all its elements unified and at a tiny scale,
the house appears considerably larger than its actual size. The facade
is like a condensed Norman streetscape, and its picturesqueness is
accentuated in a seemingly casual manner, almost as if it were a stage
set (Fig. 63). This playful, mannered quality is balanced by the taut,
rectilinear articulation and reductive simplicity of its elements, aspects
that are similar to recent English work, especially that of Charles
Voysey.

118

63. Houses on the Rue de Paris, Vitré, Brittany. Late nineteenth-century photograph in a scrapbook compiled by Bernard Maybeck. (CED Documents Collection)

There was no obvious precedent for the house's six-story rear portion (Fig. 64). Polk designed it as a loose piling of masses, with balconies and terraces, suggesting an accumulation of hillside shacks. The reference here is to the mid-nineteenth-century houses clustered on the slopes of Telegraph Hill and other promontories, which had been favored haunts of artists for several decades. The composition particularly recalls a block of cottages on Pine Street erected by the Austrian consul, Edmund Vischer, where he maintained a studio and published his famous *Pictorial California* (1870) (Fig. 65). Considered to be among San Francisco's "most romantic retreat[s]," the complex sheltered a small colony of writers, painters, and diplomats. Beyond the street lay interior courts with lush, unkempt gardens reached by

119

64. Williams-Polk house, view from northeast. (California Historical Society)

65. Edmund Vischer houses, San Francisco, mid-nineteenth century; burned 1906.
D. H. Burnham & Company's Merchants Exchange (1904–1905) in background.
(California Historical Society)

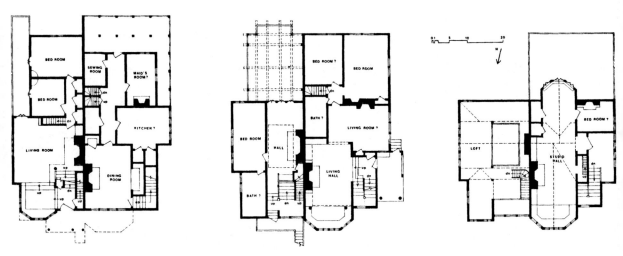

66. Williams-Polk house, author's reconstruction of original plans.
(Drawn by Kim Spurgeon Fly)

narrow, stepped passages—it was "a veritable wilderness," now tenuously perched at the edge of the expanding commercial center.[17] Polk's design proclaimed Russian Hill's growing prominence as a Bohemian enclave, with this new house as the dominant landmark.

The site on Russian Hill was not only small and steep, but it was also in a conspicuous location without abutting buildings. It had to serve the diverse needs of the elderly Mrs. Williams and the five Polks—all on a low budget. The design frankly admits its meager cost, enriching what could have been commonplace with rustic imagery that forges a link between foreign and local traditions to create a picturesque artists' compound. The solution is also notable as a departure from most houses in the region, which were designed as if the ground were level, thus demanding the inclusion of one or more ungainly basement stories at the low end. Polk's spirited accommodation to the hillside marked a new attitude toward the landscape that would have a far-reaching impact on the area's residential architecture in succeeding decades.

The Williams-Polk house interior reveals the architect's facility in using the most sophisticated American planning techniques for moderate-sized city houses (Fig. 66). Space constantly changes—expansive, then constricted; cavernous, then flooded with light. In Polk's unit the minuscule foyer empties down a stair into the dining room and, to one side, leads up to what is both a stair hall and living room (Fig. 67). In one corner stands an ornate fireplace, which seems

121

67. Williams-Polk house, living room in Polk unit. Photograph taken
after main stair was encased. (Courtesy George Livermore)

too large for the space, with a hearth wrapping around to another flight
up to Willis Polk's and his brother Daniel's quarters. The stair breaks
momentarily at a porchlike landing almost two stories high, then narrows
in an ascent to a hall no bigger than a ship's cabin. A well above this
space reveals a rustic loft, while French doors at the opposite end open
onto a broad terrace with a panoramic view of the city (Fig. 68). The
tension established between restricted and flowing space is intensified
by a duality of scale. Most details are simple and are proportioned to
the miniature size of the rooms, while the fireplaces and a few other
elements are large and elaborate. The fireplaces dominate their respective spaces but do not overpower them, since each one is located near
the threshold of yet another area, leading the eye beyond the immediate
confines of the room.

The interior's richness is further enhanced by a play between

68. Williams-Polk house, upstairs living hall in Polk unit. Photograph taken
after extension of room behind twin posts. (Courtesy George Livermore)

fancy and plain elements. Elegant classical details, which owe much
of their inspiration to Stanford White's decorative work, are offset by
large areas of unadorned redwood boards. The treatment is simplest in
the lofts, which were probably used for both work and entertaining
(Fig. 69). These rooms impart the rustic character associated with
garret spaces that have been converted into artists' studios. The evenings
Polk spent fraternizing with artists in New York no doubt gave him a
taste for this Bohemian atmosphere. But the Russian Hill house resists
appearing extemporaneous through careful composition of its elements,
so that even the simplest room has a clear order. The juxtaposition
evident here of rustic and refined qualities, large and small scale, and
seemingly casual and formal composition would remain an important
characteristic of both Polk's and Coxhead's work throughout the decade.
The two architects also gave the principal spaces in their rustic houses

123

a dramatic relationship with the landscape beyond. Ranges of windows, projecting bays, raised sitting areas, lowered ceilings, and other devices were used to emphasize the transition between indoors and out and to accentuate the often spectacular views.

For all their richness, one senses that the interiors designed by Polk and Coxhead were based as much on the activities they would house as on their visual relationships. Polk's floor plans are seldom of interest strictly as designs; they often look awkward, suggesting that he developed them as matrices for space by thinking in three dimensions rather than in two. Interiors with complex and elaborate features were no doubt intended to compensate for the meager furnishings of many of his clients. Yet these spaces are accommodating. Their flourishes are a backdrop to human activity and seem as appropriate to everyday routine as to special occasions.

Polk orchestrated the play between contrasting qualities in a somewhat different manner in the alterations he designed in 1893 for a small Italianate cottage situated on an adjacent property. The owner,

69. Williams-Polk house, studio loft in Williams unit. (Author)

Katherine Atkinson, was Gelett Burgess's cousin and a well-known supporter of local literary efforts. For several decades her house had been a favorite gathering place among artists, writers, and kindred spirits. Polk's remodeling was modest, yet it resulted in a major transformation by making a small house seem grand, with discrete spaces that are simultaneously integral parts in a circuitous sequence. Each room is tiny and is adorned with classical details in redwood—scaled to acknowledge the diminutive confines while imparting the elegance of an English country house (Figs. 70, 71). Thresholds are placed at the corners, enhancing a sense of spatial continuity. No terminating focus exists at either end of this sequence. In the hall a stair winds up to the second floor through a tiny arcade, and in the dining room an oversized fireplace, medieval in character, is set off to one side, abutting a dark passage to the pantry and a china cabinet that is the most sumptuous appointment in the house.

The plain, unpretentious exterior of the Atkinson house was left virtually intact. Polk admired the straightforward simplicity of such buildings, and his client valued her cottage's historical associa-

70. Polk & Polk. Katherine Atkinson house, San Francisco, 1893, alterations. Entry hall. (Author)

125

71. Atkinson house, dining room. (Private collection)

tions. He designed a plaque commemorating Atkinson's parents as the builders and bearing the date of construction (1853) to be placed over the front door, omitting any reference to the alterations. At about the same time, Bruce Porter probably designed the informal garden, enclosing the yard with an assortment of trees and thick shrubs. A classical balustrade and a delicately rendered wrought-iron gate separated this verdant enclave from the street.[18] The total effect imparts a sense of both ordered elegance and elements that had been accumulated over time.

Polk sought to enhance this dichotomy in subsequent proposals for Russian Hill. In 1894 he suggested that the path (platted as Vallejo Street) leading to the hill's summit be remade into a series of terraces, as if it were the central axis of an Italian garden. Then, about two years later, he advised Horatio Livermore, a rich Oakland businessman, to remodel an adjacent house in a manner that avoided any reference to formality.[19] Livermore and other residents devised yards with much the same unaffected, rural character as the Atkinson property. In little more than a decade, Russian Hill had become "a veritable wilderness" rising amid San Francisco's dense urban fabric (Fig. 72). Reached by long flights of steps and narrow paths, with plants growing

126

72. San Francisco, Russian Hill, view from southeast, ca. 1896.
(California Historical Society)

over everything in sight, the compound conveyed a sense of age, even slight decay. Its cultivated rusticity, laced with urbane counterpoints, suggested an old, remote, somewhat neglected residential quarter on the fringe of a European city rather than a pastoral retreat. The arrival of the Livermores and other socially prominent families signified that this setting now appealed to the well-to-do, as well as to artists and others of limited means. Russian Hill's character remained an anomaly only in degree; it had a considerable influence on new work in other parts of the metropolis.

The rustic city house enjoyed its greatest popularity in Pacific Heights. Straddling the northern slope of the Western Addition, with a panoramic view of the Bay and Golden Gate, this district was San Francisco's most fashionable new quarter. The construction of suburban dwellings on compact lots prevailed here. The streetscape was varied because of the mixture of large, moderate-sized, and even quite modest freestanding houses. Some blocks were more stylish than others, but even the costliest houses were never far removed from the humbler examples.

127

Coxhead began to receive commissions for small houses in Pacific Heights at about the time of Polk's first work on Russian Hill. Coxhead's earliest designs, such as that for friend James McGauley (1891), adhere to the prevailing pattern in their use of suburban imagery. McGauley's house is, in effect, a transplanted English cottage. By 1893 an important shift occurred in Coxhead's approach, evident in the adjacent residence built for himself and Almeric (Fig. 73). Like the Williams-Polk house, it exploits a difficult site to achieve a dramatic effect. The design is also a more sophisticated interpretation of English precedents than was McGauley's. The narrow street frontage is accentuated by a towerlike facade that has a taut, abstract quality. The bands of little windows set flush against the surface were probably inspired by recent London work of Shaw and others. However, the composition is more simplified and softened than English models, in keeping with the building's size and materials. The west elevation, facing McGauley's yard, with its dominant horizontality and rural character, contrasts with the facade and underscores the transition from public to private space. Expanses of shingled wall and roof surfaces, interrupted only by the simplest window articulation, extend from a pivotal clustering of elements grouped around the front door. The composition may well

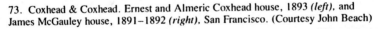

73. Coxhead & Coxhead. Ernest and Almeric Coxhead house, 1893 *(left)*, and James McGauley house, 1891–1892 *(right)*, San Francisco. (Courtesy John Beach)

74. Coxhead house, rear view. (Courtesy John Beach)

have been inspired by Voysey's early projects, but Coxhead's version is more compact and mannered at its focal point and less regimented elsewhere.[20] Toward the rear, the house looks somewhat like a Surrey barn that has been remodeled in a straightforward way, lacking the studied poise of the street facade (Fig. 74). Front and rear are set in opposition, while the overriding simplicity of detail lends cohesiveness to the whole. Both the imagery and the studied casualness present in this design owe a major debt to English arts-and-crafts work, which became a guidepost for Coxhead's work during the next several years.[21] But neither Coxhead nor Polk considered the Arts and Crafts Movement to be a discrete entity; instead they appear to have viewed it as a potent source for expression in rustic design—an updated equivalent of the Shingle Style—that was appropriate to the design of modest houses.

Coxhead's plans remained more American. In his own residence there is an ever-changing path up to and through the premises, inspired by Polk's work but developed in a different way. The entrance is reached by a series of winding steps and landings that become progressively constricted, with the final run wedged between a retaining wall and the basement, as if it were an alley in an Italian hill town

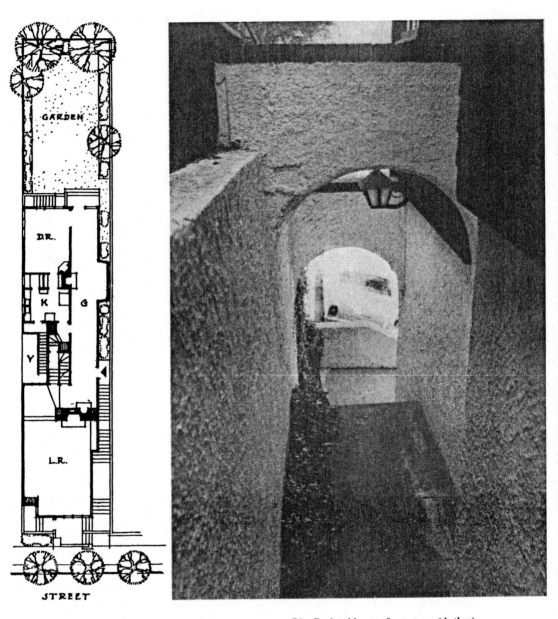

75. Coxhead house, plan.
(Drawn by Howard Moise)

76. Coxhead house, front steps. (Author)

(Figs. 75, 76). A transition occurs at the front door, spatially echoing the change in character between the front and rear portions of the house. Inside, the emphasis is wholly horizontal. The long gallery, the plan's one English component, is unlike its prototypes in that it generates a sense of continuity while dramatizing the site's narrow form through variations in space and light (Fig. 77). From the dark vestibule

130

the corridor gradually becomes brighter, expanding into a glazed bay that serves as a secondary sitting area, with a borrowed vista of McGauley's yard. The gallery brightens further at the end, where windows on two sides open into a secluded garden. In the other direction the space unfolds more rapidly, lapping down a broad turn of steps in a circuitous path to the living room. Although the stair is directly opposite the entrance, it is encased so as not to interrupt the horizontal emphasis. The living room is unusually large for a house of this size and is made even more expansive by grandly scaled redwood paneling and beams (Fig. 78). The living room windows are placed only at the corners, and each one is at a different height. Like a periscope, the highest window bank catches a segment of the McGauley house. At the far corner, the platform and attendant bench offer an observation deck from which to view houses across the street and catch glimpses of the Bay beyond. Paralleling the Williams-Polk house interiors, the sequence and manipulation of each zone imply an extension of space, mitigating the property's narrow confines.

77. Coxhead house, gallery. (Author)

78. Coxhead house, living room. (Author)

An equally unconventional solution is present in the Charles Murdock house around the corner, which Coxhead had designed several months earlier. A native of Boston, Murdock moved to California in 1855 and became a widely respected elder of the intellectual community. Murdock ran a small printing business; he considered bookmaking an art and was patronized by some of the region's most gifted writers. Among his friends were Bret Harte, Robert Louis Stevenson, John Muir, and William Keith. While active in the Unitarian church, he had been married by Joseph Worcester and frequently attended his services. Murdock was also an ardent supporter of the younger generation, including Bruce Porter, Gelett Burgess, and Coxhead. Since Murdock, like many of his friends, could not afford to spend much for his house, it was designed with about as much floor area as Coxhead's residence, and at an even lower cost.[22]

The studied asymmetry of the facade recalls those of E. W. Godwin's well-known artists' houses in Chelsea from a decade earlier,

132

79. Coxhead & Coxhead.
Charles Murdock house,
San Francisco, 1893.
(Courtesy Marguerite Murdock)

80. Houses in Burford, Oxfordshire. (Author)

but here the relationship among elements is only implied (Fig. 79).[23] Set amid a sea of shingles, each opening has a different scale and treatment, and both side elevations abandon ordered composition. The house is a picturesque but basically utilitarian box. In this respect, it bears closer affinity to the small postmedieval dwellings that line the streets of many English towns more than to its urbane London counterparts (Fig. 80).

The exterior gives little clue as to what occurs inside, where the rooms are at split levels set around a tiny central stair (Figs. 81, 82). This skylit vertical core, rendered as if it were a Georgian hall, comes as a complete surprise. Taking a cue from Shaw's plan for 42 Netherhall Gardens, Coxhead placed the stair at the end of a dark, simple, and, like everything else, miniaturized gallery. In the living room above, ornateness and simplicity confront one another in a richly carved fireplace surround isolated by plaster walls that were originally covered with brown paper (Fig. 83).

By the mid-1890s, the idea of the rustic city house began to win acceptance among well-to-do businessmen. Following Horatio Livermore's move to Russian Hill, where a rustic ambience predominated, several contemporaries commissioned sizable rustic houses in Pacific Heights, where such work was still a novelty. These houses are

81. Murdock house, author's reconstruction of original plan.
(Drawn by Kim Spurgeon Fly)

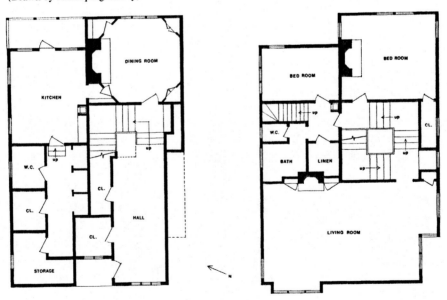

82. Murdock house, entrance
hall and staircase. (Author)

83. Murdock house, living room. (Author)

not only larger, but also more elaborate and formal in their expression. At the same time, they possess the same unconventional mix of disparate qualities found in their less expensive counterparts. The house Coxhead designed for insurance broker Russell Osborn is an important example of the larger type (Fig. 84). Inspiration for the exterior appears to have come from seventeenth-century English tradesmen's houses,

84. Coxhead & Coxhead. Russell Osborn house, San Francisco, 1896.
(Photo John Beach)

85. House, Ashburton, Devon, seventeenth century. (Horace Field and Michael Bunney, *English Domestic Architecture of the XVII and XVIII Centuries*, p. 151)

where classical details and order are mixed with late medieval verticality and picturesqueness (Fig. 85). These dual characteristics are emphasized in the Osborn house, with rustic and refined elements isolated from one another. Elaborate, overscaled Georgian details are concentrated in a single projecting bay, forming an emphatic center axis that stands alone on a large, shingled wall surface. The formal, symmetrical composition and grand scale are opposed by an awkward side bay, which looks like an afterthought but which helps to enliven the elevation and is an integral part of the plan.

All suggestion of rustic informality is abandoned on the interior. Even more than in the Murdock house, the typically English device of arranging spaces of different character in a sequence that elicits surprise and delight is used here. The unfolding of grand allusions behind a placid facade in relatively confined quarters was a favorite eighteenth-century contrivance, one that was now being used by Shaw and his followers in their London houses.[24] Here the effect is intensified by the constricted approach from a low, dark vestibule up a straight flight of steps to a skylit central hall, patterned after much larger ones in Georgian country houses (Figs. 86, 87). In the hall, thick, deeply undercut corner moldings bulge from the wall, colliding with one another at junctures and vying for space. But these elements

137

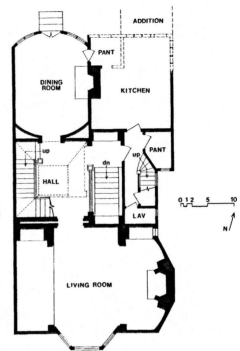

86. Osborn house, plan.
(Drawn by Kim Spurgeon Fly)

87. Osborn house, main hall. (Author)

88. Osborn house, living room. (Author)

also transform each plane into a giant panel, unrelieved save for small paired windows set at the upper level. The large scale and sense of abstractness is reinforced by the continuous molding on the staircase soffit, which seems to float as it directs the eye diagonally upward. Directly above is a delicate, even fragile, balustrade that contrasts with the adjacent features and with a robust counterpart that screens the stairwell running down to the entrance level. Restlessness also pervades the living room, where Baroque fluidity is combined with Georgian reserve in a most unusual fashion (Fig. 88). The plan itself seems agitated, with great spaces compressed to fit the confines of the lot. Yet a sense of axial order and continuity is maintained by the diagonal alignment of front and rear bay windows with the hall thresholds (Fig. 89).

The design's complexities appear to stem from more than aesthetic factors. Coxhead had to work with a relatively low budget of about $8,000.[25] The layout thus conforms to the existing grade, with the entrance level only one room deep and the main floor meeting the slope at the rear. Under these conditions, a straight flight of stairs was the most inexpensive way to connect the two levels. The kitchen had to be adjacent to the dining room, rather than below as was common with an English basement plan. Hence, the main rooms could neither

139

be axially aligned nor reached by a grand staircase from the entrance. Cost was also a likely factor in the inexpensive exterior treatment, which allowed more money to be spent on the fittings inside. Nevertheless, the fact that such imagery was used on an otherwise formal townhouse indicates the increasing respectability of rustic expression.

Appearance, more than cost, was no doubt the principal factor in Polk's unobtrusive design of the exterior for William Dimond's house (1895) (Fig. 90). A prominent figure in business and civic affairs, Dimond came to the region in 1867 and became the head of one of the largest shipping companies on the West Coast. His house was not much larger than Osborn's, but it was more than twice as expensive. Furthermore, it was located on one of the most fashionable blocks in Pacific Heights, surrounded by more ostentatious dwellings. Although descriptions of the interior indicate that it was quite ornate, no sign of such treatment is given on the exterior.[26] Like the Osborn house, the composition is essentially formal but is rendered with more understatement, using thin moldings and stock sash. Only the aediculae around the living room window and entrance depart from this simplicity, and even they are related to other parts with unexpected casualness.

Coxhead's and Polk's earlier rustic houses had drawn little

89. Osborn house, view from living room toward hall. (Author)

90. Polk & Polk. William Dimond house, San Francisco, 1895–1896;
demolished 1971. (Photo John Beach)

attention from the local press, but the unconventional appearance of a
prominent residence like Dimond's attracted considerable notice. The
San Francisco Chronicle commented favorably on its sparing use of
details, contrasting this treatment with the ornateness common to many
of the city's Colonial Revival houses.[27] The design was influential in
popularizing the rustic city house. Over the next decade, its imagery
would be widely used in new sections of Pacific Heights. As with
McKim, Mead & White's Shingle Style resort villas of the previous
decade, the rustic city house was innovative and distinct by virtue of
its special programmatic conditions. Neither Coxhead nor Polk conceived
of such work as the only, or even the prevalent, form of expression for
urban districts. Their designs were a conspicuous departure from the
norm, while at the same time they were unobtrusive, even background,
components within the neighborhood context. These dwellings represent one facet of two architects' search for an inclusive order culled
from several forms of expression.

141

VI

COXHEAD AND POLK: Rustic Suburban and Country Houses

Especially in the modern American country houses of not excessive cost is there to be found a remarkable combination of careful, logical and artistic planning, in which comfort, health and convenience are admirably provided for, with charming and picturesque exteriors, inviting and full of character. In these houses there is doubtless much to criticize; but the faults are those of a nascent and virile art.
A.D.F. Hamlin, *Architectural Record*, October–December 1891

MANY OF the commissions Coxhead and Polk received during the 1890s were for moderate-sized houses in suburban and rural areas outside San Francisco. In general, this work resembles their rustic city houses in its picturesqueness, vernacular-inspired imagery, and often in its complex, unorthodox treatment. Though such residences were conducive to the regional setting and responsive to the growing taste for rusticity, they do not constitute a distinct type like the rustic city house, for the programmatic conditions were more varied. Inspiration for these designs came from broad tendencies in British and American domestic architecture more than from specific examples. In capturing the spirit of this "nascent and virile art," the two architects created some of the most interesting residential work of the decade.

Hamlin's enthusiasm for the informal American house was well justified, yet most examples in the East and Midwest designed in the 1890s lacked the same degree of inventiveness that had characterized earlier efforts. Many architects, such as John Calvin Stevens, worked with variations on established rustic modes. In their hands, the Shingle Style continued into the twentieth century with little significant change. McKim, Mead & White, and some other firms that had been leading designers of rustic houses during the 1880s, now concentrated on larger buildings and more formal modes of expression. Many young architects also preferred classical precedent, turning to picturesque sources only when necessary. Others, including Peabody & Stearns, and Cram, Goodhue & Ferguson, developed new forms of rustic expression, often rendered in a dry manner with rather literal details, inspired by sources such as English Tudor architecture. Informal domestic architecture in the 1890s often was based on eighteenth-century American sources, emphasizing unobtrusiveness and subduing picturesque irregularities. In general, small and moderate-sized American houses were discreet and genteel, but were no match for the creative work of arts-and-crafts architects like Charles Voysey, Edwin Lutyens, and Edward Prior. Not until the Arts and Crafts Movement brought a new sense of purpose to the mainstream of American residential design in the early 1900s would a significant body of rustic work be produced to match the best of the Shingle Style houses built fifteen years earlier.[1]

From their isolated position, Coxhead and Polk kept abreast of these new tendencies. Their informal suburban and country houses reflect the taste for quiet order found in other American work. But they also seem to have been more aware of, and certainly more receptive to, the English arts-and-crafts developments than were most of their colleagues in other regions, resulting in work that was often freer and more eccentric. Like the rustic city house, these designs appear at once sophisticated and slightly innocent, perhaps even naive, encompassing dissimilar qualities that echo the convergence of many worlds in the Bay Area itself. They offer an enthusiastic gesture to San Francisco's cosmopolitan air and also to the rustic ambience that was being cultivated in outlying communities.

During the 1890s, there was a decisive change in attitudes toward suburban development in the Bay Area, which stemmed in part from the rapid growth of outlying communities. Towns were beginning to undergo a transformation from semi-isolated hamlets, serving a small resident populace and a few rich families that owned country places nearby, to links in an ever-expanding network of urban satellites. Up until this time, the metropolis had been confined to a relatively compact area surrounded by open country. Now, with improving transportation systems, concentrated development was encompassing a much larger area, as it was, in fact, throughout the nation.[2] The natural landscape was threatened with change, and as a result of public sensitivity, organized efforts were launched to enhance the land's rusticity through suburban development.

Before the 1890s, virtually all of San Francisco's suburbs adhered to the standard nineteenth-century American grid. Flat land was considered the most desirable property. House lots were often larger

91. Berkeley, Dwight Way looking east from Claremont Avenue,
ca. 1890. (California Historical Society)

than those in San Francisco and, with a sunnier climate, they supported
more foliage. But, except for a backdrop of hills and, in some instances,
views of the Bay, these suburban enclaves were like hundreds of others
in the country (Fig. 91).

Departures from the prevailing pattern first occurred in Marin
County. Situated just north of the Golden Gate, this area possesses
some of the most picturesque natural landscape in the region. As early
as 1869, cottage lots were platted on the steep slopes above Sausalito,
a fishing village with views over the Bay and San Francisco beyond.
The undertaking was soon abandoned, however; even construction
several years later of the North Pacific Coast Railroad, with its ferry
connections to the city, failed to attract many new residents. Not until
the mid-1880s was a significant accumulation of houses erected on the
site.[3] Sausalito's increasing appeal, coupled with more frequent ferry
service, encouraged the establishment of two new residential communities further afield: Mill Valley, originally named Eastland, was platted in 1889, and Belvedere was laid out during the next two years.
Each enterprise was spearheaded by a consortium of San Francisco
businessmen who selected the site primarily because of its natural
beauty. Located at the foot of Mt. Tamalpais, Mill Valley straddles a

winding creek amid forests and rolling hills (Fig. 92). Belvedere occupies a narrow, hilly peninsula, affording panoramic views in all directions (Fig. 93). Streets were platted in conformance with the terrain, pathways formed an integral part of the circulation system, and in Mill Valley forest reserves were set aside.

Both Mill Valley and Belvedere were laid out by a young civil engineer, Michael O'Shaughnessy. Trained in his native Ireland, O'Shaughnessy may have already been familiar with naturalistic planning principles before immigrating in 1885. Mill Valley was his first known design for a residential community, and he successfully adapted the romantic ideal to the tight, rugged terrain of Marin County.[4] An informal setting was clearly sought by his employers; both groups had dismissed engineers who failed to work sympathetically with the sites. Moreover, the developers served as the local governments for some years after lots began to be sold, in order to ensure that the character they had envisioned would be brought to fruition.[5]

92. Mill Valley, general view looking northwest, Mt. Tamalpais in background, ca. 1900. (Mill Valley Public Library)

145

93. Michael O'Shaughnessy. Plan of Belvedere, 1890. Belvedere Land Company Map #3. (Courtesy Scott Polland)

Mill Valley and Belvedere were fashioned after the few well-known romantic suburbs east of the Mississippi. Contemporary accounts of Belvedere often compared it to Pierre Lorrilard's Tuxedo Park (1885).[6] However, the steep-sloping topography of Mill Valley and Belvedere permitted only very narrow roads, scaled like those of European hill towns. The land was not conducive to large houses, since lots were relatively small and often included sharp changes in grade, allowing both privacy and views. These communities also served a dual function—suburb and resort—that affected both their overall character and house design.

Marin County had attracted excursionists for several decades. Many people sought the pleasures of the resort hotels erected in the area during the 1870s and 1880s. Other vacationers camped in secluded tracts that were scarcely less wild than those found in the mountain regions further north. Initially, people who loved this unspoiled beauty but were tired of forfeiting the comforts of home and of traveling long distances for their vacation were drawn to Mill Valley and Belvedere. In contrast to the structured routine of the resort hotel, life in these two communities was informal. The *San Francisco Call* noted that Mill Valley's residents wanted "a place nearby where they can get close to nature—not an artificial park, but nature unadorned." Marin County was likened to a great natural reserve, and Mill Valley was said to offer "scenery as beautiful, as varied, and as well worth going to see as the Alps."[7] Mill Valley citizens planted thousands of trees within the first decade, transforming meadowland into forest. An equally ambitious landscaping campaign was launched on Belvedere, which had supported little more than scrubby growth when it was platted. The earliest houses were small, inexpensive, and unpretentious, with simple interiors, similar to those of summer cabins in mountain areas (Fig. 94).

The first year-round residence in Mill Valley was constructed within two years of the initial subdivision plat; houses erected for the same purpose appeared in Belvedere shortly thereafter. The proximity to San Francisco, combined with the mild, sunny climate, led many summer residents to use their simpler cottages as suburban retreats.

94. Belvedere, general view looking west, ca. 1900. (Courtesy Belvedere Land Company)

Society columns in the city's weekly newspapers indicate that people often opened their houses by late March and remained until late October. This practice became routine for perhaps several hundred of the city's well-to-do residents during the 1890s. Spending much of the year in these woodsy enclaves further nourished the taste for rusticity and induced relaxed patterns of living that have been identified with the Bay Area ever since.

The idea of the rustic suburb spread quickly. Among the most important later developments was Burlingame Park (now part of Hillsborough), located near the small town of San Mateo. The area was graced with a gently rolling pastoral landscape where rich San Franciscans had been building country places since the 1860s.[8] Burlingame Park was developed by Francis Newlands, a former United States senator and a trustee of the vast Sharon estate. Newlands envisioned a country club, race track, park, and game preserve for residents in the hope that the development would become the "Tuxedo of the West." To promote sales, an initial tract was laid out by Richard Hammond, among the state's most respected civil engineers. John McLaren, superintendent of Golden Gate Park, prepared an extensive landscape plan. Page Brown collaborated on the project, designing five houses that would set the style for future work (Fig. 95). In spite of these

95. Richard Hammond and Michael O'Shaughnessy. Plan of Burlingame Park (now Hillsborough), 1893, 1894. (Bancroft Library)

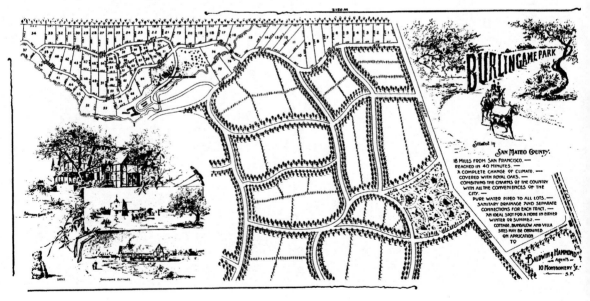

148

improvements, the subdivision, which was located on flat, open land, failed to attract many purchasers. Newlands persisted, and with the aid of several prominent young businessmen, he established a hunt and polo club on the more picturesque adjacent terrain to the west. He then sponsored a second subdivision, laid out by O'Shaughnessy alongside the clubhouse grounds, which was an instant success.

Within a few years Burlingame Park became the region's most fashionable suburb. Although the new residents were rich, they were determined to avoid the ostentatiousness of the nearby country houses built by their parents' generation.[9] Brown's design for the clubhouse, intended to recall an Elizabethan inn, provided a model in its picturesqueness, unpretentiousness, and subordination to the natural setting, which remained virtually untouched (Fig. 96). Brown also designed the first residence, for Joseph D. Grant. It is a spirited interpretation of the north tower of Stokesay Castle in Shropshire, here transformed

96. A. Page Brown. Burlingame Country Club, Hillsborough, 1893–1894; demolished. *(Monarch Souvenir of Sunset City and Sunset Scenes)*

into a tree house reached by a bridge, with its great hall perched above the forest of live oaks (Fig. 97).[10] Most later dwellings were less imaginative, but they did respect the verdant landscape, the feature that gave the community its image and appeal.

Burlingame Park's success as a playground for the rich provided the rustic suburb with its ultimate sanction among San Franciscans. Similar affluent enclaves, such as Ross, grew during the 1890s, even though none of these communities had a master plan. A rustic ambience was also aggressively cultivated by Berkeley residents. Even where picturesque natural features were not present, rusticity was nurtured through architecture and landscaping. Neither Coxhead nor Polk enjoyed the advantages Brown had in Burlingame Park, where he helped establish the development's general character and designed many of its buildings. Nevertheless, the two architects were affected by the increasing taste for rustic design, and their houses afforded some of the most influential manifestations of that taste during its formative years.

Among Coxhead's early suburban house commissions was the residence of a young Napa banker, E. Wiler Churchill (1892) (Fig. 98).[11] The scheme is a picturesquely composed, mannered tribute to the Shingle Style, with open, flowing spaces inside. The departures are just as pronounced. On the facade, overscaled elements depart from precedent and resist the confines of the building's form. The elevation is horizontally divided into two disparate zones. At the lower level, herringbone brick panels with molded wood surrounds and delicate lead-pane windows form a tapestry of rectilinear patterns. A hulking, barnlike mass looms overhead, topped with a bowed roof that laps around the dormers like a thatch roof. A sense of vertical continuity is provided by the tower, but even it is tenuously poised on a base of four Tuscan columns. At the other end, a large window panel is at once a projecting bay and an extension of the upper zone. Its ambiguous role is heightened by the lateral continuation of the wall plane as an enclosed porch that otherwise seems incidental to the mass.

The emphatic division of the facade into two zones does not correspond to the floor levels inside. The main rooms are raised several feet above the entry, a device Coxhead sometimes used to enrich spatial sequence and to secure privacy from the street. The second story is placed well above the exterior projection. Only the height of the tower soffit matches the spatial disposition behind it. The plan is

97. A. Page Brown. Joseph Grant house, Hillsborough, 1894–1895; burned 1909.
(Courtesy Sheila Mack)

98. Coxhead & Coxhead. E. Wiler Churchill house, Napa, 1892; altered.
(*Overland Monthly,* April 1902, p. 807)

hardly an afterthought; it is the most remarkable feature of the design (Fig. 99). A single bi-level space, serving as hall, stairwell, and living room, extends the length of the front. Broad flights of stairs run from the cavernous vestibule up to the hall and then back to the mezzanine above, where the tower becomes an expansive, semicircular alcove. Another flight of steps passes along a glazed bay up to the bedrooms

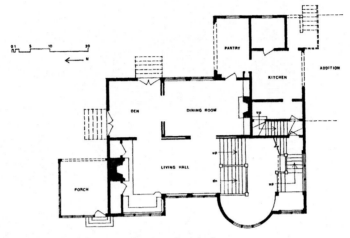

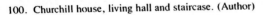

99. Churchill house, author's reconstruction of original plan. (Drawn by Kim Spurgeon Fly)

100. Churchill house, living hall and staircase. (Author)

101. Churchill house, living hall and dining room from library. (Author)

(Fig. 100). Sheathed in unmolded redwood paneling, this main room is like a great Tudor hall that has been abstracted and given a relaxed spatial flow. At either end, window bays extend nearly from floor to ceiling. The wall plane in between is penetrated by stretches of windows and by the mezzanine alcove to form alternating bands of solid and void. Wide thresholds connect to the dining room and study, where the woodwork stops at the lintel so that the partition walls read as screens, defining, but not fully enclosing, the space (Fig. 101). The sophistication of this open plan would seldom be matched until Frank Lloyd Wright's Prairie houses after the turn of the century.

The mannered forms and spatial freedom of the Churchill house are developed within a more historicizing, English-inspired framework for the residence of Andrew Carrigan, which was probably designed a few months later.[12] Located atop a grassy knoll amid open fields in the Ross Valley, the exterior composition is controlled, with an eclectic assemblage of elements subordinated to the long, rectangular block (Fig. 102). A deep side porch both extends and erodes this mass. An enormous adjacent bay bulges out to provide a focal point, agitated by stepped windows that march up to the far corner, there to be halted by a sham buttress. The rest of the composition is calm and almost symmetrical, with a small Tuscan portico affording a focal point for

153

this unobtrusive ordering of elements. The Carrigan house conveys a sense of age to a greater degree than in Coxhead's previous designs. The eccentric Tudor bay, capped by a Georgian cornice and braced by a medieval buttress, the Tuscan columns, and the bowed dormers are all actors in a pictorial play, as if a simple English barn had been modified and transformed into a small manor house over the course of several centuries. Coxhead had produced such accumulative effects in some of his ecclesiastical buildings, but never in so forthright a manner. Here, each part remains a fragment, and cohesiveness is expressed as an artful, understated collage, possibly influenced by the example of Phillip Webb and other English arts-and-crafts architects. Little precedent existed for this approach in the United States, where the Shingle Style and other contemporary rustic modes tended to unify rather than

102. Coxhead & Coxhead. Andrew Carrigan house, San Anselmo, ca. 1892; altered. (Courtesy John Beach)

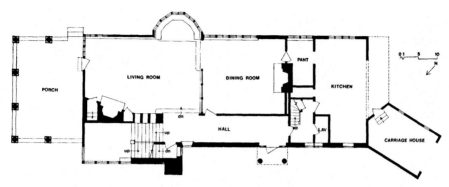

103. Carrigan house, plan. (Drawn by Kim Spurgeon Fly)

104. Charles F. A. Voysey. M. H. Lakin house, Bishops Itchington, Warwickshire, 1888. Plan. (*British Architect,* October 9, 1888)

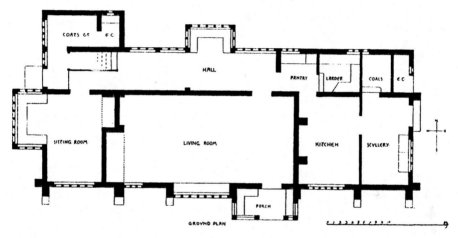

particularize diverse historical references.

The plan employs a linear arrangement of rooms off a long gallery that was no doubt inspired by published work of Voysey (Figs. 103, 104). Yet the handling of the space is entirely different, emphasizing an American taste for openness. Wide thresholds, large banks of corner windows, and an angled fireplace contribute to the sense of continuity (Figs. 105, 106). Restrained, elegant, and classicizing redwood panels form a thin membrane that enhances this effect. The living and dining rooms are essentially a single space, partitioned only by removable panels set between carved posts. Slight changes in level and window height differentiate the two zones; however, the glazing also forms a band that ties the zones together and, projecting out as a voluminous bay at the juncture of the two rooms, implies an extension

155

105. Carrigan house, living room and stair from hall. (Author)

106. Carrigan house, living room. (Author)

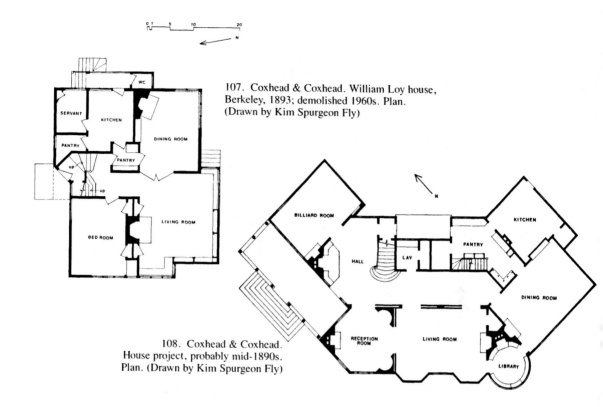

107. Coxhead & Coxhead. William Loy house, Berkeley, 1893; demolished 1960s. Plan. (Drawn by Kim Spurgeon Fly)

108. Coxhead & Coxhead. House project, probably mid-1890s. Plan. (Drawn by Kim Spurgeon Fly)

of space into the landscape. The ground floor's pervasive horizontality continues up to the stair landing, glazed as if it were a porch and sufficiently large to accommodate a secondary sitting area.

With the Churchill and Carrigan houses, Coxhead showed his mastery of the open plan, but he did not pursue this manner of arranging space as an end unto itself. A number of the residential schemes he produced during the same period are more contained and sometimes more formal. For example, the very small residence for William Loy in Berkeley (1893) has a tight, compact plan, and each space is treated as a discrete entity, with both the entry and circulation core limited to a tiny stair hall (Fig. 107). And, in an unrealized proposal for a suburban house many times larger, each space receives its own character (Fig. 108). The sequence is elaborate and the relationships complex, with movement alternating between circuitous and axial paths. Differing programmatic conditions were a major inducement for such diversity, but so was the architect's appetite for experimentation; Coxhead was seemingly never content with developing variations on a given idea for more than two or three projects.

157

109. Coxhead & Coxhead. Beta Theta Pi fraternity house, Berkeley,
1893–1894; altered. (Courtesy John Beach)

110. Malines, Belgium, commercial district. (*American Architect*, September 13, 1890)

158

Even the variations with which Coxhead experimented could assume markedly different forms. The notions of age evident in the Carrigan house appear again in the Beta Theta Pi fraternity house in Berkeley (1893), but here the mass is divided into four parts, each treated as if it were an individual building along a street in a northern European town (Figs. 109, 110). Opposing masses—the tall stuccoed "tower" and the low pavilion adjacent to it—are balanced by the comparatively unobtrusive shingled wings at either end. The four sections are staggered so that the building's aspect changes considerably when viewed from different angles. In contrast to many of Coxhead's other buildings, the external differentiation reflects distinct internal functions.[13]

The low budget of the Loy house permitted neither a division into distinct masses nor the use of elaborate, historicizing details.[14] Clad in shingles, the exterior supports the simplest of elements without any decorative embellishment (Fig. 111). The idea of modifications over time is conveyed with the same apparent casualness present in Polk's work. On the street front, two dissimilar window bays abut, and while they constitute a single wall plane, each looks like it was added to the main block at a different time. Around the corner, a boxy extension containing the stairwell hovers over the main entrance and rudely interrupts the sweep of the gable as if it were an afterthought conceived in strictly utilitarian terms. Despite appearances, these protrusions are integral to the plan and important components of the composition.

111. Loy house, side view. (Courtesy Loy Chamberlin)

159

112. Coxhead & Coxhead. Ernest and Almeric Coxhead house, San Mateo,
ca. 1893. (Courtesy John Beach)

Coxhead relied almost entirely on English rural vernacular
sources for the imagery of his rustic suburban houses, but he showed
no inclination toward developing specific regional references, as did
many of his English colleagues. For his own suburban house in San
Mateo (ca. 1893), Coxhead created an idealized version of the half-
timber cottage: picturesque, slightly irregular, even a little awkward,
yet controlled by the encompassing double-bowed roof, with each
element clearly articulated by surface timberwork to form a crisp,
linear pattern (Fig. 112).[15] The effect is studied and abstract in a
manner similar to Voysey's recent work. But Coxhead was not seeking
a standard idiom in his adaptation of the English cottage, which was
both generalized and multifaceted. A design, probably dating from the
late 1890s, isolates each element amid mural wall surfaces. Here, a
complex form is used with an X-shaped plan that breaks into a panoply
of gables midway up the side (Fig. 113). The idea must have come
from schemes by Edward Prior, which were having an important influence on English domestic architecture at that time; but the interpretation, in its form, detail, and absence of regional ties, was Coxhead's
own.

Coxhead was far enough removed from his homeland and suffi-

113. Coxhead & Coxhead. House project, probably late 1890s. (Courtesy John Beach)

ciently independent in his ideas to shun literal transplantings of the English cottage. No single English architect's influence or tendency pervades his work. One senses his nostalgia for English architecture, but also a certain detachment from it. These are not English houses so much as they are American ones that impart sensitivity to English character. They assimilate the arts-and-crafts free spirit. They offer lyrical homage to the modest, idiosyncratic character of picturesque vernacular buildings. These qualities are tempered by the taste for classical order, but they also exhibit a spatial adventurousness that distinguishes the best late nineteenth-century domestic architecture in the United States. Selecting, combining, and modifying precedent, Coxhead worked as a Californian—gathering inspiration from different worlds, which in his hands became something quite at home in the modern cosmopolis.

Many of Polk's houses also possess a vernacular-inspired spontaneity that was shared with the English Arts and Crafts Movement and was no doubt reinforced by Coxhead's example. Like Coxhead, he delighted in placing elaborate decorative details on otherwise unassuming forms. However, his designs were often more extemporaneous

161

114. Polk & Polk. Villa Veneta, John Kilgarif house, Sausalito, 1893; altered. (Courtesy Mr. and Mrs. William Riley)

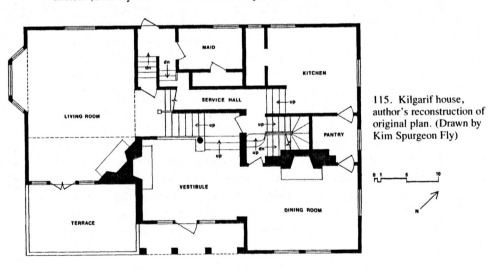

115. Kilgarif house, author's reconstruction of original plan. (Drawn by Kim Spurgeon Fly)

in effect—playful collages that seem impulsively assembled, yet also purposeful and responsive to programmatic conditions. In other instances, the results were subdued, sometimes even severe. Polk's vocabulary was broader than Coxhead's. He was more prone to exper-

162

iment with different historical sources. Furthermore, the scope of his residential work is greater, ranging from tiny suburban cottages to extensive mountain retreats.

Several of Polk's commissions during the first half of the 1890s were for houses in Marin County. The year-round residence of a San Francisco insurance broker, John Kilgarif (1893), is a good example of his freewheeling play with divergent elements (Fig. 114). On the main elevation, an overscaled entrance portal, decked in Venetian Gothic tracery, is placed right at the edge of the block. The second-story windows form a symmetrical grouping, even though it is neither centrally placed nor aligned with the components beneath. What appears to be a service wing on one side actually contains the living room, the grandest space in the house. The ambiguity continues in the plan (Fig. 115). As a diagram, it forms a rectangle, evenly divided into three parts with the entrance on center; however, each section is set progressively further back, creating a diagonal spatial sequence ascending to the living room. At this point, the ceremonious passage culminates in a barrel-vaulted space. Here, the walls are punctured by windows that are too big and peel back at the entry to form a low, shallow alcove that opens onto a terrace and reveals a panoramic view of the Bay (Figs. 116, 117).

An equally spirited hillside residence was designed for Valentine Rey in Belvedere (1893). Like Murdock, Rey was a businessman with a keen interest in the arts. He was being groomed to head the family firm, Britton and Rey, preeminent among the region's photography and lithography studios. Through its prints, the company deserved much of the credit for making the beauties of northern California's landscape well known during the late nineteenth century. Rey had grown up in a Victorian cottage on Russian Hill not far from Polk's house, and his familiarity with the architect's work there may well have led to the commission. Rey was also one of the earliest full-time residents of Belvedere and an ardent supporter of its rustic development. Rey's wife was a painter who had studied under William Keith, and she also had a love for the region's natural scenery and its early Hispanic architecture.[16]

Located on a superb site, originally with an unbroken view in all directions, the Rey house is without defined front, side, or rear elevations. A dual approach from above and below terminates at the small entry terrace, shielded by a pergola, which modestly punctuates the low, dense foliage. The house follows the slope of the land and is arranged on split levels, a configuration that is expressed on the exte-

163

116. Kilgarif house, living room. (Author)

117. Kilgarif house, living room looking toward stair hall and original porch. (Author)

rior as two distinct masses casually joined (Fig. 118). Its picturesque form, low profile, plain stucco wall surfaces, and red tile roof all suggest vernacular farmhouses in Spain and Italy, sources that were just beginning to interest American architects (Fig. 119). The projecting porch makes an unprecedented reference to buildings of the Mexican-American period in Monterey, for which Mrs. Rey had a particular fondness.[17] The freedom with which these sources are interpreted— reduced to simple, geometric forms and softened by trellises and vines— is similar to Irving Gill's work of some fifteen years later. At the same time, the Rey house is thoroughly eclectic, orchestrating diverse allusions in a complex, yet loose, pictorial assemblage. Polk's intentions are revealed overtly at the front door, which is flanked by two cartoons

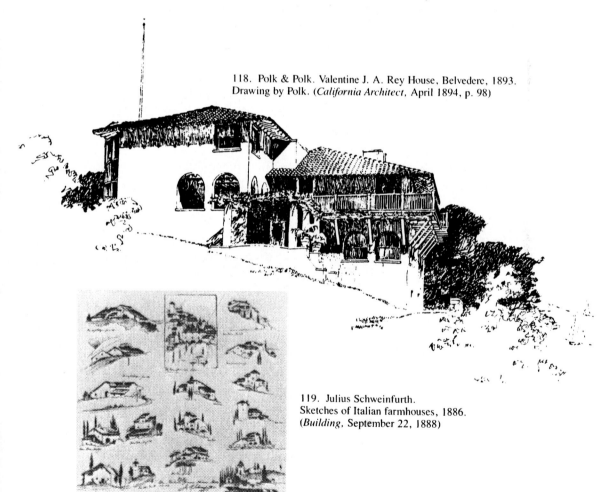

118. Polk & Polk. Valentine J. A. Rey House, Belvedere, 1893. Drawing by Polk. (*California Architect*, April 1894, p. 98)

119. Julius Schweinfurth.
Sketches of Italian farmhouses, 1886.
(*Building*, September 22, 1888)

165

of Pedro Huizar's baptistry window at the Mission San José in San Antonio, Texas, whimsically reduced to the scale of toys (Fig. 120). Their ironic context is accentuated both by repetition and by the fact that one of them is merely a blind relief.

These tiny sculptures offer little preparation for the interior, where interconnecting spaces are embellished with rich classical details. In plan, the organization appears jumbled; in three dimensions, however, it is among Polk's most dramatic interiors (Figs. 121, 122). As with the Murdock house, the main rooms are arranged around a central core that combines stair and hall. Here, the area circumscribes a tiny light well enframed by an attenuated arcade that caricatures the court of a quattrocento palace (Fig. 123). In contrast to the linear progression of space in the Kilgarif house, the organization is centripetal, with the light well acting both as a screen and as a means of visual communication between the main rooms. Each space rests at a different level and is its own miniature world: the living room suggests a baronial hall; the family room above, a rustic mountain lodge; the master bedroom, a tower chamber (Figs. 124, 125). A dialogue is thus established between the characteristically English use of contrasting spaces to create a sequence offering surprise and delight and the American sense of spatial freedom and continuity.

Polk abandoned such complexities in smaller Marin County summer cottages. These dwellings contain little save basic accommo-

120. Rey house, entrance
detail. (Author)

166

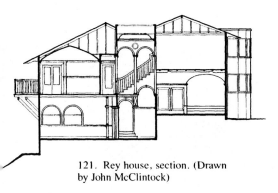

121. Rey house, section. (Drawn by John McClintock)

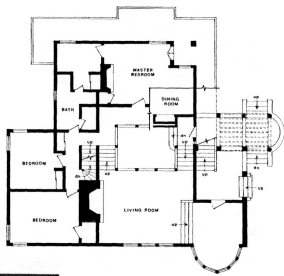

122. Rey house, plan. (Drawn by Kim Spurgeon Fly)

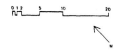

123. Rey house, stair hall. (Author)

167

124. Rey house, living room. (Author)

125. Rey house, family room. (Author)

dations, yet they are far from being ordinary. The cottage built for Alfred Moore, president of the Pacific Mining Exchange, located next to Rey's house, has a living hall occupying almost the entire main floor (Fig. 126). The idea of the tiny house as a big room may have been inspired by romantic notions of the all-purpose chamber in some pioneer cabins, but most published examples of comparably sized houses at that time divided the space into diminutive parcels. Polk's solution reflects a new concern for the special conditions of a very small dwelling. After the turn of the century, similar arrangements would become quite popular for both summer cottages and suburban residences in the region.[18] However straightforward in concept, the Moore house contains a rich collection of images. The exterior is a hybrid of an English cottage and a Swiss chalet, with the kitchen ell resembling a homesteader's cabin. Aside from this appendage, the house is symmetrical, its plan ordered by cross-axes, and many of its details inspired by late Georgian work.

The meeting of rustic and refined qualities is expressed with wit in another hall-house designed in Mill Valley for a San Francisco

126. Polk & Polk. Alfred Moore house, Belvedere, 1893; altered. Drawing by Daniel Polk. (Courtesy Mr. and Mrs. Edward Stephens)

169

127. Polk & Polk. Frank Washington house, Mill Valley, 1893; altered. (Author)

banker, Frank Washington (1893). Rising from a shacklike base, the entrance porch mimics a temple front, lacking an entablature and with decreasing intercolumniation (Fig. 127). Inside, the principal space suggests the hall of a mountain lodge (Fig. 128). Here, structure becomes ballet: the hammer-beam truss is transformed into a graceful arc of thin boards that leaps across the space and seems to be suspended from, rather than supporting, the roof.

Performing acrobatics with image, space, and scale, these houses embody the meeting of contrasts in the land of extremes. Just as San Francisco's proximity to the rugged natural landscape fostered the introduction of rusticity into the metropolis, so it induced the cultivation of urbane refinements in the resort suburb. Coxhead's and Polk's rustic work emphasized the delights of both worlds, weaving an array of grand illusions into a pervasively informal matrix. The presence of these two qualities was hardly unique to their designs; yet, like so many aspects of the region itself, each facet was more pronounced, the contrast more intense, than could be found in most other places.

170

128. Washington house, living room. (Author)

The richness of these rustic houses resulted as much from polarity as from synthesis.

Polk did not consider intricate manipulations of space and scale to be appropriate when a budget permitted rooms of generous size and clients sought an elaborate backdrop for their daily routine. His conviction reflected an axiom of the academic movement: program fundamentally affects character in design. Polk proved so facile in responding to the conditions of a project that his large rustic houses, located in remote parts of the state, hardly seem to be from the same hand as the much smaller residences he designed in San Francisco's suburbs.

One of Polk's major commissions of the 1890s came from San Francisco lawyer Charles Wheeler for The Bend, a hunting lodge near Mt. Shasta and the Oregon border. Wheeler was only in his mid-thirties when the complex was built. A self-made man, he was brilliant in his field, quickly rising to the top ranks of the bar, amassing a small fortune in the process. He had all the convictions of a gentleman. He crusaded for high standards of professional ethics and became a formi-

171

dable opponent of municipal corruption. He read voraciously on a wide range of topics, and devoted long hours to furthering the cause of public education. He had a passion for collecting fine art and was an avid sportsman who played as hard as he did everything else. The Bend was conceived as a retreat where Wheeler could entertain friends lavishly and lose himself amid the rugged beauties of California's wilderness.[19]

Overlooking a horseshoe bend in the McCloud River, the house sits in splendid isolation amid a virgin pine forest. From the top of the hill at the rear, the drive descends around the complex, offering a constantly changing perspective of its parts. This elliptical pattern is reversed at the entrance gates, with the house wrapping around an oblong court (Figs. 129–131). The house seems like a fortified outpost, but the river facade is broken down into a rambling group of masses, subordinate to the forest around them—a configuration allegedly prompted by Polk's efforts to spare all the large trees on the site (Fig. 132). House and landscape meet at one end, where the dining room is enveloped by an enormous porch that meets a grove of pines and

129. Willis Polk. The Bend, Charles Stetson Wheeler house, near McCloud, 1898–1899; altered. Entrance court. (Courtesy Mrs. Robert Morrow)

extends as a raised walkway, winding through the trees, to terminate at an octagonal gazebo projecting from a trunk and perched above the rushing waters of the McCloud.

No precedent existed in the West for such a grand compound. The idea may have been inspired by Bavarian hunting lodges and, almost certainly, by large camps in the Adirondack Mountains. Wheeler no doubt knew about the Adirondack camps from his friend, Southern Pacific Railroad president Collis Huntington, who had purchased one of the finest of them only three years earlier. Wheeler may well have sought to outdo such retreats, for his own was larger and more elaborate than most Adirondack camps at that time.[20] The Bend also reveals some important differences in attitude toward rusticity held by easterners on one hand and by a growing number of Californians on the other.

Like many of the Adirondack camps, The Bend is composed of separate units divided according to function; however, instead of comprising freestanding cottages informally grouped around a grand lodge, the house is a single, all-embracing complex. Its masonry construction and careful ordering of elements impart a sense of monu-

130. The Bend, entrance court. (Courtesy Mrs. Robert Morrow)

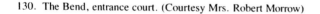

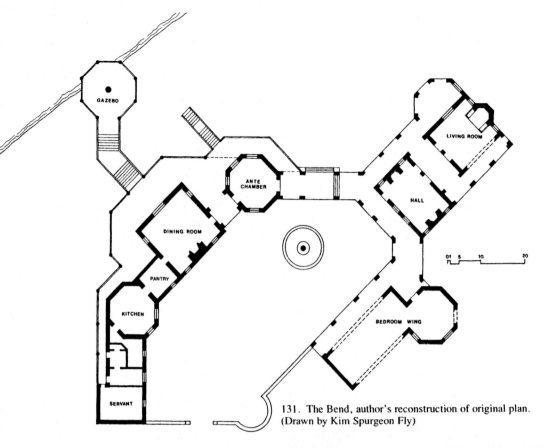

131. The Bend, author's reconstruction of original plan.
(Drawn by Kim Spurgeon Fly)

132. The Bend, view from across
McCloud River. (Courtesy Mrs.
Robert Morrow)

mentality lacking in eastern counterparts, which usually were built of
logs. The difference in character between court and river elevations
establishes a more sophisticated relationship with the site and reflects
the duality of function as both rustic retreat and urbane social center.
The interplay between these two worlds continues inside. Boldly scaled
timberwork, felled from the property and hewn and joined by hand,

174

133. The Bend, dining room. (Courtesy Mrs. Robert Morrow)

134. Camp Sagamore, William W. Durant house, near Raquette Lake, New York, 1896–1897. Living hall. (Adirondack Museum)

celebrates the primitive nature of the site. Cavernous rooms, dominated by fireplaces, convey the feeling of a medieval manor house (Fig. 133). Such allusions are balanced by the classicizing symmetry and precision with which the elements are related. The effect is entirely different from that of Adirondack camp interiors, where the sheer quantity of overscaled logs, roots, and boulders generates a sense of

175

applied decoration (Fig. 134). These are primeval versions of gilded Edwardian rooms, where rusticity was pursued with a vengeance, only to result in a rarefied display. The Bend is at once more polished and more a part of the rustic world. While life amid the wilderness was still somewhat alien to the rich New Yorkers who inhabited the camps, such an existence was sufficiently close in time and place for Californians now to be considered as a natural extension of their routine. The Bend suggests the compatibility between civilization and nature, as the largest Adirondack camps tend to perpetrate a sense of struggle and conquest.

Polk had already developed a strong, coherent means of expressing these conditions in William Bourn's Empire Cottage (1897– 1898), located in the Sierra foothills. Bourn came from a distinguished family of New England sea captains. His father had acquired a considerable fortune through shipping concerns in New York before coming to the West Coast in 1850. Bourn was the consummate entrepreneur, hard-driving, tough, innovative, and determined to make his business ventures successful beyond all predictions. (He named his country house in San Mateo County, which Polk designed in 1914–1915, Filoli—fight, love, live.) After the turn of the century, he became a leading figure in the development of utilities throughout the region, serving as president of both the San Francisco Gas and Electric and the Spring Valley Water companies. Bourn also had diverse cultural interests. Educated at Cambridge University, he was prominent in civic affairs, an early promoter of the Panama-Pacific International Exposition, president of the San Francisco Music Society, and a staunch supporter of local artists even before such patronage became fashionable. During the 1890s, Bourn and Polk became good friends. Directly or indirectly, the businessman was responsible for a large share of Polk's work over the next twenty years.[21] Bourn not only had the resources to commission important projects, he had the interest and confidence to let Polk pursue unconventional solutions.

Unlike The Bend, Bourn's mountain house was part of a working compound, built in conjunction with his efforts to rejuvenate the adjacent Empire Mine, which soon became among the largest in the country.[22] Polk's scheme included new buildings for the company and its principal employees as well as Bourn's house. Informally arranged in a parklike setting, the compound reflects its multifaceted role of country place, mountain retreat, and mining headquarters. The Empire Cottage is at once simple and complex, unpretentious and grand, rustic and classicizing. Its basic form recalls the stone cottages of the Cotswold

176

135. Willis Polk. Empire Cottage, William Bourn house, near Grass
Valley, 1897–1898. (Author)

136. Willis Polk. The Original
Empire Mine Company offices, near
Grass Valley, 1897–1898. (Author)

country, but the symmetrical composition of the main facade and the
severe treatment of details reveal a sober monumentality that alludes
to different sources (Fig. 135). Both the house and the mine offices
bear a certain kinship to mid-nineteenth-century granite commercial
buildings, then still common to many foothill towns, which likewise
were erected from the proceeds of gold. The correspondence is even
more apparent with the mine offices, where a two-story porch is patterned
after those found on commercial work in the area (Fig. 136). The
same use of massive granite walls with brick trim, executed with
straightforward simplicity, also characterizes some of the Napa Valley

177

wineries, the largest of which had been constructed by Bourn several years earlier.[23]

The plan of the house is open and informal (Fig. 137). Except for the service wing, the ground floor is a single space connected to covered porches at either end and to broad terraces on both sides; it is thus linked to the outdoors in all directions. The rooms are finished in an unusually simple manner for a house of this date, with redwood boards, exposed beams, and the plainest of trim (Fig. 138). The spaces are accommodating and wholly unpretentious, without any of

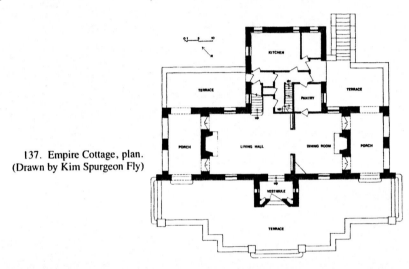

137. Empire Cottage, plan. (Drawn by Kim Spurgeon Fly)

138. Empire Cottage, living hall. (California Division of Mines and Geology)

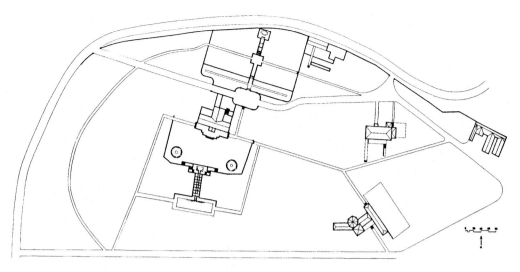

139. Empire Cottage, site plan. (Drawn by Kim Spurgeon Fly)

the play between plain and fancy elements found in Polk's suburban houses. Like The Bend, the symmetrical organization of parts and meticulous details impart a classical sense of order. Furthermore, the expansiveness of the main space, opening onto layers of terraces, suggests a great country house more than it does a mountain cabin or suburban residence.

The Bend and Empire Cottage attracted considerable attention in San Francisco. The fact that two rich and prominent citizens were constructing such costly and unconventional houses elicited nothing but praise from the press. The *San Francisco Chronicle* exclaimed that Bourn's house was "without parallel in California" and found it remarkable for having "no lathing, no plaster . . . no paint or paper." The same paper reported The Bend to be "certainly the most original dwelling in the country."[24] Such remarks were in part due to the fact that these were the first large mountain lodges erected in the state. Many of their unique qualities were in response to their programs. The deliberately primitive character of the two houses would not have been appropriate for big country places near San Francisco, where a more formal way of living was the custom. But, like the Dimond house and Burlingame Park, these two residences were conspicuous demonstrations of the respectability rustic expression was gaining in the region.

Polk gave the meeting of rustic and refined qualities a new dimension with his design for the Empire Cottage grounds executed several years later (Fig. 139).[25] The layout contains symmetrical parts composed with the elements of a formal garden, yet rendered with

179

140. Empire Cottage, entrance court. (Author)

141. Empire Cottage, garden. (Author)

great simplicity. The primary inspiration came from cinquecento villas, where both house and landscape contributed to a greater whole. Following a typical Italian practice seldom used elsewhere, entrance front and garden front are the same. Then, departing from all precedent, the approach lies in the rear. From either side, a gently curving drive ascends toward the house, the two arms meeting at an entrance court right beside the kitchen yard (Fig. 140). The formal connotations of the court are underscored by a cross-axis extending down the slope through a terraced garden. In the other direction, this line becomes an unassuming brick path that skirts the house, eventually leading to the front door. Beyond, the scheme is diagrammatic. Extending from the house is a broad grass terrace, punctuated only by two low fountains (Fig. 141). The breadth and simplicity of the space make it seem more French than Italian, like a parterre turned into a pasture. In contrast to French precedent, however, there is no continuation of orthogonal axes as vistas. The primary axis is bent, and very short in length, abruptly terminating without a focal point. Barely visible except from the terrace edge, this segment combines French and Italian elements, with a cascade emptying into a long, rectangular basin (Fig. 142). Clipped vines and

142. Empire Cottage, garden. (Author)

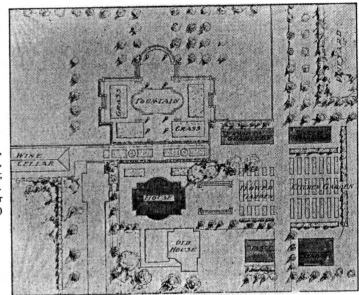

143. Willis Polk. Beaulieu,
Charles Baldwin house,
Cupertino, ca. 1900–1901;
altered. Site plan.
(*House and Garden*, December
1902, p. 617)

yew hedges reinforce the plan's geometry; otherwise no plant materials or sculpture are allowed to disturb this ordered, tranquil, unorthodox ensemble. The sequence is both ceremonious and informal, with a spectrum of worldly allusions simplified and abstracted, establishing an improbable concordance with the rugged pine forest that lies around it.

Polk's first country house to be realized in the Bay Area proper was Charles Baldwin's Beaulieu (ca. 1900–1901). The design can hardly be called rustic, but it incorporates many of the ideas expressed in the Empire Cottage. Like Bourn, Baldwin came from an old, prominent New England family and was educated abroad. Similarly, too, he developed Beaulieu as a place for both pleasure and work. A connoisseur of the arts and a devoted Francophile, Baldwin purchased a tract of rich agricultural land in the Santa Clara Valley, where he established a vineyard filled with cuttings from the Bordeaux region. Not long after marrying Ella Hobart, heiress to one of the Comstock Lode fortunes, he embarked on a program to transform what had been a simple farm complex into an elegant compound. The scheme had to be practical, for, in keeping with French custom, the Baldwins used Beaulieu as their principal residence.[26] Polk's design included a new house, staff quarters, stables, and formal grounds, all in proximity to the older buildings (Fig. 143). Perhaps because of economic constraints,

182

the Victorian farmhouse and barn, along with the recently built wine cellar, remained unaltered. Yet they are significant contributors to the overall effect, at once conspicuous and incidental to the new order, so that the whole complex appears to have been developed over the course of several generations.

Considering his love of things French, Baldwin must have stipulated some of the historical sources used. The house is patterned after an eighteenth-century *pavillon* containing only the principal rooms, with service and guest quarters located in dependencies (Figs. 144,

144. Beaulieu, garden elevation. (*House and Garden*, December 1902, p. 618)

145. Beaulieu, author's reconstruction of original plan. (Drawn by Kim Spurgeon Fly)

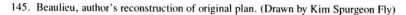
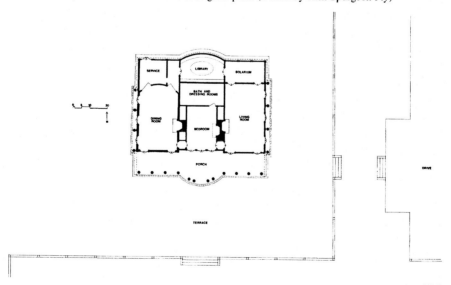

146. Beaulieu, garden. (*House and Garden*, December 1902, p. 621)

145). The interiors are detailed in the manner of Louis XVI, and the gardens are inspired by the work of Le Nôtre. The allusions are overt, but the design is still far from being a literal interpretation. The house is fronted by a deep, colonnaded porch, affording relief from the hot, dry valley climate but violating a cardinal rule of French composition by denying the facade a strong focal point. This ambiguity is accentuated by the casual relationship between the house and the approach axis, as well as by the absence of a defined entrance to the building itself. Five French doors provide a remarkably informal connection between terrace and living room. The master bedroom is set in the building's center, where the foyer normally would be located, perhaps to obtain an axial view of the garden, an arrangement reflecting the privacy that only a large country place could provide. Nevertheless, the organization is unprecedented. The passage from living to dining rooms—through a solarium, skylit library, and windowless antechamber—is circuitous, enlarging the perceived size of the building and enlivening a potentially dull plan.

184

As with the Empire Cottage, house and grounds are inseparable and the relationship between them ceremonious and informal. The gardens themselves are simplified versions of European precedent (Fig. 146). Lying close to the main house, the vineyard makes up the principal view. However, Polk offered many reminders that Beaulieu was in the West, not in France. Palm trees frame the drive at its end and continue around one side of the sunken garden. Elsewhere, live oaks, eucalyptus, and other local plant types dating from previous decades survive in informal clusters, counterpointing the geometric order of the house and its terraces. Beyond the dining room lies a large garden for flowers and vegetables, flanked by service buildings that recall ranch houses of Spanish California. The ensemble is a collage with open exchange between its dissimilar constituent parts—those old and those new, those of a working vineyard and those of a luxurious country place making the layout unusual for any part of the United States at that time.

The concept of the formal garden, still new in the United States, was being vigorously promoted at this time by architects in England and on the East Coast, who saw such work as a logical extension of the academic movement's concerns. For Americans, the two most influential advocates were the Englishmen John Sedding and Reginald Blomfield. Both men published treatises on the subject in 1892, launching a full-scale attack on the naturalistic approach that had dominated landscape design for over a century. "This vaunted naturalness of landscape gardens is a sham," Blomfield sneered; "instead of leaving nature alone, the landscapist is always struggling to make nature lend itself to his deceptions." The authors considered such design an affront to architecture. Sedding declared that "to pitch your house down on the grass with no architectural accessories about it, to link it to the soil, is to vulgarize it, to rob it of its importance, to give it the look of a pastoral farm."[27] They insisted that the formal garden was the only acceptable means by which unity between the house and its site could be achieved; the two must be conceived at one time and by the same person.

Underlying this argument was the belief that the architect alone possessed the ability to organize the landscape. Their attack was not just on naturalistic design, but on its practitioners. The design of gardens should follow the same academic principles as the design of buildings, through the use of ordered composition to create a sense of unity; subordination of the parts to the whole; simplicity; and discrete ornamental features, few in number. The authors concentrated on historic

185

147. Coxhead & Coxhead. Charles Dougherty house, near Pleasanton, 1900, project. Drawing by Coxhead. (Courtesy John Beach)

148. Stansted, Sussex, general view. (J. C. Shepard and G. A. Jellicoe, *Gardens and Design*, p. 77)

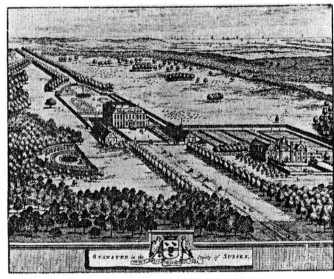

English examples to illustrate their points, but the work of other countries was not ignored. Sedding felt that the best examples of terracing were to be found in Italy, while Blomfield felt that Le Nôtre "carried the art of garden design to the highest point of development."[28]

186

Interest in these treatises in the United States was immediate. The Boston-based *Architectural Review* remarked that Sedding's and Blomfield's texts offered an invaluable lesson to Americans. In 1893, Charles Platt published two articles on the Italian garden in *Harper's Monthly* that were soon expanded into book form. By the end of the decade numerous essays on such precedents appeared in American architectural journals. In 1901, *House and Garden* was founded by two leading Philadelphia designers, Wilson Eyre and Frank Miles Day, specifically to advance the cause of formal garden design.[29] Eyre, Platt, and most other architects of this school developed their schemes according to a geometric plan. They tended to use plant materials impressionistically, inspired by the neglected state of many European gardens, and organized their plans in a straightforward manner, using the plants to provide intricate detail and patterns. Polk's method differed from these East Coast architects in that he developed casual relationships between many of the plan's components and articulated them with simple landscape features.

Two friends appear to have had an important influence on Polk's work. Bruce Porter was an avid student of garden design, and he was especially fond of English achievements in the field. Polk requested his collaboration on several schemes, of which the first to be documented was the estate of Francis Carolan in Burlingame Park (1899). Porter is credited with laying out a formal English plan and suggesting to Carolan's gardener the appropriate shapes and colors for the plants. The overall design of this and other joint ventures was probably developed by Polk, yet Porter no doubt contributed many ideas and worked directly toward their realization.[30]

Another influence on Polk's landscaping was Coxhead, who probably knew Blomfield during their student days at the Royal Academy and may well have studied English Renaissance gardens while touring Europe shortly after Blomfield's book was published.[31] Regrettably, Coxhead never saw any of his plans for country houses realized, but one project, designed just before Polk's gardens at Beaulieu and the Empire Cottage, reveals his ingenuity. The scheme was for Charles Dougherty, a rancher who owned much of the Livermore Valley, some twenty-five miles southeast of San Francisco (Fig. 147). The longitudinal axis is formed by the drive and by broad grass terraces terminating at the portico, which seems to be more a part of the garden than of the house. Straddling the ridge, walls extend from the dwelling to form a border for a grandly scaled terrace flanked by allées of cypress trees. The vocabulary is Italian, the scale French, and the character

187

comes closest to that of early eighteenth-century English examples, where vast areas of land were controlled by the simplest of devices (Fig. 148). Here is an elegant summary of the qualities then most admired in formal garden design harmoniously placed amid California's pastoral landscape.

These elaborate country places, paying homage to the classical tradition, seem to be the antithesis of the small rustic houses Coxhead and Polk designed a few years earlier, but in fact the strains are complementary, not antagonistic. The differences show a love of variety, reinforced by dissimilar programs and divergent thrusts in popular sentiment. Both formal and rustic modes of expression stemmed from a single, broad-based approach to design that was fostered by the academic movement's inclusive parameters.

VII

COXHEAD AND POLK: Large City and Country Houses

. . . the style is everywhere the same—the nineteenth-century development of the Renaissance—a style of which one phase has developed into another naturally and steadily, like any normal architectural growth, for nearly four hundred years.

Is it not almost a certainty that with the further development of studious academic architecture throughout the country there is coming a wave of Classic that will have nearly as much influence over . . . American work as it has had for centuries over Europe?

John Stewardson, *Lippincott's Magazine*, January 1896

THE ACADEMIC perception of the "Renaissance" suggested compatibility between two divergent ideas: the conservative belief that the principles of design are immutable and the liberal commitment to diverse expression. The "Renaissance" was depicted as a coherent movement, unwaivering in its adherence to the principles of order and unity. It was also inclusive, encompassing the whole classical tradition from the quattrocento to the nineteenth century, as well as transitional work such as that of Elizabethan England and vernacular examples that often showed only the indirect influence of high-style classical buildings. Moreover, the "Renaissance" had assumed somewhat different forms in each country, reflecting local traditions, materials, and tastes. By conceptualizing such broad and long-standing tradition, proponents of academic eclecticism developed a persuasive argument for an approach to design that was both structured and pluralistic.[1]

Committed to this ideological premise, Coxhead and Polk regarded themselves as classicists. Polk wrote in 1893 that most notable European architecture belonged to the classical tradition, which constituted the only viable precedent for work in the United States. Gothic design, he admitted, was an exception, but it was unsuited to the majority of modern building types. Coxhead also stressed the need for consistency in architecture by adhering to classical ideals and eschewing advocacy of "the so-called styles."[2] The postmedieval

189

vernacular sources both men used in their rustic buildings were probably viewed as part of the early Renaissance more than as the persistence of medieval traditions. When Coxhead and Polk introduced classical details and classicizing compositions into these schemes, their intention was no doubt to exploit the variations. Consistent with the academic attitude toward expression, the architects relied largely on rustic vernacular precedent when an informal, picturesque character was deemed appropriate to a building's program. With projects that invited more formal treatment they turned to elaborate, often monumental, "Renaissance" precedents. Judging by the designs they chose to publish, Coxhead and Polk were proudest of their large, costly buildings, which were of course more lucrative, more conspicuous, and more apt to further an architect's professional stature. But they also relished designing on a grand scale. Such work reveals the fallacy in the popular myth that the two architects focused just on producing a rustic architecture distinct to the region.

Coxhead's and Polk's interest in formal expression had been nurtured in their training, and was subsequently reinforced by the emergence of the classical language as the academic movement's dominant vocabulary both in the United States and England. Their initial years in California afforded few opportunities to work in a grand manner, and their early attempts were often sophomoric. But as an increasing number of large commissions came their way, they responded with no less exuberance and invention than they had done with rustic houses. During the 1890s, their work tended to become less picturesque, and the absorption of classical precedent more pronounced. The change did not signify a rejection of one world for another so much as it did a shift in emphasis and an eagerness to experiment in a different, yet compatible, vein. This move was part of a national pattern, but it was also affected by local sentiment. Just as the interest in rusticity helped to stimulate one facet of their work, so a growing identification with the glories of ancient Rome and a belief that California was destined to surpass it in cultural greatness encouraged the architects' efforts to create grand classical designs.

A sense of affinity with ancient Rome stemmed in part from similarities between the two landscapes. Beginning in the mid-nineteenth century, chroniclers remarked how much California's salubrious climate, brilliant skies, gently rolling fields, and lush agricultural valleys reminded them of pastoral Italy.[3] These resemblances fostered romantic visions of the Golden State's future. A most engaging picture of this new classical world was offered by Bayard Taylor:

190

I had another and grander dream. A hundred years had passed, and I saw the valley, not, as now, only partially tamed and reveling in the wild magnificence of Nature, but . . . humming with human life. I saw the same oaks and sycamores, but their shadows fell on mansions as fair as temples, with their white fronts and long colonnades; I saw gardens refreshed by gleaming fountains . . . palaces built to enshrine the new Art which will then have blossomed here—culture, plenty, peace, happiness everywhere.[4]

Such dreams were fueled by the doctrine of manifest destiny. Californians had made Bishop Berkeley's declaration, "Westward the course of empire," their own. Many settlers came to the West Coast convinced that it was marked for extraordinary achievements. By the turn of the century, projections of California's greatness had reached a feverish pitch. Overseas conquests reaped from the war with Spain and plans for constructing the Panama Canal seemed only to confirm the boldest of aspirations. As the gateway to a vast, rich hinterland and to the ports of the world, San Francisco was now depicted not only as a great metropolis, but as the ascendant star of the American Empire and the eventual center of Western civilization. Historian Hubert Howe Bancroft had not the slightest doubt that

always the march of intellectual development has been from east to west, and the old east dying as the new west bursts into being. . . . In the advent of progress of civilization there was first the Mediterranean, then the Atlantic, and then the Pacific, the last and greatest of all. What else is possible? Where else on this planet is man to go for his ultimate achievement?[5]

Little support existed for such notions other than undaunted, naive confidence. That Bancroft, distinguished recorder of fact, could become Bancroft, booster of inflated dreams with no apparent sense of contradiction, reveals just how far removed California was from attaining cultural preeminence. Pragmatic businessmen and aspiring intellectuals alike were captivated by the idea of eventual supremacy. The absence of established cultural traditions was not considered to be an impediment to realizing this future, and in fact California's newness was seen as an advantage. Starting afresh, its citizens could absorb the achievements of history and construct from them a base for unparalleled development. Echoing the aims of American culture in general, California's drive for supremacy was conservative, espousing adaptation rather than radical departure. In certain respects, these forecasts reflected an intensified effort to bring the state into the mainstream of American and European culture. By the 1910s, when this integration

149. A. Page Brown. Mrs. Peter Donohue house, San Francisco, 1894–1896;
no longer standing. (*Inland Architect*, July 1900)

was no longer in doubt, the self-conscious predictions of unequaled achievement in the arts evaporated, much as the self-consciousness about the state's frontier heritage had several decades earlier.[6]

Pursuing this classical ideal did not undermine, or even clash with, the contemporaneous cultivation of rusticity. Throughout much of the nineteenth and early twentieth centuries the notion of perpetuating rural, preindustrial values and of surpassing Europe's worldly splendors were often advanced by opposing forces.[7] Yet many Californians promoted both ideals. Even so passionate a devotee of rustic unpretentiousness as Joseph Worcester encouraged the planning of grand urban schemes.[8] Californians were not prone to scrutinizing closely the ramifications of their dreams. They accepted both classical and rustic ideals in the belief that the prospects for attaining them were virtually limitless.

Coxhead and Polk were inspired by the local preoccupation with the classical ideal and were instrumental in giving this impulse concrete form and direction. Both architects differed from most noteworthy members of their generation in the United States and England,

192

who tended to focus on a limited range of modes. Instead, Coxhead and Polk maintained a concern for diverse expression that encompassed the rustic and grand classical models, continuing the approach pioneered by McKim, Mead & White in the 1880s. What distinguished their effort is that it was accomplished with such skill and inventiveness.

At the beginning of the 1890s, commercial projects, such as the Hibernia Bank and the Crocker Building, were the most conspicuous harbingers of the new classical order. However, the ensuing depression greatly reduced the extent of such work until the turn of the century. Thus, houses provided the most potent symbol of the individualism that San Franciscans, in particular, regarded as the cornerstone for progress. The large wooden palaces of previous decades had fallen from favor, yet much of the initial large-scale residential work differed more in style than substance. Page Brown's design of a house for Mrs. Peter Donohue (1894–1896) is typical in lacking the strength and cohesiveness its size demanded (Fig. 149). Both its form and historical references suggest masonry construction, but the whole building is made of wood, and the results are hardly less "deceiving" than in its Victorian predecessors. Thin, linear details further contribute to an insubstantial feeling. The composition is additive on the facade, and around to one side it breaks down into a confused agglomeration. The tall foundation consummates the effect of a pastiche tenuously perched on one of San Francisco's precipitous slopes.

Polk's initial opportunity to design a large city house suffered from his lack of experience in such projects, yet the solution set a new standard for subsequent work in the city. The commission came from George W. Gibbs, one of the leading producers of iron and steel on the West Coast and a prominent figure in philanthropic affairs. Gibbs, upon retirement at age seventy, decided to erect a house that would rival those of his eastern peers—elaborate, dignified, but not ostentatious.[9] Polk drew largely from Italian Renaissance sources, then at the height of fashion in New York. The massing recalls that of a Tuscan villa, with details adapted from Raphael's Palazzo Pandolfini and a portico inspired by the Temple of Vesta at Tivoli (Fig. 150). But the elementary composition and the particularizing of its components make the facade seem more akin to mid-nineteenth-century Italianate houses than to McKim, Mead & White's work. The plan is equally conservative, with large, boxy rooms opening off a long central corridor.

Nevertheless, the Gibbs house generated a flurry of excite-

150. Polk & Polk. George W. Gibbs house, San Francisco, 1894–1895. (Author)

ment. The *San Francisco Examiner* pronounced it to be "the first classical residence in San Francisco." Enthusiasm also centered on the fact that this was among the city's earliest houses constructed entirely of stone and that almost no dwelling of comparable size matched the restraint of its exterior. The *Wave* summarized prevailing opinion, remarking that the house's "unpretentious solidity . . . cheapens the much gabled and turreted mansions surrounding it."[10] In a metropolis of wood, the Gibbs house became an instant symbol of grandeur and permanency. The scheme further set an important local precedent for the collaboration of architect and artist in developing the decorative program. Polk had Douglas Tilden design the Medusa heads for the portico—the sculptor's first commission following his return from Paris earlier that year. Bruce Porter was brought in to create the huge stained-glass window in the stair-hall landing. Lockwood de Forest, who had been a partner in one of the country's first decorative-arts studios, prepared plans for the ornamentation of some of the principal rooms. De Forest's work may not have been executed, and the whole scheme fell far short of the exquisite interiors of McKim, Mead & White's houses, which served as its conceptual model.[11] Still, the work demonstrated to rich San Franciscans that they need not entrust room design strictly to decorators, who often had little concern for architectural cohesiveness.

By 1895, both Polk and Coxhead were designing large classical projects with confidence and originality. Coxhead had just returned from an extensive tour of Europe, his first known trip outside California since 1886 and probably his first direct encounter with buildings on the Continent. Surviving sketchbooks document a visit en route to the World's Columbian Exposition in Chicago, capturing the final days of America's initial taste of the City Beautiful. He traveled through France and northern Italy, filling page after page with sketches of classical palaces, Gothic cathedrals, and vernacular cottages. He also returned to his homeland, where he may have sought out recently executed classical work of an order that had been confined to ideal projects when he was at the Royal Academy but was now a focus of attention among English architects and critics.[12]

The trip enabled Coxhead to broaden his horizons, examining firsthand historical examples he had known before only from books, prints, and photographs. But contemporary English work had the strongest impact on his own. Coxhead's designs upon his return began to reflect the exuberant, mannered, and even somewhat eccentric qualities that characterized the new English classicism. Polk was also affected by the change in Coxhead's approach, and many of his subsequent classical schemes exhibit the same spirit, irrespective of the sources used. For both men, this influence paralleled that of the English Arts and Crafts Movement; the idea was far more important than the vocabulary. Central to that idea was a sense of freedom in developing form and detail that suited the two architects' temperaments and allowed them to work in a manner not identified with New York or Paris. English classical sources bore no more direct relation to popular local analogies with ancient Rome than did the postmedieval vernacular buildings of northern Europe to the state's rustic heritage, but ancestry was not important so long as the image responded to the broad sentiment. California could indeed borrow from the world at large.

Coxhead was influenced by the spirit of the new English classicism, but he generally eschewed its repertoire of details. The Alonzo McFarland house (1895) displays an unusual combination of precedents manipulated to meet the constraints of the program, such as a modest budget of about $10,000 (Fig. 151). A sheathing of enormous painted redwood boards and stucco panels is frankly expressed as a veneer, but it helps orchestrate the grand effect. The composition and

195

151. Coxhead & Coxhead. Alonzo McFarland house, San Francisco, 1895;
parapet and dormers altered. (Author)

many of the details are derived from eighteenth-century Palladian country houses, here given proportions that would have left Burlingtonians aghast. The central zone of the facade receives the most decoration, yet its treatment remains ambiguous. Instead of suggesting a temple front as in its English models, this section is recessed and sits on an unusually high base with engaged columns squeezed between other elements. The most ornate piece is the broken pediment over the entry, which is set to one side, and the door is placed in a narrow slot dropped through the base like a utilitarian necessity. This agitated arrangement is visually contained by flanking sections that falsely appear to be at least as large as the central piece by virtue of their bold scale and comparatively simple treatment. Yet even here the windows resist being confined to the stucco panels that enframe them. The antithesis of Palladian discretion, this constant usurping of boundaries imparts a feeling of tenuousness characteristic of Italian mannerism without alluding to any particular examples. The classical language is celebrated as decoration rather than structure—emotive, imposing, and monumental in its effect. The scheme would have seemed unduly restless in a rural setting, but it is well suited to its compact site in a dense urban landscape.

196

Other manneristic devices are used to counterpoint eighteenth-century reserve in the residence Coxhead designed in 1899 for Sarah Spooner, a rich Philadelphian who had recently moved to San Francisco and devoted much of her time to collecting art (Fig. 152). In its form, the house comes very close to an ideal project presented in Robert Morris's *Rural Architecture* (1750) (Fig. 153). The facade treatment bears much greater resemblance to the engravings in such books than to buildings of that period. The wall is emphasized as a planar surface. From a distance the smooth clinker bricks offer an even texture similar to that of an engraver's hatching, and the brown sandstone trim is treated in a similar brittle fashion. The windows are isolated, with thin, dark sashes that make each unit read as a single void. Then, in total contrast, rusticated quoins articulate the corners, turning into striations over the bay fronts and bulging out into banded columns at the entrance. Tension is created by a serene particularity on one hand and an exuberant baroque plasticity on the other. Thus, favored devices of Coxhead's contemporaries in England confront Morris's pattern-book Georgian, which former schoolmate Reginald Blomfield had just denounced as "weak and pretentious" in his influ-

152. Coxhead & Coxhead. Sarah Spooner house, San Francisco, 1899–1900; altered. (Courtesy John Beach)

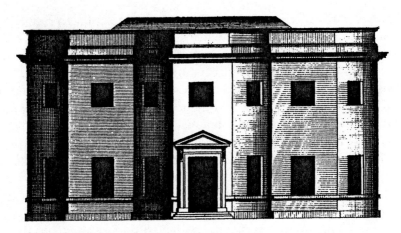

153. Robert Morris. "Structure Overlooking a Valley."
(Morris, *Rural Architecture*, plate 30)

ential book on English Renaissance architecture.[13] The irony of combining sources that were considered stylish and banal in London would not be caught by most observers on the West Coast; however, Coxhead developed a more obvious tension between the house and its setting. When viewed frontally, the facade is reserved, even prim, and its planar austerity predominates. Yet when approached from the street, the house becomes a restless series of receding forms that taunt the pedestrian classicism of its neighbors.

Among Coxhead's best-known works of the decade was a house commissioned by Irving Scott as a wedding present for his daughter, Alice, and her fiancé, James Brown. Scott was almost as important a client for Coxhead as Bourn was for Polk. The two patrons had much in common. Scott's ancestors had been members of Maryland's landed gentry since Colonial times. Scott moved to San Francisco in 1860, where he played a central role in building the Union Iron Works into the West Coast's largest shipyard. He also served as president of the Art Association and of the Mechanics Institute, as a regent of the University of California, and as a trustee of Stanford University. Scott was seen as the epitome of the industrial titan and the munificent civic leader, but he was never afraid to defy convention. An avid connoisseur of art, Scott collected works by Rembrandt, Murillo, Holbein, and Hogarth, beside which he hung canvases by Virgil Williams, Jules Tavernier, Julian Rix, and other San Franciscans. He chastised fellow citizens for indifference to local painters and to American art in general. To Scott, Coxhead was more than a provider of plans, he was an artist

198

who deserved support. The patrician and his architect became friends, and Coxhead produced some of his most imaginative work for Scott.[14]

Scott was a hard-nosed pragmatist as well as a sophisticated patron, and Alice, who shared her father's devotion to art, was no less demanding. At least seven preliminary schemes were developed before one was finally accepted in mid-1895.[15] Initially, Alice wanted to have the design look like an English half-timber house, but after several studies this idea was abandoned when her father insisted that masonry construction be used to safeguard against fire. A series of new proposals was developed, and the house was reduced in size to compensate for the added expense of the materials. Scott then demanded that the stair hall be eliminated—a difficult stipulation, since in order to utilize the sloping site to best advantage, Coxhead's design placed the floors at levels different from the fronting street. Still later changes were made when Scott decided that his daughter's choice of exterior treatment would cost too much. Coxhead used these constraints to his advantage. The final scheme is by far the strongest and most original.

The exterior combines some of the informal, picturesque qualities of English Queen Anne with the mannered exuberance of contem-

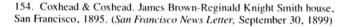

154. Coxhead & Coxhead. James Brown-Reginald Knight Smith house, San Francisco, 1895. (*San Francisco News Letter*, September 30, 1899)

porary English work (Fig. 154). A few boldly scaled elements stand out amid the placid elevations to make the house seem grand. Between rows of small, leaded windows a heavy cornice gives horizontal emphasis to an otherwise unadorned, vertical mass. A large corner bay protrudes as if it were added at the last moment, yet it also expands the perceived size of the house. On the side elevation the bay wall continues, dipping to enclose a service court where the main entrance and stair hall were originally to have been. The composition is fragmentary, offering a subtle allusion to the changes that occurred during the design's development, as if the imposing facade had been chewed away bit by bit to leave a craggy residue (Fig. 155). Coxhead indulged in similar play on the east front, which was to have been the side elevation. Here the entrance is heralded by a huge Carolean portal, whose appearance and placement are unrelated to the other elements nearby (Fig. 156). The portal is at once a centerpiece and an afterthought, as if to express defiance at having been relegated to the side street. The ambiguity is furthered by having this element enframe an open vestibule, with the

155. Brown-Knight Smith house, side view. (Courtesy John Beach)

200

156. Brown-Knight Smith house, entrance detail. (Courtesy John Beach)

front door placed to one side. The configuration is borrowed directly from Shaw's 42 Netherhall Gardens, as it was at the Murdock house, but the contrast between void and elaborate surround is new.

Inside, the layout of major spaces did not change significantly during the course of development, except for the removal of the stair hall and the reduction in room size. However, these modifications were sufficient to alter the initial straightforward sequence of spaces, so Coxhead employed devices he often used in his rustic city houses—circuitous movement, abrupt changes in dark and light zones, and elements set at a small scale—to create a sense of expansiveness. The

157. Brown-Knight Smith house, living room. (Courtesy Scott Knight Smith)

stairs rest in a barrel-vaulted tunnel enframed with heavy plaster garlands, affording a dramatic transition from the entry level to the main floor. A window floods the small landing with light near the top, where the stair then turns and spills into the living room. Here, the atmosphere is dim, restrained, and tranquil, with dignified Georgian paneling to complement the eighteenth-century furnishings. On one side, however, light pours in through two bay windows, and a great fireplace enframed by panels with carving done in the manner of Grindling Gibbons stands right in the middle (Fig. 157). The chimneypiece itself is unorthodox, with floral carving around the hearth, a carved drop placed in the middle of each panel, and a small, conventional center panel that is entirely out of scale with the rest of the ensemble. The oversized hearth, which suggests medieval precedents more than classical ones, exemplifies Coxhead's technique of freely manipulating motifs and scale to create a context quite different from that found in either historical or contemporary English work.

202

A few years later, Scott commissioned a much larger residence in Pacific Heights that would rank among the grandest on the West Coast. Unfortunately, the project proved too ambitious and had to be shelved. Scott died a few years later, and all hope for the undertaking vanished.[16] Situated atop the tallest point in Pacific Heights, with panoramic views on all sides, the scheme suggests a great baronial castle, commanding in its presence, yet aloof from everything around it (Fig. 158). Fronted by speculative residences (planned to help defer building costs), stables, and enormous retaining walls, the main house would have been barely visible from the street. Reflecting its secluded position, the building has no principal facade; each elevation is given its own identity. From the approach, the south front is understated, with an alleylike drive leading up to a small entrance squeezed between a bank of oriel windows and a utilitarian service wing (Fig. 159). The east elevation is the most imposing, sober, and forcefully arranged; yet even here a restless chord is struck. Between the symmetrical main block and a projecting wing, large and small banks of windows are set crisscross and placed against opposite corners of the connecting mass, as if to wrench the flanking sections apart.

158. Coxhead & Coxhead. Irving Scott house, San Francisco, ca. 1899, project.
Drawing probably by Coxhead. (Chicago Architectural Club, *Catalogue*, 1900)

159. Scott house, entrance elevation. Drawing probably by Coxhead.
(Private collection)

On the north side, overlooking the Golden Gate, the massing erupts into a sequence of chamfers and angled bays with a canyonlike recess right in the center (Fig. 160). To one side, a contorted stair tower rises to join the flanking wall as a parapet folded like a screen. Serving as a counterpoint, the huge polygonal bay is draped in oriels, its form echoed by a sunken pool directly below that juts out toward the street, there to be halted by a titanic wall. To achieve these effects, Coxhead intensified the abrupt changes in the existing terrain, excavating huge chunks of the northern end to create the main terrace, which rises like a bastion. The result is an accentuated reflection of San Francisco's diverse, compact topography, and a picturesqueness commensurate with the landscape, laced with classical embellishments that suggest the ideal world many people hoped San Francisco would one day become.

160. Scott house, garden elevation. Drawing probably by Coxhead.
(Private collection)

Some of the inspiration for this scheme probably came from Norman Shaw's well-published Flete (1877–1883), which set a precedent for large country houses in turn-of-the-century England. But Coxhead's eccentric use of late medieval and classical allusions comes much closer to the work of Edwin Lutyens. In its character, the Scott house resembles Lutyens's Castle Drogo (1910–1930); however, the affinity stems from shared attitudes rather than any direct correspondence. Both Coxhead's and Lutyens's defiance of tradition was founded on understanding and respect. The two architects knew that history provided ample precedent for the "liberties" that they took, and they both sought to recapture the sense of freedom and individuality of such work.[17] Their use of precedent, which was wholly consistent with academic principles, stands apart from that of many American architects of the same generation, who were becoming partial to "polite"

205

renditions of history and cleansing their work of irregularities (Fig. 161).

In another respect, however, the Scott house is very different from anything Lutyens produced. Judging from Coxhead's drawings, the design makes no attempt to emulate the exquisitely crafted fabric found in the best contemporary English work. The skills necessary to create such effects did not exist in San Francisco. Rather, his drawings suggest a tough, planar box, which is twisted, turned, and decorated with raw vigor. The effect might have been too harsh in Edwardian England, yet it seems quite at home in the land of extremes.

No realized design shows Coxhead's uninhibited use of classical precedent more fully than the residence of Edwin Tobias Earl in Los Angeles (1895–1898) (Figs. 162, 163). The house was originally designed and built as a rambling, unobtrusive shingle pile, but fire wrought extensive damage shortly before completion. Coxhead then revised the scheme, retaining the informal plan and adding new elevations inside and out.[18] In its final form, the Earl house, while still suggesting a rustic cottage, is fortified with a dense, tight wall of brick. An abstract, reductive simplicity enhances the exterior's strength, yet the effect is also made somewhat disquieting by the use of small, isolated pieces of ornament, the most conspicuous of which is a single Ionic column surrealistically supporting a tiny slice of entablature and pediment at the corner of the entrance porch.

The stripped elevations also act as a foil for the decorative performance inside. Each room is a remote world, with such striking

161. Cram, Wentworth & Goodhue. Design for a country house, ca. 1897. Drawing by Goodhue. (*Brickbuilder*, December 1897, plates 97–98)

162. Coxhead & Coxhead. Edwin Tobias Earl house, Los Angeles,
ca. 1895–1898; demolished 1957. (Courtesy John Beach)

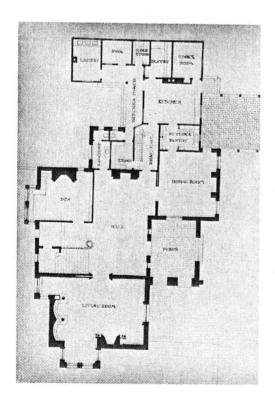

163. Earl house, plan.
(Courtesy John Beach)

207

polarities of large and small scale, and ornate and simple embellishment, that it hardly seems like a house at all. In the living room a great scrolled pediment looms above the fireplace, suspended as if it were a trophy from Baalbek hung on the wall of an art academy (Fig. 164). Its size is made even more outrageous by the low ceiling and flanking tiers of miniature orders. Across the room, Corinthian columns are isolated, again like fragments, punctuating curved bookshelves. The components are separated from their conventional context, and interact in an irregular space that is charged with contrasts between light and dark zones, plain and decorated surfaces.

The hall is no less remarkable. Huge, classicizing motifs are placed in a cavernous space with no direct source of natural light (Fig. 165). The ceiling, which meets the walls without moldings, is penetrated by three recesses so large that the lower plane becomes little more than a series of inflated plaster beams. The wainscoting, composed of colossal panels topped by a garland, adds to the sense of confinement. At one end, the fireplace mantel projects outward in alternating slices of classical regalia and dressed blocks, rising precariously above

164. Earl house, living room. (Courtesy John Beach)

165. Earl house, hall. (Courtesy John Beach)

166. Nunnery, Chichén Itzá, Mexico. (Frederick Catherwood, *Views of Ancient Monuments in Central America*, plate 21)

a pair of Serlian consoles. While precedent can be found in seventeenth- and eighteenth-century English interiors, the character of the heavy scale and the agitated, compressed decorative elements ignores the stability inherent in the classical tradition.

Mayan architecture seems to have influenced Coxhead in the design of the room. Significantly, the resemblance to the plates of

209

Frederick Catherwood's *Views of Ancient Monuments of Central America* (1844), then the major pictorial reference on the subject, are more pronounced than the resemblance to the actual buildings, which neither architect nor client had probably seen (Fig. 166). Mayan sources also are suggested in abstract form in the library fireplace (Fig. 167). Indeed, the entire room contrasts with the hall, being devoid of ornament and moldings. Bookcases, boxed beams, and wall panels are treated as planar surfaces joined at crisp, beveled corners, detailed in a manner similar to Irving Gill's simplest interiors of the next decade. The Earl house is the most sensational example of Coxhead's unorthodox sense of composition, and is the only occasion when he may have turned to non-Western sources for ideas.

Unfortunately, nothing is known about Earl's role in the project. This self-made millionaire, who was an ardent promoter of the region's special character, must have wanted a design that no local architect could provide, for securing the services of an outsider was a highly unusual course for southern Californians to take at that time.[19] Did Earl share Coxhead's love of the unconventional, desiring a house so markedly different from the norm? Or was Coxhead simply reflecting

167. Earl house, library. (Courtesy John Beach)

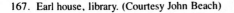

the fantasy world that Angelenos were boosting, pulling out all the stops with a nouveau riche client who believed the design to be "authentic"? Whatever the circumstances, Coxhead would never surpass the eccentricity displayed here.

Polk's use of classical precedent was equally spirited, if less extreme, even though most of his large, formal conceptions went unexecuted. Following the Gibbs house, the one opportunity Polk had to realize such a project was for William Bourn's residence in Pacific Heights. The budget was generous, over $50,000, but the site still presented a challenge. Bourn had purchased a relatively small and inexpensive lot on a side street, where far more modest dwellings and service buildings normally were located. In response to this situation, Polk designed the house with an English basement, which eliminated the need for extensive excavation and allowed the principal rooms to be placed well above the street, thus receiving more natural light and better views. The arrangement, similar to that of many large houses in eastern cities, fills almost the entire property in front and on both sides. However, since the lot abuts the rear yards of neighboring residences, three elevations are visible from the street. The exterior thus needed to have both a formal facade and an overall treatment that acknowledged its freestanding position.

Polk's design reflects this dual role, with front and side elevations that are differentiated from, but also complementary to, one another (Figs. 168, 169). The facade is rigorously ordered, but in contrast to many urban houses of comparable size, the order is implied. The repertoire of classical devices often used to achieve continuity from one zone to the next is minimal. The main floor is enunciated by a single, very large window ornately enframed; above, there is a triad of openings rendered like sharp incisions in the wall surface. These opposing strata are sandwiched between a heavily rusticated basement story and an equally pronounced cornice and attic. Contrasting materials enliven the play. Delicately carved sandstone trim rests amid expanses of rough clinker brick, which transposes the animated surface effects of shingles in rustic buildings to a monumental context. Clinker bricks afforded a rich, durable veneer that was also cheap, for the standard practice at that time was to discard them after firing. Rather than using an expensive material on the facade and turning to a less costly one for the sides, Polk employed these bricks on the whole exterior. Their textural qualities are as appropriate to the picturesque side elevations as they are to the symmetrical street front, and thus give a rare sense

211

of cohesiveness to the entire building. The studied, but seemingly casual, relationship between these elevations is equally unconventional for a house of this type. The idea may well have come from postmedieval vernacular precedent, in particular from the Eastgate House in Kent, a work Polk was familiar with from publications (Fig. 170).[20]

Passage into and through the house conveys a sense of its owner's prominence and love of power. Set beneath the living room window, the entrance is subordinated to the point of imparting an act of submission. The front door is deeply recessed and flanked by striated courses of brick that appear to eat into the sandstone trim, turning inward toward the vestibule (Fig. 171). Beyond lies a low, lavishly decorated corridor extending to the rear hall, where the main stair is

168. Polk & Polk. William Bourn house, San Francisco, 1895–1896.
(Author)

212

169. Bourn house, side elevation. (Courtesy F. Bourn Hayne)

170. Eastgate House, Rochester, Kent, sixteenth century. (*British Architect*, October 9, 1885)

213

171. Bourn house, entrance detail. (Author)

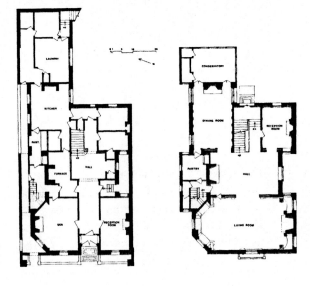

172. Bourn house, plans. (Drawn by Kim Spurgeon Fly)

173. Bourn house, entrance
hall. (Author)

174. Bourn house, den.
(CED Documents Collection)

situated in dim light. Right by the entry are two reception rooms, one
vaguely Georgian, the other aggressively rustic (Figs. 172–174). A
third, more private, upstairs reception room was for friends, but other
visitors were kept entirely apart from the principal rooms of the house.

In contrast to the warren at ground level, the main floor is
unusually open for a city house of the period. The central hall affords
the essential unifying element, with wide thresholds connecting to

215

175. Bourn house, living room. (Author)

176. Bourn house, dining room. (Author)

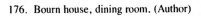

each room so that the entire layout can be perceived at once. Wood trim painted ivory forms a visual frame, defining the boundaries of the space. The wall surfaces are covered with a dreamlike landscape mural by Bruce Porter, which creates an ethereal interplay between spatial progression and pictorial illusion. The other rooms are given a strong architectural order. Elaborate, large-scale elements are accentuated by contrasts of light and dark zones (Figs. 175, 176). The effect is especially pronounced in the dining room, with all the natural light concentrated at one end where a wall of glass surrounds a massive, freestanding fireplace. The space recalls Stanford White's dining room at Kingscote in Newport, Rhode Island, updated with a contemporary taste for classical order, yet retaining a sense of freedom and of being integrated into a sequence of spaces that characterizes the best Shingle Style work.

In 1898, Bourn's mother had Polk prepare plans for a country house on her Napa Valley estate near St. Helena. The play between formal and informal qualities present in so much of Polk's and Coxhead's work is developed here on a grand scale (Fig. 177). The rambling ensemble of symmetrical, ornate facade and picturesque, simple side elevations makes a gesture to the form of the mid-nineteenth-century farmhouse that once occupied the site. In every other respect, the

177. Willis Polk. Madroño, Mrs. William Bourn, Sr., house, near St. Helena, 1898, project. Drawing by Polk. (CED Documents Collection)

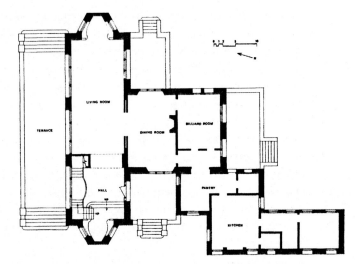

178. Madroño, plan. (Drawn
by Kim Spurgeon Fly)

scheme is a departure. Ignoring the principal facade, the approach to
the house is oblique, with the front door placed on one side of what
appears to be an ancillary terrace set between the main block and the
service wing. Inside is a two-story hall wrapped by a staircase. Beyond
the hall lies an enormous living room—the two spaces spanning over
70 feet, with grand bays containing fireplaces at each end (Fig. 178).
On the main terrace, the wall is reduced to a series of arcuated piers
that enframe windows 16 feet wide. The windows and fireplaces establish a strong biaxial symmetry, but this order is ignored elsewhere.
The effect created by large rooms that both court and defy formal
organization can only be imagined, for the project never passed beyond
the preliminary stage.[21]

In 1898, Polk also designed a town house for Charles Stetson
Wheeler, which, to judge from the sole surviving sketch, could have
ranked among the architect's most impressive works (Fig. 179). The
scheme is a big rectangular box with broad expanses of unornamented
wall surface serving as a foil for the lavish decoration concentrated at
the center. The intensity of this contrast recalls Churrigueresque work,
but the composition is Palladian, the orders mannerist, and many of
the details eighteenth-century French. Again, the entrance seems incidental, being tucked around the side and leading to a huge central hall
above in a sequence that might well have paralleled the drama of the
facade.[22]

By the turn of the century, Polk had become one of San Francisco's most fashionable architects. In addition to houses for Wheeler,

218

Charles Baldwin, and two generations of Bourns, he designed an extravagant stable compound (1899) and polo clubhouse (1901) for Francis Carolan, a leader of society sportsmen. But the prize commission came from Polk's friend William Crocker. Crocker was no less a master at business than his unscrupulous father, Charles. However, the two men had little else in common. A graduate of Andover and Yale, William was modest in demeanor; a formidable champion of economic development, political reform, and civic art; a generous philanthropist; and a maverick patron of the arts.[23] His taste for avant-garde theater and dance first generated gossip, then applause, from San Franciscans. He also inaugurated a new era in the development of country places for the region.

Crocker was one of the initial investors in Burlingame Park, where he had Page Brown design a modest classical villa for him. Only five years later, he considered the enclave too intimate and purchased some 300 acres nearby, where he planned to erect a palatial residence to rival those recently built around New York. The project caused a sensation and eventually led a number of his peers to embark on similar endeavors. What had started as a deliberately unassuming rustic suburb would be expanded by the 1910s to a tract of elegant formal compounds that eclipsed the most ambitious Victorian estates

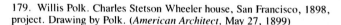

179. Willis Polk. Charles Stetson Wheeler house, San Francisco, 1898, project. Drawing by Polk. (*American Architect*, May 27, 1899)

219

constructed by the previous generation.[24] Polk's design for the Crocker house established the scale and sumptuousness that would characterize this new wave of building, but no other plans for the development matched its originality (Fig. 180). The garden facade is composed in an epic yet simple manner that is similar to the west elevation of Norman Shaw's Chesters (1891–1893), though Polk was probably not familiar with that design. In other respects, the scheme is analogous to late baroque Italian palaces, with sweeping curves that orchestrate taut stucco wall surfaces and delicate details which capture the play of light and shadow. The effect is animated and sensuous, and is in marked contrast to the rugged delineation of masses found in contemporary baroque-inspired houses by Shaw and East Coast architects. Posed against a panoramic landscape with the Bay far below, the scheme would have been a splendid fulfillment of the dream of implanting the classical legacy on fresh soil.

180. Willis Polk. William Crocker house, Hillsborough, 1899, project. Drawing by Polk. (*American Architect*, October 5, 1901)

220

VIII

COXHEAD AND POLK: Civic Projects

When as a Nation we are convinced that art is indeed a thing of first importance and priceless value, then American art . . . will have an unhampered path before it. . . . And when art eventually profits, the whole nation will profit with it.
Mariana van Rensselaer, *Forum,* December 1892

FOR A CITY of its size and importance, San Francisco was conspicuously lacking in civic amenities until after the turn of the century. Years of political corruption augmented by widespread apathy made citizens mistrustful of city officials and reluctant to approve bond issues for public works. In 1890, the editor of the *California Architect* lamented that no other major city was so poorly represented with public buildings.[1] Work had started on an immense City Hall in 1871, but appropriations were meager and construction sporadic. Over two decades elapsed before the pile was completed. Even then, the results were disappointing to many people. Removed from the commercial center and set in the middle of a squalid neighborhood, the new City Hall was considered to be as much a symbol of graft as one of municipal improvement. Public buildings were few in number, undistinguished in appearance, and hopelessly inadequate for the growing city's needs. The dearth of other facilities was just as pronounced. Aside from a handful of squares, little or no open space was reserved for public use. Golden Gate Park had been conceived as a great urban recreation ground patterned after New York's Central Park, but it lay at the western edge of the city, remote from most residential areas. In 1866 Frederick Law Olmsted prepared plans for a park system in the Western Addition, but the proposal was soon forgotten. San Francisco had few impressive streets, no grand monuments, and inadequate public service.[2]

The climate for change improved markedly during the 1890s, when small citizens' groups began to call for political reform, public enlightenment, and urban embellishment. A new generation of businessmen and philanthropists, along with young architects, artists, and intellectuals, became increasingly committed to the notion that physical improvements could provide a cornerstone for future progress. Unless the Victorian metropolis was transformed into a city beautiful, they believed, the region could never flourish as a great cultural center.

Polk was one of the most energetic promoters of civic improvement; he considered it perhaps the architect's highest calling. Even though he had a tiny practice and little experience in large-scale planning, Polk, as well as Coxhead and Maybeck, was enthralled with the potential of grand urban projects. All three architects developed conceptually audacious designs. Almost none of this work was executed. Nevertheless, the innovation it represents, together with reforms carried out in municipal government, made San Francisco an important arena of activity for the City Beautiful Movement during its formative years.

The event that made these visions of a new urban order seem so important was, of course, the 1893 World's Columbian Exposition. Even before the Chicago fair opened it became known as the Dream City, for the realization of such an enormous complex of monumental buildings seemed impossible. The design was far from radical, yet the vocabulary was still new to America and the scale was unprecedented. The academic movement had not yet produced more than a few large classical buildings. During the late 1880s, Stanford University laid the groundwork for formally arranged complexes; however, the scheme had surprisingly little influence on subsequent work. Plans for the new campuses of Columbia and New York universities were still in the preliminary design stage when the fair was completed.[3] Not only was the Exposition a pronounced departure from anything in the United States, but it had few counterparts in Europe, and nowhere had so large an ensemble been executed in a single building campaign. American observers were very conscious of this fact. Mariana van Rensselaer emphasized that it "has not been paralleled since the Rome of the Emperors . . . no place of its extent in the modern world has been so impressive, so magnificent, so imperial in its beauty." In a country notorious for valuing quantity above all else, critics hastened to add that it was not size that made the complex so momentous, but the creation of a harmonious ensemble on a grand scale. The result, one commentator noted, was the effect of silence; even with a thousand people in its midst, the setting inspired an almost spiritual tranquility that was matched by few sights in the world.[4]

Besides advancing new aesthetic standards, the fair offered organizational amenities that were at once posited as models for America's cities. The stringent control of commercial activities, the unobtrusive transportation system, the efficient methods of street cleaning, the courteous and highly disciplined police force—all were identified as important lessons in civic improvement. The Dream City was also depicted as conveying a new sense of equality among its "inhabitants"; here was a place where the people, "not the corporations and the politicians," ruled. William Dean Howells wrote a lengthy report on the fair as the only American "city" that measured up to his Utopian world of Altruria, where beauty and order were omnipresent, and commercialism and social inequality nonexistent. He concluded that "an immortal principal higher than use, higher than even beauty, is expressed in [the fair], and the time will come when [Americans] . . . will cherish it forever . . . as the earliest achievement of a real civic life." The fair "was not only a revelation, but a benediction . . . [and] a forecast of duty."[5]

Fulfilling that duty was another matter. The Columbian Exposition had little real impact on America's urban fabric until the 1900s, but in the interim, many people pressed for municipal reform so that such plans might be realized. It soon became apparent, however, that the complexion of local government could not be transformed overnight. Some people questioned the need for plans on so grand a scale, a point underscored by the economic depression that erupted before the fair closed. Most campaigns for civic adornment were concentrated on small projects which proved to be difficult enough to implement during the depression of the 1890s. That the fair afforded a polemic for urban design was seldom disputed; however, the form that its lessons should assume was far from being clear at the outset.[6]

These problems beset efforts in San Francisco no less than in other cities. Proponents of the City Beautiful were optimistic, and their vision magnanimous. However, progress was repeatedly undermined by the lack of a strong coalition among them. Visions thus remained more the dreams of individuals than a coordinated program with broad-based support. Key civic leaders also failed to realize the talents of the city's young architects.

Grand visions of the City Beautiful were harbored from the beginning of the decade. The earliest elaborate planning scheme for San Francisco came from William Randolph Hearst, whose penchant for unconventional design matched his taste for spectacular display. In 1891, when construction on the Chicago fair had only begun, the newspaperman proposed a lavish successor to be held in San Francisco in 1900. Hearst commissioned his friend Polk to prepare a schematic design that was presented in the *Examiner's* Christmas issue (Figs. 181,182). Polk's idea was daring. Unlike any previous world's fair, the complex suggests a walled city, forming a terminus to Van Ness Avenue, San Francisco's one major boulevard, thence enclosing an immense athletic field. On the other side, the building opens to embrace

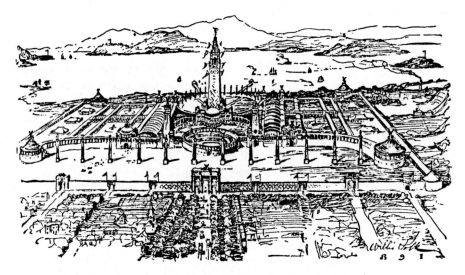

181. Willis Polk. 1900 World's Fair, San Francisco, 1891, schematic proposal done in aerial perspective. Drawing by Polk. (*Examiner*, December 25, 1891)

the Bay. The pavilions are linked to form a single building, over a mile long, broken by courtyards that offer a more intimate scale and protection from summer wind and fog. In the middle stand a cluster of amphitheaters, a domed auditorium, and towers. These and many other elements are frankly derivative, yet the organization represents a bold, ingenious departure in large-scale planning. At this stage, Polk criticized the Columbian Exposition as a whole for not possessing the unity found in its principal buildings.[7] Once the Court of Honor was completed he revised his opinion. In the meantime he conceived a spirited response to the perceived problem that elaborates upon the fair's strongest features in an original fashion. The scheme is also noteworthy because it was done before most American architects were aware of the lessons in ordered urban design that the fair would provide.

Nothing came of Polk's proposal. Hearst was regarded by many as a bombastic, extravagant publicist, and he may have been incapable of mustering initial support for the project. Twenty years elapsed before his and Polk's idea took concrete form with the Panama-Pacific Inter-

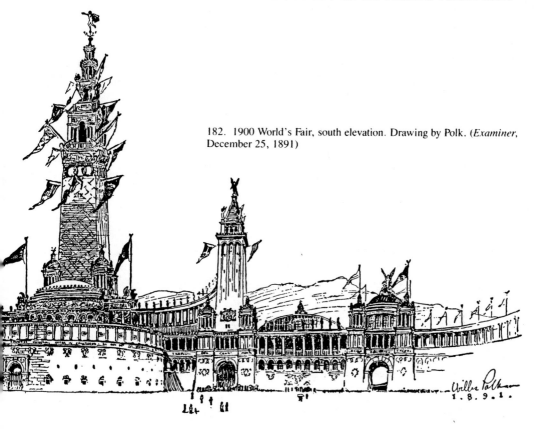

182. 1900 World's Fair, south elevation. Drawing by Polk. (*Examiner*, December 25, 1891)

national Exposition.[8] In the early 1890s, an undertaking of that size may well have been more than city leaders and the business community were ready to accept. The gap that existed between such visions and the reality of patronage became quite apparent with a sequel to the Chicago fair that *was* implemented—the California Midwinter International Exposition.

From an organizational perspective, the Midwinter fair was ambitious. Michael de Young, a state commissioner for the Columbian Exposition and Hearst's archrival in business, conceived the idea less than a year before the opening in January 1894. His plan entailed moving exhibits from Chicago and greatly expanding those devoted to California. He argued that no more effective means existed to attract large numbers of visitors to California and to give the state international publicity. The fair could be quite large with relatively little capital outlay since many of the exhibits were already assembled and an ample site was available in Golden Gate Park. Additional funds could be raised from private sources to keep the affair removed from political influence. By opening in the middle of winter, it would be a consummate demonstration of California's salubrious climate. Financial support from business patrons came quickly. Local pride swelled. The fair's *Official History* boasted that this was not a hasty regrouping from Chicago, but a "natural product of the last hundred years of California's existence."[9]

Unfortunately, de Young had no understanding of the design standards set in Chicago and refused to delegate authority in developing the fair's plan. His executive committee wanted an hexagonal layout; the park commissioners refused to accept the idea, and they asked Page Brown and Richard Hammond to prepare a new design in August 1893. Brown's proposal placed the fair's five major pavilions around a terraced rectangular court with the main entrance at one end. As the number of exhibits grew, however, the scheme was substantially modified, probably under the direction of de Young himself. John McLaren was hired for the landscaping but resigned almost at once when he discovered that he would have to cater to de Young's wishes.[10] Even sound master planning would have been hampered by the fact that the main pavilions had already been designed. An open competition, judged by de Young's committee, was conducted in July. Entrants had less than three weeks to submit proposals, and those who were selected had even less time to develop the working drawings. The committee expressed partiality to schemes they felt were characteristic of California, but aside from this amorphous stipulation no criteria

183. Willis Polk. Administration Building, California Midwinter International
Exposition, San Francisco 1893, competition entry.
Drawing by Polk. (CED Documents Collection)

were established to create a unified ensemble. Brown submitted designs
for each of the pavilions with the expressed hope that their execution
as a group would provide some cohesiveness; however, the point was
lost on the sponsors.[11]

The absence of an orchestrated plan did not prevent numerous
San Francisco architects from participating in the competition. Polk
entered, as he was especially concerned with demonstrating on the
home front the lessons of the Columbian Exposition, which he now
described as "the most beautiful example of architecture the world has
ever known."[12] His design was one of the few based on classical
precedent and the only one to treat the project as a unit. Polk ignored
the program. Instead he proposed three exhibition buildings connected
by an elliptical colonnade with an elaborate administration building as
the centerpiece. Regrettably, only his scheme for the latter building
survives. Baroque in its exuberance and Neo-Classical in its insistently
repetitive elements, the building is a giant ornament (Fig. 183). Three
round tempiettos penetrate the mass at its base and are tangent to a tall
rotunda in the middle. The rest of the exterior is all tower and dome,
broken into receding layers and laden with small-scale decoration so

227

that the building appears to be quite large. The committee expressed no interest in Polk's overall plan, but they were enticed by the theatrical administration building. Deliberations over the scheme lasted for several weeks after designs for the other buildings had been chosen. In the end, Polk lost to Page Brown, and even if his proposal had been executed, it would have been out of place in the setting that was finally constructed.[13]

The Midwinter fair's Grand Court fell far short of achieving the unity of the Columbian Exposition's Court of Honor (Fig. 184). Four architects, working independently, were responsible for the main pavilions, which were dwarfed by a central space much larger than the one Brown had proposed. The court lost virtually all definition at its head where concession stands spilled in to either side of the diminutive administration building. The grounds were laid out in a mid-nineteenth-century manner with stiff geometric patterns and clumps

184. Grand Court, California International Midwinter Exposition, 1893; demolished 1894. (San Francisco Public Library)

of plant material arranged to emphasize the particularity of each section. Amid the gardens lay large mechanical gadgets: a vatlike Electric Fountain and a scaled-down Eiffel Tower. The tower was the fair's most conspicuous feature and was the sort of amateurish replication that the planners at Chicago had labored so hard to avoid. The main pavilions supported motifs inspired by Near Eastern architecture and the California missions—imagery that the committee believed symbolized the state's unique character. The classical White City along the shores of Lake Michigan had become the exotic, polychromed Sunset City by the Golden Gate.

Supporters of the fair believed that it represented a cultural coming of age. "Well does our Exposition argue for the taste and civilization of the people, which, until recently, were regarded . . . as semi-barbarous," proclaimed James Duval Phelan, a leader in the drive for civic improvement in San Francisco. Phelan considered that "what Nature has done for California this fair has done for her people," and that "California should be what Italy and France have been. . . . San Francisco . . . should be what Venice has been and Paris is to strangers. . . . The Fair has given force and direction to the idea."[14] At that time, Phelan's viewpoint was probably shared by most of the city's prominent businessmen. Notions of grand design still took the form of a spectacle.

That spectacle elicited a very different reaction from other quarters. Boston's *Architectural Review,* then the most outspoken organ of the academic movement, stated that the fair was an object lesson in just how disastrous the results could be when the best designers were not placed in charge of the project. The use of exotic references was dismissed as banal and offered good argument for employing classical precedent in the design of large complexes.[15] Locally, no one described the scene in more acerbic terms than Polk. "As a matter of simple courtesy to the builders of the Midwinter Fair," he chided, "it will be polite to say that 'They knew better than they built,' " adding, "by the way, has it had any architects at all?" What disturbed Polk the most was the lack of unifying order. He likened the Grand Court to "a jumble of . . . A-B-C blocks [which will make] the casual observer clap his hands and laugh with glee, but the critical observer will fail to see the essay . . . [it] will not seem like a dream, but will suggest a frightful nightmare."[16] For Polk, these shortcomings were symptomatic of what had produced architectural chaos in the city over the last several decades; the Midwinter fair did not present a model for civic design, it only perpetuated the problem.

229

Polk's remarks no doubt incensed the businessmen who had struggled to realize the Sunset City. Such clashes were not uncommon. When Adolph Sutro, a rich entrepreneur and mayor from 1894 to 1897, unveiled his plans to construct a great bathhouse along the Pacific shore, Polk branded him "a menace to the public taste . . . the enemy of art . . . [and] the betrayer of Nature's trust." Shortly thereafter, he denounced the program of the University of California's new medical school competition as perpetrating an "outrageous violation of the artistic welfare of the community." Both the mayor and the board of supervisors were damned as ignorant fools for the manner in which they selected the architect of the new municipal office building and the City Hall's dome. The dome itself was "a gaudy parvenue creation . . . an outrage on decency and a permanent reflection of the taste of the city that permitted it to be built."[17] Such irreverent forays surely amused the popular audience to whom they were addressed and delighted young colleagues who shared Polk's distaste for what was being built in the region. However, some leading citizens must have regarded these insults as irresponsible accusations emanating from a band of youthful upstarts more capable of mocking the establishment than of constructive action. This sentiment could only have been reinforced by the midnight raid, staged by Gelett Burgess, Bruce Porter, and his brother, Robert, on the Cogswell Fountain, one of the city's few public monuments. Dedicated to temperance, this ornate Victorian piece was considered by the assailants to be an aesthetic and social affront. They proceeded to destroy its crowning element, a likeness of the donor, and created a small scandal in the process.[18] Among those people unamused by such antics was James Phelan.

No San Franciscan was more passionately devoted to the city than Phelan.[19] The son of a self-made millionaire, he channeled his energies, wealth, and position into advancing the idea of civic improvement. During the 1890s he embarked on a study of cities at home and abroad, focusing on public works projects and the strategies used to implement them. Along with a growing number of reformers throughout the country, Phelan believed that such projects were essential to the continued progress and vitality of the metropolis. Municipal art was neither a cosmetic nor an aristocratic indulgence, but rather a manifestation of the city's "soul." Furthermore, these projects constituted both an educational and moralizing agent capable of stirring the populace to great achievement. Phelan was as much a pragmatist as a dreamer. He believed that future greatness was impossible without first developing an honest, efficient municipal government. Launching a successful campaign for mayor, he served from 1897 to 1902 as head of a reform administration that worked tirelessly to eliminate graft and improve services.

Phelan took advantage of his position in the community to press for physical changes. In 1898 he persuaded Phoebe Apperson Hearst to fund an international competition for a master plan that the city could follow in the years to come. The competition was abandoned shortly after it was announced for reasons that remain unclear. Phelan also advocated an extension of Golden Gate Park's panhandle to Van Ness Avenue, which would provide an impressive set of landscaped boulevards, make the park more accessible to the heart of the city, and facilitate new development in the adjacent districts. While none of Phelan's proposals materialized, they did help to generate an awareness of their need and eventually led to the appointment of Daniel Burnham to prepare a master plan for San Francisco in 1904.[20]

A schematic design, almost certainly prepared at Phelan's request, suggesting how the panhandle extension might look, reveals an unfortunate weakness in his endeavors. The proposal resembles a chain of small Victorian parks, each treated more or less independently rather than as components of a long, linear space (Fig. 185). Such lackluster results were consistent with those of the Midwinter fair Phelan so admired. As a businessman, he appears to have valued architects more for their executive faculties than for their creativity. Phelan entrusted William Curlett, who headed one of the city's oldest and largest firms, to design his own buildings. Curlett was a lord of the architectural establishment, but never produced original or particularly inspired designs.[21]

Further indication of Phelan's attitude toward architecture is revealed by his role in erecting two commemorative monuments. The first he financed himself in 1896 to honor California's admission to the Union and to demonstrate locally the virtues of civic art. Douglas Tilden, recognized as the region's most talented sculptor, was charged with the design. Tilden asked Polk to collaborate, and Phelan acquiesced to the partnership but gave Polk scarcely any credit for his contribution. Several months after the unveiling, Tilden was entrusted with a much larger commission from James Donohue for a monument in memory of his father, which Phelan administered. After about a year's worth of preliminary studies, Tilden again sought Polk's assistance. Phelan was skeptical: "That agreement with Polk is all right," he advised the sculptor, "if his services are worth Two Hundred and Fifty Dollars . . . , but I would not pay it until his work is performed."[22]

231

185. Panhandle extension, San Francisco, 1899, schematic proposal.
(*Wave*, Christmas 1899, p. 27)

Phelan's response may have stemmed from an animosity toward Polk. But the civic leader also seems to have believed that an architect's talents were unnecessary for such work, and he was probably oblivious to the academic movement's idea that a union of allied arts was essential to creating monuments of aesthetic integrity. The personal and conceptual gap that existed between the businessman-politician, who so ardently crusaded for civic improvements, and the architects, who were the most capable of embodying his vision, was San Francisco's misfortune.

Progress also suffered from the absence of an organization that could champion the cause effectively. For a brief period, Polk led efforts to create such an organization through the Guild for Arts and Crafts. The Guild was founded in 1894 to combat "middle class philistinism" by advancing the ideas of William Morris, and was the first group in the country to carry the name of "arts and crafts." Comprised of painters, sculptors, and architects, its initial objective

232

was to elevate public taste through exhibitions of fine and decorative art. Bruce Porter served as secretary; Polk and Tilden were among the six directors.[23] Polk announced that the Guild would advise sponsors on the best way to conduct building competitions and drafted a resolution calling for a Board of Public Works to approve the design of all proposed municipal projects.[24] The idea represented a pioneering extension of the work performed by the municipal arts commissions founded a few years earlier in New York and Boston, which gave nonbinding opinions on the artistic merits of planned public monuments. Finally, Polk and Porter involved the Guild in sponsoring a fountain dedicated to Robert Louis Stevenson, a project patterned after those of the Fairmount Park Association in Philadelphia (1871) and the New York Municipal Art Society (1893), organizations established to donate works of civic art to their respective cities.[25]

The fountain was conceived by Bruce Porter upon hearing of the writer's death. Porter took the idea to Polk and shortly thereafter sculptor George Piper was brought in to collaborate on the project. In the tradition of the best commemorative work by McKim, Mead & White and Augustus Saint-Gaudens, the monument gives focus to its setting without being obtrusive. It also avoids the appearance of an architectural fragment, achieving an active interplay among the pedestal, inscription, and sculpture, between the broad, low basin of water in front and the ellipse of poplar trees that enframes the ensemble (Fig. 186). The proposed location in Portsmouth Square, amid the tawdry Latin Quarter once frequented by Stevenson, was intended to demonstrate the relatively new idea of adorning many portions of the city rather than just a few select places. Some observers felt that this would be the most artistic monument ever erected on the West Coast. Although the cost was only $2,000, to be raised through public subscription, it took more than three years to reach that goal. Many San Franciscans refused to donate unless the monument was erected in Golden Gate Park, defeating one of its primary purposes. A major portion of the funding was eventually secured from Stevenson admirers in the East. Adding insult to injury, the board of supervisors then rejected the design on aesthetic grounds. Infuriated, Polk introduced minor revisions and succeeded in gaining the board's approval. Sixteen months later, in October 1897, the monument was unveiled.[26]

By this time the Guild had disbanded. It had never been consulted on competitions, the drive to create a board of public works had been ignored outside the membership, and the group had even failed to solicit funds for the Stevenson fountain. An exhibit of posters and

186. Willis Polk and George
Piper. Stevenson Monument,
San Francisco, 1895–1897; altered.
(Author's collection)

books was the extent of the Guild's concrete achievements. Internal
dissension was one of the problems. Many of the artists had little
interest in civic projects, and even most of the other architects in the
city failed to rally behind Polk's initiatives. Polk himself resigned after
a heated dispute over the qualifications for membership.[27]

That Polk's efforts amounted to naught is the more regrettable
because of his somewhat novel approach to urban design. He sought
to give a new sense of order and dignity to the city, preserving the
diversity of its fabric at the same time. His concern for San Francisco's
special character, its "profusion of airy and incongruous images," is
evident in a series of renderings, made around the turn of the century,
of streetscapes and panoramas from atop Nob and Russian hills (Fig.
187). The scenes emphasize not so much picturesqueness as the myriad
intricacies of the urban fabric. Polk concentrated on conveying a general

ambience, inspired no doubt by the work of some contemporary illustrators. He was meticulous about depicting each element in the urban landscape, even in hastily drawn impressions.[28] He did not sketch scenes—or at least never published them—of Chinatown, the Latin Quarter, Telegraph Hill, or other quaint backwaters that were vibrant contributors to San Francisco's cosmopolitan character. Nor do his drawings focus on the spectacular natural setting that he and many others so admired. Instead, he concentrated on the city center—the dense, chaotic, commercial, Victorian metropolis of the last quarter-century. Polk despised the components as individual examples of architecture, yet he seems to have found their cumulative effect engaging.

Polk's draftsmanship also suggests that his interest in the harsh visual realities of San Francisco affected his approach to design. Virtually

187. Willis Polk. Drawing of San Francisco, looking southeast from the Mark Hopkins Institute of Art, 1900. (CED Documents Collection)

235

188. Willis Polk. Examiner Building, San Francisco, 1891, project. Drawing by Polk. (*California Architect*, August 1893)

all of his presentation drawings for work in the city establish an accurate physical context; the larger the project, the more its setting is revealed (Fig. 188). The technique may have been developed to enhance his designs through contrast, positing them against the decorative bombast of their neighbors. At the same time, the elegance with which these streetscapes are rendered also imparts a concern for new buildings as civic monuments in a very real sense, calculated to enrich the urban fabric rather than standing aloof from it. Polk's method, and the conception it embodies, was a pronounced departure from the prevailing practice, where perspective drawings of urban buildings constructed an ideal setting or provided no background at all.

Polk's sympathy for the idiomatic attributes of the metropolis represented a new attitude in the United States, of which the leading exponents were New Yorkers. Among the first to articulate this notion

236

in print was Royal Cortissoz, a former McKim, Mead & White employee and a staunch supporter of their work. Cortissoz's "Landmarks of Manhattan," published in 1895, began by stressing the fact that American cities were too eclectic and were developing too rapidly to imitate the official, cohesive grand designs of Europe. Throughout the article, Cortissoz emphasized groups of often highly varied buildings as the key generators of New York's memorable character. His favorite district lay around the Grand Army Plaza.

Here the triviality of the shops disappears and only the repose, the solidity, and the opulence of the public inns and private places are left. It is . . . one of the most expressive records of New York life that we have. The wealth, the luxury, the material prosperity of the town are writ across that spacious meeting of ways. It provides in perfection the atmosphere typical of "uptown."[29]

189. Birch Burdette Long. View of Fifth Avenue showing McKim, Mead & White's Tiffany Building, ca. 1900. (Avery Architectural and Fine Arts Library)

Such observations must have appealed to a populace that had grown up amid constant change and diversity and was ever more confident of its city's greatness. Perhaps one reason for the popularity of McKim, Mead & White's work was that, consciously or not, it celebrated the contemporary metropolis as much as it heralded a transformation. The mounting public regard for New York's special qualities may have induced the firm to commission a series of renderings that show completed projects as part of lively street scenes (Fig. 189). The architects' buildings are presented as gleaming symbols of a new order; but they are also genteel contributors to their settings that converse with the urban landscape.

The idea of enhancing the existing urban fabric was taken one step further when Herbert Croly openly criticized the large-scale renewal projects espoused by many City Beautiful proponents.

Just as the irregularities and discomforts and degradation of London make it a more interesting city than the monotonous machine-made regularity of the newer Paris, so no amount of elaborate and correct planning of streets, monuments, furniture and parks will of themselves make a beautiful, habitable and interesting city. The ugly actual cities of to-day make a livelier appeal to the imagination than does an ideal city, which sacrificing its ugliness on the altar of civic art, sacrifices also its character and inherent vitality.

Croly went on to argue that "a great city cannot be forced to bloom beautiful." Improvements must arise from real needs and be "guided by authentic conventions . . . and confirmed by genuine popular appreciation, in every respect the master of its resources." America had yet to reach that stage, he maintained, nor would it if proponents of civic improvement divorced themselves from the reality of the city. Croly and others who sympathized with these views were still partial to the erection of grand classical buildings, but they stressed that such work must respond to the city on its own terms. Giving greater consistency and order to the urban landscape must be achieved by meeting contemporary needs with artistic sensitivity, rather than by proposing grandiose changes in the order itself.[30]

Polk may have been exposed to these ideas in their nascent form when he worked at 57 Broadway. Whatever the source of inspiration, he was expressing this approach to urban design in his work before any articles were written on the subject. A scheme designed around 1893 was probably an exercise in how commercial architecture could respond to its multifaceted setting (Fig. 190). Only the Market

190. Willis Polk. Commercial building, Market Street, San Francisco, ca. 1893, project. Drawing by Ernest Peixotto. (*American Architect*, July 6, 1895)

191. San Francisco, Geary Street looking east from Stockton. Photograph ca. 1890, owned by Polk and probably used for study purposes. (CED Documents Collection)

239

Street site is specific; the building has neither a name nor a clearly enunciated function.[31] Unto itself, the design is unlike anything else in San Francisco. With a dense, layered composition and an abundance of heavy classical ornament, the exterior would have been quite at home in late-nineteenth-century Vienna or Berlin. Yet the overall effect indicated in Ernest Peixotto's superb rendering is to give focus to the prominent location and to serve as an ordering device for the entire area. Mass and cornice lines link to those of the flanking piles, creating a unit that emphatically defines the block. The rounded corner shaft punctuates the intersection, while echoing the curved bays on the nearby flats and offering a response to the large corner tower of the Baldwin Hotel up the street.

Several oversized photographic prints found among Polk's few surviving presentation drawings of the 1890s offer intriguing, if inconclusive, evidence of a method that he may have used to study urban projects. On one of these sheets, Polk began to draw in pen and ink over the image itself. The scene is of Point Lobos, at the western end of the city, and taken from almost the same angle as that of a sketch Polk made in 1895 depicting his proposal for the new Cliff House.[32] None of Polk's published renderings were ever copied from photographs, but these prints did enable him to examine the setting to a degree that no other means provided. Another print (26 by 19 inches) is of downtown San Francisco, two blocks away from the Market Street building study (Fig. 191). The angle the photograph was taken from is singularly appropriate for studying the appearance of a new building that might replace the dilapidated Wigwam Theatre located on the corner lot. Both the nature of this site and the coverage of the urban landscape are strikingly similar to those in Peixotto's rendering.[33] If Polk in fact used the prints this way, they allowed him to scrutinize a broad spectrum of elements—wagons, streetcars, telephone poles, lights, signs—that are shown with fidelity in his finished perspectives.

Polk's largest civic project of the decade is related to the others in idea, but it is primarily ornamental in function. The 1897 design includes a triumphal arch and peristyle enframed by small business blocks that establish an ordered spatial sequence between Page Brown's Union Depot and Ferry House (1893-1898) and the head of Market Street. The ferry building, then nearing completion, was the only monumental civic edifice to be erected in San Francisco since the City Hall was begun some twenty years earlier (Fig. 192). It provided the terminus for both heavy commuter traffic across the Bay and for the Transcontinental Railroad, being in effect San Francisco's principal

192. A. Page Brown. Union Depot and Ferry House, San Francisco, 1893–1898. (Author's collection)

gateway. Schweinfurth, who had charge of the design, patterned the facade's main block after Charles Atwood's railroad station at the Chicago fair, then the academic movement's only precedent for a building of this type in the country. Above, he placed a tower that combines aspects of those on the Piazza San Marco in Venice and the Giralda at Seville—both sources already used by Polk in his world's fair design—here rendered in a severe, almost Neo-Classical manner.[34] The tower served as a beacon, identifying the complex from across the Bay and from the further reaches on Market Street. But the building's effect was greatly diminished by the dense pierside traffic and nearby shabby structures. Polk's proposal sought to organize this congestion and subordinate it to an ensemble commensurate with the ferry building's key functional and urbanistic role.

241

At that time, the design was more ambitious in scope than any other permanent scheme proposed as a civic ornament in the country (Fig. 193). The elements are derivative, based on Charles Atwood's arch and peristyle at the Columbian Exposition's Court of Honor, and the details are even closer to Atwood's models: the arches of Constantine and Titus and the colonnade around St. Peter's Square. Yet the plan and the idea it represents are a departure. The peristyle creates an inward-looking space that also allows vistas in several directions. The arcaded buildings beyond introduce a tight, strongly defined boundary that acts as a transition between the peristyle and the city blocks. The ensemble at once controls and activates the expansive Embarcadero, filling space rather than lining it with monumental buildings. A similar effect is achieved at the approach from Market Street, a point Polk underscored in two sketches (Figs. 194,195). Under existing conditions, the ferry building was engulfed in a sea of space, unchecked by the accumulation of small buildings nearby, but in Polk's design a

193. Willis Polk. Arch, peristyle, and commercial buildings, San Francisco, 1897, project. Drawing by Polk. (CED Documents Collection)

242

194. Willis Polk. Drawing of Market Street looking northeast toward Ferry Building, 1897. (*San Francisco News Letter*, Christmas Number, 1900, p. 59)

195. Arch, peristyle and commercial buildings, view from Market Street. Drawing by Polk. (*American Architect*, August 10, 1901)

sequence of differentiated spatial zones is created. First comes the end of the street proper, defined by the arch and flanking blocks. Next comes the depot, the full impact of which can be perceived only from inside the square. The Embarcadero's breadth unfolds gradually as one passes around or through the colonnade. Each sector receives definition, yet allows the others to be seen. This intricate layering of a major urban space stands apart from the plan of the Columbian Exposition and most subsequent City Beautiful projects, where a large, central court provides the dominant order. The scheme is also unusual in that it builds upon the established urban matrix instead of attempting to eliminate it.

Polk's inspiration for this design remains a matter of conjecture. He often cited widely admired precedents for urban planning—Periclean Athens, imperial and baroque Rome, Haussmann's Paris, and the Chicago fair—none of which offers a clue. The likeliest source is one then known by few of his American colleagues: Camillo Sitte's *Der Städte-Bau nach seinen kuntslerischen Grundsätzen*, published in 1889. During the late nineteenth century, Sitte was virtually alone in advocating a return to the use of close-knit urban spaces. He repeatedly mentioned the arch, colonnade, and arcade as devices by which such spaces could receive definition and meaning. Moreover, Sitte illustrated his thesis through schematic modifications to existing urban areas rather than developing wholly new designs. Although Polk's vocabulary is different, his conceptual approach appears to be nearly identical. It is doubtful whether Polk could read German; were he aware of Sitte's text, it might well have been secondhand. But someone thought highly of the Austrian planner's work and invited him to San Francisco to advise on the location of monuments at about this time.[35] Given Polk's initiative to establish a board of public works for such undertakings and his active role in other civic efforts, it is quite possible that he was aware of Sitte's ideas. Had Polk's project been realized, it would have been a unique interpretation of the new taste for order and unity on an imperial scale. The design was received enthusiastically by many San Franciscans, even by Phelan. For the next fifteen years strategies were put forth to finance it; however, the great cost of a scheme that served no practical purpose seemed prohibitive, and nothing came of the venture.[36]

While San Francisco failed to embark on any major civic projects during the 1890s, an ideal scenario for the creation of a grand classical complex was unfolding in Berkeley. Preparations began in

1896 to secure a master plan for the University of California campus. The vision was as grand as Hearst's had been for the 1900 world's fair. Comprehensive planning had been undertaken locally a decade earlier when Leland Stanford had sought the nation's best designers to create the campus that would bear his son's name. Now his rivals in Berkeley initiated a plan that would make Stanford and all other American universities seem inconsequential. The new campus would be a city—a "City of Learning"—to manifest the highest ideals of a maturing urban culture. The program represented one of the first serious proposals in the United States to implement the City Beautiful vision on a large scale and in a permanent form.[37] The scheme had a decisive impact on subsequent plans for both urban centers and institutions throughout the country—far more impact outside the region than anything undertaken in California up to that point.

The idea was conceived by Maybeck, then an instructor of drawing at the university, who had yet to contribute much to the region's architecture. At first, his proposal was dismissed as unrealistic—a dream doomed to failure. The reaction of the university's board of regents was summarized by its newest member, Jacob Reinstein, who branded Maybeck "a freak," adding that none of the regents "regard him seriously."[38] However, Reinstein was soon seduced by the idea and became its most vigorous supporter. This brilliant, energetic young attorney now believed that building a great classical city would be the most effective way to eliminate the university's provincial aura and further its national stature. Moreover, the scheme provided an unparalleled opportunity to advance California's role as the new center of Western civilization. Maybeck's pleas for an international competition to secure the design also appealed to Reinstein; staging such an event would create widespread recognition and many of the world's most talented architects would surely vie for the chance to create such a project. The winning design would be a model for civic art and an impetus for great cultural achievements. The vision of this "city," to which all the world would turn in admiration, proved irresistible. Reinstein gloated:

Let us build not rapidly, not lavishly, but slowly, yet grandly, that there may greet the commerce which shall whiten the Golden Gate and the civilization which shall grace this western shore an architectural pile of stately and glorious buildings, which shall rival the dreams of the builders of the Columbian Exposition, which shall do honor and justice to a superb Republic, and to its most favored State, and which, even in their ruins, shall strike the beholder with wonder and rapture.[39]

In persuading the regents to reconsider, Reinstein and Maybeck defended the idea largely on practical grounds. The existing buildings, they argued, were hopelessly inadequate to meet the growing institution's needs. The image of a small agricultural college must be transformed. The fact that Stanford University, which posed a potential threat to Berkeley's academic supremacy of the West Coast, was blessed with a master plan reinforced the argument, although such comparisons were never made in public. Maybeck's underlying motivation for the competition, however, was artistic; the university master plan was more a vehicle to achieve his aims than an end unto itself. Maybeck prepared several schematic renderings for publicity purposes, which portray the new campus as a series of vast terraces filled with spiky, rather Germanic sculpture and a Pantheonlike auditorium as the crowning feature (Fig. 196). The buildings appear to be little more than a foil for the court and inappropriate for housing the functions of a large university. The conception was naive, resembling a student

196. Bernard Maybeck. University of California, Berkeley, 1896, schematic proposal. (*Wave*, November 7, 1896, p. 8)

project more than a mature work of planning. The dream was still a dream. The press dubbed the design a stage set, a forum from ancient Rome egregiously dumped on the Pacific coast without regard to need or local traditions. The thought of conducting an international competition was taken as a snub to the state's architects. "Mr. Maybeck," one journalist snapped, "has always been dreaming. He is neither of this world nor with it."[40]

But it was precisely such dreaming that carried the day. In April 1896 the regents voted unanimously to conduct a competition. That October, Phoebe Apperson Hearst, philanthropic rival of Mrs. Leland Stanford, pledged an unrestricted sum to finance the competition. The regents could not have had a better patron. Hearst's munificence for such an endeavor was unprecedented, and she possessed a deep interest in local cultural development. From the early 1890s until her death in 1919, Phoebe Hearst played as active and dynamic a role in promoting the arts as Phelan did in the drive for civic improvement.[41] She was not just a donor, but a client, sharing Maybeck's commitment to obtaining a master plan that represented the highest artistic ideals. The dream could become a reality.

Even before the money was pledged, Maybeck refused to have a direct hand in the design, but he exerted great influence on the competition and thus on the character of the design eventually selected. Maybeck seems to have had little or no exchange with Polk and other local colleagues in developing his ideas. Instead, he turned to the leaders of the academic tradition in France, whom he considered to be the most capable advisors on an enterprise of such complexity and import. With a generous stipend from Hearst, he devoted two years to the preparations. Most of his time was spent in Europe, with Paris as his headquarters. There he enlisted Julien Guadet, then the Ecole's professor of theory, to help prepare the program. Jean-Louis Pascal, who had won the Prix de Rome in 1866, assisted. Pascal conducted a major atelier for Ecole students, was a staunch ally of Guadet's, and was recognized as one of France's most eminent architects. Maybeck also selected the jurors while he was in Paris. They included Pascal; Paul Wallot, architect of the recently completed Reichstag; Norman Shaw, by then one of England's foremost classicists; and Walter Cook, a prominent New York architect who had been among the earliest American students at the Ecole.[42] Once the program was completed, Maybeck visited a number of European cities to generate interest in the undertaking, distribute information, and confer with the jurors. Even the first round of judging was conducted abroad, in Antwerp.

Not until eleven architects had been selected to compete in the final round in October 1898 did Maybeck return to the United States, and not until the second series of drawings was submitted almost a year later did the jury come to the Bay Area to inspect the site where the great City of Learning would rise.

The European orientation of this American competition was no doubt a result of Maybeck's and Reinstein's concern that it attract international participation. Had the enterprise been run from Berkeley, or even from the East Coast, response from abroad might have been meager. In addition, Maybeck still seems to have felt more at home on French soil, where he spent several stimulating years as a student, than in America, where he had experienced a decade of professional frustration. But the central reason for the international effort was probably ideological. Maybeck subscribed to the belief that great art knew no geographic boundaries and to the French academic notion that, being divorced from the immediacies of a project, the designer could be more fully devoted to its artistic fulfillment. Staging a competition in Europe for a university in California was much like giving an assignment at the Ecole for a villa on the Bosphorus or a trading post in Alaska. This detached attitude is implicit in the competition's prospectus; reading the text, one might suspect it was for a Prix de Rome project:

All the buildings which have been constructed up to the present time are to be ignored, and the grounds are to be treated as a blank space, to be filled with a single beautiful and harmonious picture as a painter fills his canvas.

There are to be no definite limitations of cost, materials, or style. All is to be left to the unfettered discretion of the designer. He is asked to record his conception of an ideal home for a University, assuming time and resources to be unlimited. He is to plan for centuries to come. There will doubtless be developments . . . in the future that will . . . require alterations . . . , but it is believed to be possible to secure a comprehensive plan so in harmony with the universal principles of architectural art, that there will be no more necessity of remodeling its broad outlines a thousand years hence, than there would be of remodeling the Parthenon, had it come down to us complete and uninjured.[43]

The competition was one of the most concerted efforts yet to bring California architecture into the mainstream of developments in leading eastern and European art centers. However, the process echoed the importation of established patterns that had characterized so much of the state's architecture in the nineteenth century. By holding the competition abroad and selecting a winner who in all probability had never been to the West Coast, California demonstrated a growing sensitivity to design, but did not show any capacity for its creation. Furthermore, the strong French overtones came when prominent American architects were concerned about transplanting French work on American soil. To some of these designers, Maybeck's incantations to Parisian authority may have seemed ever so slightly provincial.

The competition results were nevertheless admired on both sides of the Atlantic because of the project's unprecedented magnitude and the unusually high level of work chosen. Over half of the designs selected by this predominantly foreign jury were by Americans, who took four of the five prizes.[44] Both Pascal and John Belcher, who replaced Shaw in the final round, remarked that American architecture had reached the stage where it could develop and grow alongside that of Europe. First prize was awarded to the eminent French architect, Emile Bénard, but in the opinion of Belcher, implementation of this urbane scheme would afford a stimulus for departure among American designers. They would learn from his work just as Sir Christopher Wren had learned from the French over three centuries earlier.[45]

The American prizewinners had learned a great deal from the French already. At least one of the principals from each firm had attended the Ecole, most of them within the last decade.[46] Among the finalists, the Americans' work displayed the greatest debt to Prix de Rome schemes for large institutional complexes. They tended to rely on a grand and unbroken primary axis, flanked by buildings unrelenting in their symmetrical disposition, with a great auditorium, museum, or similar focal point at one end. Their compositions were simple, featuring expansive axial spaces more akin to Le Nôtre's gardens than to contemporary European urbanistic designs (Fig. 197). The order was direct, taut, and functional, with buildings arranged in a straight-forward manner and freed of the agitated details that marked late-nineteenth-century European classicism. The influence of the competition, and of the American designs in particular, was considerable. The ability of young American architects, none of whom had participated in the Chicago fair, to work with confidence on a large scale was clearly demonstrated. Their schemes helped to clarify and reinforce the formal qualities that were emerging as characteristics of American academic work. The competition helped to trigger a flurry of master plans for American universities and gave new impetus to civic projects.[47] Even the Hearst Plan itself was Americanized. Bénard's design was accepted by the regents as the official plan in December 1900;

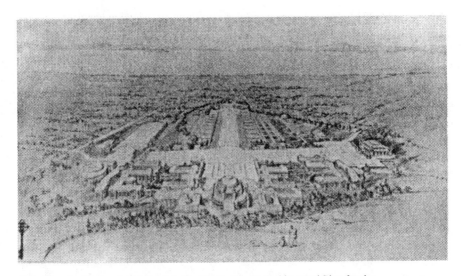

197. Howells, Stokes & Hornbostel. Phoebe A. Hearst Architectural Plan for the
University of California, Berkeley, 1899, competition entry.
(*International Competition*, p. 56)

however, the Frenchman rejected their offer to supervise its implementation. A year later, John Galen Howard, who had placed fourth, was
selected for the job. Thereafter, he introduced a series of major modifications that made the plan his own.[48]

By the time the competition ended, Bay Area residents had
developed great enthusiasm for the idea of a master plan. When the
jurors came to inspect the site and judge the final submissions, it was
treated as a major event in San Francisco, and the proposals were
lavishly displayed in the ferry depot. Before embarking to accept first
prize, Bénard was bestowed the Medal of the Legion of Honor and
was subsequently given a hero's reception in San Francisco. Belcher
remarked that this plan would surely fire the citizens of the city to
press for their own civic improvements. An elated Mayor Phelan
proclaimed that this was the dawn of a new era. As much as any event,
the competition may have impressed upon him and other local civic
leaders the importance of good design for such undertakings. The
sentiments of many leading citizens were expressed by a chronicler
who wrote:

The State faces its opportunity, and, standing before it, faces the world. We
have the chance to signalize in an enduring and monumental way our passing
into the second half-century of Statehood. Nothing would so clearly prove
our right to be here in the golden world, sheltered under the Sierra's gran-

250

deurs, and facing the Pacific Vastness, as to take from the architect's sheets this grand idea and make it a veritable utility. . . . Let California arise.[49]

Many San Francisco architects threw their support behind the plan, but not all of them were so receptive. Resentment was generated by the fact that Maybeck, who had designed almost nothing on his own, ignored all but one California colleague in orchestrating the competition. Some designers resented the foreign orientation and the abstractness of the program; others must have felt that they did not stand a chance in competing with the talent from the East Coast and Europe. Out of 105 entries, only three were from California firms—B.J.S. Cahill, Alexander Oakey, and Coxhead—and none of them placed.[50]

While Coxhead's proposal was not cited by the jury, it was among the most original designs for a large, monumental complex created in the late nineteenth century (Figs. 198–200). Rather than ordering the buildings along a central axis, Coxhead arranged them in layers that lap up the hillside. The main axis runs at right angles to these tiers and is at once underscored and denied by anchoring the major open spaces and buildings right across the center line. This complexity is furthered by a great curving street that laterally bisects the plan and forms the principal avenue. The arrangement's formality is most evident at the center, where longitudinal and curving axes intersect. From that juncture outward, the order becomes progressively

198. Coxhead & Coxhead. Hearst Plan, 1898, competition entry. (Courtesy John Beach)

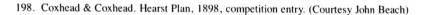

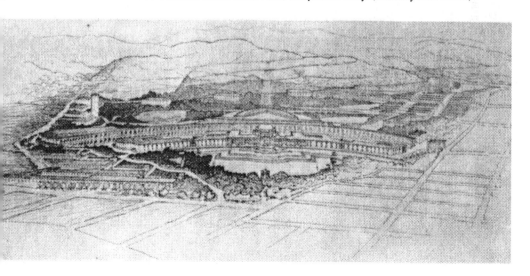

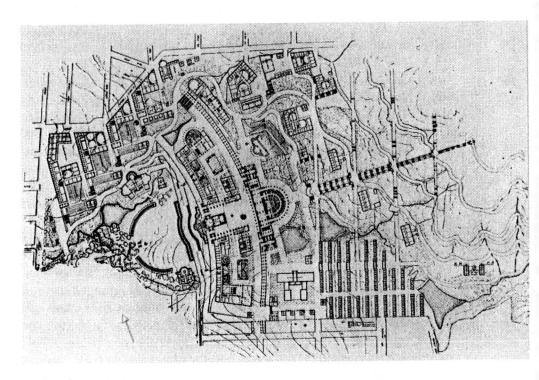

199. Coxhead & Coxhead. Hearst Plan, plan. (*Architect and Engineer,* September 1912, p. 98)

200. Coxhead & Coxhead. Hearst Plan, west elevation. (Courtesy John Beach)

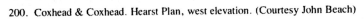

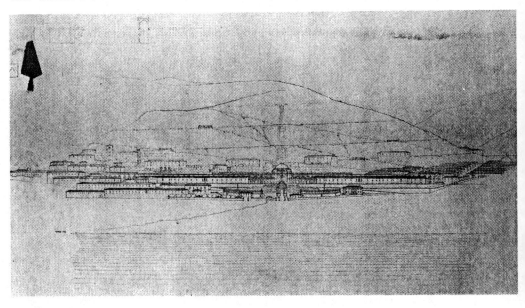

252

less rigid until it seems almost incidental at the periphery. The plan has no major entrance. The approaches are numerous, and each is carefully scaled to its immediate environs. Most of the entrances, especially those on the northern flank, appear to lead only into the compound of buildings they serve. Yet when these groups are passed, it becomes clear that they are part of a much more extensive network. Throughout his plan, Coxhead rejected virtually all the cardinal rules of composition to which the French subscribed. It is little wonder that his scheme was ignored.

Coxhead was as concerned with developing analogies between the imperial civilization of golden Rome and the upstart culture of the golden West as were Maybeck and the other competitors. Where Coxhead's scheme differs is in the specific sources he used and the way in which he interpreted them. The superimposition of dissimilar geometric orders, each emphatic in its own form yet combined to accommodate varied functions and topography, recalls reconstruction plans of antique Rome, particularly those done by Giovanni Battista Piranesi. Coxhead chose a crisp, linear rendering style similar to that used by Piranesi and later Neo-Classical architects, which was in pronounced contrast to the soft, seductive washes then popular. A section taken through the primary axis also reveals a Piranesian attitude toward Roman vaulted architecture, extravagant in its dimensions and decorative richness, yet boldly simple in its geometry and definition of space (Fig. 201). The enormous scale of the central compound, however, postdates Piranesi. Forming unbroken arcs that sweep across the campus, the main buildings are abstractions of Roman precedent enlarged to gigantic proportions, evoking the ideas, if not the forms,

201. Coxhead & Coxhead. Hearst Plan, section. (Courtesy John Beach)

of projects by French Neo-Classicists. The scheme, which is so intricate and diverse, also possesses a sublime grandeur which "even in ruins, would strike the beholder with wonder and rapture."

To balance these grand allusions, Coxhead drew from very different Italian sources for most of the building elevations, which are rendered with the utmost simplicity. The mural wall surfaces, presumably of stucco, and low-slung tile roofs, when combined with the pervasive irregularities of mass and arrangement, suggest the Italian hill towns that Coxhead had visited several years earlier. Such picturesque and informal ambience became popular in the region after 1910, but it was an anomaly around 1900 and stood in direct contrast to the embellishment of buildings in the winning schemes.[51] Coxhead's design was also different in the suggestion, in both the layout and appearance, of a community that has grown over time. The ensemble alludes to an ancient pantheon around which a town has grown since the Middle Ages, culminating in a lavish public works program during the nineteenth century. Coxhead was perhaps the only architect of his generation to apply this sense of age effectively to a large, formal plan.

This City of Learning is both an imperial city and a picturesque hill town, but it is also a city in a garden, remaining subservient to the landscape. Foliage plays an integral role throughout Coxhead's scheme and, like the plan and the buildings' character, receives varied treatment. Formal grounds abut many of the buildings in the lower section, sheltered from prevailing breezes and secluded from major circulation paths—tranquil places for thought and instruction, like the terrace gardens of a quattrocento villa. Dense groves of trees afford further seclusion, offsetting the sparse treatment and expansive wall surfaces of the buildings themselves. A cascade, which complements the scale of the central complex, extends along the primary axis up the hillside. This is among the few elements that Coxhead allowed to penetrate the upper slopes, which in most of the winning designs are broken into terraces and punctuated by monumental edifices. From below, the buildings stretch out to embrace their prospect, yet their organization converses with, rather than dominates, the setting and remains only an echo of the enframing hills (Fig. 202).

Following the natural contours of the terrain, leaving the hills open, providing shelter from the wind, employing foliage that would remain verdant the year round—all these devices express a sensitivity toward the particular qualities of the northern California landscape. The buildings would not only complement this setting in scale and color, their simple treatment would make them relatively inexpensive.

202. Coxhead & Coxhead. Hearst Plan, perspective sketch. (Courtesy John Beach)

However, one major drawback to Coxhead's scheme is that, despite its allusions, incremental construction would have been difficult with so many large buildings, and much of the design's meaning would be lost until the majority of its parts had been completed. The dormitories, arranged like barracks along one side, seem wholly incongruous with the rest of the plan. However, this was only a preliminary solution. In spite of its weak points, the design offers an elegant synthesis of the qualities with which Coxhead and Polk had experimented during the 1890s. It employs a variety of precedents, interpreting them and combining them in new ways, and it achieves a complex unity through opposition and contrast by using both formal and informal elements in its layout, buildings, and landscape plan. It is a fresh and poignant reflection of regional aspirations and the regional setting, but most importantly, it demonstrates that these qualities could be realized on a grand, urban scale.

The unique promise afforded by Coxhead's and Polk's civic designs went unfulfilled. Later monumental projects relied almost entirely on eastern models. But the cause of individual expression did not fade without a protest—from Polk, of course.

Initially, Polk reacted to the proposed competition at Berkeley with enthusiasm. While he disagreed with Maybeck's plans for an

255

open contest, he also derided those people who were against its international orientation:

All localism in the project will tend to render the results local in effect. A world-wide competition is commendable, and would be a just tribute to the liberality of our views, and the broadness of our aims. It would be a recognition of art, and art is universal.[52]

After the issuance of the program, however, Polk launched a raging attack. The elaborate procedure used to secure a design, Polk charged, was absurd, and so was the cost. Underlying his assault was an intense displeasure over the influence of the Ecole's ideology.

The teachings of the *Beaux-Arts* and the influence of its precepts have robbed endeavor of all individuality. Expression of character is minimized by artificial standards, arbitrarily set, and slavishly followed. Originality is suppressed and an art is made a profession. . . . Everything must be upon certain lines or it will not be recognized. Everything must be by rule and example, for if upon reference to the code, it does not conform, it will be regarded as unconstitutional, unacademic or not correct.

He continued:

It is doubtful whether any but the *Beaux-Arts* students or graduates . . . will be in the running in this competition, and certainly it is not in the hope that any but a *Beaux-Arts* man should be in at the death. The trustees have gone forth to seek mediocrity, and have made elaborate preparations to get it. The entire programme breathes the very air of the *Beaux-Arts*. Ideal expression or original conception of architecture suitable to California must lose its significance when poured through the academic sieve of the *Beaux-Arts*.

Polk considered the Ecole's direct influence to be inappropriate for the West Coast and fundamentally detrimental to the creative process. He was not challenging the school's emphasis on logical ordering of form and space, its partiality to the classical tradition, or its academic approach to understanding and working with the past, but he felt that the Ecole's method of instruction was by rigid, formularizing precedent and produced only "mediocrity." A few years earlier, he had praised the institution.[53] Now, having explored the classical language and formal modes of expression more fully, he joined the growing numbers of American architects who questioned the Ecole's infallibility. Indeed, his accusations are among the most scathing made at that time.

Those aspects of the Ecole that Polk criticized may well have been one of the reasons Coxhead's entry failed to place. Ironically, the design would have a significant influence on Maybeck's large classical schemes during the next two decades—in fact, a much greater influence than the more conventional winning designs. The Hearst competition demonstrated that even though Coxhead and Polk absorbed new ideas from the East Coast and Europe they did not simply reiterate current trends. Their approach found stimulus and support from what the world had to offer, but for the moment personal expression took precedence over any sense of obligation to the established norm.

IX

SCHWEINFURTH: The Cause of Regional Expression

I saw for the first time in the flesh, as it were, a roof of the genuine old Spanish tile—the very name of which is enough to make an architect's heart glow.

Imagine a long, low rambling pile of building of sturdy walls and naive distribution of voids and solids, once whitened but now stained and enriched with warm yellows and browns and greens and falling into almost unkempt decay, and crowned with the soft deep red of the hillocked tile lichened and weather beaten. . . . Behold the Mission!

John Galen Howard, letter to his mother, March 5, 1888

THE HEARST competition ranked as the most ambitious undertaking of the decade in the Bay Area's drive for cultural distinction. The event symbolized a growing desire to bring San Francisco and its environs into the orbit of great world centers. At the same time, local residents were displaying a new interest in and nostalgia for the provincial culture of Spanish America, which was part of their own heritage and added to California's distinctiveness. Many people who venerated the Spanish tradition saw California as an Eden, untarnished by the industrialized East, rather than as the ascendant center of American civilization.

During the 1890s, architecture became an important manifestation of this sentiment. San Francisco emerged as one of the first cities in the United States where regional expression was a conspicuous part of the academic movement.[1] Schweinfurth was the leading figure in this initial search for an architecture that would be closely identified with the state. His efforts won quick recognition. Many Bay Area residents took pleasure in notions of both worldly prominence and provincial quaintness; but unlike the rustic and classical ideals, these two ideas were not long destined for coexistence. By the turn of the century, Schweinfurth's cause had largely been rejected. Spanish culture had gained veneration as a segment of the past, but not as a contributor to the future.

258

The imprint of Spanish colonization had always been a conscious part of California's heritage. Americans who arrived in the state by the thousands only a few years after the end of Mexican rule held this legacy in arrogant disdain, and Hispanic culture experienced a swift decline. Even though the new inhabitants were eradicating vestiges of the past, they were also curious about what had occurred over the previous century and were concerned with offering a record of historic events. Detailed accounts of California's early days were published virtually from the inception of statehood in 1850.[2] Widespread sympathy for this colonial heritage began to coalesce in the 1870s, and over the next two decades sympathy was transformed into admiration. Like the wilderness, Hispanic culture belonged to the recent past and was threatened with extinction. To foster this sense of identity, both the memory and the image of that culture had to be perpetuated. Popular magazines, histories, novels, tourist guides, graphic representations by local artists, and eventually architecture all contributed to this process, which grew through the early twentieth century. In the rediscovery of a vanishing inheritance, much of the attention was focused on the Franciscan missions that had once reigned over the inland valleys near the California coast. These institutions were heralded as the most significant forms of Spanish settlement. They provided the best documentary record of the era, and what was left of the compounds themselves comprised the most conspicuous and picturesque tangible remains.

The enthusiasm expressed for the missions was nurtured by a romantic nostalgia for preindustrial society. As early as 1869, an article in the *American Church Review* delineated the characteristics with which the missions would generally become associated over the next decades.[3] The text depicted these compounds as outposts of civilization and as centers of culture, religious fervor, industriousness, and hospitality which had been created by humble men who endured great hardship and sacrifice to realize their objectives. Largely self-sufficient, the missions were portrayed as exemplary demonstrations of how spiritual and even material riches could be accrued without commercial exploitation. The Franciscans were seen as being "perhaps . . . the only settlers who came to a new country for purely disinterested motives." Their conduct was considered a striking contrast to the greed and lawlessness that marked American development of the region.[4]

Among the most influential literary works in generating a positive attitude toward Spanish California was Helen Hunt Jackson's

259

Ramona, published in 1884. One reviewer was quick to recognize that her thesis represented a significant shift in outlook:

Hitherto, fiction has treated California only as the seat of a new civilization. It has been delineated as the gold-digger's paradise, the adventurer's Eden, the speculator's El Dorado. "Ramona" pictures it as the Indian's lost inheritance and the Spaniard's desolated home.

Jackson's narrative of the devastation wrought by Americans offered a convincing argument that the early days of California were not only of historic interest, but a period that possessed principles of conduct and a simple, dignified way of life that contemporary society had lost. Moreover, the novel fostered the notion of compatibility between this life and the arid coastal valley landscape. The same review noted that

for the first time we see . . . what a wonderful setting the startling contrasts, fervid colors, and seemingly sterile aspects of California scenery constituted for a domestic life fashioned in harmony with them.[5]

Although the book scarcely mentioned the missions, it helped develop admiration for them. *Ramona* was fiction and the life it depicted was gone, but the derelict mission buildings still embodied the message.

These romantic associations and interest in the pastoral landscape led to a growing appreciation for the missions' physical characteristics. The *American Church Review*'s 1869 essay was again prophetic in its remarks: San Luis Rey generated "an air of beauty and magnificence"; and "there is not a fairer view in all Italy than that presented by the sunny plains of San Gabriel with the old mission buildings in their center."[6] By the 1880s, the missions, with their bold forms and picturesque silhouettes, intensified by the expansive terrain and the brilliant California sun, came to be seen as an architecture of "a superior order." They imparted a sense of age, being "among the few monuments of a country that has nothing very old." To many people, this quality was enhanced by the semiruinous condition of most of the buildings. Jackson stated that this "architecture [is] at once so simple and harmonious that, even in ruins, it is . . . the grandest in America"; and "the interior [of San Carlos Borromeo] does not yield, as a picture of sentimental ruin, to Muckross Abbey, or to any broken temple of the Roman Campagna." The interest in the missions' age was underscored by historian Frank Blackmar, who devoted a chapter to discussing their "Roman" origins in his influential study, *Spanish*

Institutions in the Southwest (1891). Early Spanish buildings, he asserted, were a mixture of ancient Roman (he was no doubt referring to Romanesque) and Moorish elements: "This primitive architecture was transplanted to America unmodified by the . . . Gothic" and there it "remains in its purest form."[7]

This erroneous lineage was matched by an equally distorted notion that the architecture of the missions was indigenous to California. Charles Shinn, a writer dedicated to promoting the state's Spanish heritage, believed that

one of the great charms of the missions is the frank simplicity everywhere visible in the work of the builders. They seem to have remembered enough of the architecture of Spain and Mexico to give them suggestions of value, and to have forgotten or ignored enough to have made their work original and fascinating.[8]

Shinn, and soon many other people, saw the missions' massive mural wall surfaces punctuated by thick buttresses and arcades, as well as their use of adobe bricks, rough plaster, and burnt clay roof tiles, as a direct expression of local conditions. If the results looked crude, they were nevertheless admired as having been wrought from the land and made with care and devotion. The missions' "honest" simplicity was felt to embody the Franciscans' cause itself.

Many of these attributes were recognized in the region's early domestic architecture as well. Descriptive accounts of ranch houses in California and Mexico published in the 1880s bolstered the image portrayed in *Ramona* of these dwellings as centers of a relaxed, accommodating life in harmony with nature. As early as 1883, one writer suggested that the hacienda should serve as a model for new California residences. Shinn praised the old houses' relationship to the land and argued that they afforded as vivid a picture of pastoral California as did the missions.[9] The appeal of Spanish-American architecture was enhanced by the proximity of many examples to towns such as Monterey, Santa Barbara, and Pasadena, which had become winter resorts in the 1880s. During the previous decade, accounts depicted these old Spanish quarters in condescending terms; a few years later, descriptions offered little but praise. Adobe houses in Monterey even became fashionable for use as winter cottages.[10]

Architects began to take note of California's Hispanic buildings only after popular interest in the subject was widespread. The

203. John Galen Howard. Sketch of a house in southern California, 1888.
(CED Docments Collection)

designers who were initially attracted to this work were for the most part young immigrants from the East and Midwest who were familiar with academic precepts. In the mid–1880s Charles Coolidge, the partner in charge of the buildings at Stanford University, is said to have admired mission architecture, but had little chance to examine it firsthand and made no overt reference to this precedent of the campus.[11] The earliest documented instance of architects studying such work in the field occurred in 1887–1888 when John Galen Howard (who had hoped to work on the Stanford design), Polk, and several other draftsmen in Los Angeles took weekend sketching trips throughout the area. Howard's surviving sketches emphasize picturesqueness and primitive simplicity—attributes that had appealed to colleagues looking at European and New England vernacular buildings over the past decade (Fig. 203).[12] The new concerns for design that expressed local conditions and for broadening the range of precedent made early California architecture seem a logical source for examination. While making forays into the countryside, both Howard and Polk experimented with references to regional work in schematic conceptions. Polk's Imaginary Mission Church (1887) is the first known design to be directly fashioned after these buildings (Fig. 204).

Los Angeles was a natural center for this activity, since the surrounding area was among the most richly endowed with Spanish-American buildings. By the early 1890s, however, the focus of interest had shifted to San Francisco. Polk sparked an appreciation for the missions among practitioners there. His short-lived *Architectural News* was the first professional magazine to publish an article on these buildings, and he may have coauthored a more extensive essay about the missions serialized in ten issues of the *California Architect* for 1891.[13] Polk's idea for the 1900 world's fair was to have a vast building with interior courtyards, a notion inspired by the mission compounds and their Spanish antecedents. He was also among the first architects to urge that the missions serve as a source for the design of the California Building at the Columbian Exposition.[14] A growing number of San Franciscans shared Polk's view. Further encouragement came from the Exposition's supervising architect, Daniel Burnham, who suggested that all southwestern states look to regional Spanish architecture for their buildings. By June 1891, members of the state committee in charge of California's exhibit indicated their partiality to the idea. When the competition for the building was formally announced seven months later, the program stipulated that the design be of the "Mission and Moorish type."[15] A new regional mode was inaugurated.

The project was unusually important to Californians. It provided the first opportunity for the state to assemble a major display of its

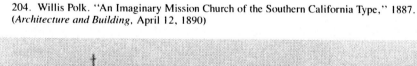

204. Willis Polk. "An Imaginary Mission Church of the Southern California Type," 1887. (*Architecture and Building*, April 12, 1890)

205. A. Page Brown. California Building, World's Columbian Exposition, Chicago, 1892–1893; demolished 1893. (*Shepp's World's Fair Photographed*, p. 351)

achievements and potential before the rest of the country. Many citizens, self-conscious about California's newness and lingering reputation as a frontier culture, saw the event as an occasion for lavish display of material progress. The second-largest state pavilion, occupying a choice site, it would stand as a unique symbol of abundant resources and promise. Previously, architects had refrained from making reference to the missions in actual projects, but now circumstances encouraged them to experiment. The competition, open to all practitioners in the state, drew entries from twenty-five firms, twenty-one of which were from San Francisco.[16] Page Brown emerged the winner. For the next several years, he and Schweinfurth would play the most conspicuous and influential role in championing the use of Hispanic precedent to create designs that would be seen as distinct to California.

A principal reason that Brown's entry was chosen may have been that it embodied the aspirations of the committee in a very literal manner. California's missions became the exterior display, just as California's products comprised the interior exhibition (Fig. 205). Grafted onto a five-part composition, then common to large public

264

buildings, was an array of elements representing the largest and best preserved of the mission compounds: San Carlos, San Antonio, Santa Barbara, and San Luis Rey. The scheme incorporated the full range of mission motifs: domed bell towers, scalloped gable ends, quatrefoil windows, round-arch arcades, mural wall surfaces finished in stucco, and low-pitch roofs covered with red clay tiles. This instant resurrection of a vocabulary that had been ignored for so long and that few people had ever seen firsthand made the California Building a great novelty and contributed to the widespread praise it received. A San Francisco critic pronounced the design to be "as typically Californian as a pyramid would be typically Egyptian or a pagoda typically Chinese. It reproduces the oldest buildings in the state which are found nowhere else." To some observers, this vocabulary seemed even more "regional" than forms associated with other places. The same review concluded:

We do not recall any other American State which can present a sample of typical architecture comparable to this. There will be New England school-houses and Western log cabins and Southern villas and the like, but there will be no such distinctive architecture as the California State building.

Scarcely less praise came from other parts of the country. Daniel Burnham called Brown's design a very scholarly production. Newspapers in New York and Chicago printed enthusiastic accounts. The unanimous sentiment of the architectural press was summarized by Montgomery Schuyler, who declared that the pavilion was "one of the noteworthy ornaments of the fair."[17] The California Building not only served as a catalyst for those people interested in creating a distinct regional mode, but as a paradigm for that mode, which would soon be called the Mission Style.

All available evidence suggests that Schweinfurth was responsible for the California Building's design and was the primary force behind redirecting Brown's office toward regional expression. Numerous contemporary accounts emphasized that the interest in using Hispanic precedent was his and credit him with creating many of the firm's most notable works in this vein. Surely Brown contributed to the process; had he not been sympathetic, he would never have allowed such efforts to become a central thrust for the office. Comparison of Schweinfurth's work for Brown and the schemes he developed independently indicate that Brown retained some control over design. Yet Schweinfurth, who was more prone to experimentation, no doubt played the dominant role.[18] He drew from a wide variety of Hispanic and vaguely related sources, but almost immediately the mission motives, which had given the firm so much recognition, were discarded.

Several explanations can be offered as to why Brown and Schweinfurth abruptly rejected the missions as a primary influence. For all its novelty, the California Building remained a collection of fragments, out of scale and out of context. Rather than unifying these references, the building's classical parti made them seem incongruous as a whole. The design also demonstrated the difficulties in adapting church forms. Elements such as the bell tower and the scalloped gable end carried ecclesiastical associations that proponents of the academic movement considered inappropriate to most contemporary building programs. Furthermore, the missions comprised but a small and provincial segment of the classical tradition in Spanish architecture. Relying on a handful of examples, peculiar to a single region and to a brief span of time, would inhibit the development of meaningful expression as it was then perceived. Many examples of the Mission Style did, in fact, have little relation to their programmatic conditions. After the turn of the century, Boston architect Frank Chouteau Brown lamented that the mode was no more than "a wave of petty 'fashion' that is endeavoring to misapply and misquote in every possible way the details of this simple 'Mission' architecture, debasing them to the petty purpose of an outside covering." Likewise, Herbert Croly reminded Californians that "the attempts which have hitherto been made to adopt the peculiarities of the Mission style to the design of contemporary American houses have been almost wholly grievous in their effects."[19] However, some architects, critics, and citizens remained intrigued with the possibilities for expression that the missions could provide. By the late 1890s, the mode had become especially favored in southern California, where it was used as an instrument to symbolize, and indeed create, a sense of regional identity.[20]

Brown and Schweinfurth had the same general objective, but they looked abroad for ideas through which to manifest it. Unlike southern California, the Bay Area had few examples of Hispanic architecture left, which facilitated the introduction of analogous substitute images. Brown and Schweinfurth also looked to precedents that were seldom, if ever, employed in other parts of the United States at that time. These factors combined to make their buildings seem unique and special to their region. As with Carrère & Hastings's Ponce de Leon Hotel, Brown and Schweinfurth introduced a spectrum of historical references that alluded to the local heritage without having direct ties.

266

206. A. Page Brown. Atkinson Building, San Francisco, 1892; burned 1906. (*American Architect*, September 30, 1893)

The architects' first work of this order was a small commercial block in San Francisco designed for Katherine Atkinson only a few months after the California Building (Fig. 206). The facade has a rigorous symmetry and bold scale that create an imposing effect, despite the modest dimensions. The abstract form evident here is even more pronounced in the original scheme for the San Francisco Polyclinic (1893), where the elements are tightly composed as overlapping rectangles and enframed by a wide surrounding wall (Fig. 207). The simple geometric order parallels the best contemporary work of Frank Lloyd Wright, but here the imagery is deliberately historicizing. Configuration, scale, and materials were inspired by the traditional small houses and shops that line the streets of numerous Spanish cities. Yet the Atkinson Building and Polyclinic also exhibit elaborate classical details seldom found on their vernacular prototypes. The interplay

207. A. Page Brown. San Francisco Polyclinic, San Francisco, 1893–1894; burned 1906. Preliminary design. Drawing probably by Schweinfurth. (*American Architect*, July 21, 1894)

between rich decoration and strong geometric forms fosters a conspicuous, rather than an unobtrusive, urbanistic role for both of these designs. In sharp contrast to their Victorian neighbors and to the character of the city as a whole, with gleaming wall surfaces of cement and white sand, the two buildings were seen as harbingers of a transformation. Brown and Schweinfurth envisioned that San Francisco might one day appear like a sun-drenched city along the Mediterranean coast—a light, airy collage of simple and pristine forms.[21]

These ideas were reflected also in the architects' urban residential projects. A group of speculative houses commissioned by William Crocker in 1892 for a site adjacent to his residence on Nob Hill was regarded at once as a model for future domestic work in the city. Two years later a more polished scheme was developed for George Roe, president of the Edison Power and Light Company, in Presidio Heights (Fig. 208). As with Coxhead's and Polk's rustic city houses, vernacular buildings provided the precedent; however, here the sources are mostly rural, taking the form of ideal Spanish and Italian farmhouses, formalized by symmetrical compositions and ornate embellishments and transposed to an urban setting. No significant differences existed between this work and the architects' dwellings for suburban areas.[22]

These designs emanating from Brown's office reflected a new attitude toward Spanish architecture. Until the mid-1880s, the prevailing opinion among architects was that work in Spain since the Middle Ages had been decadent. The more inclusive interest in the past generated by the academic movement dispelled this prejudice and resulted in a flurry of books and articles on classical, as well as medieval, Spanish buildings. The *American Architect* had nothing but praise for the most ambitious of these studies, Max Junghändel's *Die baukunst Spaniens* (1889–1898), proclaiming it to be an essential reference

208. A. Page Brown. George Roe house, San Francisco, 1894, project.
(Courtesy Sheila Mack)

209. Julius Schweinfurth.
Sketch of a house in
Seville, ca. 1886.
(Northeastern University,
courtesy Wheaton Holden)

work. Andrew Prentice's *Renaissance Architecture and Ornament in Spain* (1893) reportedly "produced . . . a sensation among students" in England when it appeared and was scarcely less popular in the United States.[23] But prior to the mid-1890s, this budding interest had little effect on actual work: the St. Augustine buildings by Carrère & Hastings were anomalies. The designs that Brown and Schweinfurth created were not only unconventional in their use of Spanish classical references but also in their focus on vernacular examples. Most published material on Spain then available concentrated on major buildings. To obtain adequate pictorial information, Schweinfurth may well have relied on sketches, and possibly on purchased prints and photographs, from his brother Julius, who had traveled to the Iberian peninsula several years earlier (Fig. 209).

Brown and Schweinfurth turned to entirely different Spanish precedents in their Midwinter fair designs. While Polk believed that a

270

210. A. Page Brown. Administration Building, California Midwinter International Exposition, San Francisco, 1893; demolished 1894. (Bancroft Library)

unified classical ensemble was the only appropriate form for the exposition, his two rivals sought the ambience of a great bazaar, using Moorish references to evoke the exoticism with which Spain had long been popularly identified. Their Administration Building drips with oversized ornament and is more of a storybook dream than a reflection of Islam's legacy (Fig. 210). Like the California Building in Chicago, the design employs historical references naively, paying little respect to context. The architects appear to have been concerned with imagery

271

for its own sake rather than with developing an integral relationship between appearance, form, and use.[24] Such projects were valuable to Schweinfurth's development, however, for they allowed him to study exotic forms of expression that would soon be tamed and integrated with other qualities.

Equally important to this formative process were two designs that introduced non-European references. The Palermo Hotel (1892) was planned for a model agricultural community situated in a corner of the hot Sacramento Valley (Fig. 211). It is perhaps the earliest project consciously designed to evoke forms found in the so-called Monterey Colonial houses and, closer by, in Mariano Vallejo's enormous hacienda begun in 1836 on the Rancho Petaluma. While the Monterey examples were as American as they were Spanish in origin, and Vallejo's residence was unusual among California haciendas, the imposing, low-slung mass, made grand with porches at each level, would soon become the archetypal image of Hispanic dwellings on the West Coast.[25] Given the corresponding nostalgia for these houses as oases of hospitality and convivial living in a remote, pastoral landscape, the Palermo Hotel's allusions no doubt seemed singularly appropriate. Yet the references are also generalized. Two-tier porches were common to hotels constructed in different parts of the country over the past several decades. Furthermore, the porches' configuration and classical details recall antebellum plantation houses in the Deep South. Thus, the references are both specific and vague, emphasizing

211. A. Page Brown. Palermo Hotel, Palermo, 1892; no longer standing. (Courtesy Sheila Mack)

212. A. Page Brown. Church of the New Jerusalem, San Francisco, 1894.
(Courtesy George Livermore)

local traditions and a degree of commonality in hotels and in the traditional architecture found in warm climates across the country.

Allusions were developed in a more abstract fashion for the Church of the New Jerusalem in San Francisco (1894–1895), one of the last designs Schweinfurth produced in Brown's office (Fig. 212). The exterior suggests several precedents; for example, the low-slung main block and ell might refer to early California ranch houses, and the arcaded entry might be derived from the missions. Contemporary accounts usually described the building in these terms.[26] However, the imagery is no less evocative of vernacular building forms in northern Spain and Italy, and only the attached campanile has a clear lineage. It is a rather literal interpretation of Lombard Romanesque design, but it is placed against the least historicizing part of the building—where brick piers flank metal-frame windows, conveying the appearance of a small industrial building. The sanctuary interior further resists a specific referential framework. No one period, place, or function comes to

273

213. Church of the New Jerusalem, sanctuary. (Courtesy Mrs. Othmar Tobisch)

214. Church of the New Jerusalem, sanctuary. (Courtesy Mrs. Othmar Tobisch)

mind so much as an image of *the* rustic hall or *the* primitive hut (Figs. 213, 214).

The client was Joseph Worcester, who has often been credited with having a major role in the design. Worcester's aesthetic preferences were reflected in the building's unobtrusive rustic character, and he may also have stipulated the incorporation of certain features. But his primary contribution was probably general ideas about what the design should be. In this respect, his attitude toward architecture may have had a greater effect on Schweinfurth than it did on Coxhead and Polk. Here, and in many of the architect's later works, a primitive simplicity appears that is a more direct embodiment of Worcester's concepts.

There is one aspect of the building that the ever-serious, self-effacing pastor surely did not suggest. Aside from the campanile, the building resembles an artists' club far more than it does a church. The combination of old vernacular and new utilitarian elements; the placement of the entrance at the rear, as if it were on an alley; the exposed, rough-hewn timberwork; board-and-batten wainscoting; landscape murals; folksy chairs (instead of pews); and dominating clinker-brick fireplace all contribute to a setting suggestive of the back rooms and lofts artists were fond of adapting into fraternal halls around the turn of the century. The resemblance to Wilson Eyre's Mask and Wig Club in Philadelphia, converted from a stable in the same year, is striking (Fig. 215).[27]

The allusion to an artists' club may well have been intentional. Worcester's parish served as an important, albeit unofficial, meeting ground for local artists and intellectuals, most of whom had little interest in Swedenborgian doctrine. The pastor's gospel of simplicity and harmony between art and nature, combined with his magnetic presence, were the generating forces. The church itself was a cooperative venture to which William Keith, Bruce Porter, and Bernard Maybeck all contributed their services.[28] More than any other building, it became a center for the region's young creative figures. The design was also a pivotal work in Schweinfurth's career, integrating his interest in regional expression with a taste for primitive rusticity inspired by Worcester. The experience had a pronounced effect on his pursuit of a distinctively Californian architecture.

Several months before the church was designed, Schweinfurth had sought to establish his own practice for the third time. The anticipated work never materialized, necessitating a temporary return to Brown's office.[29] Although he enjoyed considerable freedom there, the

215. Wilson Eyre. Mask and Wig Club, Philadelphia, 1894, 1901.
(*House and Garden*, April 1904, p. 170)

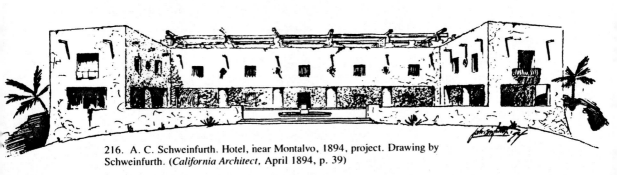

216. A. C. Schweinfurth. Hotel, near Montalvo, 1894, project. Drawing by
Schweinfurth. (*California Architect*, April 1894, p. 39)

two men may have had some serious disagreements over design
matters—reputedly Brown felt that the Church of the New Jerusalem
was not "architecture." At the same time Schweinfurth was beginning
to develop a strong personal style, producing work markedly different
from what he had done for Brown. An independent project for a hotel
near Montalvo, overlooking the southern California coast (1894), shows
his progress (Fig. 216). The sense of order and simplicity conveyed in
this design is far stronger than in any previous work. Schweinfurth
may have looked to such disparate sources as Moorish citadels, colon-

naded buildings in provincial Spanish towns, and early California courtyard houses, but the specific precedents are difficult to decipher, for they have been combined and abstracted into something quite new. In reaching this synthesis, the pueblos of New Mexico, as much as any Hispanic legacy, helped Schweinfurth to forge a bond between European and American cultures, regional expression and cultivated rusticity, exoticism and elemental simplicity.

Pueblo architecture carried many of the same associations and physical characteristics of the missions and other Spanish buildings in the Southwest. Popular interest in Pueblo Indian culture arose not long after that in the missions, with numerous articles on the subject appearing by the 1880s. Even though Pueblo culture still existed, little was known about its origins and history. Furthermore, the ways of these people differed far more from those of contemporary Western society than had the customs of Spanish settlers. Such factors contributed to the highly romantic view Anglo-Americans, and Californians in particular, had of New Mexico. Charles Fletcher Lummis, whose *Land of Poco Tiempo* (1893) was one of the most influential books in popularizing Pueblo culture, wrote:

Sun, silence, and adobe—that is New Mexico. . . . It is the Great American Mystery . . . the United States which is *not* the United States. . . . The opiate of the sun soothes to rest, the adobe is made to lean against. . . . Let us not hasten—mañana will do.

New Mexico is the anomaly of the Republic . . . a century older in European civilization than the rest, and several centuries older still in a happier semi-civilization of its own. It had its little walled cities . . . before Columbus had grand-parents-to-be; and has them yet.

Picturesque is a tame word for it. It is a picture, a romance, a dream all in one . . . a land where distance is lost, and the eye is a liar . . . the heart of Africa beating against the ribs of the Rockies.[30]

Lummis and other writers depicted the Pueblo Indians as the "most enlightened" native Americans, living in a timeless world with customs that had endured for centuries. These people were portrayed as industrious farmers and skilled craftsmen, fervently religious and lovers of peace and tranquility. Comparisons with the greed and fast-changing pace the Yankee had brought to the West were frequent.

Pueblo architecture was seen as an enduring monument to the primitive yet noble ways of its inhabitants. Even before the California missions, these adobe structures became the subject of first-hand study among architects. Around 1882 Bostonian Sylvester Baxter made an extensive tour of the state. Upon his return, he reported to fellow members of the Boston Society of Architects—Schweinfurth may well have been among them—that the pueblos afforded an important lesson in the "composition and the arrangement of great masses." Stanford White journeyed to New Mexico at about the same time and was similarly impressed with what he saw. In 1890, an article in the *American Architect* pronounced that no building in the world could be more picturesque than the terraced adobe of the pueblos (Fig. 217). Two years later a California writer went so far as to proclaim: "What castle on the Rhine . . . possesses the interest of . . . the famous ruins of New Mexico?" He added that "these ruins . . . are far more interesting than many in Europe and are the stepping stones that connect the present with the earliest days of American history."[31] The pueblos became venerated as the original American architecture, the oldest, most indigenous landmarks to be found in the country.

217. Taos Pueblo, Taos, New Mexico. (Lewis Morgan, *Houses and House-Life of American Aborigines*, facing p. 144)

The mounting admiration for the pueblos, like that for the missions, brought with it a certain contradiction. If these complexes were regarded as characteristically American buildings, they also seemed to represent the attributes of many cultures. Pueblo Indian ways were compared with those of the oldest civilizations of Central America, the Mediterranean, and the Near East. The pueblos were not only older than the adobe buildings of Spanish California, they *looked* more like their antique counterparts abroad. Probably no designer interested in New Mexico would have missed the implications of a lengthy article published in the *American Architect* in 1892. The author asserted that adobe and other forms of mud construction were as ancient a method of building for southern climates as was timber construction for northern regions; crude mud architecture ranked with the primitive hut as the ancestor of all modern building. He stressed the universality of the material and emphasized its possibilities for present-day application, concluding that California seemed to be an ideal place for the practice to be revived.[32] Even though Schweinfurth, and most of his West Coast colleagues, avoided adobe construction for practical reasons, he did cultivate the appearance of adobe as found in the pueblos for both formal and associational purposes.[33]

The opportunity for Schweinfurth to realize his ideas came from the flamboyant newspaperman William Randolph Hearst. In 1894, Hearst commissioned Brown to remodel his Sausalito residence. The project was abandoned, but a few months later Hearst retained Schweinfurth alone to design a building for the Childrens' Hospital, which was being funded by the *San Francisco Examiner.* Soon thereafter, Hearst gave his new architect a much more important assignment: the creation of a large country house. The site was on a ranch that had been acquired by his father, located in a remote section of Alameda County that had experienced little change over the past hundred years. Hearst was perhaps the first Californian who consciously revived the idea of erecting a "hacienda" that would sit amid the pastoral landscape and carry no vestiges of formal urban life. The nearest neighbors, Schweinfurth emphasized, were Mexican Indians who occupied a small settlement directly across the valley. Echoing Lummis, the architect hoped that "everything about the design would express the land of *poco tiempo* . . . where the feeling of Mañana, Mañana could be cultivated" and that everything might be carried out with "absolute simplicity." Hearst wanted a house that was "totally different in every way from the ordinary country home," and that is precisely what he got.[34]

218. A. C. Schweinfurth. Hacienda del Pozo de Verona, William Randolph Hearst-Phoebe Apperson Hearst house, near Sunol, 1895–1896; burned 1969. (Barr Ferree, *American Estates and Gardens*, p. 213)

219. Poblet Monastery, Catalonia, Spain. (Alexandre de Laborde, *Voyage pittoresque et historique de l'Espagne* I:LXXIII)

280

The Hacienda del Pozo de Verona, as it was called, incorporates many of the Hispanic and other references Schweinfurth had been experimenting with during the past four years (Fig. 218). A dichotomy in appearance and associations exists between the imposing character of a great institution and the relaxed, inviting atmosphere of a domestic retreat—two aspects evident in the client's personality. The house was often described as a Spanish or Mexican hacienda; however, its form and image are not derived from any obvious sources. Set in splendid isolation, the complex is sited like many of the missions, commanding a prospect well above the valley yet sufficiently low on the slope to be enframed by the hills above. From the approach its multitowered silhouette resembles that of a medieval Spanish monastery, underscoring its cherished seclusion (Fig. 219). Even close up, the entrance front appears to be larger than its actual size (Fig. 220). Large mural wall surfaces punctured by diminutive windows, together with the severe stepped form of the main block and walls that are sheer on one side and terraced on the other, recall the pueblos. A few conspicuous pieces of delicate wrought ironwork, a playful ghost of the interior stairs, and a richly foliated court mitigate this austerity.

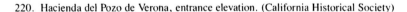

220. Hacienda del Pozo de Verona, entrance elevation. (California Historical Society)

221. Hacienda del Pozo de Verona, east elevation. (Bancroft Library)

222. Pergola at Amalfi, Italy. Late nineteenth-century photograph in a scrapbook compiled by Bernard Maybeck. (CED Documents Collection)

Facing east, the other principal elevation is almost entirely consumed by outdoor living spaces bedecked with striped awnings, potted plants, and vines. Pergolas, inspired by gardens along the Italian Riviera, are placed on all levels of the house itself as an integral part of its form (Figs. 221, 222). The Hacienda is also a place of tranquility and pleasure, romantically portrayed as if it were a vision out of *The Arabian Nights*. Practical considerations played a major role as well. The extensive wall surfaces help to shelter the indoors from the valley's hot climate, while the porches, terraces, and covered walkways catch prevailing breezes and provide panoramic vistas of the landscape.

The original plan, somewhat altered during construction, is also unorthodox (Fig. 223).[35] Following a traditional Hispanic-American practice, the court serves as a principal organizing element from which the building is entered and onto which many of the rooms open. The corridors are outside, circumscribing the court, and the depth of the house is thus limited to one room. Besides facilitating cross-ventilation, this arrangement was ideal for a client who anticipated having large numbers of visitors. With the guest rooms placed around the court away from the main portion of the house, the plan afforded privacy and created an inward-looking compound that provided a sense of community. The idea was based on the arrangements of early California courtyard houses, which were appreciated for their close relationship with nature and conduciveness to outdoor living. Schweinfurth's design established an influential precedent for the resurrection of this plan type.[36]

The Hacienda's layout also possesses a rigorous order through the use of axial symmetry that was entirely foreign to Spanish- and Mexican-American residences. The inspiration probably came from Spanish colonial military outposts (Fig. 224). San Francisco's presidio had not only been one of the most important in California, but it was considered a symbol of the region's first organized settlement, the early center of local government, and the institution that controlled the division of surrounding land.[37] The Hacienda's plan resembles the presidio not only in form but also in hierarchy, with the main block on axis with the gate and progressively less important components extending to either side. By using this organization, Schweinfurth was able to give vernacular imagery a sense of order without introducing formal or urban allusions.

On the inside, the dichotomy between openness and enclosure that characterizes the exterior is developed in a different manner. The rooms have a cavernous quality resulting from small windows, low

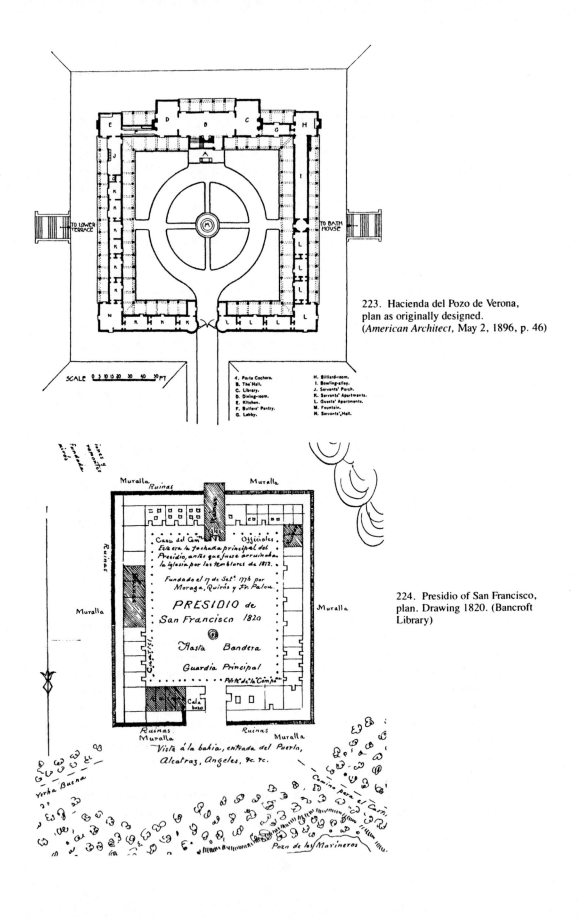

223. Hacienda del Pozo de Verona,
plan as originally designed.
(*American Architect,* May 2, 1896, p. 46)

SCALE 0 5 10 15 20 30 40 50 FT

A. Porte Cochere.
B. The Hall.
C. Library.
D. Dining-room.
E. Kitchen.
F. Butlers' Pantry.
G. Lobby.

H. Billiard-room.
I. Bowling-alley.
J. Servants' Porch.
K. Servants' Apartments.
L. Guests' Apartments.
M. Fountain.
N. Servants' Hall.

224. Presidio of San Francisco,
plan. Drawing 1820. (Bancroft
Library)

225. Hacienda del Pozo de Verona, hall. (California Historical Society)

ceilings covered with a forest of boxed beams, and a few massive elements such as the hall fireplace (Fig. 225). The generous dimensions of the main spaces, their arrangement *en filade* with wide connecting thresholds, and their pervasive horizontality afford a sense of expansiveness from within. The total effect was to have been both sumptuous and primitive. A contrast with the elaborate Spanish Renaissance paneling and furniture that Hearst had requested would have been afforded by the deliberately crude workmanship of the building fabric and by the placement of Indian pottery, baskets, and rugs. The rooms were both finished and furnished in a more elegant fashion, however, for Hearst was never able to occupy the house he had commissioned.

The property the Hacienda was built on was not Hearst's, but was owned by his mother, Phoebe, who planned to develop the ranch into a farm for orphans. Hearst initiated his project in secrecy and began construction while his mother was away. By the time she heard about her son's covert deed and was able to return to the West Coast, building had reached an advanced stage. Infuriated, Phoebe Hearst appropriated the house. The newspaperman's initial attempt to fulfill his architectural dreams was usurped at the last moment. The resulting frustration lasted for over twenty years. Not until after his mother's death in 1919 would the opportunity to commission a grand design arise again, this time with the compound at San Simeon.[38]

Fortunately, Phoebe Hearst retained Schweinfurth to complete the Hacienda. If the interior changes represented a compromise of the original idea, the additions improved the overall design. These appendages, a music room and service quarters, are separate buildings placed laterally on either side of the main block, leaving its pristine geometry intact. The two new units are picturesquely composed, offering a counterpoint to the original building's symmetry. These wings also reinforce the secondary axis which, following the topography, extends the house into the landscape while accentuating its image as a grand institutional compound. Under Phoebe Hearst, the house indeed became something of an institution. As the nerve center for her extensive philanthropic activities, it hosted dozens of prominent artists, writers, educators, and civic leaders from across the country. In its function as well as in its design, the Hacienda offered a symbol of California's energy and promise.

The Hacienda encompasses an extraordinary range of historical references that were important contributors to the design process, but not to the product as it was intended to be perceived. As with the Church of the New Jerusalem and the Montalvo hotel, the allusions here are imprecise. Schweinfurth sought to forge a link with Hispanic culture by creating a feeling rather than through overt references to specific examples. Like the best Shingle Style work, the Hacienda represents a sophisticated synthesis of things past and things new. It is a defiance of convention, a declaration of California's special qualities, just as the Shingle Style, in breaking with English Queen Anne, served conditions that were distinctly American. In both cases, reference to vernacular traditions was also a major objective, so that the results were psychologically as well as functionally accommodating. Schweinfurth described his manner as "Provincial Spanish Renaissance." He did not mean a style, but a range of expression that he believed to be the most appropriate to California.[39]

The headquarters designed for Hearst's *San Francisco Exam-*

226. A. C. Schweinfurth. Examiner Building, San Francisco, 1897–1898; burned 1906. Drawing by D. A. Gregg. (*American Architect*, February 19, 1898)

227. Joseph Pennell. Etching of Piazza di Mercato Vecchio, Florence. (William Dean Howells, *Tuscan Cities*, p. 47)

iner in 1897 was intended to be as important a statement of what a California office building should be as the Hacienda was for the California country house (Fig. 226). In contrast to the image held by many local colleagues, Schweinfurth maintained that the skyscrapers of eastern metropolises, with their tall, severe granite facades, were unsuited to the West Coast, where the climate was gentler, the pace less hectic, and the setting more provincial.[40] His response was a building swathed in rough-troweled, cream-colored stucco; crude Plateresque ornament; loggias festooned with foliage; and a pitched roof of red tiles—all devices to capture the spirit of intimately scaled southern European cities (Fig. 227). At the same time, this design is more conventional than the Hacienda, with a tripartite composition and an arrangement of details by then common to American office buildings. Schweinfurth probably saw little reason for a more radical departure because of the major advances that had occurred in the design of this building type over the past decade. Moreover, the constricted site and demanding economic conditions inherent in large commercial work precluded the degree of experimentation that was often possible in residences.

The Examiner Building also differs from the Hacienda in its use of historical references. Here the details have a clear lineage, and the sources, including the Palace of Monterey in Salamanca and the Mission San José in San Antonio, Texas, can be readily identified. Again, the context is key to understanding Schweinfurth's solution. Most practitioners of academic eclecticism regarded precise references to historical precedent to be appropriate in a major urban building, just as loosely defined vernacular references were suitable to an informal country house.[41] Schweinfurth was neither seeking the unconventional for its own sake nor developing a single mode of expression. In this respect he adhered to the eclectic mainstream by creating designs of varied character according to the circumstances of each project.

Schweinfurth's work received considerable attention at both the regional and national levels. No other San Francisco architect of his generation enjoyed so much favorable coverage in professional journals. After working on his own for only few years, he was acquiring a solid reputation. When he embarked on an extensive European tour in 1898, his success in the profession seemed assured. To close his office under these positive circumstances in order to study buildings abroad for two years was an unusual, perhaps unprecedented, step. Schweinfurth's decision reveals that however much he sought to develop a regional architecture, he wanted to do so with a broad conceptual base. Tragically, he died of pneumonia in 1900 soon after returning to

288

the United States.[42] Had he lived to resume practice, his work might have become more cosmopolitan. As it was, the appeal of his "Provincial Spanish Renaissance" in northern California was on the wane as the new century began.

A principal reason for this change in attitude may have been the war with Spain. Adopting the architecture of a country whose defeat was seen as a signifier of American ascendency as a world power would have been particularly ironic in San Francisco, where residents now coveted the attainment of a dominant cultural position. No such thoughts pervaded southern California, where the Mission Style and other modes derived from Spanish precedent enjoyed increasing popularity. But in San Francisco, the feeling of mañana, mañana was too nostalgic and too provincial to have widespread appeal for long.[43] Schweinfurth's buildings were testaments to a strong design personality, but not to a new California architecture.

Polk and several of his colleagues rejected the idea of an Hispanic-inspired architecture well before such imagery began to lose its popular appeal. In 1892, the *Wave* reported that the California Building competition had caused widespread dissatisfaction among many of San Francisco's young architects because of the stylistic requirement in its program, adding: "The 'Mission' Style is not recognized in architecture."[44] This was the first and last occasion that either Coxhead or Maybeck adopted mission imagery, and Polk did not even enter the contest. Although he had done so much to generate enthusiasm for California's Hispanic buildings, Polk became an outspoken critic of the whole trend. His fastidious remarks offer a clue as to why others were also assuming a cool attitude. Foremost among Polk's objections was the instant codification of a new "style":

When a country possesses an architectural tradition of as charming and simple a character as our pastoral missions afford is it not a pity to note the growing tendency toward its misuse upon our city streets[?]

Polk considered most examples of the Mission Style to be "hideous caricatures" that failed to express the conditions under which they were built. "The missions were not designed out of hand," he insisted, "but . . . evolved from the face of circumstances. They ought not to be basely imitated."[45]

The efforts of Schweinfurth and others to employ a wider range of precedent were no more satisfactory in Polk's opinion. He mocked

289

228. Willis Polk. Frank McCullagh house, Los Gatos, 1901. (*House and Garden*, August 1902, p. 356)

the Midwinter fair's buildings, exclaiming: "But we're to have something new at last. The new style will be East Indian, Egyptian, Moorish, Mission, Assyrian, and Conventional." Spanish Renaissance was irreverently dubbed "Spinach Reminiscence" and Schweinfurth "arrayed against the higher aims of his profession."[46] As Polk despised the mere following of East Coast trends, so he believed that attempts to create a distinct California architecture were equally superficial. The emergence of a new regional mode could only accentuate San Francisco's stigma of remoteness from major cultural centers. Polk's colleagues abstained from writing such acerbic criticism; their silence on the subject, both in print and in their work, was enough.

For all his attacks, Polk was perfectly willing to draw from Spanish California architecture, just as he used other local vernacular sources in what he considered the appropriate circumstances. Both the Rey house and the service quarters for Beaulieu are examples of such work. Imagery derived from the missions themselves pervades his 1901 design for the country residence of Frank McCullagh, a Philadelphian who was a devotee of these early ecclesiastical compounds (Figs. 228, 229). Commanding a panoramic view of the Santa Clara Valley, the house rambles amid a verdant landscape, composed as if it had been built over several centuries.[47] Generalized allusions to Mediterranean

290

229. McCullagh house, rear view. (Author)

architecture are also important contributors to the assemblage. However, the low-slung form, long arcade—the principal hallway—and the scalloped gable end at the rear make more specific reference to the missions than do most buildings by Schweinfurth. Polk's conceptual framework was different. Instead of being a polemic for regional expression, these designs represent a minor segment of a diverse oeuvre that suggests the state's cosmopolitan character more than its provincial roots.

As Polk's inclusive approach to design could entail the use of specific regional references, so Schweinfurth's pursuit of regional expression was sometimes inspired by precedents that lay wholly outside the sphere of Latin and Native American cultures. He designed several buildings that reflect the rustic ideal to which Coxhead and Polk had

291

230. A. C. Schweinfurth. James Bradford house,
San Francisco, 1896; altered. (*Overland Monthly,*
December 1900, p. 537)

contributed so much. As with these architects, Schweinfurth had clients
who were interested in the arts and wanted designs that were out of
the ordinary, but the schemes he developed are markedly different. The
residence designed for James Bradford in San Francisco (1896) is
Schweinfurth's interpretation of the rustic city house (Fig. 230). In
contrast to Coxhead's and Polk's mannered yet relatively low-key
juxtapositions of plain and fancy elements, he created a bold, imposing mass articulated with deliberate crudeness. The house makes no
direct reference to any historic precedent, or even to a general lineage
comparable to the "Spanishness" of the Montalvo hotel or the Hacienda. The main block might have been inspired by seventeenth-century
New England dwellings, with its steep roof, massive central chimney,
and saltbox addition, though the elements are placed as if they were
being viewed from the rear. And the facade, with its immense gable
end supported by trunk columns, might have been inspired by a hybrid
form of Greek Revival house common to eastern Massachusetts, with
which Schweinfurth was probably familiar from his Boston days. But

the results suggest nothing so much as an idealized primitive hut rendered with the insistent order and geometry of a Neo-Classical monument.

Similar qualities are found in the Berkeley house of Volney Moody built in the same year (Fig. 231). The stepped gables hint at the urban architecture of the Netherlands, yet they are placed in a context so different that they read primarily as geometric elements. Spilling out to converse with the rugged site, this tough, prickly mass becomes an abstract embodiment of California's primeval landscape, much as the Prairie houses of Frank Lloyd Wright offer oblique reference to the flat expanses of the Midwest. Inside, the spaces are dark and accommodating, finished in a rough fashion like Polk's Empire

231. A. C. Schweinfurth. Weltevreden, Volney Moody house, Berkeley, 1896–1897; altered. (*Architectural Review*, March 1902, p. 76)

232. Weltevreden, living room. (*Scientific American Building Edition,*
October 1898, p. 59)

Cottage, but set on suburban soil without any classicizing order or
allusions to formality (Fig. 232). As a counterpart to the sanctuary in
Worcester's church, these rooms are the epitome of primitive domestic
shelter.

Schweinfurth's last commission, the First Unitarian Church in
Berkeley (1898), is also his most sophisticated and powerful abstract
statement (Fig. 233).[48] The basic form is perhaps derived from McKim,
Mead & White's William Low house in Bristol, Rhode Island (1885–
1886), but here the facade is composed as a fragmented rectangle and
triangle, united by a circle in the center. The building is actually quite
small, commensurate with its budget of approximately $5,000 and its
residential location. Yet it has a commanding presence. The elementary components of architecture are inflated into an enormous diagram,
then softened by a rich mosaic of wood textures. Everything about the
design defies specific associations. The church is both an ancient
artifact and a break with tradition. The attempt, it seems, was to bring
together two worlds—the wilderness and the land of infinite promise.

That sentiment was expressed in a letter probably written by Schweinfurth from abroad later that year:

The people in Italy and Greece are decadent—are living in a wilderness of decay—and the beautiful things we travel so far to study and admire are works of an entirely different people from those we see today. So we in California are living in a wilderness (primeval)—. . . a wilderness of God's bountiful blessings . . . a wilderness of progress and achievement.[49]

233. A. C. Schweinfurth. First Unitarian Church, Berkeley, 1898.
(Courtesy of the Church)

X

AT THE TURN OF THE CENTURY: The New San Francisco

The Youth seemingly dies out of us as maturity comes on, and Age, we think, has its own time and its own dominant chords, a part of the sequence, perhaps, but not akin to what has gone before in motive or in meaning.
                    Gelett Burgess, *The Epi-Lark*, May 1, 1897

MAJOR CHANGES were occurring in the complexion of Bay Area architecture around 1900. Ten years earlier, a small vanguard whose ideas and methods contrasted sharply with those of the aging establishment had championed the academic cause. Now San Francisco was attracting a steady influx of talented architects, most of whom came from prominent New York offices and had attended the Ecole. A number of locally trained designers, more worldly wise than their predecessors, also were entering the field. By 1906, when conflagration destroyed a third of the city, it was well endowed with a professional corps of architects who could give form and distinction to the rebuilding campaign. The local scene became more competitive, more polished, and more prone to convention. These circumstances affected the careers of both Coxhead and Polk, each in a different way. Polk sought to embrace the corporate world. Coxhead was unable to cope, and in time he lapsed into obscurity. Bay Area architecture would never be quite the same again.

The conditions that had made San Francisco attractive to young architects around 1890 reemerged to lure a wave of new arrivals ten years later. The need for well-trained architects was again strong, and there was ample opportunity for them to establish their own businesses. Following the boom years of 1889–1891, construction declined, a tendency furthered by nationwide depression, but by 1898 recovery was strong. Investments in new buildings nearly doubled between that year and 1901, and nearly doubled again in 1902. The upsurge continued, reaching a feverish pitch from 1906 to 1909, when the city center was almost entirely rebuilt.[1] As San Francisco's commercial core expanded, there was a corresponding demand for new residential development in outlying areas.

Among the first architects of note to settle in the region after the early 1890s were Walter Bliss and William Faville, both MIT graduates and veterans of McKim, Mead & White's office. The two men formed a partnership in 1898. A native son with close ties to local society, Bliss was adept at securing major commissions. Over the next quarter-century, the firm became one of San Francisco's most prominent, creating suave renditions in McKim, Mead & White's style, much as Page Brown had done earlier.[2]

John Galen Howard was another distinguished newcomer. Since his apprentice days in southern California, he had worked in McKim's office, studied at the Ecole, and had a flourishing practice in New York. He came to the Bay Area in 1901, charged with implementing the Hearst Plan and establishing a school of architecture (the first on the West Coast) at the university. Howard also maintained a large office in the city and became a conspicuous campaigner for civic improvement.[3] Two of his assistants, Charles Peter Weeks and Julia Morgan, both trained at the Ecole and embarked on independent careers by 1905. Weeks became a well-known designer of commercial buildings. Morgan concentrated on residences and quarters for women's organizations. Although she shunned publicity, Morgan developed a substantial practice and was regarded as a leading contributor to local developments by the early 1910s.[4] Morgan was also one of several Californians who had been introduced to architecture by Maybeck at Berkeley, furthered their education in Paris, then returned to practice in the region. Another was Loring Rixford, who came back around 1900, worked briefly for Albert Pissis, and opened his own office in 1902. The most celebrated Maybeck protégés were John Bakewell and Arthur Brown, Jr., who entered a partnership in 1902. The firm earned a national reputation with its winning design for San Francisco's City Hall (1912). Of all California architects, Bakewell and Brown were regarded by their East Coast colleagues as the preeminent exemplars of Beaux Arts ideals.[5]

Many other architects flocked to San Francisco after the 1906 fire. Llewellyn Dutton came from Chicago, where he had held a prominent position in Daniel Burnham's office. Lewis Hobart, Kenneth MacDonald, George Kelham, George Applegarth, and G. Albert Lansburgh were all Ecole veterans and, except for the latter two, seasoned with experience in New York.[6] Together with several firms headed by members of the old guard—Pissis, the Reid brothers, William Curlett, and Clinton Day—these architects cornered the major share of the building market, including most important commercial and institutional commissions.

This migration greatly raised the general level of design in San Francisco. After the 1906 fire, the downtown area was rebuilt as a classical urban center—elegant, dignified, and more cohesive than most American metropolises. The new complex of civic buildings near the commercial core became one of the consummate manifestations of the City Beautiful Movement; for the first time San Francisco actually looked like a great city—a polished combination of New York and Paris, rendered by architects who considered those centers to be the epitome of urban achievement. The results of this renaissance were magnificent and at the same time conservative. The city had scores of new buildings but hardly any exceptional landmarks. The haste of reconstruction precluded a reordering of the street pattern as had been proposed in Daniel Burnham's master plan, published on the fire's eve. The prevailing mood was sober and became increasingly so after the fire, as if the city's exuberance had been buried in the ashes.[7] The fresh crop of architects was adroit in purveying fashionable modes but had little interest in innovative departures. What they transplanted from the East and abroad was more method than imagination.

The spirited use of classical precedent that characterized Coxhead's and Polk's designs over the previous decade had virtually no impact on this new work. The two older architects' buildings probably seemed a bit anachronistic to the recent arrivals. Coxhead and Polk labored over each project themselves, maintained small offices, and, despite attempts to broaden their scope, were involved mostly in residential commissions. Both men were at their creative best under the relatively isolated professional conditions of the 1890s, but now they faced stiff competition from young colleagues in the same ideological camp who were armed with impressive credentials and were skilled as managers. These circumstances seem to have made Coxhead and Polk less confident about continuing on an individualistic course.

By 1899, Polk was rebounding from bankruptcy when a chance came to expand his operations. In December he entered an association with George Washington Percy, a venerable member of the old guard, replacing Percy's design partner, F. F. Hamilton, who had died a few weeks earlier. Overnight, Polk took charge of a sizable staff and plans for numerous commercial and institutional buildings.[8] At last he could work on a large scale; however, exacting schedules and the sheer volume of work at hand forced him to delegate most tasks to others. The designs themselves were quite uneven, suggesting that Polk concentrated on a few major commissions and left others in the hands of subordinates. Percy managed the firm and attended to technical matters, but his conservative nature no doubt influenced Polk's work. Most schemes were quite conventional; Polk's personality emerged only in some details.[9] The job had other drawbacks, including the fact that Percy refused to make him a partner, and Polk often received no official credit for his work. Also, friction existed between him and older members of the office, who must have been envious of his seniority.[10]

Despite these shortcomings, Polk was bolstered by what he regarded as a rise in professional stature. He enjoyed financial security for the first time in years. A few months after entering the office, he married Christina Barreda Moore, whose father had been the Spanish ambassador to the Court of St. James. After losing their great fortune in the 1870s, the Barredas moved to San Francisco, where they remained in the social limelight even though they were reduced to modest means. Always self-conscious about his humble origins, Polk took pride in uniting with a member of such a distinguished family. The marriage may have intensified his yearning to live in a grand manner, and he became increasingly preoccupied with developing a large, business-oriented practice.[11]

His new-found security did not last long, however. Percy died in December 1900 and the firm disbanded, leaving Polk on his own again. The next move was audacious: he asked Joseph Worcester to write him a letter of introduction to Daniel Burnham, the minister's friend and cousin through marriage. Polk then proposed a partnership: he would establish a new office in San Francisco under Burnham's name. Though Burnham was flattered and thought highly of Polk's work, he rejected a collaboration with a man whom he had never met. Polk persisted, journeying to Chicago in March 1901 and striking an agreement whereby they might join forces on any large projects Polk managed to secure. When no such work was forthcoming, Polk offered to enter Burnham's Chicago office. Burnham agreed, and the Polks departed for Chicago in September 1901, remaining there for almost two years.[12]

The association with Burnham marked a turning point in Polk's career. He entered the upper stratum of the office hierarchy, designing several major projects and enjoying a favored relationship with his boss.[13] Burnham became an advisor and critic, a mentor, and a close friend. Polk had avoided patterning his work after that of any other architect, but in Burnham he found a hero. The large, multifaceted office structure, the grand scale of city planning, and the urbane formulas for commercial building design that distinguished the Chicagoan's practice—all of these became models for Polk throughout the remainder of his career. The individualism that he had articulated so defiantly in the 1890s was subsumed by his yearning for prestige and recognition.

In May 1903, the Polks sailed for Europe—it was his first trip abroad—returning to San Francisco that fall. Soon thereafter he formed a partnership with an old friend of Percy's, George Alexander Wright.[14] With his new business-minded associate, Polk hoped to capture a respectable portion of the area's expansive building market. The effort met with only moderate success, and Polk's admiration for Burnham was consequently strengthened. He often sent Burnham photographs of projects on the boards, and may have lobbied behind the scenes for hiring Burnham to prepare the San Francisco master plan. Once that commission was in hand, Polk volunteered many hours to assist in its preparation.[15]

Shortly before Burnham's plan was scheduled for distribution, the great fire destroyed the city center and many adjacent districts as well. Wright and Polk had dissolved their partnership only a few weeks before. Polk seized the opportunity to renew his proposal of heading a West Coast office for Burnham. This time Burnham was enthusiastic: he was eager to help Polk, and he believed that the conflagration had paved the way for his plan and that reconstruction would offer dozens of lucrative commissions.[16] Given virtually complete control of the new office, Polk aspired to a central role in remaking the metropolis. The alliance was successful compared to his previous ventures. Under the name of D. H. Burnham & Company, Polk secured contracts for office towers, banks, retail blocks, utility buildings, railroad stations, and the new quarters of the Pacific Union Club. Burnham's master plan was scrapped amid political scandal and the haste of rebuilding, but Polk became active in proposals for the new civic center, and he was appointed supervising architect for the Panama-Pacific International Exposition—an event that would celebrate San Francisco's spectacular comeback.[17]

In spite of these achievements, Polk's position began to erode. The volume of work never reached the level Burnham had anticipated, and poor management drove him to terminate the association in 1910. The two men remained friends. Officially, Burnham stated that Polk had earned the right to continue on his own.[18] Polk knew better. The affair was a severe blow to his pride, but it did not curb his flamboyant ways. He remained an irascible, outspoken critic of colleagues, potential clients, and politicians. His lack of diplomacy and business acumen was matched by his urge to pull conspicuous stunts—a boon to the press and a debacle for the maintenance of a sound practice. Polk never realized a major public building, and he was dismissed as the world's fair supervising architect well before its completion.[19]

Polk's conflict between his ambition to become another Daniel Burnham and his instinct to be the temperamental artist is also evident in his designs. Reorienting his efforts around the turn of the century toward a substantial volume of work led him to a greater reliance on formulas. After the two years in Chicago, he often emulated Burnham's suave classical style (Fig. 234). He was still firmly committed

234. D. H. Burnham & Company. First National Bank (now Crocker) Building,
San Francisco, 1907–1909; altered and all but lower zone scheduled for demolition.
Original Crocker Building on left. (San Francisco Public Library)

235. Willis Polk & Company. James K. Moffitt house, Piedmont, 1911–1912. (*American Architect*, April 16, 1913)

to architecture as a fine art and he never became a copyist. His best twentieth-century buildings are splendid representatives of the period, but seldom are they individually exceptional. The inventive, unorthodox, and diverse qualities that distinguished his efforts during the 1890s became much less evident. His most personal expression can be found in residences; however, he no longer had much interest in the design of the small and moderate-sized houses he had once handled with such imagination. The unconventional aspects that continued to characterize his domestic work—distorted proportions and a play between plain and fancy elements—suggest more arbitrary mannerisms than ingenious responses to the program (Fig. 235).

Only once did Polk make a substantive departure from conformity: with the glass curtain-wall facade of the Hallidie Building (1917–1918) (Fig. 236). A speculative commercial loft, the scheme defied its mundane requirements and setting to make an eloquent tribute to the imagination and gesture to the urban landscape. The reasons for this bold solution remain elusive; one can only speculate that Polk momentarily sought to be his old self again.[20] Maybeck summarized his friend's dilemma well. Polk had reserved the choicest project at the Panama-Pacific Exposition, the Palace of Fine Arts, for himself. Then, in a rare gesture of munificence, he gave it to Maybeck. Shortly

302

before the fair opened, Maybeck wrote to Polk that "you have put up a monument to your Ideals [through me] and made a sacrifice for them—there is in you a yearning for the highest Ideal . . . and I believe some morning you will wake up to cut out that other side which you seem to consider important."[21]

236. Willis Polk & Company. Hallidie Building, San Francisco, 1917–1918.
(*The Architect*, July 1918, plate 12)

That morning came too late. Polk still ranked among the region's most distinguished architects, and he enjoyed a national reputation since the early 1910s, but by the end of the decade his practice was in trouble. The few efforts after the Hallidie Building to pursue an unconventional course carry a note of desperation, and decline in new work was steady.[22] Polk's irresponsible demeanor was finally getting the best of him. Little of consequence was on the drawing boards when he died in 1924 at age fifty-seven.[23]

Coxhead's career lasted longer, but his role in local architecture waned earlier. After the 1890s, the firm seldom realized more than two or three commissions a year, most of which were still for small and moderate-sized houses. Surviving papers indicate that preliminary schemes were developed for several large residences and Episcopal churches. Coxhead continued to enter competitions for civic buildings, but he never won. Around 1911, he offered a grand proposal for the Panama-Pacific Exposition, yet it failed to elicit much interest. Polk was either unwilling or unable to secure an appointment for his friend to design even a minor fair building. The headquarters of the Home Telephone Company was Coxhead's only significant contribution to the massive rebuilding effort in San Francisco.[24]

The reasons for the architect's eclipse are difficult to pinpoint. With his retiring personality and lack of business acumen, Coxhead may have been unable to practice effectively under ever more competitive circumstances. When Irving Scott died in 1903, Coxhead lost his most important patron; never again would he find someone of comparable stature to bolster his efforts. He also suffered personal tragedy. In 1898, Coxhead married Helen Browne Hawes, the daughter of an Episcopal minister and a favorite belle of the artistic community. The union was ideal in every respect, but it came to a sudden end when Helen died giving birth to their third child around 1905. Coxhead may never have fully recovered from the loss.[25]

The decline in his practice was matched by a change in the character of Coxhead's work. He seems to have lost interest in the designs of English colleagues, which had such an influence on his work in the 1890s. Increasingly he turned to a subdued classicism that was gaining favor for residences on both the East and West coasts. Many of his newer houses possess a soft, vernacular-inspired imagery with more or less symmetrical compositions and straightforward plans. His work is also more uniform, without the diversity found in earlier years. The changes were perhaps a reaction to his failure to expand his practice; he may have sought to abstain from unorthodox uses of form, space, scale, and historical references in order to appeal to a broader, middle-class audience.

Whatever the reasons, the shift was not an improvement. Coxhead was unable to attain the refined subtleties in proportion and detail needed to elevate unobtrusive design above a pedestrian level. His attempt to be consistent seems to be imposed on the design, ignoring differences in size, cost, materials, and site. Many of his houses are attractive, commodious, and thoughtfully designed, but they lack vitality. Most schemes are also still a bit eccentric, with squat features and mannered classical details (Fig. 237). As in Polk's residential work, these qualities appear forced, more an affectation than a spirited outgrowth of a concept.[26] This aspect of Coxhead's later work also appeared, with the most bizarre results, in several competition entries for public buildings (Fig. 238).

The morning never came for Coxhead. During the 1920s he designed a few elegant Spanish Colonial Revival houses, but in a manner quite dependent upon the example of others. His brother died in 1928, and Coxhead continued to practice alone for a few years. He was seventy when he died in 1933, forgotten by most of his colleagues

237. Coxhead & Coxhead. Charles Rieber house, 1904 *(left)*, and Frederic Torrey house, 1905–1906 *(right)*, Berkeley. House in center for Lincoln Hutchinson by Morgan & Hoover, 1908. Photograph ca. 1910. (Author's collection)

238. Coxhead & Coxhead. San Francisco Sub-Treasury Building, San Francisco, 1911, competition entry. (*Architect and Engineer*, June 1911, p. 50)

and having passed his prime more than a quarter-century earlier.[27]

Polk had virtually no interest in rustic design after 1900, and Coxhead's interest now seemed equivocal, embodied primarily in the use of shingle veneers, a few hints at postmedieval vernacular sources, and an unobtrusive presence. However, both men's legacy of rustic houses from the 1890s became an important departure point for subsequent work in the region. Many of the architects who furthered the cause of rustic expression had recently been trained in local offices. At a formative stage in their careers, they witnessed the substantive changes Coxhead, Polk, and others had brought to the scene. Moreover, most members of this younger generation knew work outside the area only from secondhand sources. They turned to an immediate precedent because it was new, familiar, relatively inexpensive, and well tailored to local conditions. The rustic city houses designed by Coxhead and Polk were particularly influential, perhaps because these dwellings also seemed to constitute a unique regional type.

Among the most prolific designers in this vein was Edgar Mathews, who trained in his father's office from 1889 until he began independent practice about eight years later. Mathews's work was concentrated in Pacific Heights, where he designed numerous moderate-sized houses and apartment blocks during the early twentieth century.

306

Like Coxhead and Polk, he turned for inspiration to postmedieval urban dwellings in northern Europe; however, he avoided any tinges of unorthodoxy in his schemes. He developed a polished, unpretentious manner derived in large part from the conventions of contemporary English arts-and-crafts cottage design (Fig. 239). Herbert Croly, who championed the unobtrusive, single-focus approach of Charles Platt, identified Mathews's houses as exemplars of modest, dignified, and consistent urban residential design. His work is superb background architecture, while its very extent made Mathews perhaps the major contributor to the conspicuous presence of rustic expression in the city.[28]

Albert Farr's houses also had a significant impact on the character of San Francisco's residential districts. Born in Omaha, Farr moved to the Bay region in 1891. After about eight years of training in the offices of Clinton Day and furniture designers Howard, Belcher

239. Edgar Mathews. Stein apartments, San Francisco, before 1904. (Author)

307

240. Albert Farr. Edward Bullard, Robert Postlethwaite, and Hugh Postlethwaite houses, San Francisco, 1903; third house demolished. (Author's collection)

and Allen, he established his own practice. Farr was more experimental than Mathews, and he shared Coxhead's and Polk's interest in diversity. Early in his career, he sometimes borrowed outright from the two older architects' work, but he tempered their manipulations of composition and detail for more anonymous-looking results (Fig. 240). By the late 1900s, Farr's work owed a less overt debt to local precedent, often drawing directly from recent English arts-and-crafts examples.[29]

Several other architects were attracted to Coxhead's and Polk's use of elaborate classical elements set off against relatively plain, vernacular-inspired masses. Among the most spirited versions were those produced by John White. Beginning his tutelage as a draftsman for Henry Van Brunt and Frank Howe in Kansas City, White settled in

Berkeley during the mid-1890s, where he assisted his brother-in-law, Bernard Maybeck. By 1900, White was working for George Howard, whose partner he later became. Throughout their association, White appears to have been the principal designer.[30] He captured some of the individualistic quality present in buildings by Coxhead, Polk, and Maybeck, although his manner was somewhat more conservative and dry. Sylvain Schnaittacher also drew from their example. After graduating from the Mark Hopkins Institute of Art, he worked first for Page Brown and then for the offspring firm headed by Frank van Trees before opening his own office in 1901.[31] William Knowles was another popular designer of rustic houses in San Francisco and its suburbs. Knowles studied engineering at Stanford, then worked for Clinton Day, Brown, and Mathews, entering practice for himself around the same time as Schnaittacher. The son of a contractor who had built several projects for Coxhead, Knowles became a friend of the older architect and emulated his work on a number of occasions.[32]

Through the efforts of these architects and others like them, rustic expression became a ubiquitous feature of the regional landscape.[33] Like their more commercially oriented colleagues, they did much to raise the general standard of local design while maintaining a conservative approach. The modes they used had become well established by the early 1900s. Their plans were standard, without the innovative configurations of space and scale once practiced by Coxhead and Polk. Mathews, Farr, Knowles, and others of their generation may not have sought regionalism any more than Coxhead or Polk; yet the cumulative effect of their work was to endow the Bay Area with a rich legacy of rustic architecture that stands somewhat apart from contemporary work in other locales. In its diffused form, the rustic house adhered to basic design patterns employed elsewhere. The distinctness stems from the sheer number of picturesque yet compact dwellings placed close together, often on sloping sites. Furthermore, in no other region save coastal and mountain resorts did the use of shingles as an exterior veneer approach the popularity that it enjoyed in and around San Francisco. Finally, the houses were cohesive because they were for the most part done by architects trained in the region, of more or less the same age, who shared many values, including a rather conventional attitude toward design.

During the early twentieth century, the widespread appeal of rustic design in the Bay Area was fostered by more than local sentiment. Arts-and-crafts ideals, which had become an increasingly important influence in American artistic circles over the previous decade, were now entering the mainstream of the country's middle-class culture.[34] The Arts and Crafts Movement's concern for rustic simplicity, utilitarian value, and at least certain trappings of preindustrial society reinforced the sentiment toward the region's natural landscape and California's pioneer heritage. The rustic buildings produced in the Bay Area during the 1890s might be considered an impressive prelude to the Arts and Crafts Movement in American architecture. However, the men involved gave no indication that they considered their designs outside the broad conceptual framework of academic eclecticism. For them, the arts-and-crafts ethic was not all-consuming. Rather, it afforded an important ideological premise for the further development of certain forms of expression. The arts-and-crafts impulse gave new life to the design of rustic, picturesque buildings, the concern for which had languished somewhat since the 1880s, without significantly deviating from academic values.

The relationship that existed between the Arts and Crafts Movement and academic eclecticism in the Bay Area became widespread in the United States after 1900. The Arts and Crafts Movement was more a complement than a counterforce to academic eclecticism. Both movements were reform efforts, calling for a return to simplicity in expression, honesty in materials, beauty that was an outgrowth of practical needs, unity between architecture and the allied arts, and a harmonious order in the environment. Both were tradition-oriented movements, looking to a wide spectrum of historical precedent and seeking to restore the sense of continuity that had been interrupted by the nineteenth century, yet also concerned with adapting the lessons of the past to suit contemporary conditions. Like academic eclecticism, the Arts and Crafts Movement was an idea, not a style.[35]

Differences also existed. Proponents of the Arts and Crafts Movement tended to emphasize the moral implications of design and relationships between architecture and life more than their academic colleagues did. They also had less interest in professional education and held no allegiance to the academic tradition and its abstract design concerns. Arts-and-crafts architects normally turned to picturesque, vernacular, and rural buildings for inspiration, whereas academic architects increasingly relied on more formal precedents. Some designers, such as Irving Gill and the Greene brothers, became specialists in the arts-and-crafts realm by developing a consistent personal style much like Charles Platt or Ralph Adams Cram did in the academic sector. Some academic architects, on the other hand, had little or no direct contact with the Arts and Crafts Movement. Yet divergence occurred without animosity. Contemporary literature gives no hint of contentions between the two movements. Champions of academic eclecticism appear to have considered arts-and-crafts design quite appropriate for residences and some other buildings of modest size in suburban and rural areas. Advocates of the Arts and Crafts Movement similarly respected academic designs for commercial and civic projects.[36] In practice, the two movements were never wholly discrete entities. Many architects borrowed from both, and hundreds of early-twentieth-century American buildings fit well within either category.

For the most part, the designers of rustic houses in the Bay Area during the early twentieth century took this middle-of-the-road approach. The inspiration they derived from local sources and arts-and-crafts work elsewhere affected their treatment of more or less standard form and space configurations. With some changes in materials, and minor adjustments to the composition and historical references, many of their buildings would no longer appear "rustic" or "arts-and-crafts," but rather "Georgian" or "Spanish Colonial." However, one architect among them showed much more concern for arts-and-crafts and academic principles as generators of different, if complementary, forms of expression. He worked with facility in, and commitment to, both realms, and continued the spirit of freedom and inventiveness exercised by Coxhead and Polk during the 1890s. Maybeck, far more than his colleagues who were just beginning practice, built upon the special attitude toward design that marked earlier efforts and contributed to a legacy of more than regional consequence.

XI

MAYBECK: The Struggle for "Brief Moments of Eternal Conciliation"

There is something bigger and more worthwhile than the things we see about us, the things we live by and strive for. There is an undiscovered beauty, a divine excellence, just beyond us. Let us stand on tiptoe, forgetting the nearer things, and grasp of it what we may.

Bernard Maybeck, *San Francisco Call*, June 21, 1923

MAYBECK'S MATURING approach to design was complex and filled with dichotomies. He was perhaps as knowledgeable in design theory as any American architect of his generation, yet he seemed unintellectual, offering homespun explanations for his methods. He was engrossed in a world of dreams but also could be fascinated by mundane architectural problems. He was seldom inclined to accept normative precedents, but at the same time his outlook was that of a traditionalist, steeped in the practices of the Ecole des Beaux Arts. He obeyed the academic position; he also defied it. His perspective was broad and encompassed divergent attitudes. The result was a multifaceted oeuvre so diverse that it suggests a continual struggle to find "an undiscovered beauty."

Maybeck was over thirty when he received his first independent commission, and he did not begin to practice in earnest until the turn of the century. The formative stage of his career lasted through the mid-1900s. Though he never ceased experimenting, the conceptual parameters of his search were established by that time. Coxhead's and Polk's early work was a major source of inspiration. Unlike them, however, Maybeck remained detached from the ever more competitive and convention-prone architectural scene and oblivious to professional recognition. Much of his activity was centered in Berkeley, which was emerging as an important center for creative endeavors in the region.

Around 1900, Berkeley was still a small town, with clusters of wood houses, verdant gardens, and dirt streets surrounded by grassy hills and rolling countryside. Its quaint atmosphere, combined with the prestigious University of California in its midst, appealed to those who sought both tranquility and cultural stimulus. Many residents worked in San Francisco and saw Berkeley as their refuge. Old quarters of the metropolis, which had been the haven of artists and kindred spirits, were giving way to commercial development, and all such enclaves, save portions of Russian and Telegraph hills, were destroyed in the 1906 fire. San Francisco's new residential districts were filling up, and the land was becoming increasingly expensive. Berkeley now seemed to harbor the youthful, naive aspects of culture that San Francisco was losing. The town was also becoming more accessible, as an extensive network of electric streetcar lines was constructed in the East Bay communities during the 1890s. The Key Route, a combination train and ferry system, opened in 1903, cutting transit time to San Francisco by almost half.[1] Berkeley's population had more than doubled between 1890 and 1900, yet remained relatively modest at 13,000. Over the next decade it soared to 40,000, and many of the features that made the town attractive were consequently threatened. Residents who escaped to Berkeley in the 1890s were among the earliest to seek the preservation of its rustic ambience.

Spearheading the campaign to save Berkeley's physical beauties was the Hillside Club. Originally a women's group founded in 1898 to protect the sector just north of the university campus, the club was reorganized four years later to include men and to address development concerns in numerous portions of the community. Soon the club became a major civic force, and its policies enjoyed widespread influence. In the tradition of American village improvement societies, the Hillside Club lobbied for better streets, sidewalks, tree-planting programs, and the treatment of residential lots as harmonious gardens.[2] The group sponsored lectures, held at least one exhibition (of Japanese prints), and collected a reference library. It followed the precedents set in Mill Valley and Belvedere, arguing for development that was sensitive to the existing landscape and that would enhance its rustic qualities. However, one aspect of the club's endeavors was unusual: from its inception it was as concerned with architecture as it was with planning. After the reorganization, it strenuously promoted general guidelines for house design. The Berkeley dwelling should be formed in a certain image—rustic, picturesque, commodious, unobtrusive— that respected the setting and reflected a moralistic attitude toward

313

life. The member most responsible for propagating this local gospel on architecture was Charles Keeler.

Keeler began his career in the early 1890s as a naturalist, but his interests rapidly broadened. By the mid-1900s, he was the most vocal champion of arts-and-crafts ideals in the region. Much like his southern California friend, Charles Fletcher Lummis, Keeler preached a sermon heavily laced with state promotionalism.[3] Both men were entrepreneurs of ideas rather than intellectuals. Keeler's activities were closer to those of the chamber of commerce than to the work of his exemplar, William Morris. He viewed the rustic house as a conspicuous manifestation of his beliefs and a key instrument for their encouragement. It was he who first considered such dwellings to be a unique regional phenomenon.

Nothing is more significant of the hold which real culture is gaining in California than the growing appreciation of the simple life. . . . It is most strikingly objectified in a certain type of house which is quite distinct to California—a type developed by a little group of homemakers and architects along thoroughly rational lines. These houses are painted with uncovered shingles, brick or plaster with open timber work and are characterized within by a careful study of proportions and extreme simplicity of finish.[4]

A regional architecture? Keeler did not elaborate on the point. In 1904, he codified his message in a booklet, *The Simple Home*, although precise definitions were not his concern here either. The text was intended to advance the Hillside Club's broad architectural objectives among Berkeley residents.[5] Appealing to artistic sensibilities, middle-class moral values, and local chauvinism, Keeler's cause met with great success. The rustic house became closely identified with the town through the sheer number of examples that were erected, block after block, within its precincts (Fig. 241).

Keeler's interest in architecture was nurtured by Maybeck. He adopted many of Maybeck's convictions, was his first client, and his constant supporter. *The Simple Home* was dedicated to Maybeck, who was active in the Hillside Club, having designed its quarters in 1906. Maybeck prepared a small leaflet on hillside residential architecture for the club to distribute (1907) and served a term as the organization's president (1909–1910). Keeler's efforts helped to make Maybeck the dean of rustic architecture in Berkeley; Maybeck's ideas became a source of communal inspiration, and his buildings became the model for many others. In this folksy atmosphere, bolstered by a promotion-

241. Berkeley, general view looking north from vicinity of Ridge Road and
Scenic Way, before 1923. (CED Documents Collection)

alism for which he had little concern, Maybeck was happy and prosperous. It is among the ironies of his career that he thrived under such
circumstances, for his ideas and work had much broader implications.

Until the mid-1890s, Maybeck showed no promise of becoming a distinguished architect or even one who practiced. Since leaving
New York in 1888, he had held no noteworthy positions. Eager to
work on his own, he entered several competitions and solicited clients
but had yet to realize a project. He had scant interest in the regalia of
an aspiring practitioner. He was an unvarnished Bohemian, bearded
and balding, suited in baggy clothes, adhering to a diet of vegetables
cooked on a handmade stove, secluded with his family in a modest

315

house that was being erected piecemeal in Berkeley's outskirts. Through his university classes in descriptive geometry and an informal course in design theory conducted at home after hours, however, he managed to acquire a flock of admiring students. He also began to gain an audience among the town's permanent residents. Much of his appeal no doubt stemmed from the fact that he shunned "high-brow talk." For him, discussing design was like telling a story, and his imagination transformed everything into an event. Family life was studded with pageants. Once he started to practice, he took delight in "classifying" a client's personality according to some historical period in architecture, which he then used as a basis for developing the appropriate character of the scheme itself.[6]

Maybeck was deeply concerned with human emotions. The house, he told Keeler, "should . . . be an expression of the life and the spirit which is to be lived within."[7] He regarded architecture as a setting for people's activities, and more important to him than any aesthetic objective was how people responded to architecture. He cast himself as a missionary—humble, self-effacing, yet determined to convert those around him to his visions. And for all his apparent naiveté, he could be very persuasive. In the mid-1890s, he was like a lovable high school art teacher: adept at inspiring novices to his lofty ideals, sage yet modest, experienced yet earthy. Bolstered by a small band of local devotees, he created eccentric designs which to seasoned practitioners must have seemed barely competent.

Maybeck's first commission was for Keeler's residence. A preliminary study done around 1894 or 1895 does not suggest the hand of a well-trained architect (Fig. 242).[8] The principal elevation consists of four unrelated parts with elements that seem either too tall or too short, too wide or too narrow, as if an amateur were attempting to imitate Coxhead's recently completed Beta Theta Pi house, located a block away. The scheme's childlike innocence is heightened by the fact that it does not resemble a contemporary house so much as it bears the characteristics of "house" as the child perceives it: a big roof, prominent chimney, and little windows floating amid large, undefined wall areas. Maybeck was still struggling to resolve his adolescent love of fantasy with the ideas he had nurtured over the past decade. Part of his difficulty stemmed from his resistance to the use of accepted models. While Coxhead and Polk tended to build upon precedents that they admired, developing them in new ways, Maybeck often sought to rethink the whole idea. Keeler later recalled that the architect was adamant about returning to what he believed were the "first princi-

242. Bernard Maybeck. Charles Keeler house, Berkeley, preliminary design, ca. 1894–1895. Drawing probably by Maybeck. (Courtesy Dimitri Shipounoff)

243. Keeler house as built, 1895. (CED Documents Collection)

ples" of design, "going back to the fundamentals that have been forgotten."[9] Furthermore, Maybeck turned to divergent ideas for inspiration. He was more familiar with and interested in design theory than were his San Francisco colleagues. As guides in his search, he drew much from the writings of Viollet-le-Duc and Semper, as well as from the principles he had learned at the Ecole.[10]

The Keeler house was an important trial run for Maybeck. By the final design stage, he had begun to coalesce his thoughts and translate them into a coherent scheme, enriched by examples provided by Coxhead and Polk. As built, the house retains the basic composition

317

used earlier, but it is much more refined (Fig. 243). A stair tower, with
a roof identical to those over the projecting bays at either end, helps
tie the parts together while it eases the transition between the one- and
three-story sections. As in Polk's Russian Hill house, the repetition
and alignment of windows further unifies the design without mitigating
its casual appearance. The exterior is a logical outgrowth of the floor
plan, but offers little indication of how the plan is ordered (Fig. 244).
The spatial treatment is unorthodox, eventful, and well tailored to the
client's needs. Directly off the entry is an expansive dining room
where the Keelers often held soirees. The comparatively small living
room is prominently placed, yet set apart in its own wing for intimate
family gatherings—the center of the "home life" that Keeler championed so arduously in his book. Adjacent is a tiny library where
Keeler could lose himself in writing. Each room is distinct, but also
forms an extension of the navelike hall to create a coherent spatial
sequence (Fig. 245).[11]

Another lesson learned from Coxhead and Polk is the use of
diminutively scaled elements to make a small, inexpensive design
seem grand. Yet Maybeck achieved this illusion by using exposed
structure, a method that was of little interest to either Coxhead or
Polk. The inspiration for it no doubt came from the *Fachwerk* of
postmedieval houses in western Germany, where his parents were
raised and where Maybeck himself had spent a memorable summer
between sessions at the Ecole. The correspondence in imagery is
furthered by his use of steep, flared roofs and small, banded casement

244. Keeler house, author's reconstruction of original plan. (Drawn
by Kim Spurgeon Fly)

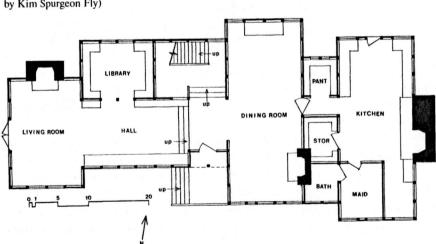

245. Keeler house, hall and living room. (Charles Keeler, *The Simple Home*, p. 47)

windows. Maybeck referred to this, and several similar residences he designed over the next two years, as "Gothic houses," paying homage to his ancestral land just as Coxhead had done with the English cottage (Fig. 246). However, the clustering of varied masses, each emphasized by its own roof, is more analogous to small German castles than to farmers' or merchants' houses, and thus the illusion of great size is fostered. The exterior gives no hint of the structural form, a major break with historic precedent. Even the existence of a solid frame is denied by the tiered range of windows across the master bedroom bay and the strapped windows around the corners. All the structure is inside, whereas few members save the floor beams were exposed in the prototypical interiors.

The Keeler interior is also a pronounced departure from convention in American house design. Few examples of wooden architecture in the United States have a structure that is so integral and intricate a part of the spatial order. Virtually all the structural components are left open to view. In the living room, hall, stair tower, and master bedroom, the posts and connecting rafters, extending well

319

246. House, Osnabrück, Westphalia, early seventeenth century. (*Blätter für Architektur und Kunsthandwerk*, May 1899, plate 45)

below the wall plates, create a veritable forest of timberwork, at once elemental and elegant, lofty and compact, structural and decorative. If this synthesis reflects the design concerns of Maybeck's former teacher, Jules André, it offers nothing short of a testimonial to Viollet-le-Duc's maxim that "Architecture and Construction must be . . . practiced simultaneously; Construction is the means, Architecture is the result."

The use of structure was no doubt further inspired by Viollet's concept of Gothic church construction. The distinguishing characteristic of the system, he argued, was a network of "independent" vertical supports that carried the entire load; the walls were merely enclosure, free from pressure and thrust.[12] Maybeck translated this idea into timber, eschewing the balloon frame for closely spaced posts to which the rafters are tied. The relationship is analogous to that of a Gothic church, in which a membrane of glass might fill the space between the spring line of each vault (Fig. 247). Both the imagery and the structural rationale behind it gave Maybeck good cause to label the house Gothic.

The rooms of the Keeler house also reflect Viollet's fascination with the products of "primitive" cultures. For Viollet, primitivism represented a germinal stage of human development that displayed intuitive intelligence and energy lost in the work of more sophisticated societies. The house has the potential to evoke the wooden building traditions of numerous primitive cultures, including non-western ones, several of which Keeler would illustrate in *The Simple Home*.[13] This

247. Keeler house, original master bedroom. (Author)

generalization embodies an underlying theme in Viollet's history of domestic architecture. He depicts the Aryan hut, originating in the Himalayas at the dawn of civilization, as a principal source for the building techniques employed from Asia to Europe. The differences between one culture and another are marked, yet the same vigorous, primitive spirit persistently reappears. The timberwork in the Keeler house conjures up an array of examples described by the theorist, ranging from the delicate intricacy of ancient Chinese architecture to the particularized clarity of ancient Greek models, a "primitive" culture for which both Viollet and Maybeck had a special fondness.[14]

Gottfried Semper provided an equally important conceptual framework for Maybeck's efforts. Like Viollet, Semper sought to advance a rational, systematic method for analyzing form based on the artifacts of past cultures. However, the two men's views differed in many respects, and Semper openly derided Viollet's rationalism. Viollet focused on structure as the generator of architecture, Semper on archetypal elements derived from function. Semper's *Der Stil* afforded both a more universal and a more specific base from which Maybeck could develop his ideas:[15] Viollet was primarily interested in historic buildings that were considered important monuments, constructed in masonry and, from the Middle Ages on, located in his own country. Viollet's writings are heavily tinged with the mid-nineteenth-century preoccupation with developing a new style. Semper was far less concerned with newness. He subordinated chronological development to his categories of textiles, ceramics, carpentry, masonry, and metallurgy. These categories transcended time and place in a more concrete way than did Viollet's principles of rational construction. Semper's theory carried no nationalistic overtones, but he discussed precedents of more immediate interest to Maybeck. A number of pages of *Der Stil* analyze the wooden folk architecture of central Europe, work that would serve as the principal model for Maybeck's rustic houses throughout his career.

In contrast to the prevailing French belief, Semper argued that traditional timber construction in central Europe was not of medieval origin, but essentially a continuation of practices employed in antiquity that were based on four irreducible elements of architecture—hearth, platform, roof, and enclosure—all present in the primitive hut. He maintained that the most consequential innovation in medieval timber architecture was the steep-pitched roof, which had originated in Nordic countries and had been transmitted to France and then to Germany by the Normans. Semper included a cross section of the twelfth-century

248. Borgund stave church,
Søgne, Norway, twelfth century.
Section. (Gottfried Semper,
Der Stil, p. 306)

Borgund stave church to illustrate the type in what he regarded as its
purest surviving form (Fig. 248).[16] Here, as in the Keeler house, the
roof is an essential contributor to the interior space. More important,
the structure is completely enclosed by, and separated from, the skin.
Seen through Semperian glasses, Maybeck's design is a German "Gothic
house" purified, more "medieval" than anything to be found in
Germany. The scheme's simplicity and abstractness also tend to
underscore Semper's four elements. Besides separating structure and

323

skin, the roof and wall frames are expressed as an integral system. Here, and in several other houses designed soon afterward, Maybeck set the building on a platform, raised well above ground level—in a climate where such a practice was unnecessary—supported by braced posts rather than the usual masonry foundation, and enveloped in a veneer of shingled boards (Fig. 249). Like several of his contemporaries, Maybeck may have regarded *Der Stil* as something of a building manual, expressing the "first principles" of design in an elementary manner Semper himself never advocated.[17]

Thus the Keeler house embodies ideas on medieval form derived from Semper and on medieval structure derived from Viollet, while reflecting the attitudes of both men on primitive architecture in general. Maybeck also drew from recent local examples of rustic houses designed by Coxhead and Polk, yet he used this inspiration to create a house unlike any other in the United States or Europe. After years of groping, even up to the preliminary stages of the Keeler commission, he achieved a solution that is remarkably sophisticated for an architect's

249. Bernard Maybeck. Williston Davis house, Berkeley, 1897; demolished. Section. (Drawn by Kim Spurgeon Fly)

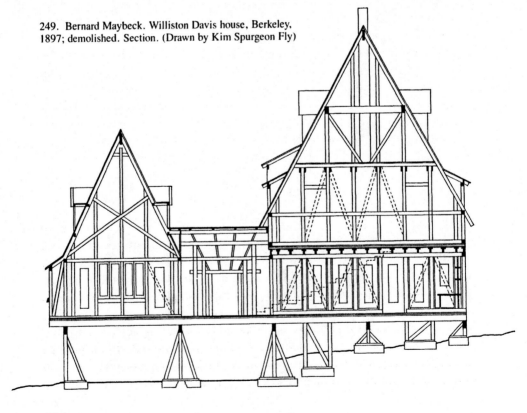

first executed project. Its richness of expression could have provided a base for years of further development. Maybeck continued to work in this vein, but only for a short period.

The two schemes that used ideas introduced in the Keeler house were for a schoolteacher, William Hall (1896), and a book-keeper, Williston Davis (1897). Both clients knew Keeler, who persuaded them to build on lots near his own dwelling in order to create an enclave of compatible architecture and to set a standard for residential design in the community.[18] Yet during these same years Maybeck was active in promoting his dream for the new university campus, a dream that would eradicate most of the existing naturalistic landscape for a grand classical compound sited only a block away from the Keeler group. These simultaneous, seemingly contradictory ventures epito-mize the breadth of the architect's concerns from the beginning to the end of his practice. Like Coxhead and Polk, Maybeck embraced both the classical and picturesque traditions, developing myriad forms of expression within each realm. In so doing he carried the practice of eclectic diversity further than did most American designers of the period.

The theoretical foundation for Maybeck's work was similarly unusual in scope. While he took much from Viollet and Semper, who were then influential among Europe's modernists, Maybeck was equally committed to the principles of the academic tradition.[19] The fact that these sources entailed many conflicting ideas was probably of little concern to him, since he had no motivation to conform to a polemic. He mined a spectrum of theoretical approaches, disregarding as many of their tenets as he followed, in order to nourish his insatiable curi-osity and appetite for experimentation. This impulse received a substantial boost from the months that he spent abroad managing the Hearst competition at the century's close.

Maybeck had not been in Europe since he had left the Ecole in 1886. Finances had limited his student travels to the environs of Paris, southern France, and western Germany. Now, with more experience, a broader perspective, and ample time and money, he could examine a wide range of European architecture. He went to most of the conti-nent's great cities, was received by leaders of the profession at each stop, and probably took excursions into the countryside between scheduled meetings.[20] He made frequent visits to the Ecole and its ateliers, attending lectures and renewing old acquaintances. The months abroad not only expanded Maybeck's horizons, they were a pilgrimage to reaffirm the principles of design he had been taught over a decade ago. Moreover, he could now converse with Julien Guadet and others as a colleague rather than as a pupil. Since leaving New York in 1888, he had had few opportunities to discuss architecture with distinguished elders in the field.

Maybeck's reverence for the academic tradition had never waivered, but his ability to express its principles lacked aplomb up though the mid-1890s. The impressionistic studies of the Berkeley campus plan are loaded with academic rhetoric, but they lack a strong order or sense of purpose. That Maybeck was cognizant of this short-coming is apparent in his refusal to design the project, turning instead to Guadet, the bulwark of academic theory, for assistance. Guadet believed that no formulas existed in architecture and that beautiful work resulted from the designer's sense of proportion and ability to compose elements. Guided by an encyclopedic interest in precedent, Guadet's beliefs corresponded to Maybeck's own inclinations. At the same time, the Frenchman was unrelenting in his logic and conserva-tive in his taste. He had no tolerance for architectural effects concocted independently of structural order. He disparaged the exuberant mannerisms that characterized much contemporary French design and the tendency among Ecole students to create plans consisting of elegant patterns created at the expense of fully developing the scheme as a three-dimensional entity. He believed that it was impossible for archi-tects to design well in a picturesque vein—picturesqueness could only result from accretions made to the urban landscape. He condemned any suggestion of instability or tenuousness, accident or eccentricity in buildings. Examples used in his lectures that fell outside the classi-cal tradition were often lauded for their classicizing attributes. Order, regularity, symmetry, and straightforward expression mattered to Guadet above all else.[21]

Guadet's no-nonsense attitude toward design was just the medicine Maybeck needed at this stage of his career. The experience gave him a final dose of discipline in composing space and form, using principles that, Guadet reiterated, were present in all meritorious work and should be applied to all design problems. The Frenchman's influence is most obvious in a competition entry for the Oakland Public Library done shortly after Maybeck returned to California (Fig. 250). The facade, forthright and slightly abstract, is a textbook study in Beaux Arts compositional technique. Many of its details are derived from southern French Romanesque sources, which Maybeck and Guadet admired for their strong classicizing qualities. The scheme also offers

250. Bernard Maybeck. Public Library, Oakland, 1900, competition entry (?).
Drawing by Maybeck. (CED Documents Collection)

a tribute to the clean simplicity of work by Henri Labrouste and his
followers (including Guadet, who won the 1864 Grand Prix with a
precedent-breaking Romanesque design).[22] The principal departures
from French conventions are the dropped cornice and layers of glazed
tile and brick that are arranged independently of the arcuated parti.
Together with the stucco surfaces below, these components emphasize
the exterior as a covering, a Semperian skin, that exists apart from the
structure underneath. The scheme served as a rite of passage for
Maybeck; never again would he adhere to Beaux Arts models so
closely. However, the sense of discipline this design represents would
characterize much of his later work.

Maybeck's progress is apparent in a schematic design for the
University Hospital in San Francisco (1903) (Figs. 251, 252). Like his
1896 renderings for the Berkeley campus, this project was prepared as
part of a funding campaign.[23] The program is much more specific than
at Berkeley, but the most important difference is the confident and
inventive manner with which the complexities of a large institutional
compound are organized to form a coherent ensemble. The pavilion
plan, taken from current French practice, clearly expresses its functional components, each in separate buildings. Flanking the entrance,
two private wards are the most conspicuous parts. Behind them are
the administration building, the nurses' quarters, the main wards, and

327

251. Bernard Maybeck. University of California Hospital, San Francisco, 1903, schematic design. Drawing by Maybeck. (CED Documents Collection)

252. University Hospital, site plan. Drawing by Maybeck. (*The Need for a University Hospital,* frontispiece, Bancroft Library)

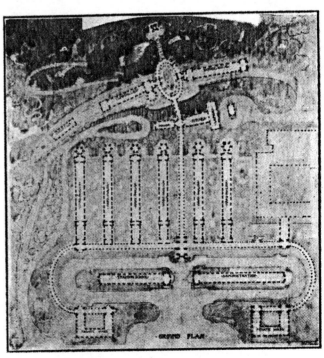

finally the kitchen and heating plant. Up the hill lies the secluded instructional nucleus.

The whole layout of the hospital is imbued with a neat axial order and a more or less symmetrical disposition, yet it contains enough variety to avoid the sense of a monotonous institution. Unity is furthered by the rhythmic pattern of simple roof lines and the repetition of small elements across the elevations. Much of the organization comes right from Guadet's lectures, but it also departs from Beaux Arts conventions in several respects. Unlike most French hospitals of comparable size, the buildings are not planned around a primary linear or centralized open space.[24] The spatial order is diffused in a manner perhaps inspired by Polk's project for the terminus of Market Street and Coxhead's Hearst competition entry. The administration building and nurses' quarters occupy the middle of a hippodrome, created by a two-tiered arcade that allows convenient movement of patients and screens this public zone from the main wards beyond. A connecting arcade runs up the primary axis to the service and instructional facilities. This network of passageways makes the outdoor areas more intimate and secluded, while allowing visual connections between zones. Extensive landscaping, as in Coxhead's Berkeley plan, further dilutes the space and mitigates the effect of unornamented stucco wall surfaces. The arrangement suggests a sequence, but only with movement through the complex does its total order unfold.

If the scheme is diffuse, it also contains an extravagant focal point. Punctuating the approach, two false fronts flank an ornate fountain. The composition is part triumphal arch and part Pantheon, with an exuberant modeling of form that recalls the monuments of baroque Rome. Strictly decorative in function, it gives the complex a public image, as would the centerpiece of Maybeck's Palace of Fine Arts a decade later.[25]

The effect of the fountain is not only a sham, as Guadet would see it, but also flagrantly disregards the French belief that such grand embellishment is inappropriate in all but the most important public institutions. Furthermore, the hospital's layout is an early indication of Maybeck's interest in making the plan a beautiful pattern unto itself, an objective Guadet heartily denounced. Maybeck subscribed to the academic concern for making the plan express "any series of human movements." However, he felt that the plan should also be developed as if it were an elegant piece of jewelry, for the total conception to be beautiful. In Maybeck's mind, these two facets were intimately related. To accommodate the most mundane functions, "canning pineapples, for instance, [the plan] should look like an abstract painting, like the choreography for a ballet."[26]

The University Hospital was the first of several grand complexes that Maybeck hoped to design. Among them only the Palace of Fine Arts would be executed, and it was literally a gift from his friend Polk.[27] Maybeck's earthy demeanor, his dreamlike visions, his lack of interest in business, politics, or even professional advancement made him an improbable candidate for the large commissions he coveted. The promise afforded by his inventive interpretations of the classical language on a grand scale went largely unfulfilled. It was a great loss for San Francisco. But fortunately, Maybeck now had the chance to realize his ideas in other, more modest projects.

Maybeck received new commissions soon after his return from Europe in the latter months of 1898. During the next decade he designed more than sixty-five projects, close to fifty of which were built. In 1902, he opened a San Francisco office and soon established a partnership with his brother-in-law, Mark White, who concentrated on the technical aspects of the business.[28] The following year, Maybeck resigned his academic post. John Galen Howard, who had been charged with establishing a school of architecture at Berkeley in addition to implementing the campus master plan, had little sympathy for Maybeck's ideas and had no desire to retain him as an instructor. Maybeck would never teach again, but the absence of a pedagogical outlet did not seem to bother him greatly. He had taught when little chance existed to develop his ideas on the drawing board. Now that the opportunity was at hand, he channeled all his energies into practice.

While headquartered in San Francisco, Maybeck was still known as a Berkeley architect. Over half of his commissions during the 1900s were in Berkeley, the great majority of them for small and moderate-sized houses. His clientele was evenly divided between university professors on one hand and businessmen and professionals on the other. Few people in the latter category were as distinguished as those who came to Coxhead and Polk in the 1890s. Some clients no doubt employed Maybeck because of the extraordinary qualities with which he could endow a modest residence. Others were probably unaware of his special talent, regarding him more as a well-known designer of the commodious rustic dwellings that Keeler eulogized. Whatever the specific reasons, the inexpensive, informal suburban house remained the primary vehicle for his experimentation.

Maybeck continued to draw much of his inspiration for this

253. Bernard Maybeck. William Reiger house, Berkeley, 1899; demolished 1950s. (CED Documents Collection)

254. Houses, Viterbo, Italy. Late nineteenth-century photograph in a scrapbook compiled by Maybeck. (CED Documents Collection)

work from postmedieval vernacular buildings in central Europe. However, he seldom used the examples from western Germany that had been a mainstay in his designs of the mid-1890s. Having just toured other parts of the continent and collected numerous photographs in the process, he created a panoply of references to folk architecture from northern Italy to Bavaria. His interest in these sources was not so much scholarly as it was pictorial. They became a means to broaden and enrich his vocabulary. The regions he was most interested in possessed natural features somewhat analogous to the Bay Area, where grassy slopes were enframed by hills and mountains. Maybeck also may have been attracted to these sources, as Coxhead and Polk had been to others a decade before, because they were not generally used by American architects at that time. Free from the constraints of convention, he could utilize historic precedent in his own manner. Yet the very range of allusions which he developed suggests that Maybeck, like Coxhead and Polk, had no interest in creating a distinct regional mode.[29]

One of Maybeck's first projects after returning from abroad was a house for a San Francisco manufacturer, William Reiger, located adjacent to Keeler's residence (Fig. 253).[30] The scheme is a pronounced departure from the others in the enclave, with a series of tall, chunky blocks that straddle the slope and are capped by a low roof. The general effect was probably inspired by houses in northern Italian hill towns, pictures of which Maybeck had just collected (Fig. 254). The walls convey a similar sense of massiveness, softened by shingles instead of exposed rubble. But here the roof is like a parasol, delicately poised above the sheer wall planes, supported by what looks like a flimsy structural outrigging—more oriental than European in character.[31]

Echoing the approach to design that Coxhead and Polk had practiced in the 1890s, Maybeck seldom experimented with a thematic idea for long. After introducing an idea in a scheme, he might combine it with others in a new project, transforming the context, and then abandon the initial conception altogether in subsequent work. The residence for classics professor Isaac Flagg (1900–1901) continues the idea of a sheer wall tenuously surmounted by a wide, projecting roof, but otherwise the design is very different from the Reiger house (Fig. 255). The compositional predilections of Guadet and the Ecole emerge in the nearly symmetrical plan and elevations and in the studied arrangement of even minor details. At the same time, the proportions are playfully distorted. Squat window clusters, accentuated by hoods and flower boxes, confront an elongated entrance and an attic

255. Bernard Maybeck. Isaac
Flagg house, Berkeley, 1900–1901.
(Author)

emphasized by board-and-batten siding and thin struts. A general, yet
at once apparent, reference is made to Swiss chalets, which for several
decades had been a prototype for rustic houses in northern Europe.
There, the prevailing tendency was to exaggerate the chalet's ornate
structural components and superimpose them on irregular masses for
picturesque effects. In contrast, the Flagg house is a pared-down and
abstracted chalet, its attic and roof more akin to that of a large Swiss
barn, while the whole is given an implicit order through a classicizing,
mannered composition.

Soon afterward, Maybeck designed a smaller chalet for law professor George Boke. Its compositional regularity is even more emphatic, broken only by the entrance porch to one side (Fig. 256). The sheer wall is replaced by a profusion of projecting elements: windows, porches, balconies, the stair hall, and the entire second story. Everything appears to be structural: a lower zone of squared logs (in reality a veneer) with a light, cross-braced frame above. The surfaces are agitated, textured, and decorated. References to the chalet are quite literal, and they are intensified by being piled on so compact a building.[32] The same basic composition is used for the house of San Jose physician Howard Gates (1904), but in another vocabulary and to different effect (Fig. 257). Again, the form is a tight box with a pronounced living room window in its center. The symmetry of the whole is broken by the entrance at one end, and the mass is abbreviated by tucking the bedrooms directly under the roof. However, the exterior surfaces are utterly plain, interrupted only by a few overscaled classical details. The result is a hybrid: an Italian farmhouse made over into a gentleman's retreat, at once modest and grand.

256. Bernard Maybeck. George Boke house, Berkeley, 1901–1902.
(CED Documents Collection)

257. Maybeck & White. Howard
Gates house, San Jose, 1904.
(*Architectural Record*,
November 1916, p. 488)

258. Maybeck & White. Frederick Farrington house, Berkeley, 1904;
burned 1923. (*Sunset Magazine*, December 1906, p. 142)

335

By the mid-1900s, Maybeck returned to developing asymmetrical, picturesque masses for many of his houses. Among the finest examples was one designed for education professor Frederick Farrington in 1905 (Fig. 258). The form consists of two parallel, interlocking blocks, one two stories high, the other three stories high and deeply recessed. Heavy roof supports, windows that break up the roof line, and wood frame projections complicate the assemblage. These features contrast with expanses of unadorned stucco wall surface, broad roofs, and a clear, often symmetrical, ordering of elements in each section. The references are general, conjuring up images of rural architecture in Bavaria, Switzerland, and Italy. Vague allusions, heavy scale, austere details, and a strong underlying geometry make the exterior monumental without compromising its picturesque folk character.

The apparent casualness of folk architecture predominates in the house of a Berkeley physician, William Underhill (1907) (Fig. 259). The composition appears haphazard, with plain boxes, sheathed in stucco, board and batten, and shakes, strung together around the rear yard. A tapering boulder chimney, with an elaborate cap of clay tiles and galvanized iron, vies for attention with the adjacent belvedere. The building seems like a transplant from the Alps, yet it also recalls local hillside shanties, such as the one the Maybecks occupied in the early 1890s.[33] The image of a peasant's house erected over time was

259. Maybeck & White. William Underhill house, Berkeley, 1907; burned 1923. (Courtesy Bertha Underhill)

probably never carried further by an architect than it was here.

Maybeck composed space as diversely as he did exteriors. A number of his rustic houses are essentially symmetrical, with the entrance in the center and the main rooms to either side. In other instances, the arrangement is informal, with the entrance near a corner and often a short flight of steps leading to the main floor, where the principal rooms form a varied sequence. Sometimes aspects of these two basic types are combined: rooms are axially aligned, but with pronounced differences in size, height, and floor level; or a circuituous approach leads to axially aligned rooms. The spaces are sometimes open and flowing, other times contained. The exterior configuration does not necessarily relate to the interior arrangement. For example, in Flagg's house the order is axial, while in Boke's it is circuituous. The principal rooms of the Farrington house form the arms of a rough cross around a two-story well, whereas those of the Underhill house are as informally organized as the elevations suggest.[34]

Site, budget, the client's needs, and personality all contributed to the diverse expression found in Maybeck's work. He relished the constraints imposed by programmatic factors, declaring that what most architects regarded as problems were really opportunities. No job was too small or too trivial for his attention, even when it entailed assisting a friend free of charge.[35] His receptivity stemmed from his affable, generous nature and his love for people, but the underlying motivation was the urge to experiment. Significantly, his theoretical inspiration came from architects who had no concern for "styles" in a categorical sense and who resisted the limitations of following any one set of precedents, even those they most admired. The patterns in Maybeck's work are so varied that it is difficult to believe that he began a new project with much preconception as to how the scheme should be developed. What little is known about his design method reinforces this notion.

Maybeck's practices stemmed from his training in Paris, where the general idea was developed quickly and then many subsequent hours were spent on refinements.[36] However, he carried the inception process further. Initially, numerous generalized form studies were made, not in pencil or ink but in charcoal and later in pastel, on huge sheets of paper so that they could be scrutinized from a distance and easily modified. Like a sculptor working in clay, Maybeck modeled his forms with complete flexibility. From these vague, impressionistic renderings, the scheme gradually became focused, then was developed in detail. Maybeck accorded himself more freedom than did most of his colleagues. He also faced a greater challenge, however, since he did not rely on standard compositional formats. Ignoring these conventions, smudging swaths of carbon on paper, he made the design process intensely personal. Having digested the programmatic concerns, he was off in a world of his own, guided by instinct and imagination. An acquaintance of later years speculated that to Maybeck, conceiving a design was more important than realizing the project.[37]

However much delight he took in this initial stage, Maybeck's work also reveals a great concern for execution. As a youth he had witnessed the craft of furniture-making in his father's shop and subsequently in the New York office of Pottier & Stymus. A knowledge of materials and sensitivity to their potential became an inherent part of his attitude toward design. He took pride in the handmade qualities of the family's house in Berkeley. Subsequent projects also reveal a penchant for individual craft. Maybeck spent many hours on the site supervising construction, and later, when painting and stencilwork were incorporated into his interior schemes, he often performed the task himself.[38]

Semper's writings helped focus Maybeck's concern for building craft. In *Der Stil*, materials were seen as major contributors to form, constituting the basis for the industrial arts. Semper emphasized crafts not for their materials as such, but because he believed they provided the key to the laws of architecture. His underlying thesis, that the laws governing crafts and architecture are the same, may well have had the greatest impact in shaping Maybeck's views. Viollet's writings were also influential. In both the *Dictionnaire* and the *Entretiens* Viollet repeatedly emphasized the construction process as a craft and principal contributor to the building's spirit. Viollet believed that in the past creativity and discipline in design came from the builder. His hero was the anonymous, free, resourceful artisan who had allegedly conceived *and* constructed the works of the greatest epochs.[39] His portrayal of the artist as a liberated craftsman probably inspired Maybeck, as it reinforced his own inclinations. Maybeck coveted freedom—the freedom to experiment and to express his ideas in a very personal way, through the design process and through the realized product. His approach precluded anonymity, yet it entailed little concern for self-aggrandizement.

Maybeck also probably found inspiration in the writings of Morris and Ruskin. Ruskin's passion for the effects of age on buildings as well as for the imperfections of handmade work may have had a major impact on Maybeck's designs. Morris's commitment to simplicity and usefulness in objects seems to have been just as influential. Joseph Worcester's concerns underscored arts-and-crafts ideals locally. Keeler described Maybeck's initial encounter with the minister's Piedmont cottage in the early 1890s as being "a revelation . . . that profoundly affected his whole artistic outlook."[40] Though Keeler exaggerated, Worcester's attitude toward design served as a catalyst for Maybeck, just as it did for Coxhead, Polk, and Schweinfurth, demonstrating how Morrisonian ideals could be implanted on western soil.

Yet English theory appears to have supported Maybeck's opinions on craft and the building art more than it helped to mold them. His primary allegiances remained to France, where he had been trained, and to Germany, the home of his ancestors. He took nothing from English arts-and-crafts design itself and very little from English vernacular sources.[41] Besides his national biases, Maybeck may have regarded contemporary English work as being too idealized in its tribute to the Middle Ages, too contrived in its picturesqueness, and too undisciplined in its planning.

Maybeck did not express much interest in current avant-garde design on the continent either, even though it was inspired by both the English example and the writings of Viollet and Semper. While in Vienna, he was taken to one of the early Secessionist exhibitions, which he criticized on several counts. The designs were too individualistic; in rejecting the past, they could be only a passing fashion. They were elegant as pictures, yet lacked strength in composition. From an academic viewpoint, Maybeck regarded these schemes as possessing no clear conceptual order.[42] The assessment was staunchly conservative. Still, his refusal to be seduced by such new currents may have contributed to the originality of his own work. Inspired by theorists who sought a return to what they believed were the fundamental principles of design and by vernacular sources, Maybeck's rustic architecture is fresh and rugged, without a trace of fin-de-siècle confection. In some cases his ideas were expressed with an apparent casualness that comes closer to the character of a primitive hut than most arts-and-crafts architects dared to venture. In other instances his designs are controlled by a rigorous order, borrowed from the academic tradition, that was an anathema to many proponents of either the arts-and-crafts or early modernist causes.

Maybeck continued to employ structure as a principal ordering device and as a means of celebrating the craft of architecture in his early-twentieth-century work. But he also became more experimental and prone to taking liberties with rationalist constructs. Unlike Viollet, he had no interest in developing a structural system that could accommodate a variety of conditions. His attitude toward structure was, in fact, rather ambivalent. Few contemporaries gave so much emphasis to exposed structure, particularly on the interiors of small buildings. Maybeck was fascinated by the expressive potential of structural elements, yet he never acquired much knowledge of structural principles, nor did he see the need for an architect to do so. Structure was an integral component of design, but not the primary one. Reflecting his academic background, he believed that architecture and engineering were separate fields, and that engineering was subservient. Anyone competent at calculations could become an engineer, but designing was an art and remained in the province of the architect. For Maybeck, structure was at once a serious concern and a plaything.[43]

The outrigging of the Reiger house gives an early indication of Maybeck's evolving attitude. The members have a life of their own that defies a logical exposition of load and support. The same idea was taken further in the more or less contemporaneous Town and Gown Club in Berkeley. It was originally a tall, unadorned box with a structural cage that bursts out near the top, extending nearly 6 feet from the wall plane. This network projects just as far into the upstairs assembly room, where it appears to hang from the roof (Fig. 260). The intricacy of this system recalls Viollet's description of ancient Chinese houses, yet it lacks a hierarchy and seems fragmental. The effect is much like that of the axonometric sectional drawings Viollet used to illustrate timber framing methods. What the Frenchman devised as a diagram to explain structural complexities is translated by Maybeck into a maze that obscures the rationale of its parts.[44] The relationship of structure to space is made all the more tenuous by the absence of revealed posts. Instead, the paneling and fireplace are improbably elongated, as if they hung from the beams and had stretched by the force of their own weight.

Structure is closely integrated with space in the women's reception hall that Phoebe Hearst commissioned for the university in 1899. The expressive devices that Maybeck concocted here were no less unorthodox than were those in the much smaller clubhouse. On the exterior, the building suggests a factory—a bulky container, its upper corners baffled as if they were ventilating units for some enormous mechanical apparatus, and the stack for the underground heating plant, prominently stationed on one side, rendered as an obelisk (Fig.

340

260. Bernard Maybeck. Town and Gown Club, Berkeley, 1899 (altered).
Assembly hall (altered). (Author)

261). The exterior composition also resembles numerous nineteenth-century railroad terminals, with the shed's form expressed on the facade, flanked by vertical elements and encased by relatively simple side elevations. This analogy continues inside, where the "shed" becomes a grand space supported by arched beams and the roof is gouged by skylights (Fig. 262). These allusions are made ambiguous

261. Bernard Maybeck. Hearst Hall, University of California, Berkeley, 1899; moved 1901, burned 1922. (CED Documents Collection)

262. Hearst Hall, assembly hall. (CED Documents Collection)

by Maybeck's use of materials, for the entire building is framed and sheathed in wood. Large shakes coat the exterior much the way asbestos tiles were used on factories. The laminated beams inside are formed like masonry arches, and their scale suggests iron. They appear to be a complete structural system, braced by relieving arches, accentuated by shake "voussoirs." However, the beams actually begin a full story below, and the floor of the main hall serves as a structural tie. This floor, in turn, is supported by a web of cross beams, struts, and posts, creating the type of labyrinthine space that might be in the bowels of a railroad terminal (Fig. 263).

The scheme patently rejects the French concept of *caractère*—that a building's composition and expression should suggest its use—and, to a certain extent, the arts-and-crafts passion for truth in materials. It can be read as a manifesto against Viollet's advocacy of iron construction, something in which Maybeck had no interest, thus giving nineteenth-century forms a preindustrial aura. On the other hand, it is a celebration of Semper's four elements—roof, floor, hearth (here a stage), and skin—each of which is treated as a discrete entity. The

263. Hearst Hall, dining room. (CED Documents Collection)

264. Maybeck & White.
Wyntoon, Phoebe Hearst
house, near McCloud,
1902–1903; burned 1933.
(*American Homes and Gardens*,
February 1906, p. 100)

effect seems both almost primeval and very sophisticated, even modern. This dichotomy is perhaps appropriate for a building that had to be an extraordinary place, the scene for theatricals as well as receptions, and a gallery for the valuable collection of tapestries, rugs, paintings, and furniture donated by the patron. Its unorthodox design was also responsive to stipulations that it be temporary and be erected on a shoestring budget of about $20,000. Maybeck apparently did not consider this to be a serious work. Nevertheless, the design reveals the priority he gave to creating a mood and the brilliance with which he could resolve a constrained program.[45]

Low cost and impermanence were by no means the only factors that set Maybeck's taste for fantasy into motion. Wyntoon, a mountain lodge for Phoebe Hearst designed three years after the reception hall, is a good example. This was the architect's grandest commission to date. Located on the McCloud River near The Bend, Wyntoon far surpassed its neighbor in size and sumptuousness (Fig. 264). Maybeck had an unlimited budget—the house cost about $100,000—and in fact, he had almost no restrictions.[46] Like Viollet's reconstructed chateau at Pierrefonds, Wyntoon embodies a host of dreams about what a medieval castle should be. Here the imagery is German, yet the effect is ebullient, with a pyramidal mass topped by layers of fanning roofs as on Japanese castles. Each part seems either compressed or elongated, the forms constantly changing and their surfaces agitated like a giant exaggeration in a Flemish Renaissance painting.

The "Gothic" living room inside is also a flight of the imagination, with allusions to both a medieval church and a baronial hall (Fig. 265). In creating this hybrid, Maybeck disregarded almost everything Viollet set down as the essence of Gothic construction. The roof is unrelieved by trusses, and its beams thrust their weight down to thick masonry walls. These surfaces are punctured by large, widely spaced arcuated openings. The configuration approximates a Roman basilica more than a medieval church, as does its structural effect, entirely static and here without vaults. Indeed, the function of the elements seems ambiguous; they are both massive and formed like huge cutouts arranged for a theatrical performance. The freestanding fireplace, backlighted by a stained-glass window, along with Hearst's tapestry collection, augment this pageant of props. The play continues with passage backstage, through a warren of dark corridors and cham-

265. Wyntoon, living hall. (*American Homes and Gardens*, February 1906, p. 101)

266. Wyntoon, dining hall. (*American Homes and Gardens*, February 1906, p. 80)

bers, up a circular stair to the dining hall (Fig. 266). Here the space is confined by immense walls, like the inner defenses of a bastion. However, they peel away on two sides for floor-to-ceiling windows that enframe vistas of the river in one direction and the mountain slope in the other.

At Wyntoon, Maybeck choreographed more than the plan, imparting to the composition the splendid and savage aspects of the Middle Ages with a Germanic flair for drama. He sought to capture the essence of the setting, with a palace "suggestive of pastry and perfume" that conversed with the "hoary forest" and the rugged terrain.[47] While he snubbed Viollet's notions of structural propriety, Maybeck reflected the Frenchman's love of architecture's emotional qualities. In the first chapter of the *Entretiens*, Viollet asserted that "Art is an instinct—a craving of the mind." He queried:

Which of us has not experienced . . . certain emotions, such . . . as a sense of grandeur, of sadness, of secret dread, of pride, joy, hope, or regret? It

346

would even appear that the further the arts are removed from the imitation of nature, the more they are calculated to strike certain deep-seated chords in the soul . . . the sight of a noble building, will often produce such a perturbation of the nerves that tears start to the eyes, and we experience a sensation of heat or cold; though we are unable to describe the nature of the feeling which moves us. This is our artistic instinct.[48]

A few pages later, he described the impact that a building could have on the imagination. It is a remembrance from childhood, perhaps somewhat embellished, when he was taken to Notre Dame in Paris. Inside, his gaze became fixed on the southern rose window, through which the sun was pouring. When the organist began to play, Viollet could only think of the notes as emanating from the stained glass— light, color, music in an inextricable symphony.

Maybeck himself would later recall the experience that first directed his interest toward architecture. He had gone to Paris to study furniture design; however, he soon became fascinated by buildings after hearing the choir sing in Saint-Germain-des-Prés. Through the music the church began to have meaning, and he returned to it again and again. Perhaps more than any other event, it made him decide to apply for admission to the Ecole. The importance he placed on architecture's emotional content is further revealed in the only lengthy essay he wrote about one of his own buildings, the Palace of Fine Arts. Most of the piece is devoted to explaining the design's "atmosphere" and the sensations it was calculated to generate: "sadness modified by the feeling that beauty has a soothing influence." Shortly before the Palace was constructed, he told William Gray Purcell: "You cannot produce a living architecture as a system of applied logic. Architecture is life-poetry; the logic is not something to be caught by intellectual machinery however clever its cogs and shifts. Architecture is the imprint of a greater logic of Man and Nature which no smart brain can take apart and make simpler."[49]

While Viollet believed that the emotional impact of architecture was divorced from nature, Semper indicated that art could be the highest form of transcendental communication with nature. In this respect, Semper's thoughts were probably more influential on Maybeck than Viollet's. Viollet argued that architecture is ultimately guided by reason, but Semper saw design as part of a cosmic natural phenomenon. In the introduction to *Der Stil* he speculated that nature was the source of great beauty but also of "sublime fear." It afforded a "confusion of charms . . . and incomprehensible laws," compounded by the "endless struggle" of all living things to survive.

347

Then there is the element of chance, the illogical, the absurd, which we encounter on every step. . . . There is the deep . . . and storm-ridden world of our own emotions; passions at war with each other and with fate . . . imagination opposing reality; foolishness at war with itself and the cosmos; nothing but confusion. The arts, by bringing these struggles to a conclusion, can . . . [draw] us out of our torment into brief moments of eternal conciliation. It is these moods which have given rise to lyrical, subjective and dramatic manifestations in art.

The enchantment, which captivates the spirit through art in all its different forms and manifestations, is *beauty*.

Moreover, the elements [which create beauty] must proceed from the laws of nature and correspond to these, for . . . art . . . can . . . do no other than follow the dictates of natural phenomena and create its form even if only through following the eternal law which moves through all the realm of nature.[50]

267. Maybeck & White. George Newhall house, San Francisco, extensive remodeling 1904, 1906; no longer standing. Entry hall. (Courtesy Jacomena Maybeck)

The beauty of metaphysical enchantment, evoking the wonders of nature, was as important to Maybeck as the abstract beauty of form that was so central to the academic tradition. At Wyntoon, he matched the "modern" concern for proportion with the ethereal suggestions of "pastry and perfume."

Maybeck did not always attain a rapprochement between these forces. An important, if little known, example of where his imagination held the upper hand is the extensive interior remodeling scheme for George Newhall's San Francisco residence (Figs. 267, 268). The client, a partner in a major shipping and insurance firm, president of a ferry company, and head of the Chamber of Commerce, imposed no financial restrictions on the project. His grand Victorian house was moved to a more accommodating site in Pacific Heights and the rooms

268. Newhall house, entry hall. (Courtesy Jacomena Maybeck)

269. Newhall house, dining room entry. (Courtesy Jacomena Maybeck)

completely remade.[51] Under these conditions, Maybeck became a decorator *de luxe*, with a design that recalls the exuberance of work done for Plum and for Carrère & Hastings. Ornamental embellishment, overscaled like Coxhead's, runs riot on the ceiling and along the walls, spilling onto the floor as a stair landing formed by three intersecting circles. The leaden quality of the decoration is matched by a playful disregard for structural expression. In the entry hall, exaggerated ornamental features consume the surfaces and attendant space. A giant molding drops to enframe the stairwell and complement the wall panels on one side. These surrounds are but secondary elements, dominated by the ceiling where deep recesses and lowered beams, probably located where walls once stood, are coated with floral carving. The resultant visual weight is received by clusters of little columns, several of which march up the stair treds as pure decorative conceits. Elsewhere pilasters become elongated panels, some meeting beams but also overlapping others that merely flank thresholds. All the compression seems to be borne by the stair landing—low, very wide, with a thick base and fat balustrade.

In the dining room, the walls are made dark by a floor-to-ceiling covering of silk (Fig. 269). Amid this expanse rest classical

350

fragments, including an enormous fireplace derived from early French Renaissance models, but exaggerated beyond anything Coxhead designed for the Earl house. On the other side stands an aedicula, top-heavy and stretched to accommodate its threshold. Above is a coffered ceiling, its surface so encrusted that the whole affair appears to be consumed by moisture and in an active process of decay, threatening the make-believe world it is supposed to protect. The ensemble is a vision of a palace from San Francisco's gilded age, more extravagant, gaudy, and outrageous than any decor concocted for the bonanza kings. Yet it is also more worldly. With swaths of embellishment painted ivory and gold, the hall captures the lavish pictorial effect of seventeenth- and eighteenth-century tapestries, for which Maybeck had created settings in the Hearst projects several years earlier (Fig. 270).[52] The rooms are not architecture, but rather a sequence of moods, and they reflect Maybeck's own childlike delight in sheer opulence; perhaps they even playfully accentuate a client's desire for Old World splendor at any price.

270. G. Audran. "The Swoon of Esther," ca. seventeenth-century tapestry in the Galleria degli Arazzi, Florence. Alinari photograph in a scrapbook compiled by Bernard Maybeck. (CED Documents Collection)

271. Maybeck & White. Golden Temple of Wine, California viticulture exhibit,
Louisiana Purchase Exposition, St. Louis, 1904; demolished.
(*Sunset Magazine*, March 1905, p. 490)

The thin line between celebrating this naive awe and its exploitation for commercial purposes is evident in Maybeck's design for the California viticulture exhibit at the 1904 Louisiana Purchase Exposition (Fig. 271). Its centerpiece is a tempietto of giant herms, painted gold. Above their Bacchus heads, painted ivory, is a convex entablature, with wine bottles for a frieze. On the edge of the cornice (a big tabletop), a sloth of little bears (the state animal) quaff the rewards of a prize vintage. On the ground lies a quartet of kegs, each one some 12 feet high, enveloped by Hydra-like capitals, garlands, and consoles (again, all painted gold) that slither around cased displays. The exhibit is like a show on the Midway, then the only place where such immense grotesqueries were considered admissible. But the critics from Italy, Spain, and the Golden State all declared enthusiastically that it was among the most "artistic" presentations they had seen.[53]

352

How Maybeck conceived the idea is uncertain. The man so at home in an earthy peasant's cottage would also gleefully accept enormous Packard touring cars as gifts from a client. And Maybeck had no reservations about comparing one of his automobile showrooms for that client to the crypts of early Christian churches, or its service ramps to the ziggurats of ancient Babylon.[54] In certain respects, he was a lot like Semper, captivated by the elemental in a quest for reason while relishing decorative splendors and struggling throughout to find "brief moments of eternal conciliation" through beauty in art.

Maybeck's demeanor makes him an unlikely candidate for intellectual torment. Yet his architecture evidences struggle as well as delight. The diversity of his work and the constant experimentation it represents reveal a fascination with so much in the world. There was always "something bigger and more worthwhile." He never rested in his efforts to discover it all and maybe was never satisfied with what he found. From indulgent forays into purely decorative classicism, he could plunge into a lean, lucid rational world. No sooner had the Newhall interiors been finished than he created a house out of exposed concrete for geology professor Andrew Lawson (1907) (Fig. 272). Its symmetry, unadorned elements, and planar wall surfaces make it bolder than most schemes then realized by European modernist colleagues.

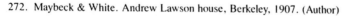

272. Maybeck & White. Andrew Lawson house, Berkeley, 1907. (Author)

353

For a moment, Maybeck eulogized the call for experimentation with new forms of expression derived from new structural materials that Viollet had launched several decades before. The Lawson house is a spirited interpretation of an ancient Roman villa, but these fanciful allusions are discreet compared to the no-nonsense rendition of abstract form.

Maybeck's first dozen years of practice, up to about 1908, established the tone of his career. For several years thereafter, he attained greater synthesis with the buildings that would eventually make him famous: the Chick and Roos houses, the First Church of Christ Scientist, and the Palace of Fine Arts. Each of these projects, in a different way, offered a masterful resolution, but this time period was an interlude. For the remainder of his long career, the search continued, often in a more fragmentary vein.

If his searching was indeed a continual struggle, it was one that gave Maybeck pleasure. Like a child learning how to walk, Maybeck never relented and was enthralled by the task. He did not mind that his adventure departed from conventional paths, perpetrating a reputation of eccentricity. He was never defeated by the fact that the large-scale projects that he coveted almost always eluded him. He did not seem to care that he lacked professional stature beyond a coterie of local admirers until late in life. He continued on the course set by Coxhead and Polk a few years before. He looked to the world at large, learning much from the past and the present. He was sensitive to new tendencies in design and divergent theoretical positions, assimilating them and defying them at the same time. His defiance was in fact the most pronounced, resulting in work that is unlike that of any other architect.

Maybeck also had an impact on the future. His individualism has been a major source of inspiration to designers in the Bay Area from the early twentieth century to the present. His rustic buildings in particular have fostered a local tradition.[55] At its best, this tendency has furthered San Francisco's role as an architectural center, with designs based on understanding and creativity, not subservience and parochialism. It is an inheritance of attitude more than one of physical form. For that reason, San Francisco has been one of the few places where several generations of modernists have looked to a tradition-oriented architecture from the recent past for ideas.

Because of modernist rhetoric, Coxhead, Polk, Schweinfurth, and Maybeck have often been depicted as renegades, but their departures from convention must be viewed from within the context of the academic movement. All four architects believed in that movement's basic tenets and objectives while they expressed those beliefs with independent spirits. The special character of their work stems from a shared approach that encompassed obedience and rebellion, respect for the past and freedom from it, urbanity and innocence, and a relishing of things simple and grand, straightforward and complex. They were part of the academic movement, which often encouraged conformity; however, the importance of their contribution is that they refused to conform. Through their efforts, San Francisco was no longer removed from the mainstream of architecture, but became a place that achieved its own presence. Burgess's hope was fulfilled. One of the strengths of this work, as well as a source of its charm, is that, in stepping away from the edge of the world, it did not step too far.

NOTES

LIST OF FREQUENTLY USED ABBREVIATIONS

AABN	*American Architect and Building News* (1876–1909); *American Architect* (1909–1936)
A&B	*Building* (1882–1890); *Architecture and Building* (1890–1899)
A&E	*Architect and Contractor of California* (1905); *Architect and Engineer of California* (1905–1955)
AN	*Architectural News*
AR	*Architectural Record*
ARev	*Architectural Review*
ARev(B)	*Architectural Review* (Boston)
BA	*British Architect*
BB	*Brickbuilder*
BL	Bancroft Library, University of California at Berkeley
BN	*Building News*
CABN	*California Architect and Building Record* (1880–1882); *California Architect and Building News* (1882–1900)
Call	*San Francisco Call*
CED Docs	Documents Collection, College of Environmental Design, University of California at Berkeley
Ch	*San Francisco Chronicle*
CHSL	California Historical Society Library, San Francisco
Ex	*San Francisco Examiner*
H&G	*House and Garden*
HB	*House Beautiful*
IA	*Inland Architect and Builder* (1883–1888); *Inland Architect and News Record* (1888–1908)
JSAH	*Journal of the Society of Architectural Historians*
LADH	*Los Angeles Daily Herald*
LSFD	*Langley's San Francisco Directory; Crocker-Langley San Francisco Directory*
OM	*Overland Monthly*
OW	*Land of Sunshine* (1894–1901); *Out West* (1901–1923)
PCA	*Pacific Coast Architect* (1911–1915, 1923–1929); *The Architect* (1915–1919); *Building Review* (1919–1923)

357

RIBA	Royal Institute of British Architects
SABE	*Scientific American Architects' and Builders' Edition* (1885–1895); *Scientific American Building Edition* (1895–1905)
SFMR	*San Francisco Municipal Reports*
SFNL	*San Francisco News Letter and California Advertiser*
TT	*Town Talk*
WABN	*Western Architect and Building News*
Brown Scrapbooks	Scrapbooks of photographs of work by A. Page Brown in possession of Sheila Mack, Los Angeles
Brown Scrapbooks CHS	Scrapbooks of newspaper clippings concerning A. Page Brown, California Historical Society, San Francisco
Coxhead Papers	Photographs and drawings of work by Ernest Coxhead in possession of John Beach, Berkeley
McCormick Papers	Letters from A. Page Brown to Nettie Fowler McCormick and Cyrus McCormick, Jr., State Historical Society of Wisconsin, Madison
Polk Papers	Photographs, drawings, and correspondence concerning Willis Polk, Documents Collection, College of Environmental Design, University of California at Berkeley

INTRODUCTION

1. James Bryce, *The American Commonwealth* (London and New York, 1888), 3: 223.

2. Gelett Burgess, "On the Edge of the World," *Sunset Magazine,* August 1902, pp. 233–234.

3. Harold Kirker, *California's Architectural Frontier,* reprint ed. (Santa Barbara and Salt Lake City, 1973); Kirker, "California Architecture and Its Relation to Contemporary Trends in Europe and America," *California Historical Quarterly,* Winter 1972, pp. 289–305. Kirker maintains that these qualities have continued to characterize architecture in California up to the present day, a notion that this study refutes.

4. Few essays have gone so far as to suggest the existence of a regional style. Some of the accounts that, in various ways, have sought to delineate the regional qualities of Bay Area architecture are: Lewis Mumford, "The Skyline," *The New Yorker,* October 11, 1947, pp. 94–99, reprinted in *The Museum of Modern Art Bulletin,* Spring 1948, p. 2; *Domestic Architecture of the San Francisco Bay Region* (San Francisco, 1949); Elizabeth Thompson, "The Early Domestic Architecture of the San Francisco Bay Region," *JSAH,* October 1951, pp. 15–21; Leslie Freudenheim and Elisabeth Sussman, *Building with Nature* (Santa Barbara and Salt Lake City, 1974); David Gebhard, "Introduction: The Bay Area Tradition," and John Beach, "The Bay Area Tradition 1890–1918," in Sally Woodbridge, ed., *Bay Area Houses* (New York, 1976) pp. 3–98.

5. Cities that have served as headquarters for a number of the country's most distinguished architects for at least several generations include Boston, New York, and Philadelphia. The foundations were laid for Chicago to join this league in the 1880s, for San Francisco in the 1890s, and for Los Angeles in the 1900s. Since that time, no other American metropolis has emerged to equal their importance in this respect.

6. John Beach's essay cited in n. 2 is the most detailed and informative. A complete list of material on the subject is given in the Bibliography.

7. Discussion of surviving material is contained in the introduction to the Bibliography.

CHAPTER I

1. This chapter is a shortened and otherwise slightly revised version of the author's "Academic Eclecticism in American Architecture," *Winterthur Portfolio*, Spring 1982, pp. 55–82, which includes a discussion of nomenclature used at the turn of the century and in recent decades. The article quotes more extensively from the period's literature and should be consulted for many references not cited in the notes below.

2. A.D.F. Hamlin, "The Battle of the Styles," *AR*, January–March 1892, p. 268.

3. Peter Collins, *Changing Ideals in Modern Architecture* (London, 1965), esp. chap. 13; Robert Macleod, *Style and Society: Architectural Ideology in Britain 1835–1914* (London, 1971), chaps. 1, 2; Nikolaus Pevsner, *Some Architectural Writers of the Nineteenth Century* (Oxford, 1972), esp. chap. 22; Richard Guy Wilson, "American Architecture and the Search for a National Style in the 1870s," *Nineteenth Century*, Autumn 1977, pp. 74–80; and Wilson, "The Early Work of Charles F. McKim: Country House Commissions," *Winterthur Portfolio*, Autumn 1979, pp. 235–267.

4. Ralph Adams Cram, *Church Building* (Boston, 1901), p. 13.

5. See, for instance, James Fergusson, *A History of All Countries' Architecture*, 2nd ed. (London, 1874), 1: xiv. Fergusson's bias may have been a significant factor in the writing of new general texts published in the 1890s, where a more objective view is presented. The most influential was Bannister Fletcher's *A History of Architecture on the Comparative Method* (London, 1896). See also A.D.F. Hamlin, *A Text-Book of the History of Architecture* (New York, 1896).

6. Hamlin, "Architectural Design," *A&B*, December 31, 1887, p. 222.

7. Cram, "Style in American Architecture," *AR*, September 1913, p. 237.

8. The most complete argument for academic ideals in English is Geoffrey Scott's *The Architecture of Humanism* (London, 1914). Written well over a decade after the academic movement had become widely accepted in England and the United States, the text was a reasoned defense of ideas that were familiar to its audience. The major treatise on academic design is Julien Guadet, *Eléments et théories de l'architecture*, 4 vols. (Paris, 1905).

9. Herbert Croly, "The Architectural Work of Charles A. Platt," *AR*, March 1904, pp. 240–241.

10. The best recent discussion of the subject is contained in Richard Guy Wilson et al., *The American Renaissance 1876–1918* (New York, 1979), chaps. 6–8.

11. Cram, "Good and Bad Modern Gothic," *ARev*(B), October 1899, p. 116.

12. See, for example, H. Langford Warren, "The Influence of France Upon American Architecture," American Institute of Architects 33rd annual convention, *Journal of Proceedings*, 1899, p. 82.

13. Some specific qualities of Victorian architecture that contemporary architects disliked and the vehemence with which their opinions were expressed are evident in several of the "Architectural Aberrations" series published in *AR*. See also Cram's "Good and Bad Modern Gothic," pp. 115–119.

14. Mariana van Rensselaer, "Recent Architecture in America," *Century*, May 1884, pp. 51, 52.

15. Hamlin, "The Difficulties of Modern Architecture," *AR*, October–December 1891, p. 139.

16. Croly, "Art and Life," *AR*, October–December 1891, pp. 224–227.

17. See, for instance: Cram, "The Case Against the Ecole des Beaux-Arts," *AABN*, December 26, 1896, pp. 107–109; Cram, "An Architectural Comment," *ARev*(B), February 1899, p. 18; "Architectural Education in America," *Engineering Magazine*, April 1894, pp. 39–45 and May 1894, pp. 154–161; Warren, "Influence of France," and Walter Cook, "Recent Progress in Architectural Design," American Institute of Architects 34th annual convention, *Journal of Proceedings*, 1900, p. 96.

18. Hamlin, "The Influence of the Ecole des Beaux-Arts on Our Architectural Education," *AR*, April 1908, p. 246.

19. Van Rensselaer, "The Development of American Homes," *Forum*, January 1892, p. 675.

20. Wilson cites the centennial year, 1876, as the beginning of the movement (*American Renaissance*, p. 63). Yet, with few exceptions, work designed during the remainder of that decade was still decidedly Victorian in character. The year 1880 comes closer to being the pivotal time of change.

21. Richard Morris Hunt also played an important role in the movement's formative years by the example of such buildings as the William K. Vanderbilt house in New York. However, his work appears to have been considerably less influential than that of McKim, Mead & White in establishing the parameters of expression for the new movement. Further study of the matter is needed and will be facilitated by the wealth of information contained in Paul Baker's *Richard Morris Hunt* (Cambridge, Mass., and London, 1980).

22. Vincent Scully, *The Shingle Style* (New Haven, 1955). See also his essay in *The Architectural Heritage of Newport, Rhode Island, 1640–1915* (Cambridge, Mass., 1952).

23. Charles Baldwin, *Stanford White* (New York, 1931), pp. 85–86; Lawrence White, *Sketches and Designs by Stanford White* (New York, 1920). Many photographs of such buildings, presumably purchased by White while on tour, remain in possession of his descendants.

24. Van Rensselaer, "American Country Dwellings," *Century*, May 1886, pp. 18–19.

25. Richardson set an important precedent in this respect with his suburban libraries. The subject was discussed by David Van Zanten in a paper delivered before the 29th annual meeting of the Society of Architectural Historians, 1976; a synopsis appears in *JSAH*, December 1976, pp. 284–285.

26. Van Rensselaer, "American Country Dwellings," pp. 18–19; and in the same series: June 1886, p. 206; July 1886, pp. 422–423; and Price, "The Suburban House," *Scribner's*, July 1890, pp. 6–7.

27. Joseph Wells, a draftsman in the McKim, Mead & White office at the time, is frequently credited with the design of the Villard houses. Wilson argues convincingly that McKim, not Wells, was responsible for this major commission in "Charles F. McKim and the Development of the American Renaissance: A Study in Architecture and Culture" (Ph.D. diss., University of Michigan, 1972), pp. 247–252. See also Leland Roth's review of Mosette Broderick and William Shopsin, *The Villard Houses*, in *JSAH*, March 1982, p. 73. Recent work by Wilson and Roth has provided an essential basis for analyzing McKim, Mead & White's role in American architecture. In addition to Wilson's dissertation and his essays in *American Renaissance*, see his "Early Work of McKim," pp. 235–267. Roth's contributions include: "The Urban Architecture of McKim, Mead and White, 1870–1910" (Ph.D. diss., Yale University, 1973); "McKim, Mead and White Reappraised," in *A Monograph of the Work of McKim, Mead and White, 1879–1915*, reprint ed. (New York, 1973), pp. 11–57; *The Architecture of McKim, Mead and White, 1870–1920: A Building List* (New York, 1978); and "Three Industrial Towns by McKim, Mead and White," *JSAH*, December 1979, pp. 317–347.

28. For contemporary discussion of the problem, see van Rensselaer, "Recent Architecture in America," *Century*, February 1886, pp. 548–558. Russell Sturgis, in "The Works of McKim, Mead and White," *AR*, Great American Architects series, May 1895, pp. 61–63, discussed several of these houses, expressing regret that more of the firm's work was not done in a similarly free manner. He failed to realize the reasons such liberties were taken in some cases and not in others.

29. Illustrative examples of McKim, Mead & White's office buildings of the 1880s include the American Safe Deposit Company and Columbia Bank (1882) and the Goelet Building (1886) in New York, and the New York Life Insurance Company Building (1887–1890) in Kansas City. St. Peter's Episcopal Church (1886–1892) in Morristown, New Jersey, is similar in character to St. Paul's in Stockbridge and should be contrasted with their Methodist Episcopal Church (1882–1887) in Baltimore and the Judson Memorial (Baptist) Church (1888–1893) in New York. The best pictorial sources for McKim, Mead & White's work include Sturgis's

article cited in n. 28 above; *A Monograph of the Work of McKim, Mead and White 1879–1915,* reprint ed. (New York, 1973); and Roth, *The Architecture of McKim, Mead and White 1870–1920.*

30. Van Rensselaer, "Recent Architecture in America," *Century,* February 1886, p. 557.

31. Van Rensselaer, "Recent Architecture in America," *Century,* January 1885, p. 323.

32. Hamlin, "Battle of the Styles," p. 410; "Architecture," *Forum,* July 1895, pp. 59, 60; and "The Modern Architectural Problem Discussed from the Professional Point of View," *Craftsman,* June 1905, p. 331.

33. See, for example: George Sheldon, *Artistic Country Seats,* 4 vols. (New York, 1886); van Rensselaer, "American Country Dwellings"; and Price, "The Suburban House."

34. As quoted in Baldwin, *White,* pp. 156–157. The exact date of the design remains uncertain. The Indian Industrial (Ramona) School was founded in April 1885. The school's 1887–1888 *Catalogue* mentions that a considerable portion of the money needed to build White's scheme had already been raised. However, the school relocated late in 1887, and the project was never realized. I am grateful to James H. Purdy of the State Records Center and Archives, Santa Fe, for this information.

35. Paul Turner, *The Founders & The Architects* (Stanford, Calif., 1976). Olmsted was perhaps the most concerned with expressing regional qualities in the plan, buildings, and use of plant material. However, he too thought in terms of foreign analogies; he suggested that some of the best precedents for both plan and buildings were in Syria, Greece, Italy, and Spain. Olmsted sent his assistant, Henry Codman, to the Mediterranean basin to study vernacular architecture and plants for the project. See Laura Wood Roper, *FLO: A Biography of Frederick Law Olmsted* (Baltimore and London, 1973), pp. 410 ff. I am indebted to David Streatfield for additional information on the subject.

36. *Florida the American Riviera, St. Augustine the Winter Newport* (New York, 1887) pp. 19–24; *AABN,* August 25, 1888, pp. 87–88; Carl Condit, "The Pioneer Concrete Buildings of St. Augustine," *Progressive Architecture,* September 1971, pp. 128–131; Thomas Graham, "Flagler's Magnificent Hotel Ponce de Leon," *Florida Historical Quarterly,* July 1975, pp. 1–17. Bernard Maybeck is frequently credited with playing a major role in the hotel's design; however, he did not enter Carrère & Hastings's office until construction was well under way (see chap. 2). Other buildings in the complex are: the Alcazar Hotel (1886–1888), Grace Methodist Episcopal Church (1887–1888), and the Flagler Memorial Presbyterian Church (1889–1890).

37. Cope's interest in regional precedent is noted in Edgar Seeler, "Walter Cope, Architect," *ARev*(B), December 1902, pp. 293–295. For accounts of their collegiate work, see: Cram, "The Work of Messrs. Cope and Stewardson," *AR,* November 1904, pp. 409–438; and Buford Pickens and Margaretta Darnall, *Washington University in St. Louis; Its Design and Architecture* (St. Louis, 1978).

38. The T Square Club exhibition catalogues illustrate the interest that young designers had in regional architecture beginning in the 1890s. For accounts of later work, see: Thomas Nolan, "The Suburban Dwelling and Country Villa—Recent Philadelphia Architecture," *AR,* March 1911, pp. 236–264; C. Matlack Price, "The Development of a National Architecture: The Pennsylvania Type," *Arts and Decoration,* September 1913, pp. 363–366; and Price, *The Practical Book of Architecture* (Philadelphia and London, 1916) chap. 8.

39. H. Langford Warren, "The Year's Architecture," Boston Architectural Club, *Catalogue,* 1899, p. 17.

40. Frank Chouteau Brown, "Boston Suburban Architecture," *AR,* April 1907, pp. 240–242.

41. Walter Cook, "Recent Progress," p. 94.

42. Hamlin, "Battle of the Styles," January–March 1892, p. 275 and April–June 1892, p. 409.

43. Early examples of such work published in *AABN* include: Joseph Merrill house, Little Boars Head, New Hampshire (June 29, 1895); Public Library, Fall River, Massachusetts (October 26, 1895); competition entry for the City Hall, New York (May 9, 1896); Methodist Episcopal

Church, Newton, Massachusetts (January 15, 1898); and design for a tropical church (September 17, 1898). See also: Montgomery Schuyler, "The Works of Cram, Goodhue and Ferguson," *AR*, January 1911, pp. 1–72; Goodhue, *Mexican Memories* (New York, 1892); Cram, "An Architectural Experiment," *AR*, July–September 1898, pp. 82–91; and Cram, *Impressions of Japanese Architecture* (New York and Boston, 1930).

44. Croly, "Charles A. Platt," p. 244.

45. Thomas Hastings, "The Relations of Life to Style in Architecture," *Harper's Monthly*, May 1894, pp. 958, 962.

46. A. L. Brockway, "The Influence of the French School of Design Upon Architecture in America," American Institute of Architects 33rd annual convention, *Journal of Proceedings*, 1899, p. 70.

CHAPTER II

1. Concerning Hunt's role, see Paul Baker, *Richard Morris Hunt* (Cambridge, Mass. and London, 1980), esp. pp. 98–107. For a sampling of contemporary articles on the subject, see: H. Langford Warren, "The Use and Abuse of Precedent," *ARev*(B), February 13, 1893, pp. 11–15 and April 3, 1893, pp. 21–25; Robert Andrews, "The Broadest Use of Precedent," *ARev*(B), May 15, 1893, pp. 31–36; Henry Marshall, "The Education of an Architect," *AR*, July–September 1895, pp. 82–92; and Henry Van Brunt, "The Growth of Characteristic Architectural Style in the United States," in William Coles, ed., *Architecture and Society: Selected Essays of Henry Van Brunt* (Cambridge, Mass., 1969), pp. 319–327.

2. Details concerning the Coxhead family have been gleaned from the Census of England and Wales, 1851, 1861, and 1871; the Calendar of the Grants of Probate and Letters of Administration made in the Probate Registries of the High Court of Justice in England; will records; and local directories.

3. Coxhead's apprenticeship with Wallis is documented in his application for membership in the Royal Institute of British Architects, *Recommendations and Declarations of Associates*, vol. 7, entry 122, RIBA Library. Concerning Wallis's career, see: George Chambers, *East Bourne Memories of the Victorian Period . . .* (Eastbourne, 1910), pp. 134, 201; and *Eastbourne Standard*, Special Illustrated Edition of the Royal Visit, July 3, 1883, p. 19. I am grateful to Richard Crook, who has researched the nineteenth-century development of Eastbourne extensively, for sharing much additional information with me.

4. These drawings have been preserved in the architect's papers.

5. Coxhead's employment with Chancellor is documented in his application for RIBA membership cited in n. 3 above. Concerning Chancellor, see *RIBA Journal*, February 1918, pp. 89–90. Numerous preparatory drawings for Chancellor's book survive in Coxhead's papers. On contemporary attitudes toward early classical tombs, see Edward Tarver, "English Monuments of the 16th & 17th Centuries," RIBA, *Transactions*, session 1883–1884, pp. 34–49.

6. Ottery St. Mary underwent some minor restoration work by William Butterfield in 1849, but its medieval character was left largely intact. Coxhead's description of the church was published in *BN*, March 27, 1885, p. 488. I am grateful to David Pearce, Secretary, Society for the Protection of Ancient Buildings, London, for a search through membership records to see whether Chancellor or Coxhead had any formal connection with the Society.

7. The Royal Academy's Registers state that Coxhead was admitted as a Probationer on July 3, 1883 and admitted into the Lower School on December 31, 1883; no record exists of his entrance to the Upper School. Coxhead's application for membership in the RIBA, dated May 5, 1886, notes he was still enrolled. Academy regulations stipulated that if students in architecture had not entered the Upper School after three years, they would be terminated. Reference to Coxhead's association with the Academy ceases about three years after his admission. The Architectural Association's catalogues ("Brown Books") list Coxhead as a

member from the sessions of 1884–1885 through those of 1887–1888. Apparently he attended classes there for about two years, passing the RIBA qualifying exam in March 1886. The RIBA's Minutes of Ordinary Meetings, sessions 1885–1886 to 1893–1894, record that Coxhead was proposed as an Associate on May 31, 1886, elected on November 1 the same year, and dropped from membership on March 17, 1890, because he had not paid his dues.

8. Reginald Blomfield, *Memoirs of an Architect* (London, 1932), pp. 37–43. See also: Robert Macleod, *Style and Society: Architectural Ideology in Britain 1835–1914* (London 1971), pp. 88–90; and Sidney Hutchinson, *The History of the Royal Academy, 1768–1968* (London, 1968). A detailed description of the curriculum is contained in the Academy's *Laws* (London, 1881), pp. 6–31. John Summerson, *The Architectural Association 1847–1947* (London, n.d.), pp. 16–20, provides a synopsis of its educational program at that time. See also the Association's "Brown Books" and RIBA, *Proceedings*, session 1882–1883, no. 3, pp. 27 ff.

9. Macleod, *Style and Society*, pp. 88–97.

10. Some of the major large-scale classical designs done in England during the 1880s were by students competing for the Tite Prize sponsored by the RIBA. The programs for 1880–1881 and 1883–1884 were for monumental entrance halls to a Royal Exchange and Royal Palace, respectively. See *BN*, May 27, 1881 and May 23, 1884 for illustrations.

11. These sketches are contained in Coxhead's papers.

12. A biographical account in *An Illustrated History of Los Angeles County* (Chicago, 1889), p. 725, states that Coxhead arrived in southern California during the spring of 1886; however, a sketchbook with drawings made in England and with dates noted through July 1886 shows this statement to be incorrect. Although Coxhead was elected to the RIBA in November, he may have already departed for the United States. *LADH*, January 30, 1887, mentions Coxhead as secretary of the corporation of Epiphany Mission, suggesting he had been in residence for several months. No information about Almeric's education or employment prior to settling in Los Angeles has been found.

13. During this three-year period, approximately eleven new Episcopal churches were built between Santa Barbara and San Diego, of which seven were designed by Coxhead. Those churches designed by other architects were mostly the farthest from Los Angeles. Many of the buildings Coxhead designed were missions, for which the bishop himself acted as the client. Kip devoted much of his energy to developing the church organization in southern California from the mid-1870s until 1890. Concerning Kip, see: Kevin Starr, *Americans and the California Dream* (New York, 1973), pp. 83–85; and Rev. D. O. Kelley, *History of the Diocese in California* (San Francisco, 1915). See also chap. 4, n. 35.

14. *BA*, March 6, 1885, p. 114. See also: Arnold Lewis, *American Victorian Architecture* (New York, 1975), p. 3; and James Kornwolf, *M. H. Baillie Scott and the Arts and Crafts Movement* (Baltimore and London, 1972), pp. 34–36.

15. The commission was originally given to London architect Arthur Edmund Street, whose design was published in *SABE*, September 1889, p. 47. Coxhead's initial role may have been as supervising architect, but subsequently he gained complete charge of the project and totally redesigned the church, keeping only Street's basic form. For additional information on the building, see Donald Crocker, "The Church of the Angels," in *Within the Vale of Annandale* (Pasadena, 1968), pp. 38–42.

16. The major biographical sources for W. W. Polk are: L. U. Reavis, *The Railway and River Systems of the City of St. Louis. . . .* (St. Louis, 1879), supplement, pp. 35–36; W. H. Polk, *Polk Family and Kinsmen* (Louisville, Ky., 1912), pp. 582–587; and his obituary in the *St. Louis Globe-Democrat*, December 1, 1906.

Willis Polk's parents were Kentuckians and he always claimed to be a native of that state; however, the state census for 1870, Lexington, Kentucky, Ward #2, p. 18, lists Illinois as his state of birth. Reavis's chronicle on W. W. Polk's frequent moves notes that between 1866 and 1869 the family lived in Platte County, Missouri; Leavenworth, Kansas; Indiana; Jacksonville, Illinois; and Ludlow, Kentucky. The Grantee Index of Deeds for Morgan County, Illinois, bk. 4, p. 577, documents that W. W. Polk purchased property in Jacksonville on

November 6, 1867, about a month after Polk was born. The town's birth records do not exist prior to 1878. While the evidence is circumstantial, Jacksonville was almost certainly his place of birth.

17. Reavis, *Railway and River Systems,* p. 36, notes that the Polks moved to Lexington, Kentucky, in 1869; Humboldt, Kansas, in 1871; Kansas City, Missouri, in 1873; and St. Louis later in the same year. The details of Polk's years in the latter city are from his own recollections as written by Pauline Jacobson in "The Whip of Discontent," *Sunset,* April 1922, pp. 29–30, 56–58. In that account, Polk claimed that his father was crippled with rheumatism, forcing him (Polk) to start earning money for the family at age six. Polk went on to recall that he won an 1882 competition for a schoolhouse in Hope, Arkansas, and subsequently started his own practice there. However, according to Edward O'Day, "Varied Types—Willis Polk," *TT,* February 25, 1911, p. 7, the family moved to Hot Springs, Arkansas, to alleviate W. W. Polk's rheumatism. There father and son began to collaborate on design and construction work, and Polk won the school competition several years after the move.

On Polk was a notorious exaggerator and did not hesitate to concoct stories about his youth to cultivate a Horatio Alger image. No two biographical accounts of his early years are the same, and none of them is wholly accurate. Whenever possible, I have sought to verify details through local directories, census records, contemporary newspaper accounts, contract notices, published drawings, and other reliable sources.

18. *Architecture and Society,* p. 154. Concerning Van Brunt's attitude toward education, see: his letter to the editors in *Technology Architectural Review,* April 15, 1888, p. 11; "The Education of an Architect," *Technology Architectural Review,* October 31, 1890, pp. 31–33, and November 29, 1890, pp. 37–39; and "Richard Morris Hunt," in *Architecture and Society,* pp. 328–341.

19. Van Brunt, "Henry Hobson Richardson, Architect," in *Architecture and Society,* pp. 170–179. For comparison with Van Brunt's Richardsonian work of the late 1880s, see figs. 57, 59, 60, 61 in the same book.

20. A biographical sketch in *Master Hands in the Affairs of the Pacific Coast* (San Francisco, 1892), p. 309, states that Polk moved to Washington following his appointment by President Cleveland to serve as consulting architect for the United States exhibit at the 1889 Exposition Universelle in Paris. Evidence documenting the appointment has yet to be found; however, correspondence in Polk's papers verifies that he worked in Washington at about this time. One of these letters, from Walker Fuller of the U.S. Department of Agriculture, dated November 20, 1890, inquires: "Is that tall young Englishman with you, you once brought to see me?" Fuller cannot remember the man's name, but thinks an example of his work was published in Polk's *AN.* The man in question may well have been Coxhead, whose work was illustrated in the magazine. The circumstances under which the two architects met are unknown, but it seems likely that Polk would not have moved to Los Angeles without some prior arrangements for a job. A drawing for Polk's scheme for "An Imaginary Mission Church of Southern California Type" (Fig. 205) suggests that he had moved to that region by the late months of 1887. Published drawings by Polk of Coxhead designs include: the English Lutheran Church, Los Angeles (*AABN,* May 19, 1888); houses in Los Angeles and Santa Monica (*AABN,* July 7, 1888); and, perhaps, a project for the San Diego YMCA (*AABN,* February 25, 1888).

Subsequently, Polk may only have been touring the San Francisco area, but while there he made measured drawings of an eighteenth-century piano in Oakland (*AABN,* September 21, 1889). Polk's return to Kansas City is documented by his design for the First Presbyterian Church, Liberty, Missouri (*AABN,* August 24, 1889). The cornerstone was laid in November 1888, by which time he had already left for New York. Apparently the job was done in collaboration with, and supervised by, his father, since W. W. Polk and Son are the architects of record. I am grateful to Frank Littleford of Liberty for information concerning the church.

21. See n. 20 and the List of Buildings and Projects.

22. Howard to his mother, June 3, 1888 and May 13, 1888, Howard Papers, BL.

23. O'Day, "Varied Types," p. 7; interview with Chesley Bonestell, October 1972. Ware describes his course in "The Study of Architectural History at Columbia College," *School of Mines Quarterly,* November 1895, pp. 56–67. Polk may have been one of the first draftsmen whom

Ware permitted to audit the program; see Ware, "Professional Draftsmen as Special Students in the School of Architecture," *School of Mines Quarterly,* July 1897, pp. 422–429. See also David De Long, "William R. Ware and the Pursuit of Suitability: 1881–1903," in Richard Oliver, ed., *The Making of an Architect: 1881–1891* (New York, 1981), pp. 13–21.

24. *Master Hands,* p. 309. Polk worked on Atwood's competition entry for the New York City Hall, published in *A&B,* December 29, 1888; Polk's signature as delineator appears in copies among his papers. Another illustration of the tower, probably drawn by Polk later, was published in *AABN,* February 1, 1890.

25. Born December 1859 in Ellisburg, New York, Arthur Page Brown attended Cornell's school of architecture for one year (1878–1879). Apparently he entered McKim, Mead & White's office shortly after it was founded in 1879, left for a brief period, then returned by October 1882. In 1883–1884, he took an extensive tour of Europe, including stops in London, Paris, Rome, Florence, and Venice. He rejoined the McKim office in May 1884 and soon thereafter began to do work for Mrs. McCormick on the side. He opened his own office that December. A detailed account of Brown's practice during the mid-1880s is revealed in his letters to Mrs. McCormick, Nettie Fowler McCormick Papers, State Historical Society Library, Madison, Wisconsin (hereafter, McCormick Papers). For a synopsis of her role in his career, see the author's "The Patron as Philanthropist: Mrs. Cyrus McCormick and A. Page Brown," *JSAH,* October 1974, p. 236.

26. Charles Baldwin, *Stanford White* (New York, 1931), p. 115. See also: Leland Roth, *The Architecture of McKim, Mead & White 1870–1920: A Building List* (New York, 1978), pp. xxiv–xxv; and Richard Guy Wilson et al., *The American Renaissance 1876–1918* (New York, 1979). Polk's fraternization with these men is noted in O'Day, "Varied Types," p. 7; and his lasting friendship with many of them confirmed in an interview with Chesley Bonestell, April 1972.

27. D. Morris Kurtz, *Auburn, New York: Its Facilities and Resources* (Auburn, 1884), p. 106; Elliott Storke, *History of Cayuga County, New York. . . .* (Syracuse, 1879), p. 175; Stephen Neitz and Wheaton Holden, *Julius A. Schweinfurth* (Boston, 1975), p. 1.

28. "Charles F. Schweinfurth," *Architectural Reviewer,* September 30, 1897, pp. 80–115; and Neitz, *Schweinfurth.*

29. Concerning Peabody's attitude toward early New England architecture, see Vincent Scully, *The Shingle Style* (New Haven, 1955), pp. 42–46.

30. Wheaton Holden, "The Peabody Touch: Peabody and Stearns of Boston, 1870–1917," *JSAH,* May 1973, p. 120, and figs. 13, 16, 20, 23.

31. In a letter to Mrs. McCormick, dated February 2, 1885, Brown states that Schweinfurth has recently arrived from Boston, adding: "Mr. Peabody's school is very different from Mr. McKim's, but I have great hopes for my assistant. . . ." Brown mentions that he has made a rough sketch for a new project and that Schweinfurth is assisting him in developing the scheme. Other correspondence that helps reveal Schweinfurth's role are to Mrs. McCormick, August 13, 1886 and July 10, 1887; and to Cyrus H. McCormick May 17, 1886, McCormick Papers.

   That Schweinfurth had a major role in the design of the Princeton Museum was related to the author by Schweinfurth's niece, the late Mrs. Pembroke Woods, in a November 1975 telephone interview. For illustrations of the Peabody & Stearns works cited, see Holden, "Peabody Touch," figs. 4, 20.

32. A. Page Brown to Mrs. Cyrus McCormick, June 22, 1886, McCormick Papers; obituary, *AABN,* October 20, 1900, p. 22; "The Later Work of A. C. Schweinfurth, Architect 1864–1900," *ARev*(B), March 1902, p. 76.

33. "What One Architect Says," *WABN,* February 1890, pp. 179–180.

34. Much later, Maybeck recalled that he first met Polk in Kansas City ca. 1890 (Bernard Maybeck, "Willis Polk," *AABN,* November 5, 1924, p. 422). This story is accepted by Kenneth Cardwell in *Bernard Maybeck* (Santa Barbara and Salt Lake City, 1977), p. 26. However, the last known time Polk resided there was around the middle of 1888 (see n. 20), when Maybeck was employed by Carrère & Hastings in New York. Both Maybeck and Polk

were in the latter city between the fall of 1888 and the following summer, each working for firms headed by former McKim, Mead & White draftsmen, who kept close ties with the parent firm. Under these circumstances, it is likely that New York was where the two first met. Polk may well have suggested Kansas City as a place where Maybeck could begin independent practice and given him introductions to his family and to his friend John White, whose sister, Annie, married Maybeck in October 1890.

35. The basic details of Maybeck's youth and training are in Cardwell, *Maybeck*, chaps. 1, 2.

36. Given the elder Maybeck's business and cultural interests, it is very possible that Semper's writings were a subject of discussion among family and friends. Concerning Semper, see: Joseph Rykwert, "Semper and the Conception of Style," in *Gottfried Semper und die Mitte des 19. Jahrhunderts* (Basel and Stuttgart, 1976), pp. 68–81; Rosemarie Bletter, "On Martin Frölich's Gottfried Semper," *Oppositions*, October 1974, pp. 146–153; Nikolaus Pevsner, *Some Architectural Writers of the Nineteenth Century* (Oxford, 1972), chap. 24; and L. D. Ettlinger, "On Science, Industry and Art: Some Theories of Gottfried Semper," *ARev*, July 1964, pp. 57–60.
   Notice of Maybeck's forthcoming translation of *Der Stil* appeared in *AN*, January 1891, p. 23. No further issues of the magazine were published (see chap. 4). Had *AN* continued, it is doubtful that Semper's voluminous tome would have been included in its entirety. No clue exists as to what portions Maybeck intended to translate.

37. J. Guadet, "Notice sur la vie et les ouvrages de M. André," *L'Architecture*, 1890, pp. 419–421, 429–431. For illustrations of the Natural History Museum, see *Révue Générale de l'Architecture*, 1883, plates 59–61 and 1884, plates 35, 36.

38. Concerning Viollet-le-Duc and Guadet at the Ecole, see Donald Drew Egbert, *The Beaux-Arts Tradition in French Architecture* (Princeton, 1980), pp. 64–66. Egbert notes that Guadet himself assimilated many of Viollet's ideas about structure. Maybeck's association with Guadet is discussed here in chaps. 7 and 10. The importance of Viollet's writings for Maybeck is noted in William Jordy, *American Buildings and Their Architects* (Garden City, N.Y., 1972), 3: 280. I am grateful to Allan Temko, who talked with Maybeck at great length after World War II, for sharing additional insights on this connection with me.

39. Frederick Nichols, "A Visit with Bernard Maybeck," *JSAH*, October 1952, p. 31.

40. Maybeck often mentioned his work on the Ponce de Leon Hotel; see Nichols, "Visit." However, he did not play the major role in its design that many historians have suggested. According to Thomas Graham, "Flagler's Magnificent Ponce de Leon," *Florida Historical Quarterly*, July 1975, p. 4, construction began during the summer of 1885. Maybeck did not join the office until the following year. By this time it is likely that full-sized details for the exterior were well under way. Interior details, generally the last feature of a work of this magnitude to be developed, were very possibly from Maybeck's hand. Illustration of the plan and other rooms are in *AABN*, August 25, 1888, June 13, 1896, June 20, 1896, and July 18, 1896.

41. The Alcazar was intended as a collection of shops at ground level with moderately priced rooms on the floors above; however, it was soon converted into a full-fledged hotel. The semicircular arcade was never executed. The original design is illustrated in Cardwell, *Maybeck*, p. 22, although the rendering is not by Maybeck as there claimed.

42. Some of the ebullient character of these buildings was in part due to Hastings, as evidenced not only by the Ponce, but also by work done after Maybeck left the office, such as the Tenney house, Methuen, Massachusetts (*AABN*, November 22, 1890); the Mail and Express Building, New York (*A&B*, February 18, 1893); and their competition entry for the American Surety Company Building, New York (*AABN*, February, 17 1894). After around 1890, most of the firm's work became more subdued, if still lavishly ornamented. Both Hastings and Maybeck may have had a predilection for fantasy and reinforced this tendency in one another while they were associated.

43. "The St. Louis City Hall Competition," *IA*, March 1890, pp. 36–37. Maybeck entered the competition with Kansas City architects Fassett & Russell. The association was probably one of convenience, since Fassett & Russell also entered alone, preparing a scheme entirely

different from that described by Ware. Carrère & Hastings also submitted a design, whose character was rather restrained.

CHAPTER III

1. James Bryce, *The American Commonwealth* (London and New York, 1888), 3: 227.

2. Ibid., p. 228.

3. Judd Kahn, *Imperial San Francisco* (Lincoln, Neb., and London, 1979), p. 25. The best recent histories of San Francisco before 1900 are: Gunther Barth, *Instant Cities* (New York, 1973); and Roger Lotchin, *San Francisco 1846–1856: From Hamlet to City* (New York, 1974).

4. William Bishop, *Old Mexico and Her Lost Provinces* (New York, 1883), p. 333; Samuel Williams, "The City of the Golden Gate," *Scribner's*, July 1875, p. 266; C. W. Elliott, "Life in Great Cities—San Francisco," *Putnam's*, May 1868, pp. 558–559.

5. David Starr Jordan, "California and Californians," *Atlantic Monthly*, December 1898, pp. 793–794; Willis Polk, "The Western Addition," *Wave*, January 28, 1893, p. 16.

6. J. W. Buel, *Metropolitan Life Unveiled* (St. Louis, 1882), p. 337; Julian Ralph, "San Francisco Through Eastern Eyes," *Harper's Weekly*, February 6, 1892, p. 135; Robert Louis Stevenson, "A Modern Cosmopolis," *Magazine of Art*, 1883, p. 275. See also: Annie Morris, "A Glimpse of San Francisco," *Lippincott's*, June 1870, p. 645; Joseph Carey, *By the Golden Gate* (Albany, New York, 1902), pp. 56–57; John Hittell, *A Guide Book to San Francisco* (San Francisco, 1888), pp. 20–21; Charles Greene, "A Prowl for the Picturesque," *OM*, August 1895, p. 207; and William Simpson Morris, *Meeting the Sun: A Journey all Round the World . . .* (London, 1874), p. 348.

7. Gelett Burgess, *Bayside Bohemia: Fin de Siècle San Francisco and Its Little Magazines* (San Francisco, 1957), p. 13. See also Will Irwin, *The City That Was: A Requiem for Old San Francisco* (New York, 1906).

8. Henry Morford, *Morford's Scenery and Sensation Hand-Book of the Pacific Railroads and California* (New York, 1878), p. 200; Bishop, *Old Mexico*, pp. 326–327. See also: Stevenson, "Modern Cosmopolis," p. 276; Greene, "Prowl for the Picturesque," pp. 205–210; Elodine Hughes, "Hills and Corners of San Francisco," *The Californian Illustrated Magazine*, December 1893, pp. 63–71; J. M. Scanland, "Curious Houses of San Francisco," *OM*, June 1904, pp. 470–475; "Old Landmarks of San Francisco," *Ch*, September 18, 1898; and "Relics from Early Days," *Ex*, February 12, 1893. Not all accounts offered favorable comment; see, for example, "The Needs of San Francisco," *SFNL*, June 1, 1895, p. 2.

9. Williams, "City of the Golden Gate," p. 266. See also: Ralph, "San Francisco," p. 135; Benjamin Avery, *California Pictures in Prose and Verse* (New York, 1878), pp. 240–241, 247; Horace Bushnell, *California: Its Characteristics and Prospects* (San Francisco, 1858), p. 7; and *Doxey's Guide to San Francisco and Vicinity . . .* (San Francisco, 1881), pp. 66 ff.

10. Douglas Tilden, "Art and What California Should Do About Her," *OM*, May 1892, p. 509. See also: Ralph, "San Francisco," p. 135; *Argonaut*, March 24, 1890, p. 11; and *Call*, July 24, 1893.

11. Franklin Walker, *San Francisco's Literary Frontier* (New York, 1939). Other important texts on San Francisco's cultural climate in the nineteenth century include: Kevin Starr, *Americans and the California Dream* (New York, 1973); Louis Wright, *Culture on the Moving Frontier* (Bloomington, Ind., 1955), chap. 4; and Oscar Lewis, *Bay Window Bohemia* (Garden City, N.Y., 1956). See also Robert Ditzler, "Bohemianism in San Francisco at the Turn of the Century" (M.A. thesis, University of Washington, 1966).

12. John Walker, "The San Francisco Art Association," in *Art in California* (San Francisco, 1916), pp. 97–101; Kate Hall, "The Mark Hopkins Institute of Art," *OM*, December 1897,

pp. 539–548; *Artist-Teachers and Pupils, San Francisco Art Association and California School of Design; the First Fifty Years, 1871–1921* (San Francisco, 1971).

13. Gertrude Atherton, *Adventures of a Novelist* (New York, 1932), p. 132. Aside from this and other reminiscences, such as Amelia Neville's *The Fantastic City* (Boston and New York, 1932), most chronicles of San Francisco society in the nineteenth century focus on the richest and often the most notorious parvenus. Entries in biographical dictionaries, city histories, and family histories offer some of the most valuable information on other notable figures.

14. Concerning Tilden, see: Mildred Albronda, *Douglas Tilden: Portrait of a Deaf Sculptor* (Silver Spring, Md., 1980); William Armes, "California Artists III. Douglas Tilden, Sculptor," *OM*, February 1898, pp. 142–153; "Douglas Tilden," *OM*, November 1906, pp. 329–336. On Peters, see "Charles Rollo Peters," in Gene Hailey, ed., "California Art Research," Abstract from W.P.A. Project 2874, typescript (San Francisco, 1937), 9: 61–90. On Peixotto, see: Raymond Rush, "A California Illustrator," *Wave*, October 24, 1896, p. 9; and Peter Robertson, "Peixotto and His Work," *OW*, August 1903, pp. 133–144. A detailed account of Porter's career has yet to be written. I am grateful to his daughter, Catherine Porter Short; goddaughter, Phoebe Brown; and Mrs. Lockwood de Forest for giving me much useful information about him. For Burgess, see: Joseph Backus, "Gelett Burgess: A Biography of the Man Who Wrote 'The Purple Cow' " (Ph.D. diss., University of California at Berkeley, 1961); and Burgess, *Bayside Bohemia*. For Norris's journalistic activities: *Frank Norris of "The Wave," Stories and Sketches From the San Francisco Weekly* (San Francisco, 1931).

15. Regarding Keith, see: Brother [Fidelis] Cornelius, *Keith, Old Master of California*, 2 vols. (New York, 1942, 1956); and Charles Keeler, "The American Turner: William Keith and His Work," *OW*, May 1898, pp. 253–259. Worcester's role is discussed here in chap. 5.

16. Some of the projects on which the architects and artists collaborated are discussed in the following chapters. A brief but superb account of how life in San Francisco could inhibit artistic productivity is offered in Starr, *California Dream*, pp. 260–261. For a sampling of the numerous optimistic projections for the development of art in the region, see: James Phelan, "The Old World Judged by the New," *OM*, April 1891, p. 429; Charles Keeler, "The Passing of the Wild and Woolly West," *Ch*, January 1, 1903; John Galen Howard, "Outdoor Life and the Fine Arts," in *Nature and Science on the Pacific Coast* (San Francisco, 1915); *Art in California* (San Francisco, 1916); and Porter Garnett, "California's Place in Art," *California's Magazine*, 1916, pp. 39–46.

17. See chap. 9.

18. Harold Kirker, *California's Architectural Frontier*, reprint ed. (Santa Barbara and Salt Lake City, 1973), chaps. 3 and 4, provides an excellent introduction to the work of this era; for illustrations of the Montgomery Block and West End Hotel, see figs. 18 and 32. For illustration of the Parrott house, see Lucius Beebe and Charles Clegg, *San Francisco's Golden Era* (Berkeley, 1960), p. 122.

19. Willis Polk, " 'The Artists' Choice,' " *Wave*, October 1, 1892, p. 8; Polk, "The New Dome and the Western Addition," *Wave*, April 14, 1894, p. 9; Ernest Peixotto, "Architecture in San Francisco," *OM*, May 1893, pp. 451–452; Agnes Buchanan, "Some Early Business Buildings of San Francisco," *AR*, July 1906, pp. 15–32.

20. Stevenson, "Modern Cosmopolis," p. 274; Charles Lummis, "The Right Hand of the Continent," *OW*, January 1903, p. 7.

21. "California Bricks," *CABN*, May 1880, p. 13; "San Francisco—Building Materials on the Pacific Coast," *AABN*, September 17, 1892, pp. 178–179; "Healthful Brick Residences—Hollow Walls," *CABN*, May 1880, p. 13; "Brick Residences Should Be Painted," *CABN*, March 1889, p. 35; Newton Tharp, "The Advantages of Masonry over Wood in Architecture," *SFNL*, Christmas 1901, p. 43; Charles Peter Weeks, "Brickwork on the Pacific Slope," *BB*, September 1904, p. 178.

22. "San Francisco's Wooden Houses," *CABN*, November 1887, p. 148; see also W. N. Lockington, "A Chapter on Architecture," *OM*, September 1875, pp. 281–284.

23. [Gelett Burgess], "Architectural Shams," *Wave*, August 15, 1891, p. 6; A. Page Brown,

"Architecture in California," *Ch,* December 30, 1894; Peixotto, "Architecture in San Francisco," p. 462.

24. Willis Polk, "The Western Addition," *Wave,* January 28, 1893, p. 16; Polk, "The New City Hall Tower," *Wave,* July 15, 1893, p. 16.

25. Kirker, *Frontier;* and Kirker, "California Architecture and Its Relation to Contemporary Trends in Europe and America," *California Historical Quarterly,* Winter 1972, pp. 289–305. For other recent accounts of Victorian architecture in San Francisco, see: Joseph Baird, *Time's Wondrous Changes* (San Francisco, 1963), pp. 23–35; David Gebhard and Hariette Von Breton, *1868–1968: Architecture in California* (Santa Barbara, 1968), pp. 8–10; Carol Olwell and Judith Waldhorn, *A Gift to the Street* (San Francisco, 1976); Judith Waldhorn and Sally Woodbridge, *Victoria's Legacy* (San Francisco, 1978); and David Gebhard et al., *Samuel and Joseph Cather Newsom* (Santa Barbara, 1979).

26. An invaluable list of biographical references for these men is contained in Kirker, *Frontier,* pp. 203–216. Useful pictorial sources that identify their work by name include: *CABN,* which began publication in 1880; and *Artistic Homes of California* (San Francisco, ca. 1889).

George Washington Percy was a notable exception to this lack of innovation. Together with the contractor Ernest Ransome, Percy developed some pioneering methods of reinforced-concrete construction during the 1880s and 1890s. Ransome has usually been given the credit for this work (e.g., Stephen Jacobs, "California Contemporaries of Frank Lloyd Wright, 1885–1915," in *Problems of the 19th and 20th Centuries* [Princeton, 1963], 4: 40–43; and Peter Collins, *Concrete: A New Vision in Architecture* [London, 1959], pp. 61–64). However, Percy appears to have played a key role. See, for example: his "Practical Application of Iron and Concrete to Resist Transverse Strains," *A&B,* September 1888, pp. 69–71 and September 8, 1888, pp. 77–79; and his "Concrete Construction," *CABN,* February 1894, pp. 14–17. Percy was later associated with Polk (see chap. 10).

27. Paul Turner, *The Founders and Their Architects* (Stanford, Calif., 1976), pp. 21 ff; see also Turner, "The Library That Never Was," *Imprint of the Stanford University Libraries Associates,* April 1976, pp. 4–13.

Earlier, Bruce Price designed houses for J. V. Coleman in San Francisco (1885) (*Artistic Homes,* plate 27); for William Henry Howard in San Mateo County (1886–1887) (Bruce Price, *A Large Country House: Modern Architecture No. 1,* [New York, 1887]); and for Frederick Sharon and Joseph D. Grant nearby (ca. 1886). The latter two projects were never realized.

28. "Stately Buildings," *Wasp,* February 8, 1890, p. 4. See also "The Artists are Voting," *Call,* September 10, 1892. A good summary of the development of commercial architecture in San Francisco is contained in Charles Hall Page, *Splendid Survivors* (San Francisco, 1979), pp. 23–61. Hearst subsequently went to Polk to prepare a less ambitious plan for the Examiner Building and finally commissioned Schweinfurth to design an even smaller scheme, which was executed. These designs are discussed in chaps. 8 and 9, respectively. For further details on Burnham & Root's San Francisco work, see Donald Hoffman, *The Architecture of John Wellborn Root* (Baltimore and London, 1973), pp. 127–129, 200, 204, 206–208. The firm also extensively remodeled a ranch house for William Wehner near San Jose; see *CABN,* April 1889, p. 59.

29. Illustration of Wood's California Hotel is contained in *CABN,* April 1889, supplement. On the Reid brothers, see "The Work of the Reid Brothers, Architects," *A&E,* November 1910, pp. 36–69. The Hibernia Bank is illustrated in Kirker, *Frontier,* fig. 58; and Page, *Splendid Survivors,* p. 28. For examples of Pissis's earlier work, see: *CABN,* February 15, 1889, p. 20; and May 1890. See also "The Work of Albert Pissis, Architect," *A&E,* July 1909, pp. 35–67.

CHAPTER IV

1. A letter from Brown to Mrs. McCormick, September 14, 1886, McCormick Papers, states:

"I have thought quite seriously of going to Chicago—and opening an office there—as there must be a better chance than for a man here—and the cost of living much less."

Brown probably first met members of the Crocker family through a friend of Mrs. McCormick's, Henry Alexander, who was instrumental in securing several commissions for the architect at Princeton College. Alexander's son, Charles, married Charles Crocker's daughter, Harriet. Brown extensively remodeled the couple's summer cottage in Rumson, New Jersey (1885).

Brown's obituary, *AABN*, February 8, 1896, p. 57, notes "family reasons" caused him to move to San Francisco; however, no evidence has been found to substantiate this claim. Instead, *Wave*, December 19, 1891, p. 35, states that Brown came to supervise construction of the Crocker tomb. Work on the Old People's Home was under way by July 14, 1889, indicating that it too had been designed while Brown was still in New York. The prospects for other projects were no doubt imminent as well. *A&B*, June 22, 1889, p. 204, notes that Brown had left for San Francisco to open a branch office, while maintaining one in New York; and *Ch*, July 14, 1889, states that Brown was "temporarily established in this city." Presentation drawings dated as late as 1892 refer to both offices, but this was probably done for publicity purposes. After moving to the West Coast, Brown never had an active practice in the East. A letter in the Princeton University archives from Brown to Professor William Libby, Jr., dated March 14, 1890, indicates that he had turned over his East Coast projects to Stratton & Ellingwood in New York.

2. Later work commissioned by Crocker is discussed below and in chap. 9. Crocker was also a friend of Polk's (see chap. 7).

3. *SFNL*, January 25, 1896, p. 18; *Wave*, January 25, 1896, p. 6. See also *Wave*, October 19, 1895, p. 6.

4. See, for example, the Builders' Exchange (*CABN*, December 1895) and the California Building (*Ch*, April 7, 1895), both in San Francisco.

5. For writings on Oakey, see *A&E*, February 1916, p. 10; for Rousseau, see *National Cyclopedia of American Biography*, 19: 378; for Mathisen, see: *Wave*, July 2, 1892, p. 3; and Elliot Evans, "Burlingame Station and the Architects Howard and Mathisen," in *Festschrift: A Collection of Essays on Architectural History* (Salem, Oreg., 1978), pp. 63–67; for Schnaittacher, see *Davis' Commercial Encyclopedia* (Berkeley, 1911), p. 217; and for Miller, see *Davis' Commercial Encyclopedia*, p. 228. The work of Knowles and Schnaittacher is discussed in chap. 10. Miller's best-known buildings were done in partnership with Timothy Pfleuger during the 1920s and 1930s.

Kenneth Cardwell, *Bernard Maybeck* (Santa Barbara and Salt Lake City, 1977), p. 29, maintains that Edward Swain worked for Brown; however, Swain established his own office in 1877. He assumed the duties of supervising architect for Brown's Union Depot and Ferry House after the latter's death, but no evidence of an association between the two men has been found.

Brown's obituary in *Ex*, January 22, 1896, states that Schweinfurth would probably receive most of Brown's business; however, others emerged as the principal beneficiaries. Mathisen and George Howard took over Brown's office suite in the Crocker Building, and Van Trees appears to have procured the majority of outstanding projects.

6. *Wave*, December 19, 1891, p. 35, and January 25, 1896, p. 6; *Argonaut*, January 27, 1896, p. 10; *AABN*, February 8, 1896, pp. 57–58; Charles Peters Weeks, "Brickwork on the Pacific Slope," *BB*, September 1904, p. 178.

7. For illustrations of the Appleton house, Goelet Building, Yo-semite Apartments, and Exchange Building, see Leland Roth, *Architecture of McKim, Mead and White, 1870–1920: A Building List* (New York and London, 1978), figs. 75, 327, 581, 796. I am grateful to Professor Roth for bringing the Union Pacific Hospital to my attention.

8. Concerning Schweinfurth's role in Brown's office, see *Ch*, February 26, 1894, which cites Trinity Church and the Union Depot and Ferry House, as well as the Administration Building, Manufacturers and Liberal Arts Building, and a number of small pavilions at the California Midwinter International Exposition to be among the many of "his conceptions." Besides Schweinfurth's acerbic letter to the editor of *WABN* discussed in chap. 2, two letters published

in the *Wave*, November 28, 1896, p. 3, and February 13, 1897, p. 3, shed some light on his personality.

9. New York architect William Halsey Wood was commissioned to design the building (*Ch*, October 31, 1891), but shortly after he submitted the preliminary scheme, a competition was held. Coxhead entered it, and photographs of the design survive in his papers.

10. Cardwell's account of Maybeck's early years in San Francisco (*Maybeck*, pp. 26–35) omits some important details and appears to be inaccurate in several places. Documented information that Cardwell does not cover follows in generally chronological order. A note in *Ch*, May 11, 1903, states Maybeck came to the city to work for Brown on the Crocker Building, the preliminary plans of which were completed in January 1890. Later, Polk recalled that both he and Maybeck assisted Brown with the design (*Ex*, November 1, 1919). Contracts for the building began to be let in July 1890; Polk left the office about a month later. Maybeck's contribution, then, probably involved the development of details during the advanced stages of design.
    Cardwell notes that by May 1890, Maybeck was in Salt Lake City supervising a project for Wright & Sanders and that he was married in Kansas City on October 29 of that year and returned to San Francisco immediately thereafter. The 1891 edition of *LSFD*, published in May, lists him as a designer for Plum. That June, plans were announced for a school of architecture established under the auspices of the local chapter of the American Institute of Architects' Sketch Club, with Maybeck as its head (*Wave*, June 20, 1891, p. 6), a project that was never realized. The following January, Maybeck teamed up with Mathisen to enter the competition for the California Building at the World's Columbian Exposition, with Mathisen as the architect of record. The partnership between Maybeck, Mathisen, and George Howard was announced six months later (*Wave*, July 2, 1892, p. 3); but it is uncertain whether Maybeck ever actually worked with the other two men, since all known designs are by Mathisen and Howard only.
    Cardwell told the author that Maybeck once described to him going to Chicago to help supervise construction of the California Building, which Brown had designed. However, construction did not begin until early July 1892, by which time Maybeck had formed the partnership with Mathisen and Howard. Peter B. Wight was the building's supervising architect. Maybeck may have continued to work for Brown, but if he visited the site in an official capacity, it must have been only for brief periods. The 1892 edition of *LSFD* lists Maybeck as an "architect" at 23 Post Street, the same address as Brown's office. Maybeck may well have worked in the office for the better part of that year. Around December 1892, he entered the competition for the French Hospital in San Francisco (*CABN*, January 1893, p. 7).
    Cardwell also stated that William Loy's daughter told him that Maybeck had once told her about his assisting Coxhead with the plans for Loy's house, the contracts for which were let in March 1893 (see chap. 6). The 1894 edition of *LSFD* lists Maybeck as a draftsman for Julius Krafft; however, he is also known to have had a hand in Brown's design for the Church of the New Jerusalem, the plans for which were completed in August 1894 (see chap. 9). He joined the University of California faculty in September 1894; an account published two years later notes that he left Brown's office to take this job, suffering a very substantial reduction in salary in the process (*Wave*, October 9, 1896, p. 7).

11. *Wave*, November 28, 1896, p. 3; see also "The University Competition," *Wave*, February 13, 1897, p. 3.
    A description of Maybeck in the 1890s is provided in Charles Keeler's recollections, "Friends Bearing Torches," unpublished manuscript, begun 1934, Keeler Papers, BL, pp. 223 ff., a small portion of which is quoted in Leslie Freudenheim and Elisabeth Sussman, *Building with Nature* (Santa Barbara and Salt Lake City, 1974), p. 43.
    Notice that Maybeck's house was in construction appears in the *Berkeley Daily Herald*, May 5, 1892. According to Cardwell, *Maybeck*, pp. 37–39, the house was originally one story and was added to several times over the next decade; however, a description in the *Wave*, May 9, 1896, p. 7, notes that it already looked like a "chalet," with a ladder rather than a staircase connecting the second floor. Keeler, in "Friends Bearing Torches," remembered that the house contained a handmade stove. In an October 1974 interview, one of Maybeck's clients, the late Mrs. Leon Roos, recalled that the front door entered directly into the kitchen. The house has been extensively remodeled, but study of the fabric suggests an

12. The partnership was established by September 1890, the date that appears on the office stamp contained on a detail sheet for an architrave in the architects' office (Polk Papers). A large portion of the firm's work was in Oakland, Alameda, and Berkeley, where Gamble had numerous connections. Later, Polk did work for Horatio Livermore and Charles Eels, both friends of the Gamble family. *LSFD* lists Gamble as a "salesman" in 1893, a "house decorator" in 1894, and a "decorator" in 1895. George Livermore, who knew Gamble in later years, informed me that he cannot recall Gamble having an occupation.

13. Notice of the partnership's formation is contained in *Ch*, October 26, 1892. At first the firm was known simply by the name of each principal; however, this was soon changed to the more manageable title of Polk & Polk. W. W. Polk prepared plans for the Centenary Methodist Episcopal Church in San Francisco, illustrated in the *Pacific Methodist Advocate*, December 24, 1891, p. 7. Subsequently, Willis Polk prepared an entirely different scheme which was accepted some two months later. In a March 1972 interview, Chesley Bonestell recalled a revealing anecdote about the Polks' relationship that had been told to him by Coxhead: on one occasion when W. W. Polk was out of town, Willis had the firm name on the office door changed to read "Willis Polk and Father."

Daniel Polk's sketch of a church, probably Calvary Presbyterian in Kansas City, designed by his father and illustrated in *AABN*, June 21, 1890, indicates he was working for W. W. Polk prior to moving to San Francisco. His design for an imaginary mountain house was published in *AN*, December 1890. For other examples of his renderings, see: *CABN*, November 1892; February 1894; April 1894 (p. 41); and May 1894. He had a hand in the Alfred Moore house in Belvedere (see chap. 6), and he designed a small house in Kansas City for Annie Barnard, illustrated in *CABN*, June 1892. The Polks acted as general contractors for the San Francisco houses of Adam Grant and William Joliffe.

14. Apparently, W. W. Polk retired due to illness; see *Call*, February 13, 1896. Regarding Daniel's vaudeville career, see *Call*, April 4, 1899. Subsequently he worked in McKim, Mead & White's office for three months in 1902 (Charles Moore, *Life and Times of Charles Follen McKim* [Boston and New York, 1929], p. 334). *Trow's New York City Directory* lists him as an "architect" from 1903 to 1905. He died in almost total obscurity in Jersey City several years later (*AABN*, February 26, 1908, p. 17). On Willis Polk's bankruptcy, see *Call*, July 31, 1897, which lists rent due his mother to be among his outstanding debts. See also: *Call*, August 26, 1896; August 29, 1896; and January 24, 1898.

15. Addison Mizner, *The Many Mizners* (New York, 1932), pp. 74–75. Accounts of some of Polk's escapades are contained in *Wave*, August 1, 1891, p. 1; August 8, 1891, p. 2; December 5, 1891, pp. 1–2; May 21, 1892, pp. 1–2; June 4, 1892, p. 2; July 16, 1892, p. 11; August 13, 1892, p. 6; October 8, 1892, pp. 5, 6–7; February 4, 1893, p. 4; December 28, 1895, p. 6; *Call*, July 13, 1893; and *SFNL*, September 7, 1895, p. 12.

16. Polk's surviving correspondence indicates that he sent copies of *AN* to the editors of *AABN* and *IA* as well as to acquaintances in Washington, D. C. A galley sheet probably intended for the never-published February 1891 issue reprints a letter from R. C. McLean, *IA* editor: "Let me congratulate you on your journalistic venture. It is great and will catch the draftsmen as it should the architects. Always count on me and the Inland as a friend to you and the paper." *Ch*, November 21, 1890, states that Henry Merritt assisted Polk in editing *AN*.

The popular story that Polk voluntarily stopped publishing *AN* and took a trip with the subscription money appears to be invalid. A letter to Polk from William J. Marsh, April 10, 1891, suggests financial difficulties were the cause. This is also indicated in an undated letter from Polk to *CABN* proposing an arrangement under which the two magazines would be merged, *his* staff would assume editorial control, and the other magazine would assume his printer's debt of $730 (Polk Papers).

For discussion of the interest Polk and others had in the missions, see chap. 9. Regarding Maybeck and Semper, see chaps. 2 and 11.

17. Willis Polk, "A Matter of Taste," *Wave*, November 12, 1892, p. 16. These and other essays written for the magazine are reprinted in the author's *A Matter of Taste: Willis Polk's Writings*

on Architecture in The Wave (San Francisco, 1979). Cardwell, *Maybeck*, p. 38, believes that one or more letters about San Francisco architecture published in *AABN* between January 2, 1892 and August 10, 1895 may have been by Polk. If all of them were written by the same person, Polk was not the author. Not only does the style of writing differ from his, but some of the opinions expressed are in direct opposition to those in Polk's *Wave* articles, and the last letter discusses a European tour which Polk did not make.

18. Polk, "A Matter of Taste"; and "Our Colonial Craze," *Ex*, September 13, 1891. For a more sympathetic view of Newsom's work, see David Gebhard et al., *Samuel and Joseph Cather Newsom* (Santa Barbara, 1979).

19. Polk, "Our Colonial Craze"; "Tendency of San Francisco Architecture," *Wave*, September 30, 1893, p. 9; and "Western Addition, Second Edition," unpublished typescript, Polk Papers. Polk's friend Ernest Peixotto was more specific in questioning whether use of the Colonial Revival mode was appropriate locally; see "Architecture in California," *OM*, May 1893, p. 462. Ironically, Polk had defended the Towne house design when the *Wave* published unfavorable comments about it in 1890; quoted in Cardwell, *Maybeck*, p. 34. At the time Polk launched his invectives against the building, prevailing opinion held it to be among San Francisco's major landmarks; see, for instance, *SFNL*, May 9, 1891.

20. Willis Polk, "The New City Hall Tower," *Wave*, July 15, 1893, p. 6; and "The New Postoffice," *Wave*, February 6, p. 7. Polk was not the only architect to criticize the Post Office design; see: *Ch*, November 20, 1896; and *CABN*, November 1896, pp. 123–124. For illustration of the design, see *AABN*, February 6, 1897.

21. See his 1890 project for a house in San Francisco, illustrated in Harold Kirker, *California's Architectural Frontier*, reprint ed. (Santa Barbara and Salt Lake City, 1973), fig. 57.

22. Willis Polk, untitled handwritten manuscript, Polk Papers.

23. Between 1889 and 1892 Coxhead prepared designs for eleven Episcopal churches in northern California, six of which were executed according to his plans.

24. The partnership of Coxhead & Coxhead is first listed in the 1891 edition of *LSFD*. Very little is known about Almeric's specific office responsibilities. The 1899 to 1901 editions of *LSFD* list him as residing in Los Angeles, where he was probably supervising work by the firm then in progress. He was clearly interested in design, and after moving to Berkeley around 1902, he became active in community improvement efforts of the Hillside Club (see chap. 11). See also Almeric's article, "The Telephone Exchange," *A&E*, August 1909, pp. 35–46. According to Alfred Roller, who worked for the firm in later years, Almeric had a terrible temper and a somewhat stormy working relationship with contractors and clients. I am grateful to John Beach for this information.

25. *Ch*, November 20, 1896.

26. Coxhead seems to have acquired a sizable collection of books. Among the volumes found among his papers in 1974 were: P. M. Letarouilly, *Edifices de Rome moderne . . .* (Boston, n.d.); A. L. Tuckerman, *Renaissance Architecture in Italy*, 2 vols. (New York, 1891); Andrew Prentice, *Renaissance Architecture and Ornament in Spain* (London, 1893); Ambrose Ledru, *La cathédrale St. Julien du Mans* (1890); J. Britton and A. Pugin, *Public Buildings of London*, 2 vols. (London, 1825, 1828); James Fergusson, *History of the Modern Styles of Architecture*, 2nd ed. (London, 1873); and Colen Campbell, *Vitruvius Britannicus*, 3 vols. (London, 1715–1725).

27. Chesley Bonestell, Mrs. Lockwood de Forest, Elizabeth Knight Smith, and Mr. and Mrs. Scott Knight Smith, all of whom knew Coxhead at various times after 1910, have kindly shared their recollections with me, giving valuable insight into the architect's personality.

28. A copy of the scheme is in Coxhead's papers and is reproduced in the author's "Architects on the Edge of the World . . ." (Ph.D. diss., University of California at Berkeley, 1977), fig. 47.

29. R. Phené Spiers, *Architecture East and West* (London, 1905); see also George Aitchison, "Byzantine Architecture," *AR*, July–September 1891, pp. 82–95.

30. For a history of the parish, see Rev. D. O. Kelley, *History of the Diocese in California* (San Francisco, 1915), pp. 343, 356, which notes that the church was built largely on the initiative of its rector, E. B. Spaulding. Spaulding subsequently commissioned Coxhead to design the chapels for two new missions: Holy Innocents in San Francisco and St. John the Evangelist, Del Monte. St. John's cost around $45,000. Page Brown's much smaller additions to Grace Church in San Francisco cost almost half that amount, while his somewhat larger, but still relatively simple design for Trinity Church ran well over $100,000. Cram's famous All Saints' Church, Ashmont, in Boston (1892–1894), which is approximately the same size as St. John's, cost some $70,000.

31. Peixotto, "Architecture in California," pp. 456–457.

32. Coxhead, "Church Planning," *AN*, November 1890, p. 6.

33. *Ch*, June 28, 1891. The account states that the church was designed so as to look complete in the event that the spires were never built, which turned out to be the case. For background on the parish, see: Kelley, *History of the Diocese*, pp. 343–344; and *Ch*, January 24, 1901.

34. Compare, for example, with Henry Wilson's slightly later designs for the Church of St. Andrew, Boscombe, and St. Augustine's Church, Highgate, illustrated in *Academy Architecture*, 1895, p. 24, and 1896, p. 3, respectively.

35. Coxhead's patronage from the Episcopal church through the early 1890s appears to have been in large part due to Bishop Kip. Beginning in 1888, a drive was launched to create the position of assistant bishop, who would be responsible for operations in southern California. This effort may well have influenced Coxhead's decision to relocate in San Francisco, where the diocese was headquartered. The position was filled in 1890; thereafter Kip concentrated his efforts in northern California. Kip died in 1893, and Coxhead designed his tomb, which was constructed two years later. By this time, commissions from the church had fallen off sharply, and little substantive work of this nature came his way in later years.

CHAPTER V

1. [Willis Polk], *AN*, December 1890, p. 11.

2. Mariana van Rensselaer, "Recent Architecture in America, City Dwellings," *Century*, October 1883, p. 557.

3. Ibid., p. 548. See also: A.D.F. Hamlin, "Architectural Art," *Forum*, July–September 1902, p. 100; Barr Ferree, "Artistic Domestic Architecture in America," *New England Magazine*, June 1895, pp. 451–466; Herbert Croly, "The Renovation of the New York Brownstone District," *AR*, June 1903, pp. 555–571; John Wellborn Root, "The City House in the West," *Scribner's*, October 1890, pp. 416–434; and Russell Sturgis, "The Building of the Modern City House," *Harper's Monthly*, March 1899, especially pp. 581 ff.

4. No record exists of the architectural journals to which Coxhead subscribed, except *AABN*, numerous illustrations from which survive in his papers. The frequent correspondence between aspects of his designs and work then appearing in magazines such as *The Architect, Building News*, and *British Architect* suggests that he had access to such publications. Sometime in the late 1880s, Polk drew sketches for a stable and a country club (see *A&B*, April 12, 1890) that are direct copies of the Smithfield Cocoa House and the restored Old Falcon Inn, both in Chester, England, as they were depicted in *BN*, February 6, 1885 and April 30, 1886, respectively. Either Polk searched out the journal on his own or, more likely, made use of Coxhead's copies.

5. A good contemporary description of some of these factors is contained in Herbert Croly, "An Architect of Residences in San Francisco," *AR*, July 1906, pp. 47, 52–53.

6. Albert Evans, *A la California* (San Francisco, 1873), p. 221. See also Benjamin Avery, *California Pictures in Prose and Verse* (New York, 1878), especially chap. 1. Kevin Starr's *Americans and the California Dream* (New York, 1973), chap. 6, is invaluable for understand-

ing the significance of the wilderness for Californians during the latter half of the nineteenth century. Among the most well-known summer cabins owned by San Franciscans was that of Virgil Williams in Silvarado Springs; it was frequently used by his friend Robert Louis Stevenson, who there wrote his famous short story "Silvarado Squatters" (1883). Polk, Bruce Porter, Gelett Burgess, and others rented several such abodes, all of which they called Camp Ha Ha. While staying in one of them, they conceived their irreverent magazine, *The Lark*.

7. Concerning the early years of the Sierra Club, see: Starr, *California Dream*, pp. 189–190, and Holway Jones, "History of the Sierra Club, 1892–1926" (M.A. thesis, University of California at Berkeley, 1956), chap. 1. Polk's original drawing for the Sierra Club shield is preserved in his papers. The best account of the Bohemian Club's early years is *A Chronicle of Our Years, Commemorating the 75th Anniversary of the Founding of the Bohemian Club of San Francisco* (San Francisco, 1947). See also Porter Garnett, ed., *The Grove Plays of the Bohemian Club*, 3 vols. (San Francisco, 1918).

8. Perhaps the earliest essay to depict Worcester as being a central influence on Coxhead, Polk, and others of their generation is Charles Keeler's "Municipal Art in American Cities: San Francisco," *Craftsman*, August 1905, p. 592. See also: Elizabeth Thompson, "The Early Domestic Architecture of the San Francisco Bay Region," *JSAH*, October 1951, p. 18; and Stephen Jacobs, "California Contemporaries of Frank Lloyd Wright," in *Problems of the 19th and 20th Centuries* (Princeton, 1963), p. 37. A detailed account of Worcester's architectural interests is contained in Leslie Freudenheim and Elisabeth Sussman, *Building with Nature* (Santa Barbara and Salt Lake City, 1974), chap. 1. The authors ascribe undue importance to the minister's own houses as prototypes for the rustic work of the 1890s and thereafter, however. The most valuable documents concerning Worcester's life and interests are: Alfred Worcester, "Rev. Joseph Worcester; A Memoir and Extracts from His Letters" (unpublished typescript, n.d.), and a remembrance by Edmund H. Sears, dated June 26, 1930—both in possession of Mrs. Othmar Tobisch, Berkeley. I am grateful to Mrs. Tobisch and to Sturla Einarsson for sharing these and other materials on Worcester with me. Other useful sources include: *New-Church Messenger*, September 24, 1913, pp. 194–200; Brother [Fidelis] Cornelius, *Keith, Old Master of California* (New York, 1942), chap. 24; a sixteen-volume set of scrapbooks and bound periodicals, mostly pertaining to architecture, in CED Docs; letters from Daniel Burnham (a cousin through marriage), Burnham Papers, Art Institute of Chicago Library; and letters from Worcester to John Galen Howard and George Howison in their respective papers, BL.

9. Further discussion and pictorial coverage of the house is contained in Freudenheim and Sussman, *Building*, chap. 1. Illustrations from both the *New York Sketch-Book* and *AABN* are contained in Worcester's scrapbooks cited in n. 8 above.

10. The designer of the Marshall houses has yet to be discovered. Freudenheim and Sussman date the residences 1887, apparently on the basis of a letter from Worcester to Mrs. Marshall that year advising her to build. However, San Francisco Water Department records show that application for water service for the three houses was filed on July 7, 1889, which is probably about the time they were completed. Normally, wood-frame houses of this size required less than six months to construct. Under the circumstances, it is doubtful whether work was begun before 1889. The authors also date Worcester's house 1888–1890 and have documented that Worcester moved into the dwelling about September 1890. No explanation for the earlier date is given. For the same reasons cited above, it is doubtful that work was begun much before the early months of 1890.

11. A wealth of valuable information on the prevailing attitude toward redwood can be found in issues of *CABN* during the 1880s. Among the more useful articles are: "Redwood," October 1886, pp. 153–154; "California Woods," March 1887, pp. 37–38; "California Veneers," October 1887, p. 130; "Redwood," October 1887, p. 133; "Redwood and Its Future," October 1887, p. 135; and "Pine vs. Redwood," January 1888, p. 2. Another important source, still to be thoroughly examined, is the periodical *Pacific Coast Wood and Iron*.

12. Works by McKim, Mead & White that incorporated California redwood on the interior include: Tilton house (1881–1882) and Goelet house (1882–1883) in Newport; Newcomb house (1880–1881) and Cook house (1885) in Elberon, New Jersey; Cheever house (1885–1886) in Far Rockaway, New York; and Choate house (1884–1887) in Stockbridge, Massa-

chusetts. Clarence Luce also used the material in his Josephs house (1882–1883) in Middletown, Rhode Island. Mention of the presence of redwood in all these buildings except the Tilton house is contained in George Sheldon's *Artistic Country Seats . . .* (New York, 1886). By the close of the decade, Californians became somewhat embarrassed by untreated redwood's popularity in the East, as *CABN,* January 1888, p. 2, indicates:

People here appreciate redwood less than do those of the Eastern States. There it is considered one of the most valuable woods for ornamental purposes and is now used in the interior finish of fine houses. The idea has been copied to a certain extent by builders here.

13. Two of Coxhead's surviving churches in southern California use redwood on their interiors: Church of the Messiah, Santa Ana, and Church of the Epiphany, Los Angeles (both 1888–1889). The material was also employed in his St. Augustine-by-the-Sea, Santa Monica (1887–1888) and may well have been present in other, nonextant buildings.

14. Worcester commissioned Brown to design his church in San Francisco (see chap. 9). Worcester also appears to have had Bruce Porter prepare plans for the quarters of the Society for Helping Boys at 2225 Mariposa Street, of which both men served as director. The fireplace surround in Worcester's living room is nearly identical to one Polk designed around 1890 for Worcester's friend George Howison, the plans for which are in Polk's papers. An undated letter from Worcester to Howison in Howison's papers (BL) reveals that Howison had originally gone to Brown, who replied that he was too busy to take on the job but suggested that Worcester do it. Howison must have commissioned Polk shortly thereafter.

15. See chap. 6.

16. No contract notices for the house were published, suggesting that the Polks did most, if not all, of the work themselves. San Francisco Water Department records show that water service began in September 1892, probably about the time of initial occupancy. The interiors of the Polk apartment were not completed until the following year—1893 being inscribed as part of the decorative woodwork over the dining room fireplace.

   The story about Polk's securing half of the property was told to Mrs. Max Stern by George Wright (Daisy Polk's lawyer) when she and her husband purchased the Polk side of the house in 1924. Shortly after Willis Polk moved out in 1900, the family's unit was divided into several apartments, sustaining considerable changes in the process. Already an addition had been made to the top floor of the Williams unit. Polk's involvement in these changes is unknown. The plans shown in Fig. 66 are based on old photographs and detailed examination of the existing fabric.

17. "Old Landmarks of San Francisco," *Ch,* September 18, 1898. See also chap. 3, n. 8.

18. Joseph Backus, "Gelett Burgess: A Biography of the Man Who Wrote 'The Purple Cow' " (Ph.D. diss., University of California at Berkeley, 1961), p. 141, states the garden was laid out in 1894. The current owner, who has known the house since the 1910s, recalled that Porter was always given credit for the garden. Porter also designed the stained-glass window originally located in the dining room bay. He frequently collaborated with Polk on work and was also a friend of Atkinson's. A photograph of the gates is contained in a scrapbook Coxhead kept of his own work; no other evidence to substantiate the connection has been found. However, Coxhead did design the additions to her Atkinson Building (ca. 1902) (see chap. 9).

19. Polk's proposal for terracing is contained in a letter to Irving Scott (who subsequently became one of Coxhead's most important clients), dated October 26, 1894 (Polk Papers). Some twenty years later, Horatio Livermore had Polk design a set of ramps, stairs, and balustrade for the Jones Street approach to the block. Horatio Livermore's wife told her grandson, George, that Polk had been involved with the ca. 1897 alterations to the family house; however, photographs of work done at that time suggest that neither Polk nor any other architect actually designed the changes. Instead, he probably served as an informal consultant. Polk was responsible for alterations made ca. 1891 for himself and his family prior to construction of their own residence next door. See *OM,* May 1893, p. 460, for an illustration.

20. For comparison, see: Shaw's 42 Netherhall Gardens, London (1887–1888), illustrated in *The Architect,* March 7, 1890; and Voysey's "A Country House with Octagonal Hall" (ca. 1888), illustrated in *BA,* April 5, 1889.

21. The similarities between a number of Coxhead's designs and contemporaneous published English work is so strong that he must have had access to one or more of that country's architectural magazines (see n. 4 above). Whether he had any closer contact with architects such as Voysey, through correspondence or mutual friends in England, is unknown.

22. The approximate cost of Coxhead's house was $5,500; Murdock's, $4,200. Concerning Murdock, see: *Davis' Commercial Encyclopedia* (Berkeley, 1911), p. 67; Backus, "Burgess," pp. 155–157; and Charles Murdock, *A Backward Glance at Eighty, Recollections and Comment* (San Francisco, 1921). I am grateful to his daughter, Marguerite Murdock, for supplying me with much useful information about the house.

23. For illustration, see Mark Girouard, *Sweetness and Light: The 'Queen Anne' Movement 1860–1900* (Oxford, 1977), figs. 165–168.

24. See, for instance, the hall of Shaw's 170 Queen's Gate, illustrated in *The Architect*, June 2, 1891; and Andrew Saint, *Richard Norman Shaw* (New Haven, 1976), fig. 186.

25. The precise cost of the house is unknown. One contract notice published in *CABN*, July 1896, p. 84, quotes a figure of $4,597 excluding "Plumbing, mantles, etc." Such work, coupled with Coxhead's 7 percent commission, would probably not have been more than equal to the base cost.

26. *Ch*, August 8, 1895, and *Wave*, March 14, 1896, p. 10. For further information on Dimond, see: "Defenders of the Union," *OM*, April 1896, pp. 455–456; and W. H. Murray, *The Builders of a Great City* (San Francisco, 1891).

27. *Ch*, August 8, 1895.

CHAPTER VI

1. Articles dealing with American suburban houses published during the 1890s include: Bruce Price, "The Suburban House," *Scribner's*, July 1890, pp. 3–19; Mariana van Rensselaer, "The Development of American Homes," *Forum*, January 1892, pp. 667–676; and Barr Ferree, "Artistic Domestic Architecture in America," *New England Magazine*, June 1895, pp. 451–466. For good illustration of McKim, Mead & White's rustic houses of the period, see Mosette Broderick, "A Place Where Nobody Goes: The Early Work of McKim, Mead & White and the Development of the South Shore of Long Island," in Helen Searing, ed., *In Search of Modern Architecture, A Tribute to Henry-Russell Hitchcock* (New York and Cambridge, Mass., 1982), pp. 185–205.

   Further study may reveal a substantial body of rustic suburban and country houses designed during the 1890s that are of major importance; however, the period's literature does not indicate this. A major exception to this generality outside the Bay Region is the work of Wilson Eyre, who drew much inspiration from contemporary English arts-and-crafts design. See: Alfred Githens, "Wilson Eyre, Jr.: His Work," *Architectural Annual*, 1900, pp. 121–184; and Julian Millard, "The Work of Wilson Eyre," *AR*, October 1903, pp. 282–325.

2. Mel Scott, *The San Francisco Bay Area* (Berkeley and Los Angeles, 1959), especially chaps. 4 and 5.

3. *Sausalito News*, February 12, 1885; *Ch*, May 26, 1889; *Sausalito News*, January 9, 1897; *California Illustrated, A Guide for Tourists and Settlers* (San Francisco, 1891), p. 59. I am grateful to Helen Van Cleve Park for sharing with me her large collection of notes copied from contemporary sources on Sausalito, Mill Valley, and other Marin County communities.

4. Little is known about O'Shaughnessy's early career, but he laid out at least one other rustic suburb, Burlingame Park, discussed below. Basic biographical information can be found in *Who's Who in California* (San Francisco, 1929), p. 266. After the mid-1890s, most of his work centered on the development of the region's utilities; see Scott, *San Francisco Bay Area*, pp. 167–168.

5. Concerning Mill Valley, see: *Argonaut*, August 4, 1890, p. 7; *Ex*, March 22, 1896; *Sausalito News*, January 9, 1897; and *Mill Valley Record*, September 21, 1960. On Belvedere, see:

Wave, March 21, 1891, p. 14; *SFNL*, August 15, 1891, p. 29; Daniel O'Connell, *Belvedere, A Picturesque Situation for Residential and Summer Houses* . . . (n.p., n.d.), p. 5; *Souvenir of Belvedere* (San Francisco, n.d.). Much additional information is contained in the Belvedere Land Company's records, which I was graciously permitted to examine.

6. *Argonaut*, April 20, 1891, p. 11; *Wave*, March 20, 1891, p. 14.

7. *Wave*, May 2, 1891, p. 9; *Call*, May 18, 1890, sect. 9, pp. 3–4; Charles Keeler, *San Francisco and Thereabout* (San Francisco, 1902), p. 90; *Sausalito News*, April 8, 1892. See also Marin County Journal, *Souvenir of Marin County California* (San Francisco, 1893).

8. "San Mateo," *California Home and Farm*, April 1889, pp. 2–5; *Ex*, June 2, 1889; Phillip Alexander and Charles Hamm, *History of San Mateo County* (Burlingame, Calif., 1916), pp. 42 ff. Illustration of some of the area's Victorian country houses is contained in Donald Ringler, "Hillsborough-San Mateo Mansions," *La Peninsula*, Winter 1976.

9. *Wave*, February 11, 1893, p. 6; March 18, 1893, p. 6; and October 20, 1894, pp. 7–8; *Ch*, December 7, 1894, and June 4, 1899; *Redwood City Democrat*, March 30, 1893; and Brown Scrapbooks, CHS. Concerning the community's later development, see: A. J. Wells, "Down the Peninsula," *Sunset*, July 1909, pp. 102–105; William de Jung, "San Mateo County," *OW*, February 1902, pp. 223–233; Henry Spencer, "Democracy DeLuxe," *Sunset*, May 1915, pp. 935–946; and Elizabeth Burns, "The Enduring Affluent Suburb," *Landscape*, 1980, pp. 33–41. Useful pictorial supplements include: Janet Nelson and Fran Meyer, *Ranchos "Victorian"* (Hillsborough [?], Calif., 1966); and Betty McGlynn, "The Celebrated Burlingame Country Club," *La Peninsula*, Fall 1973.

10. Kenneth Cardwell, in *Bernard Maybeck* (Santa Barbara and Salt Lake City, 1977), p. 35, suggests that Maybeck might have designed the house on the basis of its similarity to the work he did in Berkeley several years later. The conception is quite unlike others produced by the office. Construction began around late October 1894, so Maybeck could have worked on at least the preliminary design before leaving the office in September. The house was described as "English" at that time, and its reference to Stokesay Castle seems much stronger than to the postmedieval vernacular houses of western Germany from which Maybeck drew in subsequent years (see chap. 11). The few surviving photographs also indicate that the details were consistent with Brown's other work and markedly different from Maybeck's own. Thus, whether Maybeck contributed to the scheme or not remains a matter of conjecture.

11. An extensive search conducted by John Beach and myself failed to uncover written documentation that Coxhead designed the Churchill house. However, careful examination of the building's design, including its details, reveals too many similarities in personal style for the house to have come from another architect's hand. The unusual plan is much the same in its basic arrangement as that of Coxhead's own house in San Mateo. An even greater affinity exists with the David Greenleaf house in Alameda (ca. 1892), illustrated in Sally Woodbridge, ed., *Bay Area Houses* (New York, 1976), pp. 30–31 (there it is incorrectly spelled Greenlease). Indeed, the two houses are identical, save for details and a few aspects of their plans. Yet no written documentation exists for the Greenleaf house either. The closest thing to proof is contained in J. Cather Newsom's *Modern Homes of California* (San Francisco, 1893), where he cites Coxhead as among the architects whose work is illustrated and where a photograph of the Greenleaf house is included. It is the only house in Newsom's book that could possibly have been designed by Coxhead. The Greenleaf house is also too individual a solution and bears too many of Coxhead's stylistic traits to suggest that it was designed by another architect copying the Churchill house.

12. The exact date of the Carrigan house remains uncertain. The residence was not completed by July 1892, when *SFNL* noted that Carrigan would be renting a house nearby for the summer; but it probably was by May 1893, when *LSFD* listed him as a resident of San Rafael, of which the Ross Valley was then a part.

13. The building has served as offices for the University of California since World War II; no original plans have been found. According to Stirling Gorrill, who lived there while it was a fraternity in the 1930s, the southern wing (at the right in Fig. 109) housed a den with study rooms above; the adjacent section contained a large, barrel-vaulted living hall; the tall, stuccoed portion included the original dining room with bedrooms above; and the northern wing held the kitchen and additional bedrooms.

14. The client's grandson, Loy Chamberlin, possesses Coxhead's bill, which shows the total cost was $4,155.65, including the architect's 7 percent commission for plans, specifications, and details. The bill also indicates that work on the project began as early as January 1890. Maybeck may have had a role in the design; see chap. 4, n. 10.

15. Again, the house's exact date is unknown. The deed for the property was filed in the San Mateo County Recorder's Office on May 11, 1891. The similarity in its plan with those of the Churchill and Greenleaf houses suggests that it was built at about the same time, that is, within a year or two of the property's purchase. Both Coxhead and his brother Almeric were bachelors at this time and their place of residence remained San Francisco. The San Mateo house was used as a second dwelling until Ernest Coxhead moved there permanently ca. 1903. The motivation behind its construction may well have been to advertise the firm's work in hopes of securing commissions in Burlingame Park and other fashionable suburban developments nearby.

16. Rey's son, the late Britton Rey, and granddaughter, Jane van Kuelen, kindly furnished me with information concerning the family.

17. Mrs. Rey's mentor, William Keith, was among the first California artists to express an interest in the state's Hispanic architecture; see Brother [Fidelis] Cornelius, *Keith, Old Master of California* (New York, 1942), pp. 112–113. Several sketches of Monterey buildings drawn by Mrs. Rey in the late 1880s are in the possession of Jane van Kuelen.

18. Mira Maclay, "The Maybeck One Room House," *Sunset*, July 1923, pp. 65–66, 80; and Cardwell, *Maybeck*, especially chap. 8. For illustration of a more typical plan for small summer cottages, see *SABE*, August 1896, p. 30.

19. *Ch*, March 16, 1899; and *Memorial Notices upon the Death of Charles Stetson Wheeler* (San Francisco, 1924). Wheeler's great-granddaughter, Mrs. Robert Morrow, and Donald McLaughlin gave me many invaluable details concerning both client and house.

20. At that time most Adirondack camps were still quite modest; however, the term was assuming a new meaning, comparable to that of a "cottage" in Newport, with the construction of elaborate compounds by William Durant on and near Raquette Lake. See: Craig Gilborn, *Durant: The Fortunes and Woodland Camps of a Family in the Adirondacks* (Sylvan Lake, N.Y., 1981); Harvey Kaiser, *Great Camps of the Adirondacks* (Boston, 1982), especially chaps. 5, 6, 9; and Harold Hochschild, *Life and Leisure in the Adirondack Backwoods* (Blue Mountain Lake, N.Y., 1962), especially chaps. 1, 3.

      All of these buildings, including The Bend, would soon be eclipsed by Phoebe Hearst's Wyntoon (1902–1903), designed by Maybeck; see chap. 11. According to Donald McLaughlin, Wyntoon was located on Wheeler's property. Mrs. Hearst, a friend and client, was given permission to construct a "bungalow" on the premises. Wheeler was reportedly outraged when he discovered the scope of her plans. The land was not purchased by the Hearst family until much later.

21. Polk prepared two designs for Bourn's mother's house in St. Helena (ca. 1890 and 1898) (see chap. 7), and another for Bourn himself nearby (1894). None of these schemes was executed. Other commissions include Bourn's houses in San Francisco (1895–1896) (see chap. 7) and Woodside (1914–1916). Polk also designed a number of buildings for the Spring Valley Water Company and the San Francisco (later Pacific) Gas and Electric Company, as well as the new quarters of the Pacific Union Club, at a time when Bourn was either president of or active in these organizations. Much of the credit should probably go to Bourn for Polk's chairing the Architectural Committee for the Panama-Pacific International Exposition. Bourn's nephew, F. Bourn Hayne, and Chesley Bonestell provided me with much useful information concerning the friendship between the two men.

22. Charles Bohakel, *A History of the Empire Mine at Grass Valley* (Nevada City, Calif., 1968).

23. For illustration, see Harold Kirker, *California's Architectural Frontier*, reprint ed. (Santa Barbara and Salt Lake City, 1973), fig. 56.

24. *Ch*, May 2, 1897 and March 16, 1899.

25. Surviving preliminary drawings for the grounds in Polk's papers were prepared while he was in partnership with George Alexander Wright (1904–1906); however, the orientation of the

house away from the road and the temporary nature of earlier landscaping suggest the basic form of this layout was conceived at the same time as the house itself. One sheet from the 1904–1906 period, delineating a planting scheme, was prepared by the elusive San Francisco landscape designer Oscar Prager. Polk's friend Bruce Porter may also have contributed to the design; see n. 30.

26. *Call*, May 16, 1896 and July 8, 1896; and *Argonaut*, December 6, 1946, p. 11. A brief and somewhat inaccurate history of Beaulieu is contained in *The Trianon Awaits*, California History Center, Local History Studies, vol. 14 (Cupertino, Calif., 1973).

27. Reginald Blomfield and F. Inigo Thomas, *The Formal Garden in England* (London, 1892), p. 13; John Sedding, *Garden-Craft Old and New* (London and New York, 1892), p. 156.

28. Blomfield and Thomas, *Formal Garden*, pp. 19, 58–59; Sedding, *Garden-Craft*, p. 161.

29. *ARev*(B), June 13, 1892, pp. 53–55; Charles Platt, *Italian Gardens* (New York, 1894). See also: Morris Reynolds, "The Villas of Rome," *ARev*(B), January–March 1897, pp. 256–288; R. Clipson Sturgis, "The Garden as an Adjunct to Architecture," *ARev*(B), March 20, 1898, pp. 21–24; and Elizabeth Champney, "The Chateau Gardens of André Le Nôtre," *ARev*(B), June 10, 1898, pp. 31–34.

30. "The Carolan Stables, Finest in California," *Ch*, March 25, 1900. Porter appears to have designed the grounds when Polk remodeled Katherine Atkinson's house; see chap. 5. He may well have collaborated on the garden plans of the Empire Cottage and Beaulieu discussed above. Other documented landscape work includes the gardens at Filoli, William Bourn's country place at Woodside, and those at New Place, William Crocker's Hillsborough residence.

31. For discussion of Coxhead's tour, see chap. 7, n. 12.

CHAPTER VII

1. For a sampling of contemporary uses of the term "Renaissance," see: Mariana van Rensselaer, "The Development of the American Home," *Forum*, January 1892, pp. 673–674; George Sheldon, *Artistic Country-Seats*, 4 vols. (New York, 1886); Bruce Price, "The Suburban House," *Scribner's*, July 1890, p. 18; Thomas Hastings, "The Relations of Life to Style in Architecture," *Harper's Monthly*, May 1894, p. 957; Joy Wheeler Dow, *American Renaissance* (New York, 1904); and "The Work of Messrs. Carrère and Hastings," *AR*, January 1912, pp. 1–21.

2. Willis Polk, "Tendency of San Francisco Architecture," *Wave*, September 30, 1893, p. 9; Ernest Coxhead, "A Village Church: Cost Fifty Thousand Dollars," *BB*, September 1899, p. 156.

3. Kevin Starr, *Americans and the California Dream* (New York, 1973), pp. 375 ff.

4. Bayard Taylor, *New Pictures for California* (New York, 1894), as quoted in George Wharton James, *California Romantic and Beautiful* (Boston, 1914), p. 6.

5. Hubert Howe Bancroft, *Some Cities and San Francisco . . .* (New York, 1907), pp. 24–25.

6. See, for instance, Bruce Porter, "The Beginning of Art in California," in *Art in California* (San Francisco, 1916), pp. 21–32.

7. Morton and Lucia White, *The Intellectual Versus the City* (Cambridge, Mass., 1962).

8. Worcester's scrapbooks in CED Docs reveal the breadth of his interests in architecture. An entire volume is devoted to material on the Hearst Plan for the University of California. The minister's surviving correspondence with John Galen Howard, Howard Papers, BL, indicates that his interest in the competition was not entirely passive. Worcester was also a staunch admirer of the work done by his nephew through marriage, Daniel Burnham, and in 1900 he facilitated an introduction to the Chicago architect for his friend Polk; see chap. 10.

9. Concerning Gibbs, see *Ch*, November 16, 1895; and George Gibbs, *The Gibbs Family of*

Rhode Island and Some Related Families (New York, 1933). Gibbs died less than a month after moving into the house.

10. *Ch*, July 16, 1894; *Wave*, October 19, 1895, p. 10. To my knowledge only two other residences in San Francisco were constructed entirely of stone at that time: the James Flood house, designed by Augustus Laver (1886), and the Henry Crocker house, designed by the New York architect Frank Freeman (1890–1891). Work began on an equally large stone dwelling, designed by Edward Swain for William Whittier, a few months after plans for the Gibbs house were announced.

11. Documentation for the collaborating artists' work is contained in *Ex*, August 17, 1894; *Wave*, October 19, 1894, p. 10; and *Ch*, May 11, 1895. The first account mentions that de Forest designed an "arabesque" scheme for the library, suggesting something quite different from the executed design. The third account credits de Forest with having designed the interior woodwork, which may be correct, as the main rooms are rather unlike others done by Polk during the period. More precise documentation has yet to be found.

12. Places recorded in his sketchbooks include: Paris, Fontainebleau, Chartres, Versailles, Blois, Rouen, Cluny, Tours, Verona, Florence, Venice, Siena, Rome, and Assisi. The notion that Coxhead might have seen new examples of English classicism, such as Belcher and Pite's Institute of Chartered Accountants in London (1888–1893), a building then the subject of considerable attention and controversy, is hypothetical. No evidence exists that he even went to London during his tour, and thus his sources for such work may have been limited to architectural periodicals and photographs.

13. Reginald Blomfield, *History of Renaissance Architecture in England, 1500–1800* (London, 1897), 2:316.

14. The best biographical account of Scott is contained in Hubert Howe Bancroft, *Chronicles of the Builders of the Commonwealth*, 7 vols. (San Francisco, 1891–1892), 1:440–493. See also Charles Lummis, "The Passing of a Man," *OW*, July 1903, pp. 57–65. For additional information on Scott's interests in art, see: *Wave*, May 16, 1891, p. 7; and *American Art Annual*, 1907–1908, pp. 34–35.

15. James Brown and Alice Scott were married in June 1895; he died the following April, having lived in the house for only a few weeks. Several years later, she married a pediatrician, Reginald Knight Smith. I am grateful to her daughter, Elizabeth Knight Smith, for providing me with much useful information about the house and its design history.

16. The exact date of the project remains uncertain. According to Elizabeth Knight Smith, it was designed in the late 1890s. The scheme was completed in time for one of Coxhead's renderings to be published in the Chicago Architectural Club's 1900 *Catalogue*. *Ch*, June 9, 1900, notes that Scott had reached an agreement with neighbors regarding the location of party walls for "his contemplated residence."

17. The photographs and prints then collected by architects, or in contemporary monographs such as Charles Latham's *In English Homes* . . . , 2 vols. (London and New York, 1904, 1906), reveal the breadth of subject matter that interested them.

18. This series of events is documented by several photographs in Coxhead's papers, some taken shortly after the fire and others taken of the house as completed.

19. Concerning Earl, see: *Men of Achievement in the Great Southwest* . . . (Los Angeles, 1904), pp. 78–80; "Makers of Los Angeles," *OW*, April 1909, p. 359; and John McGroarty, *Los Angeles from the Mountains to the Sea.* . . , 3 vols. (Chicago and New York, 1921), 3: 339, 906–908.

20. Polk was unquestionably familiar with this building, for he fell just short of replicating its facade for the William Boericke house in San Francisco (1891). See *CABN*, May 1894, for an illustration.

21. Mrs. Bourn may not have shared her son's enthusiasm for Polk's work. Some two years after the original farmhouse burned, she commissioned Polk to develop plans for a new residence, but the project was soon shelved. Subsequently, she turned to Percy & Hamilton for the design of her house in San Francisco (1892–1893). After Polk's second proposal for the St. Helena

house, the job was given to a Napa architect, W. H. Corlett.

22. Cost seems to have precluded its realization; Wheeler purchased a more modest dwelling, designed by Samuel Newsom for O. D. Baldwin (1893).

23. David Warren Ryder, *"Great Citizen": A Biography of William H. Crocker* (San Francisco, 1962).

24. *Ch*, April 22, 1899; *TT*, May 17, 1902, p. 5. Concerning subsequent developments in the area, see references cited in chap. 6, n. 8, n. 9. Over a decade elapsed before Crocker, or anyone else, would construct so grand a house. Polk made extensive revisions to his scheme in 1905; photographs of the model are in Polk's papers. For unknown reasons Crocker turned to Lewis Hobart to prepare the final design (ca. 1907).

CHAPTER VIII

1. *CABN*, February 18, 1890, p. 14.

2. For a general discussion of the city's public buildings and parks in the nineteenth century, see: Mel Scott, *The San Francisco Bay Area* (Berkeley and Los Angeles, 1959), pp. 51–53, 97–98; Judd Kahn, *Imperial San Francisco* (Lincoln, Nebraska, and London, 1979), pp. 67–69; and Harold Kirker, *California's Architectural Frontier*, reprint ed. (Santa Barbara and Salt Lake City, 1973), pp. 97–98. For illustrations of City Hall, see: Joseph Baird, *Time's Wondrous Changes* (San Francisco, 1962), plates 37, 38; and the author's *A Matter of Taste; Willis Polk's Writings on Architecture in The Wave* (San Francisco, 1979), figs. 8, 13. Besides City Hall, San Francisco's only major public building in 1890 was Alfred Mullett's Greek Revival United States Branch Mint (1869–1874). Work began on Shea & Shea's Hall of Justice in 1896. The site was selected for a new Post Office in 1891, and plans were presented five years later; however, the building was not completed until 1905; see chap. 4. The best historical account of Golden Gate Park is David Streatfield, "Shifting Sands, 'Verdant Umbrageousness,' and 'the People's Park'": Public Open Space in San Francisco, 1886–1893," *Development Series* (University of Washington, 1975), pp. 15–36. See also Raymond Clary, *The Making of Golden Gate Park* (San Francisco, 1980).

3. Paul Turner, *The Founders & the Architects* (Stanford, Calif., 1978); Francesco Passanti, "The Design of Columbia in the 1890s: McKim and His Client," *JSAH*, May 1977, pp. 69–84. The master plan for New York University is illustrated in Leland Roth, *Architecture of McKim, Mead and White 1870–1920: A Building List* (New York, 1978), fig. 598.

4. Mariana van Rensselaer, "The Artistic Triumph of the Fair Builders," *Forum*, December 1892, p. 528; H. C. Bunner, "The Making of the White City," *Scribner's*, October 1892, pp. 406–407.

5. John Adams, "What a Great City Might Be—A Lesson from the White City," *New England Magazine*, March 1896, pp. 10, 12; William Dean Howells, *Letters of an Altrurian Traveller*, reprint ed. (Gainesville, Fla., 1961), p. 34.

6. See, for example: Adams, "What a Great City Might Be," pp. 9–10; P. B. Wight, "The Great Exhibition Reviewed," *AABN*, December 30, 1893, p. 159; van Rensselaer, "Artistic Triumph," p. 531; Henry Van Brunt, "The Columbian Exposition and American Civilization," and "Two Interpretations of National Architecture," in William Coles, ed., *Architecture and Society* (Cambridge, Mass., 1969), pp. 305–318, 360; Montgomery Schuyler, "Last Words about the World's Fair," in William Jordy and Ralph Coe, eds., *American Architecture and Other Writings*, paperback ed., (New York, 1964), pp. 275–293; Thomas Hines, *Burnham of Chicago: Architect and Planner* (New York, 1974), pp. 116–124, 141–142; and David Burg, *Chicago's White City of 1893* (Lexington, Ky., 1976), pp. 297 ff. Of the many recent accounts of the City Beautiful Movement, few have devoted much attention to its nascent stage. One exception is Jon Peterson's "The City Beautiful Movement: Forgotten Origins and Lost Meanings," *Journal of Urban History*, August 1976, pp. 415–434.

7. Willis Polk, "A Professional Glance at the World's Fair Structures in Chicago," *Ex*, Decem-

ber 25, 1891. At that time, Polk could have known the Chicago fair's design only through sketches, none of which fully conveyed the Court of Honor's effect. The aspect Polk criticized most was the informal character given to other parts of the plan.

8. In its basic conception, form, and site, Polk's scheme is so similar to the Panama-Pacific International Exposition of 1915 that it is probable he had a greater hand in its design than has generally been assumed. Polk's role as supervising architect of the exhibition is briefly discussed in chap. 10.

9. *Official History of the California Midwinter International Exposition* (San Francisco, 1894), p. 25. See also: Phil Weaver, Jr., "The California Midwinter International Exposition," *OM*, November 1893, pp. 449–462; Marcus Wiggin, "California's Midwinter Fair," *Harper's Weekly*, September 23, 1893; and Gunther Barth, "California Midwinter International Exposition," in *West Coast Expositions and Galas*, no. 2 (San Francisco, 1970).

10. Concerning Brown's plan, see *Call*, August 16, 1893; it is illustrated in *Ch*, August 17, 1893. The design must have been altered soon thereafter as the groundbreaking occurred on August 24. Michael O'Shaughnessy's name appears as chief engineer on official maps; however, his role was probably confined to executing de Young's ideas. McLaren's brief association is noted in Raymond Clary, *The Making of Golden Gate Park* (San Francisco, 1980), p. 77.

11. *Ch*, July 10, 1893; July 17, 1893; July 18, 1893; July 22, 1893; July 29, 1893; July 31, 1893; August 6, 1893; *Official History*, p. 25; and *Call*, August 6, 1893.

12. Willis Polk, "Ungrateful Chicago," undated typescript (ca. 1893), CED Docs.

13. Descriptions of Polk's entry in *Ch* and *Call*, August 6, 1893, are sufficiently different to suggest that he submitted two designs. A plan found with his drawings of the Administration Building, illustrated in Fig. 183 and now in his papers, corresponds to the *Call's* account and shows a layout for the Administration Building quite different from that depicted in Fig. 183. Another drawing shows the Administration Building depicted in Fig. 183 and the prize-winning designs for the remaining pavilions using Brown's master plan. Announcement of the jury's prolonged deliberation of the Administration Building design and of their final selection of Brown's entry is in *Ch*, August 17, 1893 and September 2, 1893. For discussion of Brown's scheme, see chap. 9.

14. James Phelan, "Is the Midwinter Fair A Benefit?" *OM*, April 1894, p. 392.

15. *ARev*(B), May 15, 1894, p. 38.

16. Willis Polk, "Sunset City Discords," *Wave*, December 2, 1893, p. 13.

17. Willis Polk, "Mr. Sutro's Baths," *Wave*, November 3, 1894, p. 5; *Call*, February 14, 1896; Polk, "The Architect and the Mayor," *Wave*, July 29, 1893, p. 16; Polk, "The New Dome and the Western Addition," *Wave*, April 14, 1894, p. 9.

18. Joseph Backus, "Gelett Burgess: A Biography of the Man Who Wrote 'The Purple Cow' " (Ph.D. diss., University of California at Berkeley, 1961), p. 131; Gelett Burgess, *Bayside Bohemia* (San Francisco, 1954), p. v. The incident caused Burgess's dismissal from the University of California, where he had been employed as a drafting instructor. The action eventually led him to pursue the writing career that made him famous.

19. The best coverage of Phelan's civic activities during the 1890s is contained in Kahn, *Imperial San Francisco*, chap. 3; see also Kevin Starr, *Americans and the California Dream* (New York, 1973), pp. 249–253.

20. *Ex*, December 4, 1898, in Phelan scrapbooks, BL, vol. 7, p. 163. See also: Phelan scrapbooks, 7: 197; 9: 118; and 10: 102–112; "A Chain of Parks for San Francisco," *Wave*, Christmas 1899, p. 27; *SFMR*, 1898–1899, appendix, pp. 572–596. Concerning the Burnham Plan, see chap. 10.

21. Curlett's firm designed the Phelan Branch Library (ca. 1902), the Phelan Building (1908), several speculative commercial blocks for the Phelan estate in San Francisco, and Montalvo, Phelan's country house in Saratoga (1912). Two of the speculative buildings designed during the 1890s are illustrated in *CABN*, October 1896 and June 1899.

22. Letter from Phelan to Tilden, December 28, 1898, as quoted in a letter from Gladys Tilden

to the author, February 27, 1975. I am grateful to Miss Tilden for supplying me with much useful material concerning her father's association with Polk.

On the Admission Day monument, see: *Wave*, October 24, 1896, p. 4; *SFMR*, 1896–1897, pp. 391–393; and Phelan scrapbooks, BL, 4: 101, 110. On the Donohue monument, see Phelan scrapbooks, 5: 13. For illustrations, see Charles Hall Page, *Splendid Survivors* (San Francisco, 1979), pp. 239–240.

23. Information on the Guild is meager. Officers and directors are listed on its stationery, copies of which are in Polk's papers. See also: *Wave*, November 17, 1894, p. 17; November 24, 1894, p. 7; December 15, 1894, p. 10; *Ch*, January 19, 1896; and Austin Lewis, "The 'Arts and Crafts': Its First Exhibition in the City," *OM*, March 1896, pp. 292–302.

24. *Call*, February 14, 1896. The resolution calling for establishment of a Board of Public Works is written in Polk's hand and is contained in his papers. No evidence has been found to confirm whether or not the Guild adopted this proposal.

25. Regarding the Fine Arts Federation in New York (1896) and the Boston Arts Commission (1890), see "Public Art in American Cities," *Municipal Affairs*, March 1898, pp. 9–11. On the Fairmount Park Association, see "Public Art," pp. 2–3. On the Municipal Art Society in New York, see: Lillie French, "Municipal Art," *Harper's Weekly*, April 22, 1893, p. 371; Edward Bell, "Art in Municipal Decoration," *Harper's Weekly*, April 28, 1894, p. 401; "The Embellishment of Cities," *Harper's Weekly*, March 19, 1898, p. 282; "Public Art," pp. 7–9; "Art for the City," *Nation*, May 30, 1901, pp. 428–429; W. T. Larned, "The American Municipal Art Movement," *Chautauquan*, August 1903, p. 467; and Harvey Kantor, "The City Beautiful Movement in New York," *New-York Historical Society Quarterly*, April 1973, pp. 149–171.

26. *Wave*, January 5, 1895, p. 8; *Call*, February 29, 1896; *SFMR*, 1896–1897, appendix, pp. 451–455; "The Stevenson Monument," *OM*, December 1897, pp. 528–530; "The City's New Fountains," *Mark Hopkins Institute Review of Art*, September 1900, pp. 7–10; Robert O'Brien, "The Sketch on the Tablecloth," *Ch*, December 23, 1949, 3: 5.

27. *Wave*, February 16, 1895, p. 9.

28. Other renderings of the urban landscape drawn by Polk can be found in: Chicago Architectural Club, *Catalogue*, 1903; Charles Maginnis, "The Pen-and-Ink Perspective," *ARev*(B), December 1904, p. 245; Charles Moore, *Daniel H. Burnham, Architect, Planner of Cities*, 2 vols. (Boston and New York, 1921), opposite p. 207; and in Polk's papers.

29. Royal Cortissoz, "Landmarks of Manhattan," *Scribner's*, November 1895, p. 534. See also Mariana van Rensselaer, "Picturesque New York," *Century*, December 1892, pp. 168–171.

30. Herbert Croly, "What is Civic Art?," *AR*, July 1904, pp. 47–52.

31. Virtually all buildings of any size constructed along the eastern part of Market Street during the late nineteenth and early twentieth centuries contained offices, department stores, or hotels. Based on its appearance, this design could be either for a hotel or an apartment house. However, it does not have a large, clearly defined entrance as was the standard for these building types, nor does the building's form correlate with the wedge-shaped gore lot at the corner of Market, Ellis, and Stockton streets, the site it occupies in Peixotto's rendering.

32. These drawings and prints were rolled together in the former drafting room of Polk's Russian Hill house, from which he moved in 1900. They appear to have been left undisturbed until they were discovered in 1977 by a tenant, Mrs. Walter Jennings, who donated them to CED Docs. Polk's rendering of the Cliff House was published in *Ex*, January 6, 1895.

33. The Wigwam Theatre was located at the southeast corner of Stockton and Geary streets. No known project by Polk was designed for this site; however, he may well have used, or intended to use, the setting for study purposes.

34. Polk has long been credited with assisting Brown on the ferry building's design, but no evidence of his participation has been found among the voluminous documents pertaining to the project. Furthermore, Polk's frequent written attacks on Brown's work during this period make it highly unlikely that the two men would have collaborated. *Ch*, February 26, 1894, credits Schweinfurth with having designed the building while in Brown's office. Following

Brown's death in 1896, Edward R. Swain assumed the post of supervising architect. Polk's almost contemporaneous proposal for the arch and peristyle is no doubt the source of the confused attribution.

Both Schweinfurth and Polk were partial to the Giralda tower and its American offspring on McKim, Mead & White's Madison Square Garden. Schweinfurth used these sources for his Grand Market in Lima; see chap. 9, n. 24. Later, Polk offered variations in proposals for additions to the Chronicle Building (ca. 1913) and for a new Crocker Building (1919–1922) in San Francisco.

35. George R. Collins and Christiane Crasemann Collins, *Camillo Sitte and the Birth of Modern City Planning* (New York, 1965), p. 12. No further details regarding the invitation have been found. Sitte died in 1903, and it is doubtful whether anyone in San Francisco would have asked him to offer such advice before the mid-1890s.

36. See, for instance: *Ch*, March 25, 1889, p. 7; Bernard Maybeck, "A Dream that Might be Realized," *Merchants' Association Review*, November 1903, pp. 1–2; and Willis Polk, "Arch and Peristyle for Lower Market Street," *A&E*, July 1910, pp. 60–61.

37. The only earlier known examples are the master plans for Stanford, Columbia, and New York universities; see n. 3 above.

38. A. C. Schweinfurth, letter to the editor, *Wave*, November 28, 1896, p. 3.

39. *CABN*, January 1896, p. 2.

40. *Wave*, May 2, 1896, p. 3; and February 13, 1897, p. 3. Another illustration of Maybeck's scheme is contained in Kenneth Cardwell, *Bernard Maybeck* (Santa Barbara and Salt Lake City, 1977), p. 41.

41. Cardwell, *Maybeck*, pp. 40–41, suggests that Phoebe Hearst may have precipitated the idea of a master plan when she went to the university's president, Martin Kellogg, in late 1895 with a proposal to donate a building for the Department of Mining in memory of her husband. Kellogg, in turn, asked Maybeck to make sketches of what such a building could look like. However, announcement of Hearst's funding the construction of a mining building was not made for another year and a half (*Wave*, April 16, 1897, p. 3). It is perhaps more likely that once Maybeck's idea became public, Hearst was encouraged by her son, who had already harbored dreams of a world's fair and was more interested in architecture, to underwrite the competition. Phoebe Hearst was also a sophisticated patron, far more so than Mrs. Stanford. See Paul Turner, "The Library That Never Was," *Imprint of the Stanford Libraries Associates*, April 1976, pp. 4–13. For additional background on the competition, see: Loren Partridge, *John Galen Howard and the Berkeley Campus* (Berkeley, 1978), chap. 3; and *The International Competition for the Phoebe Hearst Architectural Plan* (San Francisco, 1899).

A detailed analysis of Phoebe Hearst's life has yet to be written. The standard biography, commissioned by William Randolph Hearst, is Winifred Bonfils, *The Life and Personality of Phoebe Apperson Hearst* (San Francisco, 1928).

42. Reinstein also served on the jury as the university's representative. The one San Francisco architect whose services Maybeck acknowledged was Albert Pissis. Besides Maybeck himself, Pissis was probably the only designer then practicing in the region to have attended the Ecole.

43. *International Competition*, pp. 8, 10.

44. Namely: J. H. Freedlander; Howard & Cauldwell; Howells, Stokes & Hornbostel; Lord, Hewlett & Hull; and Whitney Warren (all New York); Despradelle & Codman (Boston); Emile Bénard; Héraud & Eichmuller; and Barbaud & Bauhain (all Paris); F. Bluntschli (Zurich); and Rudolph Dick (Vienna). The winners included Bénard and all the Americans except Freedlander and Warren.

45. "The International Competition for the Phoebe A. Hearst Plan for the University of California," *Architectural Annual*, 1900, pp. 56–58. Not everyone agreed. The noted German architect, Max Junghändel, derided the choice, labeling Bénard's scheme "un-American," adding that the design should not be another "Chicago World's Fair." See Kenneth Cardwell and William Hays, "Fifty Years from Now," *California Monthly*, April 1954, p. 22. Bénard's scheme is illustrated in Cardwell, *Maybeck*, p. 45.

385

46. Namely: John Galen Howard, I. N. Phelps Stokes, Joseph C. Hornblower, James M. Hewlett, and Constant Désiré Despradelle.

47. Academic institutions that conducted competitions for their master plans around the turn of the century included the United States Naval and Military academies, Washington University, Carnegie Technical Schools, and the Johns Hopkins University. See also John Burchard and Albert Bush-Brown, *The Architecture of America* (New York, 1961), pp. 224–228.

48. Partridge, *John Galen Howard*, chaps. 4–7.

49. Edward Payne, "The City of Education," *OM*, October 1899, p. 361. See also: "The Visit of the Jurors in the Hearst Architectural Competition," *University Chronicle*, October 1899, pp. 3–17; *CABN*, September 20, 1899, pp. 97–98; and "San Francisco Chapter of Architects Entertain Mons. Bénard at the Bohemian Club Rooms," *CABN*, December 1899, pp. 134–136.

    Phelan's short-lived project for a San Francisco master plan secured through an international competition was based directly on the Berkeley precedent. Several years later, he pressed for securing the services of Daniel Burnham for the plan. Whether he sought the Chicagoan because of his distinguished record in design or because of his national prestige remains unknown.

50. The competition's regulations stipulated that the names of those architects who entered would remain confidential; only the winners' identities would be revealed. Much later, Cahill recalled that Coxhead and Oakey, in association with J. M. Dunn, had been the only other entrants from the state (B.J.S. Cahill, "Adventurings in the Monumental," *A&E*, August 1918, p. 54). Cahill's scheme was published in *AABN*, July 29, 1899.

51. During the 1890s, Schweinfurth also looked to vernacular precedents in Mediterranean countries for inspiration. However, he used these sources in a somewhat different way; see chap. 9.

52. Willis Polk, "The University Competition," *Wave*, November 7, 1896, p. 3.

53. Willis Polk, "The University Competition," *Wave*, January 29, 1898, p. 2.

CHAPTER IX

1. Two other cities that were important in this respect prior to 1900 were Philadelphia (see chap. 1) and Los Angeles.

2. See, for instance, Frank Soulé, John Gibson, and James Nisbet, *The Annals of San Francisco . . .* (New York, 1855).

3. "The Old Romish Missions in California," *American Church Review*, July 1869, pp. 253–267.

4. Agnes Manning, "San Carlos de Monterey," *OM*, July 1884, p. 43. Similar interpretations written before 1890 include: B.C., "The Story of the California Missions," *Month*, September–October 1872, pp. 169–199; "Centennial Sketches: II—The Early Spanish Settlement of California," *Appleton's Journal*, January 22, 1876, pp. 105–107; "The Early Catholic Missions of California," *Catholic World*, October 1880, pp. 111–120; H.[elen] H.[unt], "Father Junipero and His Work," *Century*, May 1883, pp. 3–18, and June 1883, pp. 199–215; and Mary Graham, "San Carlos del Carmelo," *OM*, September 1884, pp. 292–296. A lengthy account of nineteenth-century attitudes toward the missions is provided in Karen Weitze, "Origins and Early Development of the Mission Revival in California" (Ph.D. diss., Stanford University, 1978), chap. 1.

5. Albion Tourgée, "A Study in Civilization," *North American Review*, September 1886, p. 249.

6. "Old Romish Missions," pp. 254, 257.

7. "Early Catholic Missions," p. 115; James Steele, *Old California Days* (Chicago, 1889), p.

48; H.[unt], "Father Junipero," p. 199; Frank Blackmar, *Spanish Institutions in the Southwest* (Baltimore, 1891), p. 127.

8. Charles Shinn, "Mission Bells," *OM*, January 1892, pp. 4–5.

9. Susan Power, "Pacific Home-Making," *OM*, May 1833, pp. 459–462; Charles Shinn, "Spanish Pioneer Houses of California," *Magazine of American History*, May 1890, pp. 353–360. See also: Charles Nordhoff, *California for Health, Pleasure and Residence* (New York, 1882), chap. 17; Steele, *Old Californian Days*, chap. 6; and Blackmar, *Spanish Institutions*, chap. 12.

10. Josephine Clifford, "Modern Monterey," *The Californian*, July 1880, p. 80. See also: Caroline Churchill, . . . *Sketches of Travel in California* . . .(Chicago, 1887), p. 224; Clara Brown, "La Ciudad de la Regna de Los Angeles," *OM*, June 1883, pp. 579–583; Edward Roberts, "Two Seaports of New Spain," *OM*, December 1884, pp. 561–575; Edward Roberts, "Santa Barbara," *Art Journal*, January 1887, pp. 10–13; and Charles Shinn, "Los Angeles—Studies of a Century of Change," *OM*, March 1889, pp. 225–234.

11. See chap. 1.

12. Accounts of these trips were written by Howard in a number of letters to his mother (Howard Papers, BL). Some of his southern California sketches are in this collection and in CED Docs, and three of them were published in *AABN*, March 16, 1889. Among the other draftsmen Howard mentioned were "Moore," "Hunt," and "Arthur Brown." Moore was probably Lester Moore, credited by George Wharton James with being one of the earliest proponents of the Mission Style in southern California ("The Influence of the 'Mission Style' upon Civic and Domestic Architecture in Modern California," *Craftsman*, February 1904, p. 462). Hunt may well have been Sumner Hunt, who also played a leading role in fostering the mode in that region. The identity of Arthur Brown remains unclear. Howard stated that he was eighteen and working in the office of Caukin & Haas. Thus he was probably not Arthur Brown, Jr., who grew up in the Bay Area and who was thirteen at that time; and he was certainly not Arthur Page Brown, who was twenty-eight and well established in practice for himself in New York. Howard made no mention of Coxhead; however, that architect's surviving sketchbooks reveal that he made drawings of the Mission Santa Barbara and other Spanish buildings in 1889.

13. Henry Merritt, "Old California Missions," *AN*, November 1890, pp. 7–9 and December 1890, pp. 14–16. The sketches accompanying the *CABN* series (May–December 1891) are signed "Très," except for the last in the series, which is signed by Charles Mitchell, a Polk employee at that time. Some of the drawings appear to have come from another hand and closely resemble Polk's rendering style. According to local tradition, Polk did make a tour of the state not long after *AN* folded in January 1891.

14. *AN*, January 1891, p. 4. Polk was also probably instrumental in selecting this project for the Sketch Club of San Francisco's monthly competition for January 1891, reported in *AN*, November 1890, p. 10.

15. Some of the most useful information concerning the competition can be found in *Ch*, especially May 18, 1891 and January 13, 1892. See also: California World's Fair Commission, *California at the World's Columbian Exposition, 1893* (Sacramento, 1894); and *California's Monthly World's Fair Magazine*, 1891–1892. The term "Moorish" carried rather vague connotations at that time. Many people were under the impression that the missions contained elements of Moorish design. Often, too, the term was used to describe any elements in Spanish architecture that seemed exotic. According to Weitze, "Early Development of the Mission Revival," pp. 94 ff., another competition for the California Building had been held in 1891, but it was not nearly as important or influential as that conducted the following year.

16. A complete list of entrants is published in *California's Monthly World's Fair Magazine*, February 1892, p. 60. A few of the prominent old San Francisco firms entered, including Pissis & Moore, Mooser & Cuthbertson, and Samuel Newsom. Among the younger competitors were Coxhead, Joachim Mathisen and Bernard Maybeck, Newton Tharp, and Daniel Polk. Only three firms from Los Angeles entered.

17. "Typical Architecture," *Ch*, February 13, 1892; letter from Brown to Mrs. McCormick,

March 14, 1893, McCormick Papers; Montgomery Schuyler, "State Buildings at the World's Fair," *AR*, July–September 1893, p. 61. See also: *Ex*, February 12, 1892; and *Ch*, April 21, 1893.

18. Schweinfurth's role in Brown's office is discussed in chap. 4. Contemporary accounts that cite Schweinfurth's great interest in Spanish California architecture include: *AABN*, October 20, 1900, p. 22; *IA*, November 1900, p. 32; and "The Later Work of A. C. Schweinfurth, Architect," *ARev*(B), March 1902, p. 76. The first of the above citations gives Schweinfurth, together with Brown, credit for the design of the California Building. Kenneth Cardwell, *Bernard Maybeck* (Santa Barbara and Salt Lake City, 1977), pp. 94 ff., suggests that Maybeck had a hand in the project's design. This attribution is based on the similarity of the central dome to that of Carrère & Hastings's Ponce de Leon Hotel (to which Maybeck did *not* make a major contribution; see chap. 2., n. 40). However, Brown and Schweinfurth frequently looked to the Ponce de Leon Hotel as a source of ideas for their California work. Furthermore, Maybeck entered the competition separately, collaborating with Joachim Mathisen (see chap. 4, n. 10). Given these circumstances, it is unlikely that Maybeck had a significant role, if indeed any, in designing Brown's scheme.

19. Frank Chouteau Brown, "Boston Suburban Architecture," *AR*, April 1907, p. 254; Herbert Croly, "The California Country House," *A&E*, December 1906, pp. 24–25.
 "Mission Style" was the most commonly used term in the late nineteenth and early twentieth centuries, as opposed to the much more recent "Mission Revival." Both terms have been applied loosely to identify a wide range of buildings that possess some allusions to Spanish architecture. This is confusing because a large amount of work designed between the 1890s and 1920s relied heavily on the imagery of the missions themselves and are often quite different from the work of Schweinfurth and others. Like the term "Colonial Revival," "Mission Style" and "Mission Revival" need more precise definition. For recent analyses of the mode, see: Harold Kirker, *California's Architectural Frontier*, reprint ed. (Santa Barbara and Salt Lake City, 1973), pp. 121–127; David Gebhard, "The Spanish Colonial Revival in Southern California (1895–1930)," *JSAH*, May 1967, pp. 131–147; Gebhard, "Architectural Imagery, the Mission and California," *Harvard Architectural Review*, Spring 1980, pp. 137–145; and Weitze, "Early Development of the Mission Revival."

20. Contemporary articles on the subject include: Arthur Benton, "The California Mission and Its Influence Upon Pacific Coast Architecture," *A&E*, February 1911, pp. 63, 71, 75; Charles Lummis, "The Lesson of the Adobe," *OW*, March 1895, pp. 65–67; Benton, "Architecture for the Southwest," *OW*, February 1896, pp. 126–130; George Wharton James, "The Influence of the 'Mission Style' upon Civic and Domestic Architecture of Modern California," *Craftsman*, February 1904, pp. 458–469; William Phillips Comstock, "Modern Mission Architecture in Southern California," *A&B*, May 1905, pp. 337–352; James, "The Mission Style in Modern Architecture," *Indoors and Out*, May–September 1907, pp. 51–59, 119–124, 186–193, 223–238, 271–275; W. L. B. Jenney, "The Old California Missions and Their Influence on Modern Design," *IA*, February–June 1906, pp. 7, 23, 35, 71–72.

21. A. Page Brown, "Architecture in California," *Ch*, December 30, 1894; "An Ideal Summer Home," *Wave*, March 13, 1897, p. 6.

22. Concerning the Crocker houses, see: *Wave*, February 4, 1893, p. 5, and March 25, 1893, p. 6; and *Ch*, March 25, 1893. The houses were not constructed, no doubt due to rising land values in the district. Examples of surburban work include houses for Frank Douty in San Mateo (1894) and Edward Eyre in Menlo Park (ca. 1894). See also Brown's Sainte Claire Club in San Jose (1893–1894), illustrated in *AABN*, February 1, 1896. Five speculative houses for Crocker in Santa Barbara (1894–1895) employ scalloped gable ends and other mission motifs, perhaps because they are located close to that town's famous mission church.

23. *AABN*, December 21, 1889, pp. 291–292; Andrew Prentice, *Renaissance Architecture and Ornament in Spain*, reprint ed. (London, 1970), p. 11. See also: Robert Gibson, "Spanish Architecture," *AABN*, October 13, 1881–August 9, 1884; and H. Saladin, "Spanish Architecture," *AABN*, May 30, June 27, 1891.

24. Nor can it be argued that such treatment was given just to temporary exhibition buildings. Similar qualities pervade one of Brown's largest projects of the decade, a market hall for Lima, Peru, illustrated in *A&B*, November 12, 1892.

25. Harold Kirker, *California's Architectural Frontier;* David Gebhard, "The Monterey Tradition; History Reordered," *New Mexico Studies in the Fine Arts,* 1982, pp. 14–19.

26. "A Church at San Francisco, Cal.," *SABE,* August 1899, p. 35; Mabel Craft, "A Sermon in Church Building," *HB,* February 1901, p. 126; "The Most Picturesque Church in the Country," *Ch,* April 7, 1901. See also "A Departure in Church Building . . . ," *Craftsman,* June 1906, pp. 330–334. For a recent, though somewhat inaccurate account, see Leslie Freudenheim and Elisabeth Sussman, *Building with Nature* (Santa Barbara and Salt Lake City, 1974), pp. 20–30.

27. For contemporary accounts of this and other such clubhouses, see: John Stone, "The Dutch Room of the Grolier Club," *HB,* July 1897, pp. 29–32; Spencer Roberts, "The Mask and Wig Club," *HB,* January 1899, pp. 72–74; Helen Henderson, "The Artistic Home of the Mask and Wig Club," *H&G,* April 1904, pp. 168–174; "Two Decades of Club History," T Square Club, *Catalogue,* 1903–1904, pp. 11–16; and "The Town Room in Boston," *Indoors and Out,* February 1905, pp. 229–231.

28. Porter designed one of the stained-glass windows and perhaps the garden. Keith was responsible for the murals. Maybeck has usually been given credit for the building itself, but Schweinfurth was the key figure according to Bruce Porter in an interview with Elizabeth Thompson conducted shortly before his death. I am most grateful to Mrs. Thompson for this information. Porter also stated that Maybeck played a minor role in the project. The fact that identical chairs have been found in some of Maybeck's houses has led to the commonly held conclusion that he designed these pieces. The chairs were especially designed for the church and were then produced in some quantity for sale by the Forbes Manufacturing Company of San Francisco (interview with Willis Forbes, July 1975). Comparison with both Maybeck's early furniture designs and with Schweinfurth's work suggests that Schweinfurth more likely was responsible for them. On the other hand, the small side table pictured in Fig. 213 is similar to Maybeck's work of the period.

    In the mid-1890s, one of these chairs was sent to a New York furniture manufacturer, Joseph P. McHugh, who used it as a model for his "mission" pieces. McHugh's products, in turn, became a major source for Gustav Stickley's Craftsman furniture. See: "San Francisco the Home of Mission Type of Furniture," *A&E,* August 1906, p. 68; Alwyn Covell, "The Real Place of Mission Furniture," *Good Furniture,* March 1915, pp. 359–362; and R. J. Clark, Introduction to *Mission Furniture and How To Make It,* by M. H. Windsor, reprint ed. (Santa Barbara and Salt Lake City, 1976), pp. 6–7.

29. Announcement that Schweinfurth had begun to work for himself is in *Ch,* February 26, 1894. Thereafter, the practice was probably never officially terminated, but another year would elapse before any independent commission would be realized. Prior to that time, only two projects are known to have been designed by him: a hotel in Montalvo and a "winter residence" in Santa Barbara. Given these circumstances, Schweinfurth must have maintained some sort of an association with Brown under which the Church of the New Jerusalem and other work was designed.

30. Charles Lummis, *The Land of Poco Tiempo* (New York, 1893), pp. 3–5. Other valuable accounts of the pueblos include: C. N. Holford, "Oriental Resemblances in New Mexico," *Kansas City Review of Science and Industry,* February 1881, pp. 602–605; "Ancient Pueblos of New Mexico and Arizona," *Harper's Monthly,* August 1875, pp. 327–333; Major W. L. Powell, "The Pueblo Indians," *Potter's American Monthly,* March 1878, pp. 226–230; Lewis Morgan, *Houses and House-Life of the American Aborigines* (Washington, D.C., 1881), chap. 6; Victor Mindeleff, "A Study of Pueblo Architecture . . . ," in *Eighth Annual Report of the Bureau of Ethnology* . . . (Washington, D.C., 1891), pp. 3–228; and A. F. Bandelier, *Final Report, Hemenway Southwest Archaeological Expedition,* Papers of the Archaeological Institute of America, Vol. V, 1890.

31. Sylvester Baxter, "Zuni Revisited," *AABN,* March 17, 1883, p. 124; Frederick Ober, "Acoma, A Picturesque Pueblo," *AABN,* August 2, 1890, p. 67; Henry Mason, "Some American Ruins," *Californian Illustrated Magazine,* February 1892, p. 197. See also: "The Terraced Cities of New Mexico," *AABN,* July 23, 1881, p. 37; and "A New Mexico Pueblo," *AABN,* November 29, 1884, p. 258. Regarding White's visit to New Mexico, see chap. 1.

32. William Simpson, "Mud: A Material of Persian and Eastern Architecture," *AABN,* July 2,

1892, pp. 9–12, and July 9, 1892, pp. 25–27.

33. One unusual case of adobe construction during the 1890s was for Las Tejas, the residence of W. Allston Hayne, Jr., in Montecito (1894). The house, now altered beyond recognition, was one story, with an open central court and low red-tiled roof. Hayne served as his own contractor in this novel venture, but surviving plans in possession of his son, F. Bourn Hayne, indicate that the services of an architect (whose identity remains unknown) were procured. A preliminary set of plans by a different hand also exists, and these just may be by Schweinfurth and for the "winter residence" in n. 29 above. For illustrations of the house, see Constance Austin, "Some Modern Adobes," *OM*, October 1908, pp. 324–327.

34. Letter from Schweinfurth to Edward H. Clarke, December 20, 189[5], Phoebe Hearst Papers, BL.

35. As realized, the two lateral arms of the house were reduced to about half of their proposed length and the rooms running along the front were eliminated, leaving only a wall and gate turrets. No doubt implemented as an economy measure, these modifications changed the appearance of the house considerably. That Schweinfurth considered the executed plan to be a compromise is suggested by the fact that he submitted the original layout for publication.

36. Charles Lummis, "The Patio," *OW*, June 1895, pp. 12–16; Lummis, "The Grand Veranda," *OW*, July 1895, pp. 63–67; Arthur Benton, "The Patio," *OW*, August 1897, pp. 108–112; Lummis, "The Greatest California Patio House," *Country Life in America*, October 1904, pp. 533–540. The only earlier California house to incorporate the revived concept of a central court that I know was Las Tejas, described in n. 33 above.

37. Major George Elliot, "The Presidio of San Francisco," *OM*, April 1870, pp. 336–344; Blackmar, *Spanish Institutions*, chap. 9.

38. This account was told to Mrs. George Eastham by Ann Apperson Flint, Phoebe Hearst's niece and witness to the confrontation. I am grateful to Mrs. Eastham for sharing the information with me. Concerning Hearst and San Simeon, see the author's "Julia Morgan: Some Introductory Notes," *Perspecta 15*, 1975, pp. 21–23. See also W. A. Swanberg, *Citizen Hearst* (New York, 1961), pp. 67–68, 414–415.

39. "An Ideal Summer Home," p. 6. Other contemporary accounts of the Hacienda include: "Hacienda del Poso de Verona," *CABN*, September 1899, p. 108; E. V. Matignon, "Hacienda del Poso de Verona," *Ch*, February 4, 1900; "The Hearst Country Seat at Pleasanton, Cal.," *SABE*, July 1900, pp. 8–9, 16; Barr Ferree, *American Estates and Gardens* (New York, 1906), pp. 211–217; Porter Garnett, *Stately Homes of California* (Boston, 1915), pp. 21–29; "Hacienda del Pozo de Verona," *Oakland Tribune Annual Number*, January 1920, pp. 50–51.

40. "An Ideal Summer Home," p. 6. See also Montgomery Schuyler, *Westward the Course of Empire* (New York, 1906), pp. 98–99. Phoebe Hearst, not her son, commissioned the building.

41. From the late 1880s on, office building design tended to employ increasingly precise historical details, even though the overall form of these structures remained distinct to the type.

42. Two watercolor sketches currently in the author's possession indicate that Schweinfurth visited Siena and Rome; see n. 49 below. The rest of his itinerary remains unknown, but it probably included Spain and other Mediterranean countries. Schweinfurth died on September 27, 1900 while visiting his wife's family in Dryden, New York.

43. A variety of Spanish references continued to be used in the Bay Area and other portions of northern California after the turn of the century. However, such work was seldom by prominent architects, nor did it enjoy a distinguished clientele. The majority of examples were designed as speculative commercial buildings (especially small apartment houses), buildings associated with tourism (railroad stations and hotels), and schools in rural communities. By the 1910s, Spanish references began to be interpreted in a more precise manner, very different in its effect, that has been identified by Gebhard as a separate mode, the Spanish Colonial Revival. See his: "Spanish Colonial Revival in Southern California," pp. 136 ff.; and *1868–1968 Architecture in California* (Santa Barbara, 1968), pp. 19–21.

44. *Wave*, February 13, 1892, p. 7.

45. "An Architectural Controversy," *Wave*, February 13, 1897, p. 3; Willis Polk, "The Possibilities of Our City," typescript of speech delivered before the Outdoor League, San Francisco, February 22, 1904, Polk Papers. See also "Polk's Idea of Mission Style," *Ch*, July 30, 1901.

46. Willis Polk, "Tendency of San Francisco Architecture," *Wave*, September 30, 1893, p. 9; Polk, "The New Postoffice," *Wave*, February 6, 1897, p. 7; and "Architectural Controversy," p. 3.

47. W. Horace Jones purchased the house from Mrs. McCullagh in 1939 and discussed its history with her at that time. According to Jones, the McCullaghs built a wood-frame house on the site ca. 1880. The grounds were cultivated for some time before Polk was commissioned to remake the dwelling. The existing house was divided into two parts, which form at least a portion of each of the present building's two-story sections. Polk's design obliterated all visual evidence of the original fabric (interview with W. Horace Jones, October 1974).

48. E. S. Gray, Volney Moody's son-in-law and the real client for the Moody house, was a prominent member of the congregation. Church records show that he asked Schweinfurth to prepare plans for the building even before an architect had been officially chosen. Gray also superintended construction of the building while Schweinfurth was in Europe. Mathisen prepared plans for the building four years earlier, but his scheme apparently proved too expensive (*Ch*, November 18, 1894). Other members of the congregation included J. S. Bunnell, Clifford McGrew, Charles Keeler (all clients of Maybeck's), and Allen Freeman (a client of Coxhead's). A number of these individuals were also members of the Hillside Club, but that organization did not in any way sponsor construction of the church, as Freudenheim and Sussman claim (*Building with Nature*, p. 59). For discussion of the Hillside Club's activities, see chap. 11.

49. "Regenerating San Francisco," *Wave*, December 17, 1898, p. 8. The letter is signed "Architectus, Florence, Nov. 10, 1898." In the brief editorial preface, the author is identified as a well-known San Francisco architect; remarks in the letter strongly suggest that he was a member of Schweinfurth's generation. Among this group, Schweinfurth is the only one known to have been abroad at that time. His sketches cited in n. 42 above document that he was in northern Italy during the latter months of 1898.

CHAPTER X

1. *Ch*, December 29, 1901; *TT*, August 1902; Rufus Steele, "How San Francisco Grows," *Sunset*, December 1904, pp. 103–117; and Mel Scott, *The San Francisco Bay Area* (Berkeley and Los Angeles, 1959), pp. 59–96, 119. A good introduction to the physical development of the city center is contained in Charles Hall Page, *Splendid Survivors* (San Francisco, 1979), pp. 23–61.

2. For a largely pictorial survey of the firm's buildings, see B.J.S. Cahill, "The Work of Bliss & Faville," *A&E*, January 1914, pp. 47–96. Little research has been conducted on this firm and most of the other firms cited below. Page, *Splendid Survivors*, pp. 49–54, gives a valuable profile of professional education and practice. The single most informative biographical reference is *Davis' Commercial Encyclopedia* (Berkeley, 1911).

3. Concerning Howard, see: Herbert Croly, "The New University of California," *AR*, March 1908, pp. 271–293; Joan Draper, "John Galen Howard and the Beaux-Arts Movement in the United States" (M.A. thesis, University of California at Berkeley, 1972); and Loren Partridge, *John Galen Howard and the Berkeley Campus* (Berkeley, 1978). Most of Howard's office records and personal papers are in BL and CED Docs.

4. On Weeks, see *Ex*, March 26, 1926 and *A&E*, April 1928, p. 122. On Morgan, see: Walter Steilberg, "Some Examples of the Work of Julia Morgan," *A&E*, November 1918, pp. 39–107; and the author's "Julia Morgan: Some Introductory Notes," *Perspecta 15*, 1975, pp. 74–86. Some of Morgan's drawings are in CED Docs. A major collection of her papers has recently been donated to California State University, San Luis Obispo.

391

5. Concerning Bakewell & Brown, see "Some Work of Bakewell & Brown, Architects," *A&E*, February 1909, pp. 34–43; and B.J.S. Cahill, "The New City Hall, San Francisco," *A&E*, August 1916, pp. 39–77. Arthur Brown's papers have recently been donated to BL.

6. Applegarth was a native of Oakland; Hobart and Lansburgh were born elsewhere, but spent part of their youth in the region. The others moved to San Francisco after they had been professionally trained. On Dutton, see: "Some Bank and Office Building Designs," *A&E*, April 1907, pp. 35–42; *Men Who Made San Francisco* (San Francisco, n.d.), p. 51. On Hobart, see: "The Work of Lewis P. Hobart," *AR*, October 1909, pp. 274–295; Louis Mullgardt, "The Architecture of Mr. Lewis P. Hobart," *A&E*, August 1915, pp. 39–89. On MacDonald, see: *Men Who Made San Francisco*, p. 267; and *A&E*, January 1938, p. 55. On Kelham, see: *Who's Who in California* (San Francisco, 1929), p. 273; and *A&E*, June 1932, p. 27. On Applegarth, see: "Some of the Work of G. A. Applegarth, *A&E*, May 1913, pp. 46–64; and Gray Brechin, "George Applegarth: Classical Creativity," Foundation for San Francisco's Architectural Heritage, *Newsletter*, Summer 1981, p. 5. On Lansburgh, see Norton Stern and William Kramer, "G. Albert Lansburgh, San Francisco's Jewish Architect from Panama," *Western States Jewish Historical Quarterly*, April 1981, pp. 210–224. I am grateful to Michael Corbett and Steven Levin for providing me with some of these references.

7. Concerning the general mood of San Franciscans in the fire's wake, see Will Irwin, *The City That Was* (New York, 1906). On the fire and reconstruction, see: A. C. David, "The New San Francisco . . . ," *AR*, January 1912, pp. 3–26; Scott, *San Francisco*, chap. 7 and pp. 154–158; Judd Kahn, *Imperial San Francisco* (Lincoln, Neb. and London, 1979), chaps. 7, 8; and Joan Draper, "The San Francisco Civic Center: Architecture, Planning and Politics" (Ph.D. diss., University of California at Berkeley, 1979).

8. *Ch*, December 16, 1899. The note stated that as of January 1, 1900, the two architects would be associated in all work then in hand and received in the future. Also mentioned is that Percy would manage office business and that Polk would have charge of design.

9. Two exceptions were the original designs for the Alexander Young Building in Honolulu and a double house for Mrs. Robert Louis Stevenson and Lloyd Osbourne in San Francisco; prints of a perspective rendering of the Young Building and a set of working drawings for the Stevenson-Osbourne house exist in Polk's papers. Other projects on which Polk appears to have focused his energies include the Hayward Building and competition entries for Mercantile Trust Company and the Mutual Savings Bank, all in San Francisco.

10. Mrs. Leland King told the author that, according to Percy's daughter, Polk wanted to be a partner. The senior architect's only response was that he made a fine *draftsman*. Henry Meyers, who trained in the office, apparently had no kind feelings toward Polk. When the firm disbanded following Percy's death, Meyers managed to take charge of work still in progress, leaving Polk without employment. Later, Meyers publicly contested Polk's no doubt legitimate claim to the design of the Hayward Building; see *A&E*, May 1911, p. 100.

11. Christina Barreda had married Charles A. Moore in 1890. Their son, Austin Percy Moore, was born the following year. He married Page Brown's daughter in 1912, later assisted Polk, and became a partner in the firm after Polk's death. Charles Moore died in 1895. The Barredas were friends of Phoebe Hearst, and it was at her Hacienda del Pozo de Verona where Polk and Christina met. For additional information on the family, see: Ethel Shorb, "Personal," *Argonaut*, July 14, 1939, p. 11; and Frederick Barreda Sherman, *From the Guadalquivir to the Golden Gate . . .* (Mill Valley, Calif., 1977).

12. Letters from Daniel Burnham to Joseph Worcester, January 26, 1901; February 23, 1901; and April 27, 1901; and letter from Burnham to Willis Polk, March 1, 1901, Burnham Papers, Library of the Art Institute of Chicago (hereafter Burnham Papers). See also: Burnham diary, 1901, Burnham Papers; *Ch*, March 16, 1901; April 6, 1901; June 29, 1901; and September 7, 1901.

13. Polk's name appears just under that of Ernest Graham, the office manager, in the title blocks of the working drawings for the Merchant's Exchange Building in San Francisco, suggesting that he was in charge of the project. Polk is cited as the designer of the main building for the First National Bank of Chicago, *TT*, September 29, 1906, p. 3. Polk also apparently designed an unexecuted scheme for the Union League in Chicago; copies of the presentation drawings

392

are in his papers. These were among the most important commissions in Burnham's office at that time. Burnham's frequent social engagements with Polk are documented in his diaries for 1902 and 1903, Burnham Papers.

14. The Polks were abroad for approximately three months; their itinerary remains unknown. The partnership with Wright was established by the time of publication of *LSFD* in May 1904. For biographical information on Wright, see Edgar A. Mathews, "Editorial," *PCA*, March 1918, p. 190.

   For a brief period in 1905 Louis Mullgardt became a partner in the firm. He and Polk were friends, but their approaches to design were too different for the association to last. Polk always spoke highly of Mullgardt's work and may have had a hand in securing for Mullgardt, who heretofore had received relatively minor commissions, the job of designing the Court of the Ages at the Panama-Pacific International Exposition. I am grateful to Chesley Bonestell and Robert Judson Clark for some of this information.

15. Letters from Burnham to Polk, October 1, 1903; October 26, 1903; October 27, 1903; November 5, 1903; November 12, 1903; February 17, 1904; February 24, 1904; March 31, 1904; April 21, 1904; August 8, 1904; March 29, 1905; April 12, 1905; May 18, 1905; November 13, 1905; and Burnham diary, 1904, Burnham Papers. Several of these letters suggest that Polk may have been active both in encouraging the Association for the Improvement and Adornment of San Francisco to select Burnham as architect of the master plan and in encouraging Burnham to undertake the project.

   Whether Polk had any influence on the proposals made in Burnham's plan is unknown. In the *Report on a Plan for San Francisco* (San Francisco, 1905), p. 211, Polk is acknowledged for his "sympathy with the whole project and his practical assistance throughout the course of the work." See also: Burnham diary, 1905, Burnham Papers; and Charles Moore, *Daniel H. Burnham, Architect, Planner of Cities*, 2 vols. (Boston and New York, 1921), 1: 231 ff. For recent analysis of the plan, see: Scott, *San Francisco*, chap. 6; Thomas Hines, *Burnham of Chicago; Architect and Planner* (New York, 1974), chap. 9; and Kahn, *Imperial San Francisco*, chap. 4.

16. Letters from Burnham to Polk May 1, 1906 and June 13, 1906, Burnham Papers. Subsequent letters indicate that Polk had almost complete control of the office; however, expenses and salaries were paid from Chicago.

17. Concerning Polk's work during this period, see: Frederick Hamilton, "The Work of Willis Polk & Company," *A&E*, April 1911, pp. 34–73; C. Matlack Price, "Notes on the Varied Work of Willis Polk," *AR*, December 1913, pp. 566–583; Willis Polk, "The Panama-Pacific Plan," *Sunset*, April 1912, pp. 487–493; and Polk's office scrapbooks in the California Historical Society and in his papers.

18. Letters from Burnham to Polk, October 4, 1907; October 19, 1907; October 29, 1907; December 7, 1907; January 24, 1908; March 25, 1908; September 19, 1908; February 18, 1909; April 27, 1909; May 7, 1909; August 2, 1909; February 16, 1910; March 17, 1910; May 21, 1910; July 27, 1910; January 28, 1911; February 13, 1911; July 19, 1911; September 1, 1911; letters from Burnham to Worcester, August 11, 1911; October 6, 1911, Burnham Papers; and *Ch*, October 26, 1910.

19. In August 1911, a preliminary architectural commission was established, consisting of Polk, John Galen Howard, Albert Pissis, William Curlett, and Clarence Ward. Shortly thereafter, Burnham and William Bourn, one of the fair's directors, proposed Polk as director of the permanent commission. Howard, Curlett, and Pissis refused to serve. Within three days, the new commission was established with Ward, William Faville, and Polk, with Polk at its head. Sometime between September and December 1912 he was replaced by George Kelham. The reasons for his dismissal remain unknown; however, considering that a close Burnham associate, Charles C. Moore, was president of the Exposition; that another Burnham associate, Edward Bennett, was chief advisor on the master plan; and that Polk's friend, William Crocker, was in charge of the building committee, Polk's actions must have been untenable.

20. Around 1911, the University of California Regents commissioned Polk to design an apartment hotel for the site. The scheme, illustrated in *Ch*, July 22, 1911, was mundane and never executed. The Regents defaulted in payments for Polk's services; he sued them in 1915.

Thus, it is unusual that they returned to him for the design of the Hallidie Building two years later.

A note in the *Oakland Tribune*, May 20, 1917, stated that the tenants wanted a glass-front building, but gave no explanation. A search through the records of the major initial tenant, Roos Atkins, and the university archives, as well as interviews with Chesley Bonestell, who was in Polk's office at that time, and Mrs. Harrison Clarke, the widow of the job captain, have uncovered no further clues. For additional material on the building, see: *Ex*, January 20, 1918; "The World's First Glass Front Building," *A&E*, April 1918, pp. 71–73; Irving F. Morrow, "The Hallidie Building," *PCA*, July 1918, pp. 40–41; and Keith W. Dills, "The Hallidie Building," *JSAH*, December 1971, pp. 323–329.

21. Letter from Maybeck to Polk, March 6, 1915, Polk Papers. For background on Polk's securing of the Palace of Fine Arts design for Maybeck, see Kenneth Cardwell, *Bernard Maybeck* (Santa Barbara and Salt Lake City, 1977), p. 141.

22. This quality is evident in several unexecuted projects. The facade of Polk's scheme for the Women's City Club in San Francisco (1923) carries a bizarre combination of glass curtain wall and Churrigueresque ornament; several drawings for the scheme are in his papers. A proposal for the Woodlawn Memorial Mausoleum in Colma (1918) is a heavy-handed attempt to replicate portions of the Palace of Fine Arts, then threatened with demolition; see *Ex*, May 17, 1918. See also proposals for the Daniel Jackling house in Hillsborough (ca. 1918), *Western Architect*, January 1919, plates 5–6.

23. Nevertheless, Polk's death was marked by an outpouring of tributes; see: "Passing of Willis Polk, Architect and Master Builder," *A&E*, September 1924, pp. 108–109; Maybeck, Letter to the Editor, *AABN*, November 5, 1924, p. 422; and Bruce Porter, "Willis Polk," *San Francisco Water*, October 1924, p. 12. William Bourn's Spring Valley Water Company published a slim, elegant commemorative booklet, *To Remember Willis Polk, Architect* (San Francisco, 1926). A monograph of his work, *Willis Polk; A Memorial Volume*, was planned under the sponsorship of Bourn, Daniel Burnham, Jr., John Bakewell, Arthur Brown, Edward Bennett, William Crocker, Jules Guerin, Maybeck, and Porter, among others. Unfortunately, the project never materialized. In addition to the sources cited in the notes above, interviews with Chesley Bonestell (March, April, and October 1972), Michael Goodman (March 1972), Emily Michels (July 1973), Leffler B. Miller (February 1972), and John O'Shea (June 1972), all of whom were in Polk's employ at various times between 1910 and 1924, have been invaluable in assessing this period of his practice.

24. Since Coxhead's office records have been destroyed, a full count of work will probably never be compiled. The estimate made here is based on research by John Beach, Anthony Bruce, and the author. Coxhead's proposal for the exposition is illustrated in *AR*, May 1911, pp. 398–399. Later he expressed bitterness over having been left out of the affair, claiming erroneously that his scheme was used, without credit, as a conceptual basis for the realized complex; see *TT*, April 24, 1915. Coxhead's eagerness for the large-scale work is also suggested by his unsolicited proposal for the redevelopment of Market Street around the ferry depot (Coxhead, "The Improvement of the Foot of Market Street, San Francisco," *A&E*, November 1914, pp. 65–66) and the publishing of his plans for the Hearst competition ("An Echo of the Phoebe Hearst Architectural Competition," *A&E*, September 1912, pp. 97–101).

Along with the main office building, the firm designed several other facilities for the Home Telephone Company during the late 1900s; see Almeric Coxhead, "The Telephone Exchange," *A&E*, August 1909, pp. 35–46. The only other known commercial building designed by Coxhead in San Francisco after the 1906 fire is the modest Continental Hotel (1907), illustrated in Page, *Splendid Survivors*, p. 124.

25. Information concerning the wedding (Polk was best man) is contained in a letter from Helen Coxhead to Mary Louise Coxhead (one of Coxhead's sisters), July 1, 1898, in possession of Helen Coxhead Strong. I am grateful to John Beach for other information concerning the family.

26. This change is dramatically suggested by the designs of adjacent houses for Bruce and Robert Porter (1903–1904) and their brother-in-law Julian Waybur (ca. 1900–1901) in San Francisco. The earlier design takes the rustic house in a new direction as a flat-roofed, symmetrical

box, unadorned save for a few wildly exaggerated and contorted classical elements in the center. The Porter house is a variation on the same idea, but one that is dry and stiff, a faint echo of its rambunctious neighbor. For an illustration, see Sally Woodbridge, ed., *Bay Area Houses* (New York, 1976), p. 34.

27. In contrast to the outpouring of tributes to Polk at the time of his death, little mention was made of Coxhead, and his work was noted only in passing. See: *Berkeley Daily Gazette*, March 28, 1933; and *A&E*, April 1933, p. 51.

28. Herbert Croly, "An Architect of Residences in San Francisco," *AR*, July 1906, p. 46–62; John Beach, "The Bay Area Tradition 1890–1918," in Woodbridge, ed., *Bay Area Houses*, pp. 60–68. See also *Oakland Daily Tribune*, December 19, 1891. Local directories are an important source of information for Mathews and the other architects cited below. Edgar's father, Julius Case Mathews, came to Oakland in 1852. His older brother, Walter, was also a prominent architect in the same city. The most distinguished member of the family was another brother, Arthur, a painter and furniture designer.

29. For a sampling of Farr's work, see: *Merchants' Association Review*, December 1903, p. 2; *A&E*, January 1907, p. 30; April 1909, pp. 72–75; December 1910, p. 49; and "Jack London's Unique Country Home," *A&E*, July 1911, pp. 49–51.

30. *Hoye's Directory of Kansas City* shows that White was employed in Van Brunt's office ca. 1886–1891. Apparently, he knew Polk well from this period. The inverse side of a photograph taken ca. 1890 is inscribed "To my chief assistant Jon White comps of Willis Polk," Polk Papers. The *LSFD* for 1904 and 1905 indicates that John joined his brother, Mark, in the firm of Maybeck and White. From 1906 to 1908, George Howard joined the office in a loose-knit association under the name of Maybeck, Howard, & White. By the latter year, the firm of Howard & White (John) was formed. A substantial number of John White's drawings are in CED Docs.

31. For biographical information, see *Davis' Commercial Encyclopedia*, p. 217.

32. For illustration of Knowles's work, see: "Three Beautiful Homes, Some Features in Residential Architecture as Shown in Recent Work of Architect Knowles," *A&E*, June 1905, pp. 29–37, 59, 61; and William Knowles, "The Garden and the Bungalow," *A&E*, November 1906, pp. 19–25. I am grateful to his son, Duncan Knowles, for supplying me with additional information.

33. The architects cited above are only those who began practice around the turn of the century and who are known to have designed some noteworthy rustic buildings about that time. Both John Galen Howard and Julia Morgan also worked in this province; see: Beach, "Bay Area Tradition," pp. 71–80; and n. 4 above. A number of other architects, such as John Hudson Thomas, Henry Gutterson, William Charles Hays, and Walter Ratcliff, began practice some years later and made a significant contribution to the region's rustic ambience. Thomas is the only one of this latter group about whom much has been written; see: Charles H. Cheney, "The Art of the Small Home," *HB*, July 1910, pp. 34–38; Thomas Gordon Smith, "John Hudson Thomas and the Progressive Spirit in Architecture 1910-1920" (M.A. thesis, University of California at Berkeley, 1975); and Beach, "Bay Area Tradition," pp. 87–98. Much additional research needs to be conducted for the full richness of the 1900s and 1910s to be revealed. Local surveys, such as that sponsored by the Berkeley Architectural Heritage Association, are a valuable step in this direction.

34. Scholarly analysis of the Arts and Crafts Movement in American architecture is just beginning. Among the most useful accounts are: H. Allen Brooks, "Chicago Architecture: Its Debt to the Arts and Crafts," *JSAH*, December 1971, pp. 312–317; Robert Judson Clark, ed., *The Arts and Crafts Movement in America 1876–1916* (Princeton, 1972); James Kornwolf, *M. H. Baillie Scott and the Arts and Crafts Movement* (Baltimore and London, 1972), pp. 344–393; Timothy Andersen, Eudorah Moore, and Robert Winter, eds., *California Design 1910* (Pasadena, 1974); Robert Winter, "The Arts and Crafts as a Social Movement," *Record of the Art Museum, Princeton University*, 1975, no. 2, pp. 36–40; and Reyner Banham, Introduction, in Randall Mackinson, *Greene and Greene: Architecture as a Fine Art* (Santa Barbara and Salt Lake City, 1977), pp. 12–23.

35. Alwyn Covell, in "The Real Place of Mission Furniture," *Good Furniture*, March 1915, pp.

359–362, emphasized that arts-and-crafts "is not really a 'style'—it is an idea." More recently, Brooks, in "Chicago Architecture," p. 312, stressed the same point.

36. See, for instance, Ralph Adams Cram's comments on work by Greene & Greene in his preface to *American Country Houses of Today* (New York, 1913), pp. III–IV; also: Aymar Embury II, *One Hundred Country Houses* (New York, 1909); and Charles Hooper, *The Country House* (Garden City, N.Y., 1913). The content of design periodicals also is revealing. Between the mid-1900s and World War I, *AR* published numerous articles on work by architects such as the Greenes, Irving Gill, Henry Mercer, and Frank Lloyd Wright. During the same period, *Craftsman* frequently included essays espousing City Beautiful objectives.

CHAPTER XI

1. The best depiction of Berkeley's character around the turn of the century is Dimitri Shipounoff's Introduction to Charles Keeler, *The Simple Home*, reprint ed. (Santa Barbara and Salt Lake City, 1979). See also: William Ferrier, *Berkeley California: The Story of the Evolution of a Hamlet into a City of Culture and Commerce* (Berkeley, 1933); Eva Carlin, ed., *A Berkeley Year; A Sheaf of Nature Essays* (Berkeley, 1898); Herman Whitaker, *Berkeley, California Illustrated* (Berkeley, ca. 1903). Concerning the development of mass-transit systems, see Mel Scott, *The San Francisco Bay Area* (Berkeley and Los Angeles, 1959), pp. 85–86, 92–93.

2. Concerning the club's history and activities, see: Shipounoff, Introduction, *Simple Home;* Leslie Freudenheim and Elisabeth Sussman, *Building with Nature* (Santa Barbara and Salt Lake City, 1974), pp. 63–74; Martin Curtis, "A Club to Beautify the Hillsides," *Ch,* January 13, 1901; Anna Simpson, "Ideal Home-Making on a Berkeley Hillside," *Ch,* August 14, 1904, Sunday supplement; Charles Keeler, "A Retrospection," *Year Book of the Hillside Club* (Berkeley, 1907), pp. 2–5; and "What the Club Advocates," *Year Book, The Hillside Club, 1911–1912* (Berkeley, ca. 1912), pp. 6–7. The club's records are on deposit at BL. On village improvement societies, see David Handlin, *The American Home: Architecture and Society, 1815–1915* (Boston and Toronto, 1979), pp. 91–116, 183–197.

3. Good background information on Keeler is supplied in Shipounoff, Introduction, *Simple Home.*

4. Charles Keeler, "The Passing of the Wild and Woolly West," *Ch,* January 1, 1903.

5. The original 1904 edition appears to have had limited distribution; copies are extremely rare. Two additional essays by Keeler on architecture are: "Municipal Art in American Cities: San Francisco," *Craftsman,* August 1905, pp. 584–600; and "Thoughts on Home Building in California," *A&E,* October 1905, pp. 19–28.

6. A. B. Wastell, "Bernard R. Maybeck," *PCA,* March 1916, p. 154; taped interview with Bernard Maybeck by Robert Schulz, KPFA, Berkeley, ca. February 1953, CED Docs, reel 1. See also Louis Stellmann, "Interesting Westerners," *Sunset,* November 1915, pp. 951–952.

7. Charles Keeler, "Friends Bearing Torches," typescript, begun 1934, Keeler Papers, BL, p. 227.

8. See Shipounoff, Introduction, *Simple Home.* pp. xix–xx, for a background on the commission. The contract notice for the house appears in the *Berkeley Gazette,* August 1, 1895, citing a cost of $2,000. Maybeck expressed interest in designing Keeler's residence several years earlier. No clues have been found to suggest a precise date for this preliminary scheme.

9. Keeler, "Friends Bearing Torches," p. 226.

10. Concerning Maybeck's acknowledged debt to Viollet, see chap. 2, n. 38. To the author's knowledge, Maybeck never mentioned the influence of Semper either in writing or in interviews. However, the fact that he was preparing to, or in the process of, translating at least portions of Semper's *Der Stil* (see chap. 2, n. 36) suggests that he held the German architect's ideas in high esteem and wished to have his American colleagues become familiar with them.

396

The importance of the Ecole for Maybeck is discussed in Kenneth Cardwell, *Bernard Maybeck* (Santa Barbara and Salt Lake City, 1977), pp. 17 ff.; and in chap. 8 and the text below herein.

11. Keeler's daughter, the late Merodine Keeler McIntyre, provided essential information and assistance in reconstructing the house's original plan. The building was extensively remodeled for apartments around the 1920s, probably by Maybeck himself.

12. Eugène Emmanuel Viollet-le-Duc, "Construction," in *Dictionnaire raisonné de l'architecture française de XIe au XVIe siècle,* trans. George Huss, *Rational Building* (New York, 1895), pp. 1, 76.

13. Viollet-le-Duc, *Rational Building,* pp. 9, 16 ff.; Viollet-le-Duc, *Discourses on Architecture,* trans. Benjamin Bucknall, reprint ed. (New York, 1959), especially pp. 31–32. Illustrations of native houses in New Zealand and Hawaii are contained in Keeler, *Simple Home.*

14. Eugène Viollet-le-Duc, *The Habitations of Man in All Ages,* trans. Benjamin Bucknall (Boston, 1876), chap. 4; Viollet-le-Duc, *Discourses,* especially pp. 31–32, 86–88, 191–192. Maybeck, in KPFA tape, reel 3, described his composing ("modeling") the design for the First Church of Christ Scientist in Berkeley (1910), "just as if I was an old Greek," no doubt referring to Viollet's portrayal of how ancient Greek temples were formed.

15. Gottfried Semper, *Der Stil in den technischen und tektonischen Künsten oder praktische Ästhetik,* 2 vols. (Frankfurt am Main, 1860, 1863). Semper's scorn for Viollet's rationalism is noted in Robin Middleton, "Viollet-le-Duc's Academic Ventures and the Entretiens sur l'Architecture," in *Gottfried Semper und die Mitte des 19. Jahrhunderts* (Basel and Stuttgart, 1976), p. 242. Might the *Entretiens* have been written to counter points made in *Der Stil,* as well as those of French academic theory?

16. Semper, *Der Stil,* 2nd rev. ed. (Munich, 1879) 2: 275 ff., 305–306.

17. Rosemarie Bletter, "On Martin Fröhlich's Gottfried Semper," *Oppositions,* October 1974, pp. 150–151.

18. Shipounoff, Introduction, *Simple Home,* pp. xxi–xxii; Kenneth Cardwell, *Maybeck,* pp. 58–61.

19. Viollet's influence on architects such as Victor Horta, Hector Guimard, and Antonio Gaudí is well known; Semper's influence on other early modernists is less so; see, for example: Bletter, "Semper," p. 149; Pieter Singelenberg, *H. P. Berlage; Idea and Style* (Utrecht, 1972), chap. 2; Joan Campbell, *The German Werkbund; The Politics of Reform in the Applied Arts* (Princeton, 1978), p. 93; and Benedetto Gravagnuolo, *Adolf Loos* (New York, 1982), pp. 38, 47–48.

20. The known facts about Maybeck's travels in Europe are contained in Cardwell, *Maybeck,* p. 43. Purchased photographs, which appear to date from the late nineteenth century, can be found in Maybeck's sole surviving scrapbook, CED Docs. They are mostly of vernacular buildings in northern France, southwestern Germany, and central Italy.

21. J. Gaudet, *Eléments et théorie de l'architecture,* 4 vols., 4th ed. (Paris, 1905), especially Livres I and II. Also Peter Collins, *Concrete: A New Vision in Architecture* (London, 1959), pp. 160–162.

22. The evidence for this design being the Oakland Public Library is circumstantial. The photograph, bearing Maybeck's initial and contained in his scrapbook, CED Docs, is otherwise unidentified. However, the scheme does correspond to descriptions of Maybeck's library design in *Ch,* April 29, 1900 and in *Oakland Tribune,* May 2, 1900. The parti also suggests a library; the size and configuration are roughly the same as those of the realized building, designed by Bliss & Faville. Moreover, the design does not correspond to any project designed by Maybeck after 1906, for which office records are fairly complete. For illustration of Gaudet's design, see Arthur Drexler, ed., *The Architecture of the Ecole des Beaux-Arts* (Cambridge, Mass., 1977), pp. 255–257.

23. *The Need of a University Hospital* (Berkeley, 1902).

24. Projects in L. Farge, *Les concours publiques d'architecture* (Paris, 1901, 1903, 1904, 1905,

1909), provide a useful basis for comparison with contemporary French hospital design.

25. Both this scheme and Coxhead's Hearst competition entry, with its curvilinear form, central domed building and enframing arcade, appear to have been important influences on the Palace of Fine Arts. Concerning that building, see: William Jordy, *American Buildings and Their Architects* (Garden City, N.Y., 1972) 3:275–300; and Cardwell, *Maybeck,* pp. 141–152.

26. Jack Arnold, "Bernard Maybeck, Architect," typescript, ca. 1949, p. 6 (author's collection); Bernard Maybeck, *Palace of Fine Arts and Lagoon: Panama-Pacific International Exposition, 1915* (San Francisco, 1915), p. 2; Maybeck, "Architecture of the Palace of Fine Arts at the Panama-Pacific International Exposition," *California's Magazine,* 1916, 2: 161–162.

27. Other large, classical projects for civic and institutional buildings are briefly discussed in Cardwell, *Maybeck,* pp. 135–141, 197–201. This aspect of Maybeck's work deserves further study. Concerning Polk's role in Maybeck's securing the Palace of Fine Arts commission, see Cardwell, *Maybeck,* p. 141.

28. This tally of Maybeck's commissions is based on the list of work in Cardwell, *Maybeck,* pp. 240–242. Cardwell also provides details on the Maybeck office.

29. Like Coxhead, Polk, and many other proponents of academic eclecticism, Maybeck was concerned with adapting precedent to regional conditions. In *Palace of Fine Arts,* p. 13, he wrote that "in the Panama-Pacific International Exposition is expressed the life of the people of California. It has its geographic stamp just as the architecture of Thibet has its geographic reason for being. This same group could not have happened in Boston or in India." He concluded: "When the people of California visit the grounds they should think of the fact that the Fair is an expression of future California cities . . . the future city of California will have the same general feeling; because it will be a California city." However, such remarks should not be interpreted as representing the desire to create a new California style. Maybeck's few essays make it clear that his interest in precedent and expression was broad. See: "The Planning of a University," *Blue and Gold* (University of California yearbook) (Berkeley, 1900), pp. 17–20; "A Dream that Might be Realized," *Merchants' Association Review,* November 1903, pp. 1–2; and "Architecture of the Palace of Fine Arts."

30. Additional information on this scheme and the Flagg, Boke, and Gates houses discussed below is contained in Cardwell, *Maybeck,* pp. 64–65, 73, 75–76, and 96.

31. A number of Maybeck's buildings possess vaguely oriental qualities imparted by structural intricacy and screenlike interior wall planes. The degree of Maybeck's interest in oriental architecture, or whether he deliberately sought to create such allusions, is unknown. In any event, his references to central European sources are much more pronounced.

32. The scheme bears a strong resemblance to a railroad freight station illustrated in *Architektonisches Skizzen,* 1855, plate 2. Mid-nineteenth-century German and French work of this nature, with which Maybeck was probably familiar from his student days abroad, was a principal source for the so-called Stick Style in the United States. It is interesting that Maybeck drew from work of this period, even though the Boke house (and two other residences built from its plans) is the only instance where a mid-nineteenth-century influence is easily traceable in his rustic designs. I am grateful to Sarah Landau for the reference.

33. A watercolor rendering of this cottage, located near Joseph Worcester's cottage in Piedmont, is reproduced in Jacomena Maybeck, *Maybeck: The Family View* (Berkeley, 1980), p. 5. A set of sketchy working drawings for the Underhill house is in CED Docs.

34. Plans for the Flagg and Boke houses appear in Cardwell, *Maybeck,* pp. 72, 75. Only a short description of the Farrington house's organization survives; see Whitaker, "Berkeley, the Beautiful," p. 143.

35. Interviews with the late Walter Steilberg, October 1974, and Marion Gorrill, November 1973. Miss Gorrill, whose aunt was Charles Keeler's wife and whose father was also among Maybeck's clients, shared a number of useful recollections with the author concerning how Maybeck would encourage friends (including her mother) to design their own houses and help them in drawing the plans. The Gorrill house at 2725 Dwight Way, Berkeley, was one such scheme. See also Cardwell, *Maybeck,* p. 68.

36. In later years, Maybeck often recounted the early months spent in André's atelier and emphasized the freedom that his patron insisted on in studying the basic design. See Cardwell, *Maybeck*, pp. 17–18.

37. Interviews with Steilberg and the late Edward Hussey, October 1974. Steilberg knew Maybeck beginning in the early 1910s; Hussey entered the office in 1930. According to Maybeck himself, KPFA tape, reel 3, large charcoal studies were made for the First Church of Christ Scientist. While documentation has yet to be found, it is likely that Maybeck used this method earlier as well. When working in the office, Hussey saved a number of these studies, which were normally discarded as a project was further developed, and they are now in CED Docs. The importance Maybeck placed on the conceptual process is noted in Arnold, "Maybeck," p. 7.

38. Interviews with Steilberg and Hussey; Arnold, "Maybeck," p. 8.

39. See, for instance: *Rational Building*, p. 43; and *Discourses*, pp. 86–88, 91–92.

40. Keeler, "Friends Bearing Torches," p. 226.

41. Cardwell suggests that English vernacular architecture was tapped as a source early in Maybeck's career, *Maybeck*, p. 77; however, there is nothing particularly English about the example cited or about other known work before Principia College, the preliminary designs of which were begun in the mid-1920s.

42. Maybeck, KPFA tape, reel 1; Cardwell, *Maybeck*, p. 43.

43. Interview with Steilberg; "No Regrets from Great Architect," *Ex*, November 2, 1926, 4: 2–3. Both the above sources refer to a period (after ca. 1910) when, as Cardwell notes, Maybeck was less interested in structural expression than he was during the 1900s. Nevertheless, the nature of work done throughout suggests that the shift was one of degree rather than of his basic conception toward structure. While Maybeck's attitude may have been somewhat cavalier, he always relied on the expertise of his partner, Mark White, who was trained as an engineer, to ensure that solutions were technically viable.

44. Jordy, *American Buildings*, p. 302, notes the similarity between such drawings by Viollet and the freestanding brackets that front the south elevation of Maybeck's First Church of Christ Scientist, but does not suggest the irony implicit in the treatment. Viollet's method of depicting structural assemblies was widely used during the second half of the nineteenth century, so that if it was a source of inspiration for Maybeck, he may not have been thinking of Viollet alone. Additional material on the building is contained in Cardwell, *Maybeck*, pp. 62–64. Although some of the same people were members of both organizations, the Town and Gown Club had no official connections with the Hillside Club as Freudenheim and Sussman, *Building with Nature*, pp. 60–61, claim.

45. William Charles Hays, "Some Interesting Buildings at the University of California," *Indoors and Out*, May 1906, p. 74, and *Ch*, December 31, 1899. Additional material on the building is contained in Cardwell, *Maybeck*, pp. 46–51, and in E. V. Matignon, "What Mrs. Hearst Will Do In 1900," *Ch*, December 31, 1899. For an excellent analysis of the importance Maybeck placed on a design's mood, see Jordy, *American Buildings*, pp. 285 ff.

46. Enos Brown, " 'Myntoon' [sic], a Mediaeval Castle in Shasta, California," *American Homes and Gardens*, February 1906, p. 100. See also: Cardwell, *Maybeck*, pp. 52–55; and above, chap. 4, n. 20.

47. "House of Mrs. Phoebe A. Hearst in Siskiyou Co., Cal.," *ARev*(B), January 1904, pp. 65–66.

48. Viollet-le-Duc, *Discourses*, pp. 17–18.

49. Esther McCoy, *Five California Architects* (New York, 1960), p. 3; Maybeck, *Palace of Fine Arts*, p. 9; and William Gray Purcell, "Bernard Maybeck; Poet of Building," typescript, 1949, CED Docs, p. 3.

50. Semper, *Der Stil*, trans. Joseph Rykwert, *Architectural Design*, June–July 1981, p. 10.

51. Enos Brown, "The Most Artistically Decorated Mansion in California," *Call*, February 24, 1907.

52. A number of photographs of such tapestries are contained in Maybeck's scrapbook cited in n. 20 above. Other rooms in the house are illustrated in *AABN*, June 17, 1905.

53. W. N. Harris, "California at St. Louis," *Sunset*, March 1905, p. 491. See also "The Sunny Land of Wine," *Merchants' Association Review*, April 1907, p. 7. Maybeck may have seen pictures of the Palais de Champagne, an exhibit at the 1900 Universal Exposition in Paris, and drawn some inspiration from it; however, his scheme is markedly different in character from others at the St. Louis Fair and from most at earlier expositions.

54. Edward Hussey recalled Maybeck's great fondness for the Packards he began to receive from Earle Anthony in the late 1920s. Concerning Maybeck's analogies for the Anthony showroom in Oakland (1928), see *The Romance of Transportation in California and the Story of the Packard Building* (Oakland, 1928), pp. 3, 5. This and other commissions from Anthony are discussed in: McCoy, *Five California Architects*, pp. 53–54; Cardwell, *Maybeck*, pp. 220–227; I.[rving] F. M.[orrow], "The Earle C. Anthony Inc. Packard Building, San Francisco," *A&E*, July 1927, pp. 60–67; Zoe Battu, " 'The Man on the Street'—Speaks of the Packard Building," *PCA*, July 1927, pp. 32–35; and Don Gillum, "The Earle C. Anthony Building, Oakland, California," *A&E*, February 1929, pp. 35–42. Further study of this work and Maybeck's attitude toward commercial architecture is needed.

55. Sally Woodbridge, ed., *Bay Area Houses* (New York, 1976), especially David Gebhard's Introduction, pp. 3–22.

BIBLIOGRAPHY

A Note on the Sources

Surviving material from the offices of Coxhead, Polk, Schweinfurth, and Maybeck is meager for the years covered in this study. Coxhead's office burned in 1906. Material he kept at home and that of later years was saved by his family until a substantial portion of it was inadvertently destroyed over a decade ago. What remains consists mostly of photographs, renderings, and travel sketches. A few of these were donated to the Bancroft Library in the 1970s. The rest is now in the possession of John Beach and constitutes by far the most valuable source for documenting Coxhead's work.

Polk left many of his early records in the family's Russian Hill house when he moved to new quarters in 1900. Most of these documents were discarded in the 1940s; the few that survived were donated several years ago to the Documents Collection, College of Environmental Design at the University of California at Berkeley. One of the most informative items is a cash book recording client payments between March 1893 and August 1896. A large collection of later drawings and memorabilia was given to Berkeley's Department of Architecture by Polk's widow in the 1930s. The drawings were placed in storage and forgotten, and most of them became damaged beyond repair. In the 1960s, the salvageable items were placed in the Documents Collection. A small number of drawings and letters (most dating from the 1890s) found by David Gebhard and myself have been added to this material. Five scrapbooks of newspaper clippings kept by Polk's office from 1906 to 1924 are at the California Historical Society Library. Copies of letters from Daniel Burnham to Polk, which document their association, are in Burham's papers at the Art Institute of Chicago Library.

None of Schweinfurth's papers are known to be extant; they were probably destroyed not long after his death in 1900. However, much of his work for Brown is recorded in two scrapbooks of photographs and sketches assembled by Brown and owned by a descendant. Two scrapbooks of newspaper clippings collected by Brown, now at the California Historical Society Library, afford detailed information on many of his West Coast projects. The most extensive source on Brown's practice through the 1880s is at the State Historical Society of Wisconsin in the form of a large collection of letters to Mrs. Cyrus McCormick and her son.

Maybeck's office, like Coxhead's, burned in 1906, and his house suffered a similar fate in 1923. Maybeck donated most of his surviving records to Berkeley's Department of Architecture shortly before his death. They form the nucleus of the Documents Collection. While coverage of work from about 1910 on is quite extensive, few items remain from the 1890s and early 1900s. Material added by Kenneth Cardwell over the past twenty years is of particular value in researching the formative period of Maybeck's long practice. Some additional pieces remain in possession of the architect's daughter-in-law, Jacomena Maybeck.

A wealth of material on other architects from the region is also contained in the Documents Collection, which has become one of the major repositories of its kind in the United States. The Bancroft Library's vast resources include some architectural documents, as well as the papers of many prominent Californians, an enormous photograph collection, and hundreds of now scarce publications. Other libraries in the Bay Area, especially those of the California Historical Society, the California Room of the San Francisco Public Library, and the San Mateo County Historical Association, are invaluable sources for related material. Many photographs, drawings, and additional documentary evidence were borrowed from current or former owners and descendants of clients.

The major architectural magazines of the period contain some work of Polk, Schweinfurth, and Brown, but very little by either Coxhead or Maybeck. Periodicals that were published in San Francisco are more informative sources. The *California Architect and Building News,* issued monthly from 1880 to 1900, is an essential record of professional activity, although it was oriented toward members of the old guard. Polk's short-lived *Architectural News* (1890–1891), the only known copy of which is in the College of Environmental Design Library, U.C. Berkeley, is an especially important record of the concerns of his generation shortly after they settled on the West Coast. The *Architect and Engineer of California,* published in San Francisco from 1905 to 1955, offers the most detailed picture of early twentieth-century regional work and some coverage of previous years. The *Pacific Coast Architect,* which commenced in 1911 and subsequently changed titles several times, becoming *California Arts and Architecture* in 1929, is less valuable for this period, but nevertheless should be consulted. Two earlier local journals are also notable: *Architect and Builder* (1894–1895) and *Art and Architecture* (1900). *The Daily Pacific Builder,* which began in 1892, lists all recorded building contracts in the region. The only known complete set of this paper was given by the publisher to the San Francisco Public Library some years ago. It was not catalogued and almost the entire run prior to 1908 has been lost. No other copies of issues from the 1890s have been found.

Several San Francisco newspapers and popular weekly magazines give even more details on work of the 1890s than do the professional journals. Coverage focuses on buildings in the city, but sometimes includes work

402

in outlying areas. Contract notices usually were published each week in the *San Francisco Chronicle*, which also contains frequent notes concerning architects' activities and short articles about buildings planned or under construction. Time permitted only spot checks in the *San Francisco Examiner* and *San Francisco Call*, both of which appear to be equally informative. The *Wave* (1891–1901) is the most valuable of the city's late nineteenth-century weekly magazines, both for architecture and for gaining a sense of local cultural attitudes. The *San Francisco News Letter* (1856–1928) frequently included photographs of houses, commercial buildings, and general views of the city from the late 1880s through the turn of the century. Such publications are now extremely rare, but microfilm copies of most of them have been made by the Bancroft Library. The San Francisco–based *Overland Monthly* (1883–1933) and its competitor, *Sunset Magazine* (1898–), occasionally printed articles on architecture, but are most useful as indicators of cultural attitudes and as pictorial records.

Most historical studies of San Francisco architecture from this period are introductory, beginning with a brief essay by Elizabeth Thompson, "Early Domestic Architecture of the San Francisco Bay Region," published in 1951. The most recent, and best, introductory pieces are by David Gebhard and John Beach in *Bay Area Houses* (1976). Gebhard's introduction seeks to clarify and elaborate on the long-standing debate about which characteristics of regional domestic architecture from the late nineteenth century to the present constitute a tradition. Beach's chapter deals with work from 1890 to 1918, making many revealing observations but including no footnotes. Harold Kirker's *California's Architectural Frontier* (1960) deals with the entire state and focuses on earlier developments. Among the most thoughtful analyses of this subject, the book provides an essential background to the late nineteenth century, particularly in its interpretation of how buildings reflect societal attitudes.

Maybeck has been the subject of numerous studies. The pioneering research was conducted by Jean Murray Bangs (Mrs. Harwell Harris) and resulted in several short essays published during the late 1940s and early 1950s. This work was continued by Esther McCoy in her classic book *Five California Architects* (1960). William Jordy's chapter on Maybeck in *American Buildings and Their Architects* (vol. 3, 1972) gives the best analysis of the designer's intentions and methods. Kenneth Cardwell's monograph, *Bernard Maybeck; Artisan, Architect, Artist* (1977) provides a detailed chronicle of his long career and much new information. Concerning Polk, my introduction to *A Matter of Taste: Willis Polk's Writings on Architecture in The Wave* (1979) outlines some thoughts developed more fully here.

Other recent work on related architectural subjects has greatly enriched the picture. Most notable among these are Gebhard's articles on the Mission Style and his *Samuel and Joseph Cather Newsom* (1979), Loren Partridge's short history of the U.C. Berkeley campus (1978), and Michael Corbett's analysis of the development of downtown San Francisco in *Splendid Survivors* (1978). To my brief essay on Julia Morgan (1975) will soon be added a major study by Sara Boutelle. Dimitri Shipounoff's introduction to the reprint edition of *The Simple Home* (1979) is the best work on Charles Keeler, the Hillside Club, and Berkeley at the turn of the century. Mel Scott's *San Francisco Bay Area* (1959) is likely to remain the basic text on the region's physical development for some time to come. *Imperial San Francisco* by Judd Kahn (1979) examines the city's urban aspirations at the turn of the century, relating physical change, economics, and politics. Gunther Barth's *Instant Cities* (1973) masterfully analyzes the forces that shaped San Francisco through the 1880s. Kevin Starr's *Americans and the California Dream* (1973) affords a vivid, engaging, and broad analysis of the state's cultural impulses during the late nineteenth and early twentieth centuries.

I have sought to give comprehensive citations of material written by and about the four architects during the period covered in this study, while selecting later writings on the basis of the insights they provide. The remaining entries are limited to publications on the region, excluding many popular works that are based on other studies and local lore. Numerous additional publications that contributed to this book are cited in the footnotes. For the sake of brevity, I have not included what would be a very long list of treatises, articles, and monographs to which architects of the period referred. Nor have I cited the myriad studies of architecture in the United States and Europe published over the past half century on which any work of this nature must depend.

UNPUBLISHED MATERIAL

Interviews

Theodore Bernardi, San Francisco, July 1977

Chesley Bonestell, Carmel, March, April, and July 1972; July 1975

The late Mrs. Robert Bowie, Mill Valley, April 1972

Phoebe Brown and Mrs. Catherine Porter Short, San Francisco, September 1974

Edward H. Clarke, San Francisco, July 1975

Mrs. Lockwood de Forest, Santa Barbara, January 1975

Mrs. George Eastham, Chico, July 1977

Joseph Esherick, Berkeley, July 1977

Willis Forbes, San Francisco, July 1975

Michael Goodman, Berkeley, March 1972

Marion Gorrill, Berkeley, November 1973

F. Bourn Hayne, St. Helena, June 1973

The late Edward Hussey, Berkeley, October 1974

W. Horace Jones, Los Gatos, October 1974

Mrs. Harold Kelley, Berkeley, October 1974

Elizabeth Knight Smith, San Francisco, July 1974

Mr. and Mrs. Scott Knight Smith, Saratoga, November 1974

Duncan Knowles, Oakland, September 1974

The late Merodine Keeler McIntyre, Mill Valley, November 1974

Donald McLaughlin, San Francisco, June 1977

Emily Michaels, San Francisco, July 1973

Leffler Miller, San Francisco, February 1972

Charles W. Moore, Los Angeles, May 1977

Marguerite Murdock, Berkeley, April 1975

John O'Shea, Oakland, June 1972

The late Britton Rey, Belvedere, August 1973

The late Mrs. Leon Roos, San Francisco, October 1974

Frederick Barreda Sherman, Mill Valley, April 1972

The late Walter Steilberg, Berkeley, February 1972, October 1974

Mrs. Max Stern, San Francisco, March 1972

Gladys Tilden, Berkeley, April 1975

Archival material

Bancroft Library, University of California at Berkeley

Gelett Burgess Correspondence and Papers

Ernest Coxhead Architectural Drawings (small collection of drawings of work and travel sketches, all post-1900)

Phoebe Apperson Hearst Correspondence and Papers (includes letters concerning the Hearst Competition and the Hacienda del Pozo de Verona)

Hillside Club Papers (minutes, pamphlets, and yearbooks)

John Galen Howard Correspondence and Papers (drawings and photographs of work, travel sketches, and letters)

George Holmes Howison Correspondence and Papers (includes letters from Worcester)

Charles A. Keeler Family Papers (includes writings and material related to Hillside Club)

James D. Phelan Correspondence and Papers (includes diaries, letters, and scrapbooks)

Bruce Porter Correspondence and Papers (includes diaries and letters)

Sharon Family Papers (includes letters from A. Page Brown)

Documents Collection, College of Environmental Design, University of California at Berkeley

Bernard Maybeck (drawings, photographs, and specifications of work; office correspondence; and scrapbook)

Willis Polk (drawings and photographs of work, renderings, paintings, scrapbooks, cash book, office furniture, and correspondence)

Joseph Worcester (fourteen scrapbooks of clippings from magazines, and photographs)

Library, Art Institute of Chicago

Daniel Burnham Papers (includes diaries and copies of office correspondence with Polk, Worcester, Phelan, and others in San Francisco).

Library, California Historical Society, San Francisco

A. Page Brown (two scrapbooks of newspaper clippings)

Willis Polk (five scrapbooks of newspaper clippings, 1906–1924)

Library, Society of California Pioneers, San Francisco

George W. Percy (scrapbook, includes clippings of work done in collaboration with Polk)

Library, State Historical Society of Wisconsin, Madison

Cyrus McCormick, Jr. Papers (includes letters from A. Page Brown)

Nettie Fowler McCormick Papers (includes letters from A. Page Brown)

Private collections

John Beach, Berkeley
Ernest Coxhead (an extensive collection of drawings and photographs of work, notebooks, travel sketches, and student projects)

Sheila Mack, Los Angeles
A. Page Brown (two scrapbooks containing mostly photographs of work)

Dissertations, theses, and other manuscripts

J. Arnold, "Bernard Maybeck, Architect." Typescript, ca. 1949, author's collection.

J. M. Backus, "Gelett Burgess: A Biography of the Man Who Wrote 'The Purple Cow,' " Ph.D. dissertation, University of California at Berkeley, 1961.

C. L. Calavan, "A. C. Schweinfurth in California 1893–1898." M.A. thesis, University of California at Santa Barbara, 1972.

R. W. Ditzler, "Bohemianism in San Francisco at the Turn of the Century," M.A. thesis, University of Washington, 1966.

J. E. Draper, "John Galen Howard and the Beaux-Arts Movement in the United States." M.A. thesis, University of California at Berkeley, 1972.

G. Hailey, ed., "California Art Research." Abstract from W.P.A. Project 2874, typescript, 20 vols., San Francisco, 1937.

W. C. Hays, "Order, Taste and Grace in Architecture." Typescript of interviews conducted by Edna Tartaul Daniel, Regional Oral History Office, Bancroft Library, University of California at Berkeley, 1968.

C. Keeler, "Friends Bearing Torches." Unfinished manuscript, (begun 1934), Keeler Papers, Bancroft Library.

R. W. Longstreth, "On the Edge of the World: Ernest Coxhead and Willis Polk in San Francisco during the 1890s." Ph.D. dissertation, University of California at Berkeley, 1977.

W. G. Purcell, "Bernard Maybeck: Poet of Building." Typescript written for Mrs. Harwell Harris, 1949, in C.E.D. Documents Collection.

R. Schulz, Taped interview with Bernard Maybeck, ca. February 1953 for KPFA, Berkeley, in C.E.D. Documents Collection.

K. J. Weitze, "Origins and Early Development of the Mission Revival in California." Ph.D. dissertation, Stanford University, 1978.

A. Worcester, "Rev. Joseph Worcester; A Memoir and Extracts from His Letters to His Nephew, Alfred Worcester." Typescript, ca. 1945, in possession of Mrs. Othmar Tobisch, Berkeley.

PUBLISHED MATERIAL

Writings by Coxhead, Maybeck, Polk, and Schweinfurth

Coxhead:

"Church Planning." *Architectural News,* November 1890, pp. 5–7; December 1890, pp. 19–20; January 1890, pp. 25–26.

"Ottery St. Mary Church, Devon." *Building News,* March 27, 1885, p. 488.

"The Telephone Exchange." *Architect and Engineer,* August 1909, pp. 35–46 (by Almeric Coxhead).

"A Village Church, Cost Fifty Thousand Dollars." *Brickbuilder,* July 1899, pp. 156–158.

Maybeck:

"Architecture of the Palace of Fine Arts at the Panama-Pacific International Exposition." *California's Magazine,* 1916, pp. 161–164.

"A Dream that Might Be Realized." *Merchants' Association Review,* November 1903, pp. 1–2.

Letter to the Editor. *American Architect,* November 5, 1924, p. 422.

Palace of Fine Arts and Lagoon, Panama-Pacific International Exposition, 1915. San Francisco: Paul Elder and Company, 1915.

"The Planning of a University." *Blue and Gold* (University of California Yearbook), 1900, pp. 17–20.

Untitled booklet on hillside house design written for the Hillside Club. Berkeley: Ricardo J. Orozco, 1907.

Polk:

"Arch and Peristyle for Lower Market Street, San Francisco." *Architect and Engineer,* July 1910, p. 61.

"The Architect and His Client." *House Beautiful,* June 1902, p. 58.

"The Architects and the Mayor." *Wave,* July 29, 1893, p. 16. (This and other *Wave* articles reprinted in *A Matter of Taste: Willis Polk's Writings on Architecture in The Wave,* cited in following section).

"Artistic Work in Buildings." *San Francisco Examiner,* November 27, 1892.

" 'The Artists' Choice,' or Why the Hibernia Bank and the Huntington House are the Most Beautiful Buildings in San Francisco." *Wave,* October 1, 1892, p. 8.

"A Brilliant Future for Art in San Francisco." In *Art in California,* pp. 77–78. San Francisco: R. L. Bernier, 1916.

"The City Beautiful." *Town Talk,* December 22, 1900, pp. 43–44.

"An Era of Good Architecture." *San Francisco News Letter,* December 22, 1900, pp. 58–60.

"How to Beautify San Francisco." *Wave,* March 10, 1900, p. 4.

"A Matter of Taste." *Wave,* November 12, 1892, p. 16.

"Mr. Sutro's Baths." *Wave,* November 3, 1894, p. 5.

"The New City Hall Tower." *Wave,* July 15, 1893, p. 16.

"The New Dome and the Western Addition." *Wave,* April 14, 1894, p. 9.

"The New Postoffice." *Wave,* February 6, 1897, p. 7.

"Our Colonial Craze." *San Francisco Examiner,* September 13, 1891.

"A Professional Glance at the World's Fair Structures in Chicago." *San Francisco Examiner,* December 25, 1891.

"Ramblings among local Artists." *Wave,* Christmas 1893.

"San Francisco Beautiful." *Wave,* April 15, 1899, p. 3.

"Stained Glass." *Wave,* November 18, 1893, p. 11.

"The Statue, the Dome and the Draughtsman." *Wave,* June 30, 1894, p. 11.

"Sunset City Discords." *Wave,* December 2, 1893, p. 13.

"Tendency in San Francisco Architecture." *Wave,* September 30, 1893, p. 9.

"The University Competition." *Wave,* November 7, 1896, p. 3.

"The University Competition." *Wave,* January 29, 1898, pp. 2–3.

"The Western Addition." *Wave,* January 29, 1895, p. 16.

Schweinfurth:

Letter to the Editor. *Wave,* November 28, 1896, p. 3.

"Regenerating San Francisco." *Wave,* December 17, 1898, p. 8. (Signed "Architectus"; the evidence of Schweinfurth's authorship is circumstantial).

"What One Architects Says." *Western Architect and Building News* (Denver), February 1890, pp. 179–180.

Writings on Coxhead, Maybeck, Polk, and Schweinfurth: Their Families and Their Work

Coxhead:

D. W. Crocker, "The Church of the Angels." In *Within the Vale of Annandale,* pp. 38–41. Pasadena: published by the author, 1968.

"An Echo of the Phoebe Hearst Architectural Competition for the University of California." *Architect and Engineer,* September 1912, pp. 97–101.

"Ernest and Almeric Coxhead." *Davis' Commercial Encyclopedia of the Pacific Southwest,* p. 219. Berkeley: Ellis A. Davis, 1911.

"Ernest Coxhead." *Architect and Engineer,* April 1933, p. 51.

"Ernest Coxhead." *An Illustrated History of Los Angeles County,* p. 725. Chicago: The Lewis Publishing Company, 1889.

Obituary of Ernest Coxhead. *Berkeley Daily Gazette,* March 28, 1933.

"Personal Glimpses, Ernest Coxhead." *Pacific Coast Architect,* September 1926, p. 53.

"Young Men's Christian Association Building, Los Angeles, California." *California Archi-*

tect, September 15, 1888, pp. 115–116.

Maybeck:

J. M. Bangs, "Bernard Ralph Maybeck, Architect, Comes Into His Own." *Architectural Record*, January 1948, pp. 72–79.

——————————, "Maybeck—Medalist." *Architectural Forum*, May 1951, pp. 160–162.

M. Bell, "Hearst Hall." *The University of California Magazine*, February 1900, pp. 10–14.

E. Brown, "The Most Artistically Decorated Mansion in California." *San Francisco Call*, February 24, 1907 (Newhall house).

——————————, " 'Myntoon' [sic], a Medieval Castle in Shasta, California." *American Homes and Gardens*, February 1906, pp. 100–102.

K. H. Cardwell, *Bernard Maybeck; Artisan, Architect, Artist*. Santa Barbara and Salt Lake City: Peregrine Smith, Inc., 1977.

—————————— and W. C. Hays, "Fifty Years from Now." *California Monthly*, April 1954, pp. 20–26.

J. Harris, "Bernard Ralph Maybeck." *Journal of the American Institute of Architects*, May 1951, pp. 221–228.

W. C. Hays, "Some Interesting Buildings at the University of California." *Indoors and Out*, May 1906, pp. 68–75.

"House of Mrs. Phoebe A. Hearst." *Architectural Review* (Boston), January 1904, pp. 64–66.

E. Howard, "Famous Californians—Bernard Ralph Maybeck." *San Francisco Call*, June 21, 1923.

W. H. Jordy, *American Buildings and Their Architects: Progressive and Academic Ideals at the Turn of the Twentieth Century*. Garden City, N.Y.: Doubleday & Company, Inc., 1972.

E. V. Matignon, "What Mrs. Hearst Will Do in 1900." *San Francisco Chronicle*, December 31, 1899.

J. Maybeck, *Maybeck: The Family View*. Berkeley: Berkeley Architectural Heritage Association, 1980.

"Maybeck to Resign." *San Francisco Chronicle*, May 11, 1903.

E. McCoy, *Five California Architects*. New York: Reinhold Publishing Corporation, 1960. Reprint ed., New York: Frederick A. Praeger, Publishers, 1975.

The Need of a University Hospital. Berkeley: The University Press, 1902.

"The New U.C.: Mr. Maybeck's Ideal of University Buildings." *Wave*, November 7, 1896, p. 8.

F. D. Nichols, "A Visit with Bernard Maybeck." *Journal of the Society of Architectural Historians*, October 1952, pp. 30–31.

"No Regrets from Great Architect." *San Francisco Examiner*, November 2, 1921, 6:2–3.

"Presentation of The Institute's Gold Medal to Bernard Ralph Maybeck." *Journal of the American Institute of Architects*, July 1951, pp. 3–7.

W. Sargent, "Bernard Maybeck." *Life Magazine*, May 17, 1948, pp. 141–142, 144, 147–148, 150, 153.

H. H. Saylor, *Architectural Styles for Country Homes*. New York: McBride, Nast & Company, 1912.

L. J. Stellmann, "Interesting Westerners." *Sunset Magazine*, November 1915, pp. 951–952.

A. B. Wastell, "Bernard R. Maybeck." *The Architect*, March 1916, p. 154.

Polk:

A. Brown, Jr., "Willis Polk." *Architect and Engineer*, September 1924, p. 109.

"A California Home, Santa Clara County." *House and Garden*, August 1902, pp. 355–359 (McCullagh house).

"The Carolan Stables, Finest in California." *San Francisco Chronicle*, March 25, 1900.

F. Hamilton, "The Work of Willis Polk & Company." *Architect and Engineer*, April 1911, pp. 34–73.

P. Jacobson, "The Whip of Discontent." *Sunset Magazine*, April 1922, pp. 29–30, 56, 58.

A. Laurie, "So You're Gone, Are You, Willis?" *San Francisco Examiner*, September 15, 1924.

R. W. Longstreth, *A Matter of Taste: Willis Polk's Writings on Architecture in The Wave*. San Francisco: Book Club of California, 1979.

B. Maybeck, "A Dream that Might Be Realized." *Merchants' Association Review*, November 1903, pp. 1–2.

———————————— , Letter to the Editor. *American Architect*, November 5, 1924, p. 422.

W. C. Morrow, "Let the Next Great World's Fair Be Held in San Francisco." *San Francisco Examiner*, December 25, 1891.

Obituary of Daniel Polk. *American Architect*, February 26, 1908, p. 17.

Obituary of W. W. Polk. *American Architect*, December 22, 1906, p. 194.

Obituary of W. W. Polk. *San Francisco Call*, December 2, 1906.

E. F. O'Day, "Varied Types—X—Willis Polk." *Town Talk*, February 25, 1911, pp. 7, 19.

"Passing of Willis Polk, Architect and Master Builder." *Architect and Engineer*, September 1924, pp. 108–109.

W. H. Polk, *Polk Family and Kinsmen*. Louisville: Bradley and Gilbert, 1912.

"Polk, Willis Jefferson," *Dictionary of American Biography*, 25: 45–46. New York: Charles Scribner's Sons, 1935.

B. Porter, "Willis Polk." *San Francisco Water*, October 1924, p. 12.

C. M. Price, "Notes on the Varied Work of Willis Polk." *Architectural Record*, December 1913, pp. 566–583.

L. U. Reavis, *The Railway and River Systems of the City of St. Louis* (Supplement). St. Louis: Woodward, Tiernan and Hale, 1879 (W. W. Polk).

F. B. Sherman, *From the Guadalquivir to the Golden Gate*. Mill Valley: privately printed, 1977.

To Remember Willis Polk, Architect. San Francisco: John Henry Nash, 1926, (edition limited to 35 copies printed for the Spring Valley Water Company).

"W. W. Polk Dies in San Francisco, Cal." *St. Louis Daily Globe-Democrat*, December 1, 1906, p. 4.

"Willis Polk." *Davis' Commercial Encyclopedia of the Pacific Southwest*, p. 208. Berkeley: Ellis A. Davis, 1911.

"Willis Polk." *Master Hands in the Affairs of the Pacific Coast*, p. 309. San Francisco: Western Historical Publishing Co., 1892.

"Willis Polk." *San Francisco, Its Builders Past and Present* I: 275–276. Chicago and San Francisco: S. J. Clarke Publishing Company, 1913.

"Willis Polk." *Wave*, December 19, 1891, pp. 33–34.

H. R. Wray, " 'Beaulieu,' Cupertino, Santa Clara County, California." *House and Garden,* December 1902, pp. 617–625.

Schweinfurth:

E. Everett, "Two Unique Structures." *Keith's Magazine,* May 1910 (First Unitarian Church).

B. Ferree, *American Estates and Gardens.* New York: Munn and Company, 1906 (Hacienda del Pozo de Verona).

"Hacienda del Pozo de Verona." *Oakland Tribune,* Annual Number, January 1920, pp. 50–51.

"The Hearst Country Seat in Pleasanton, Cal." *Scientific American Building Edition,* July 1900, p. 16.

"An Ideal Summer Home: Mrs. Hearst's 'House of the Well' at Sunol." *Wave,* March 13, 1897. p. 6.

D. M. Kurtz, *Auburn, N.Y., Its Facilities and Resources.* Auburn: The Kurtz Publishing Company, 1884 (Charles Schweinfurth).

"The Later Work of A. C. Schweinfurth, Architect 1864–1900." *Architectural Review* (Boston), February 1902, pp. 76–79.

C. F. Lummis, "The Greatest California Patio House." *Country Life in America,* October 1904, pp. 533–540, 560.

E. V. Matignon, "Hacienda del Poso de Verona." *San Francisco Chronicle,* February 4, 1900.

S. J. Neitz, W. A. Holden, eds., *Julius A. Schweinfurth Master Designer 1858–1931.* Boston: Northeastern University, 1975.

Obituary of A. C. Schweinfurth. *American Architect,* October 20, 1900, p. 22.

Obituary of A. C. Schweinfurth. *Inland Architect,* November 1900, p. 32.

"A Residence at Berkeley, Cal." *Scientific American Building Edition,* October 1898, p. 57 (Moody house).

Contemporary Writings on Architecture and Planning in the Bay Area Around the Turn of the Century

C. H. Alden, "The Historic Precedent in Pacific Coast Architecture." *Architect and Engineer,* July 1912, pp. 80–83.

Architectural Club of San Francisco, *First Annual Exhibition Catalogue.* San Francisco: C. A. Murdock & Co., 1895.

"An Architectural Controversy." *Wave,* February 13, 1897, p. 3.

Artistic Homes of California. San Francisco: San Francisco News Letter, ca. 1889 (collection of artotypes issued individually with the magazine from March 19, 1887 to March 24, 1888 and then distributed in folio form; issues vary slightly).

"The Artists are Voting." *San Francisco Call,* September 10, 1892.

A. H. Barendt, "Midwinter Exposition Buildings." *Wave,* September 9, 1893, p. 9.

A. P. Brown, "Architecture in California." *San Francisco Chronicle,* December 30, 1894.

A. F. Buchanan, "Some Early Business Buildings of San Francisco." *Architectural Record,* July 1906, pp. 15–32.

"Building Up of San Francisco." *Art and Architecture* (San Francisco), November 1900, pp. 19–31.

[G. Burgess], "Architectural Shams." *Wave,* March 20, 1897, p. 4.

D. H. Burnham and E. H. Bennett, *Report on a Plan for San Francisco.* Edited by Edward

O'Day. San Francisco: published by the City, 1905. Reprint ed. Berkeley: Urban Books, 1971.

B. J. S. Cahill, "Adventurings in the Monumental." *Architect and Engineer*, August 1918, pp. 39–97.

───────────── , "City Architecture in 1903." *San Francisco News Letter*, Christmas 1903, pp. 44–45.

───────────── , "The Local Architecture of San Francisco." *Architect and Engineer*, August 1909, pp. 77–82.

California World's Fair Commission, *California at the World's Columbian Exposition, 1893*. Sacramento: State Printing Office, 1894.

"A Chain of Parks for San Francisco." *Wave*, Christmas 1899, p. 12.

C. H. Cheney, "The Art of the Small House." *House Beautiful*, September 1910, pp. 34–38.

"The City's New Fountains." *Mark Hopkins Institute Review of Art*, September 1900, pp. 7–15.

A. B. Clark, *Art Principles in House, Furniture and Village Building*. Stanford: Stanford University Press, 1921.

M. C. Craft, "A Sermon in Church Building." *House Beautiful*, February 1901, pp. 125–132 (Church of the New Jerusalem).

H. Croly, "An Architect of Residences in San Francisco." *Architectural Record*, July 1906, pp. 47–62 (Edgar Mathews).

───────────── , "The California Country House." *Sunset Magazine*, November 1906, pp. 50–65. Reprinted as "The Country House in California." *Architectural Record*, December 1913, pp. 483–519.

───────────── , "The Promised City of San Francisco." *Architectural Record*, June 1906, pp. 425–436.

M. Curtis, "A Club to Beautify the Hillsides." *San Francisco Chronicle*, January 13, 1901.

A. C. David, "The New San Francisco: Architectural and Social Changes Wrought by Reconstruction." *Architectural Record*, January 1912, pp. 3–26.

"A Departure in Church Building—The Second New Jerusalem Church in California." *Craftsman*, June 1906, pp. 330–334.

"Designs for the New Post Office, An Architectural Curio." *San Francisco Chronicle*, November 20, 1896.

T. A. Eisen, "The Consistency of San Francisco Architecture." *California Architect*, April 1882, pp. 53–54.

P. Garnett, *Stately Homes of California*. Boston: Little, Brown & Co., 1915.

C. S. Greene, "The Hearst Architectural Competition of the University of California." *Overland Monthly*, July 1899, pp. 63–73.

"Growth of San Francisco." *San Francisco Chronicle*, January 1, 1891.

"Growth of San Francisco Since 1890, A New Era in Building Development." *San Francisco Chronicle*, January 2, 1898.

W. Hegemann, *Report of a City Plan for the Municipalities of Oakland & Berkeley*. [Oakland]: Municipal Governments of Oakland and Berkeley, 1915.

"The Hillside Cottage." *Architect and Engineer*, January 1910, p. 85.

"The Home Beautiful." *Art and Architecture* (San Francisco), October 1900, pp. 55–79.

J. G. Howard, "Building Materials in California." *For California*, May 1905, pp. 5–6.

───────────── , "Country House Architecture on the Pacific Coast." *Architectural Record*, October 1916, pp. 323–355.

——————— , "Outdoor Life and the Fine Arts." In *Nature and Science on the Pacific Coast*. San Francisco: Paul Elder & Company, 1915.

[M. Hume], *San Francisco Architecturally*. San Francisco: George F. Spaulding & Co., 1903.

M. Hunt, "Personal Sources of Pacific Coast Architectural Development." *American Architect*, January 5, 1926, pp. 51–54.

"The International Competition for the Phoebe A. Hearst Plan for the University of California." *Architectural Annual*, 1900, pp. 53–59.

A. C. Keane, "Ideal Suburbs of American Cities, California's Best Types." *Suburban Life*, January 1906, pp. 10–14.

C. Keeler, "Municipal Art in American Cities: San Francisco." *Craftsman*, August 1905, pp. 584–600.

——————— , "A Retrospection." *Yearbook of the Hillside Club*, 1907, pp. 2–5.

——————— , *The Simple Home*. San Francisco: Paul Elder & Company, 1904. Reprint ed. with introduction by Dimitri Shipounoff. Santa Barbara and Salt Lake City: Peregrine Smith, Inc., 1979.

——————— , "Thoughts on Home Building in California." *Architect and Engineer*, October 1905, pp. 19–28.

"The Most Picturesque Church in the Country." *San Francisco Chronicle*, April 7, 1901 (Church of the New Jerusalem).

"Municipal Art in San Francisco." *San Francisco Chronicle*, April 22, 1900.

J. C. Newsom, *Modern Homes of California*. San Francisco: published by the author, 1893.

A. H. Noll, "The Spanish Missions of the Pacific Coast." *American Architect*, June 5, 1897, pp. 75–76.

A. F. Oakey, "A Word to the Wise." *Overland Monthly*, August 1891, pp. 132–143.

Obituary of A. Page Brown. *American Architect*, February 8, 1896, pp. 57–58.

Obituary of A. Page Brown. *San Francisco Examiner*, January 22, 1896.

Obituary of A. Page Brown. *San Francisco News Letter*, January 25, 1896, p. 18.

Obituary of A. Page Brown. *Wave*, January 25, 1896, p. 6.

Official History of the California Midwinter International Exposition, A Descriptive Record of the Origin, Development and Success of the Great Industrial Exposition. San Francisco: H. S. Crocker & Company, 1894.

"Our State Building." *San Francisco Chronicle*, April 21, 1893.

E. B. Payne, "The City of Education." *Overland Monthly*, October 1899, pp. 353–361; November 1899, pp. 449–455.

E. Peixotto, "Architecture in San Francisco." *Overland Monthly*, May 1893, pp. 449–463.

J. D. Phelan, "Is the Midwinter Fair a Benefit?" *Overland Monthly*, April 1894, pp. 390–392.

B. Porter, "Art and Architecture." In Zoeth Skinner Eldredge, ed., *History of California*. New York: Century History Company, 1915, V: 461–484. Reprinted as "The Beginnings of Art in California." In *Art in California*. San Francisco: R. L. Bernier, 1916.

S. Power, "Pacific Home-Making." *Overland Monthly*, May 1883, pp. 459–462.

E. Roberts, "Some Architectural Effects." *Overland Monthly*, April 1894, pp. 341–351 (Midwinter Fair).

M. Robinson, "The Hillside Problem." *House Beautiful*, June 1899, pp. 30–33.

E. S. Ryder, "Old Landmarks of San Francisco." *San Francisco Chronicle*, September 18, 1898.

413

"San Francisco." *American Architect*, occasional column in nine issues between January 2, 1892 and November 4, 1893.

San Francisco Architectural Club, *Catalogue of the Second Annual Exhibition, 1902–1903*. San Francisco: C. A. Murdock & Co. [1903].

——————————— , *Catalogue of the Third Annual Exhibition, 1903–1904*. San Francisco: C. A. Murdock & Co. [1904].

"San Francisco Architecture." *Wave*, June 6, 1896, pp. 2–3.

San Francisco Art Association, *Catalogue, Spring Exhibition, 1894*. [San Francisco: 1894].

"A San Francisco Renaissance." *San Francisco Call*, August 9, 1896.

"San Francisco the Home of Mission Type of Furniture." *Architect and Engineer*, August 1906, p. 68.

"San Francisco's Wooden Houses." *California Architect*, November 1887, p. 148.

J. M. Scanland, "Curious Houses of San Francisco." *Overland Monthly*, June 1904, pp. 470–475.

M. Schuyler, "State Buildings at the World's Fair." *Architectural Record*, July–September 1893, pp. 55–71.

M. U. Seares, "Some Types of Shingle Houses." *House Beautiful*, February 1911, pp. 89–90.

A. P. Simpson, "Ideal Home-Making on a Berkeley Hillside." *San Francisco Chronicle*, July 14, 1904, Sunday Supplement.

A. W. Smith, "The Shingled House in California." *Architect and Engineer*, May 1905, pp. 17–20.

R. M. Steele, "How San Francisco Grows." *Sunset Magazine*, December 1904, pp. 103–117.

——————————— , "Making San Francisco Beautiful." *Sunset Magazine*, June 1905, pp. 117–127.

N. Tharp, "The Advantages of Masonry over Wood in Architecture." *San Francisco News Letter*, Christmas 1901, pp. 43, 46–47.

——————————— , "Architecture in San Francisco, Past and Present." *Wave*, March 10, 1900, p. 8.

——————————— , "What Bad There Is and What Good There Might Be in Inexpensive Architecture." *Overland Monthly*, December 1900, pp. 532–538.

The Trustees of the Phoebe Apperson Hearst Architectural Plan for the University of California, *The International Competition for the Phoebe Hearst Architectural Plan for the University of California*. San Francisco: H. S. Crocker Co. [ca. 1899].

"Typical Architecture." *San Francisco Chronicle*, January 13, 1892.

"The University Competition." *Wave*, February 13, 1897, p. 3.

C. P. Weeks, "Brickwork of the Pacific Slope." *Brickbuilder*, September 1904, pp. 178–180; October 1904, pp. 205–207; November 1904, pp. 235–236.

"What the Club Advocates." *Yearbook, the Hillside Club, 1911–1912*, pp. 6–7.

H. Wright, "California and Its Homes." *Architect and Engineer*, May 1905, pp. 20–26.

Recent Writings on Architecture and Planning in the Bay Area Around the Turn of the Century

T. J. Andersen, E. M. Moore, and R. W. Winter, eds., *California Design 1910*. Pasadena, California: California Design Publications, 1974. Reprint ed. Santa Barbara and Salt Lake City: Peregrine Smith, Inc., 1980.

J. A. Baird, *Time's Wondrous Changes: San Francisco Architecture, 1776–1915*. San Francisco: California Historical Society, 1962.

E. A. P. Evans, "Burlingame Station and the Architects Howard and Mathisen." In Northern Pacific Coast Chapter, Society of Architectural Historians, *Festschrift: A Collection of Essays on Architectural History.* Salem, Oregon: Your Town Press, 1978.

L. M. Freudenheim and E. S. Sussman, *Building with Nature: Roots of the San Francisco Bay Region Tradition.* Santa Barbara and Salt Lake City: Peregrine Smith, Inc., 1974.

D. Gebhard, "Architectural Imagery, the Mission and California." *The Harvard Architecture Review,* Spring 1980, pp. 137–145.

——————————— , "The Spanish Colonial Revival in Southern California (1895–1930)." *Journal of the Society of Architectural Historians,* May 1967, pp. 131–147.

——————————— and H. Von Breton, *1868–1968: Architecture in California.* Santa Barbara: The Art Galleries, University of California, Santa Barbara, 1968.

——————————— , H. Von Breton, and R. W. Winter, *Samuel and Joseph Cather Newsom: Victorian Architectural Imagery in California 1878–1908.* Santa Barbara: University of California at Santa Barbara Art Museum, 1979.

D. Gebhard et al., *A Guide to Architecture in San Francisco & Northern California.* Santa Barbara and Salt Lake City: Peregrine Smith, Inc., 1973.

S. W. Jacobs, "California Contemporaries of Frank Lloyd Wright, 1885–1915." In *Problems of the 19th and 20th Centuries, Studies in Western Art, Acts of the Twentieth International Congress of the History of Art* IV: 34–63. Princeton: Princeton University Press, 1963.

J. Kahn, *Imperial San Francisco: Politics and Planning in an American City, 1897–1906.* Lincoln and London: University of Nebraska Press, 1979.

H. Kirker, *California's Architectural Frontier, Style and Tradition in the Nineteenth Century.* San Marino, California: The Huntington Library and Art Gallery, 1960. Reprint ed. Santa Barbara and Salt Lake City: Peregrine Smith, Inc., 1973.

——————————— , "California Architecture and Its Relation to Contemporary Trends in Europe and America." *California Historical Quarterly,* Winter 1972, pp. 289–305. Reprinted in George H. Knoles, ed., *Essays and Assays: California History Reappraised.* San Francisco: California Historical Society, 1973.

R. W. Longstreth, "Julia Morgan; Some Introductory Notes." *Perspecta 15,* Yale Papers on Architecture, 1975, pp. 74–86. Reprinted as *Julia Morgan, Architect.* Berkeley: Berkeley Architectural Heritage Association, 1977.

R. Olmsted and T. H. Watkins, *Here Today: San Francisco's Architectural Heritage.* San Francisco: Chronicle Books, 1968.

C. H. Page & Associates, Inc., *Spendid Survivors: San Francisco's Downtown Architectural Heritage.* San Francisco: California Living Books, 1979.

——————————— , *Union Depot and Ferry House, San Francisco.* San Francisco: Charles Hall Page & Associates, Inc., July 1978.

L. W. Partridge, *John Galen Howard and the Berkeley Campus: Beaux-Arts Architecture in the "Athens of the West."* Berkeley: Berkeley Architectural Heritage Association, 1978.

M. Scott, *The San Francisco Bay Area: A Metropolis in Perspective.* Berkeley and Los Angeles: University of California Press, 1959.

D. Streatfield, "Shifting Sands, 'Verdant Umbrageousness,' and 'the People's Park': Public Open Space in San Francisco, 1886–1893." *Development Series,* University of Washington, 1975, pp. 15–36.

R. I. Stringham, "A Note on Antecedents and Trends in the Domestic Architecture of California." *California Historical Quarterly,* March 1946, pp. 54–56.

E. K. Thompson, "The Early Domestic Architecture of the San Francisco Bay Region." *Journal of the Society of Architectural Historians,* October 1951, pp. 15–21.

P. V. Turner, M. Vetrocq, and K. Weitze, *The Founders and the Architects: The Design of Stanford University.* Stanford: Stanford University Department of Art, 1976.

S. Woodbridge, ed., *Bay Area Houses.* New York: Oxford University Press, 1976.

Histories, Descriptions, and Other Writings on the Bay Area Around the Turn of the Century

C. S. Aiken (compiler), *California Today, San Francisco and Its Metropolis.* San Francisco: California Promotion Committee, 1903.

M. Albronda, *Douglas Tilden: Portrait of a Sculptor.* Silver Spring, Md.: T. J. Publishers, Inc., 1980.

P. W. Alexander and C. P. Hamm, *History of San Mateo County.* Burlingame, Cal.: Burlingame Publishing Company, 1916.

W. D. Armes, "California Artists—III—Douglas Tilden, Sculptor." *Overland Monthly,* February 1898, pp. 142–153.

Art in California. San Francisco: R. L. Bernier, 1916.

G. Atherton, *Adventures of a Novelist.* New York: Horace Liveright, Inc., 1932.

——————————— , *My San Francisco, A Wayward Biography.* New York and Indianapolis: Bobbs-Merrill Company, 1946.

B. P. Avery, *Californian Pictures in Prose and Verse.* New York: Hurd and Houghton, 1878.

H. H. Bancroft, *Chronicles of the Builders of the Commonwealth.* 7 vols. San Francisco: History Publishing Company, 1891–1892.

——————————— , *Some Cities and San Francisco.* New York: The Bancroft Company, 1907.

G. Barth, *Instant Cities: Urbanization and the Rise of San Francisco and Denver.* New York: Oxford University Press, 1973.

The Bay of San Francisco . . . A History. 2 vols. Chicago: Lewis Company, 1892.

"A Beautiful San Francisco Suburb." *San Francisco Chronicle,* June 4, 1899 (Burlingame Park).

[Belvedere Land Company], *Souvenir of Belvedere.* [San Francisco]: H. S. Crocker & Company, ca. 1893.

L. Beebe and C. Clegg, *San Francisco's Golden Era, A Picture History of San Francisco Before the Fire.* Berkeley: Howell-North, 1960.

H. Bingham, *In Tamal Land.* San Francisco: Calkins Publishing House, 1906.

W. H. Bishop, *Old Mexico and Her Lost Provinces.* New York: Harper & Brothers, 1883.

J. Bryce, *The American Commonwealth.* London and New York: Macmillan and Co., 1888.

G. Burgess, *Bayside Bohemia, Fin de Siècle San Francisco and Its Little Magazines.* San Francisco: Book Club of California, 1954.

——————————— , *The Heart Line, A Drama of California.* Indianapolis: Bobbs-Merrill Company, 1907.

——————————— , "On the Edge of the World." *Sunset Magazine,* August 1902, pp. 233–234.

L. F. Byington and O. Lewis, *The History of San Francisco.* 3 vols. San Francisco: S. J. Clarke Publishing Company, 1931.

G. E. Channing, "The Meeting of Extremes." *Out West,* September 1903, pp. 239–249. Continued as "What We can Learn From Rome," October 1903, pp. 357–368; November 1903, pp. 473–483; December 1903, pp. 605–616.

416

The City of San Francisco and a Glimpse of California. San Francisco: Enterprise Publishing Company, 1889.

R. H. Clary, *The Making of Golden Gate Park: The Early Years: 1865–1906*. San Francisco: California Living Books, 1980.

Brother [Fidelis] Cornelius, *Keith, Old Master of California*. 2 vols. New York: G. P. Putnam's Sons, 1942, 1956.

Davis' Commercial Encyclopedia of the Pacific Southwest. Berkeley: Ellis A. Davis, 1911.

"Douglas Tilden." *Overland Monthly*, November 1906, pp. 329–336.

Colonel A. S. Evans, *A la California: Sketches of Life in the Golden State*. San Francisco: A. L. Bancroft & Company, 1873.

J. A. Fronde, *Oceana, or England and Her Colonies*. London: Longmans, Green and Co., 1885.

P. Garnett, "California's Place in Art." *California's Magazine*, 1916, I: 39–42.

Gelett Burgess Behind the Scenes; Glimpses of Fin de Siècle San Francisco. Commentaries by Joseph M. Backus. San Francisco: Book Club of California, 1968.

K. M. Hall, "The Mark Hopkins Institute of Art." *Overland Monthly*, December 1897, pp. 539–548.

J. S. Hittell, *A History of the City of San Francisco and Incidentally of the State of California*. San Francisco: A. L. Bancroft & Company, 1878.

"The Influence of Italianate Surroundings." *Overland Monthly*, September 1904, pp. 137–140.

L. H. Irvine, *A History of the New California, Its Resources and People*. 2 vols. New York and Chicago: Lewis Publishing Company, 1902.

W. Irwin, *The City That Was*. New York: B. W. Huebsch, 1906.

G. W. James, *California Romantic and Beautiful*. Boston: Page Company, 1914.

C. Keeler, "California's Painters, Poets, Sculptors and Fiction Writers." *The World*, March 20, 1904.

——————————— , "The Land of the Olive and Pomegranate." *San Francisco Chronicle*, January 1, 1903.

——————————— , "The Passing of the Wild and Woolly West." *San Francisco Chronicle*, January 1, 1903.

——————————— , *San Francisco and Thereabout*. San Francisco: California Promotion Committee, 1902.

The Rev. D. O. Kelley, *History of the Diocese of California from 1849 to 1914*. San Francisco: Bureau of Information and Supply, 1915.

O. Lewis. *Bay Window Bohemia: An Account of the Brilliant Artistic World of Gaslit San Francisco*. Garden City, N. Y.: Doubleday & Company, Inc., 1956.

C. Lockwood, *Suddenly San Francisco: The Early Years of an Instant City*. San Francisco: California Living Books, 1978.

C. F. Lummis, "The Right Hand of the Continent." *Out West*, June 1902 to June 1903.

Marin County Journal, Souvenir of Marin County California. San Francisco: C. A. Murdock & Co., 1893.

Marin County Journal, New Era Edition. San Rafael: Marin County Journal, 1887, 1909.

E. Markham, *California the Wonderful*. New York: Hearst's International Library Company, 1914.

Master Hands in the Affairs of the Pacific Coast. San Francisco: Western Historical and Publishing Company, 1892.

417

B. L. McGlynn, "The Celebrated Burlingame Country Club." *La Peninsula,* Fall 1973 (whole issue).

B. Millard, *History of the San Francisco Bay Region.* 2 vols. Chicago, San Francisco, and New York: American Historical Society, Inc., 1924.

Modern San Francisco and the Men of To-Day. San Francisco: Western Press Association, 1906.

J. Muir, ed., *Picturesque California and the Region West of the Rocky Mountains from Alaska to Mexico.* 5 vols. New York and San Francisco: J. Dewing Co., 1888.

W. H. Murray, *The Builders of a Great City.* San Francisco: San Francisco Journal of Commerce Publishing Company, 1891.

New-Church Messenger, September 24, 1913 (issue devoted to Joseph Worcester).

C. Nordhoff, *California for Health, Pleasure and Residence.* New York: Harper & Brothers, 1882.

E. Peixotto, *Romantic California.* New York: Charles Scribner's Sons, 1910.

J. D. Phelan, *The New San Francisco.* San Francisco: 1896.

E. Pomeroy, *In Search of the Golden West: The Tourist in Western America.* New York: Alfred A. Knopf, 1957.

B. Porter, "Old and New San Francisco." *For California,* February 1904, pp. 5–6.

J. Ralph, "San Francisco Through Eastern Eyes." *Harper's Weekly,* June 2, 1892, pp. 130–135.

P. Robertson, "Peixotto and His Work." *Out West,* August 1903, pp. 133–145.

E. S. Ryder, "Mill Valley in Marin County." *San Francisco Call,* May 18, 1890, 9:3–4.

M. Schuyler, *Westward the Course of Empire.* New York: G. P. Putnam's Sons, 1906.

K. Starr, *Americans and the California Dream.* New York: Oxford University Press, 1973.

J. Steele, *Old California Days.* 2d ed. Chicago: Morrill Higgins & Co., 1892.

R. L. Stevenson, "A Modern Cosmopolis." *Magazine of Art,* 1883, pp. 272–276.

D. Tilden, "Art and What California Should Do About Her." *Overland Monthly,* May 1892, pp. 509–515.

F. Walker, *San Francisco's Literary Frontier.* New York: Alfred A. Knopf, 1939. Reprint ed. Seattle: University of Washington Press, 1969.

H. Whitaker, "Berkeley, the Beautiful." *Sunset Magazine,* December 1906, pp. 138–144.

Who's Who in California: A Biographical Dictionary, 1928–1929. San Francisco: Who's Who Publishing Company, 1929.

L. B. Wright, *Culture on the Moving Frontier.* Bloomington, Ind.: University of Indiana Press, 1955. Reprint ed. New York: Harper & Row, Publishers, 1961.

J. P. Young, *San Francisco, A History of the Pacific Coast Metropolis.* 2 vols. San Francisco and Chicago: S. J. Clarke Publishing Company, 1912.

LIST OF BUILDINGS AND PROJECTS

This catalogue includes all known work by Coxhead, Polk, Schweinfurth, and Brown through the turn of the century. Maybeck is not included since a relatively complete list of his commissions can be found in Kenneth Cardwell's monograph on the architect. Brown's work is cited because both Schweinfurth and Polk occupied key design positions in his office for most of its existence.

With few office records remaining for these architects, a complete list of their work will probably never be compiled. The entries cited below are based on ten years' research by myself and, in the case of Coxhead, also by John Beach. I have included commissions, competition entries, schematic proposals, and student projects where adequate graphic or written documentation for them can be found. Three entries under Coxhead are attributions; in each case the circumstantial evidence leaves no doubt that they are from his hand.

Among the work not cited: 1) designs in Coxhead's papers that are unidentified by client, location, and date; 2) entries in Polk's cash book from 1893 to 1896 when I was unable to determine the location and nature of work performed; 3) schemes, mostly interior remodelings, designed by Brown in the early part of his career, which are noted in his correspondence with Mrs. McCormick, but with insufficient reference to location and nature of the work; and 4) graphic designs for publications and clubs.

Wherever possible, I have included the current street address and condition of buildings. All locations are in California unless otherwise noted. The cost figures are approximate and are rounded to the nearest hundred dollars. Many of these figures are taken from contract notices published in local newspapers and journals. These figures represent a base construction cost; often the total price for a building was at least several hundred dollars more. For projects and, in some instances, executed work, the figures are published estimates.

The sources noted are mostly limited to contemporary publications (contract notices, notes, articles, and illustrations) and archival material. They have been selected for the information they provide and do not always constitute a comprehensive list. Contract notices in the *California Architect* are not included when those in newspapers reflect more accurately the date of signing and/or provide more information.

419

The dates under which the entries are grouped indicate the year in which the design was completed. In cases where construction is known to have continued into the subsequent year(s), a detailed breakdown is given. In instances where the precise date is undocumented, the year given is the most likely one based on available evidence.

Brown's last work was in 1895; Schweinfurth's in 1898. The termination date for Polk's work was set at 1901, the year he entered Daniel Burnham's office in Chicago. For purposes of consistency, the same end date is used for Coxhead, even though no particular year marks as much of a pronounced change in the orientation of his practice.

ERNEST COXHEAD

"Design for a Private Residence" 1879

Schematic design probably for a draftsmen's competition
(Source: Coxhead Papers)

"Design for a Chapel to a Public School"
(Source: Coxhead Papers)

The Building News Designing Club 1880
competition entry
(Source: Coxhead Papers)

"Design for a Country Residence" 1881

Schematic design probably for a draftsmen's competition
(Source: Coxhead Papers)

"Design for a Bank in a Country Town
including Manager's Residence" 1885

Probably student project for Royal
Academy
(Source: Coxhead Papers)

"Design for the Entrance Hall and Staircase
of a National Gallery" 1885

Probably student project for Royal
Academy
(Source: Coxhead Papers)

Bank and stores for Mr. Painter 1887

Monrovia
Extant?
Cost $7,000
(Source: *LADH*, Jan. 1, 1888)

Church of St. Augustine-by-the-Sea 1887

1227 4th Street, Santa Monica
Cost $3,500

Burned 1966
(Sources: *CABN*, Aug. 1887; *LADH*, Jan. 1, 1888)

Church of the Ascension 1887?

St. Louis Street, between Michigan
and Brooklyn, Los Angeles
Exact design date unknown
No longer standing
(Source: John Beach)

Church of the Ascension 1887

Laurel and Baldwin avenues, NE corner,
Sierra Madre
Designed 1887; built 1887–1888
Extant: altered
Cost $4,000
(Sources: *AABN*, Dec. 29, 1888; *LADH*,
Jan. 1, 1888;
church records)

Anthony Hernandez house 1887

646 North Hill Street, Los Angeles
No longer standing
Cost $4,500
(Source: *LADH*, Jan. 1, 1888)

Hutchinson house 1887

Monrovia
Extant?
Cost $2,500
(Source: *CABN*, Aug. 1887)

Powell house 1887

Boyle Heights, Los Angeles
No longer standing
Cost $2,000
(Source: *LADH*, Jan. 1, 1888)

Houses for Edward Sweetser 1887

The Palms, Los Angeles
No longer standing
Cost $15,300 for six houses of varying
    sizes
(Source: *LADH*, Jan. 1, 1888)

Lyman Thompson house   1887

Alvarado and 8th streets, Los Angeles
No longer standing
Cost $3,200
(Source: *LADH*, Jan. 1, 1888)

Young Mens' Christian Association   1887

207–211 South Broadway, Los Angeles
Designed 1887; built 1887–1888
Demolished 1920s
Cost $80,000
(Sources: *AABN*, Oct. 13, 1888; *CABN*,
    Sep. 1888;
    LADH, Jan. 1, 1888; Jan. 1, 1889)

Young Mens' Christian Association   1887

San Diego
Project
Cost $50,000
(Sources: *AABN*, Feb. 25, 1888; *LADH*,
    Jan. 1, 1888)

All Saints' Episcopal Church   1888

132 North Euclid Avenue, Pasadena
Designed 1888; built 1888–1889; tower
    not executed
Demolished early 1920s
Cost $14,000
(Sources: *AABN*, Mar. 30, 1889;
    LADH, Jan. 1, 1889; Jan. 1, 1890)

Bunker Hill Mission   1888

Bunker Hill, Los Angeles
No longer standing
Cost $2,000
(Source: *LADH*, Jan. 1, 1889)

Church of the Epiphany   1888

1808 Altura Street, Los Angeles
Extant; minor alterations
Cost $3,000
(Sources: *LADH*, Jan. 1, 1889; church
    records)

Church of the Messiah   1888

614 Bush Street, Santa Ana
Designed 1888; built 1888–1889
Extant
Cost $4,600

(Sources: *LADH*, Jan. 1, 1890; church
    records)

Commercial building for Griffin Green   1888

San Pedro Street, Los Angeles
No longer standing
Cost $9,000
(Source: *LADH*, Jan. 1, 1889)

First Presbyterian Church   1888

3rd and Arizona streets, Santa Monica
Designed 1888; built 1889
Demolished 1922
(Source: church records)

First English Lutheran Church   1888

8th and Flower streets, SE corner, Los
    Angeles
Designed 1888; built 1888–1889
Demolished 1930s
Cost $14,000
(Sources: *AABN*, May 19, 1888;
    LADH, Jan. 1, 1889; church records)

Green house   1888

10th and Olive streets, Los Angeles
Possibly house illustrated in *AABN* cited
    below
No longer standing
Cost $5,000
(Sources: *AABN*, July 7, 1888; *LADH*,
    Jan. 1, 1889)

House   1888

Santa Monica
Probably a project
(Source: *AABN*, July 7, 1888)

Schoolhouse   1888

4th and Del Mar streets, The Palms, Los
    Angeles
Demolished 1913
Cost $9,000
(Source: *LADH*, Jan. 1, 1889)

Alpheus Sturge house   1888

2345 Thomas Street, Los Angeles
Extant; house at this location appears to be
    the one Coxhead designed for Sturge,
    but full documentation lacking
(Sources: *LADH*, Jan. 1, 1889; Jan. 1,
    1890)

Christ Episcopal Church   1889

Santa Clara Avenue and Grand Street,

Alameda
Designed 1889; built 1890–1891
Burned 1959
Cost $12,500
(Sources: *PC*, Oct. 1889; *Ch*, Mar. 9, 1891)

First Congregational Church   1889

6th and Hill streets, SW corner, Los Angeles
No longer standing
Cost $14,000
(Sources: *LADH*, Jan. 1, 1890; church records)

James McKinley house   1889

508 West Adams Avenue, Los Angeles
No longer standing
Cost $4,000
(Source: *LADH*, Jan. 1, 1890)

Memorial Church of the Angels   1889

1100 Avenue 64, Los Angeles
Extensive redesign of scheme by Arthur Street
Extant; tower altered
Cost $30,000
(Sources: *AABN*, Jan. 11, 1890; May 24, 1890; *SABE*, Sept. 1889; *PC*, Oct. 1889; *LADH*, Jan. 1, 1890)

St. John's Episcopal Church   1889

El Dorado and Miner streets, Stockton
Project; church built 1891–1892 by A. Page Brown
Cost $25,000
(Sources: *PC*, June 1889; July 1889; Aug. 15, 1891; Coxhead Papers)

St. John's Episcopal Church, Guild Hall 1889

El Dorado and Miner streets, Stockton
Designed 1889; built 1889–1890
Extant; altered
Cost $10,000
(Sources: *PC*, June 1889; Oct. 1889; July 1890)

Santa Paula Academy   1889

Santa Paula Avenue, between 5th and 6th streets, Santa Paula
Demolished after 1957
Cost $9,500
(Sources: *AABN*, Nov. 9, 1889; *LADH*, Jan. 1, 1890)

Schoolhouse   1889

Boyle Heights, Los Angeles
No longer standing
Cost $9,000
(Source: *LADH*, Jan. 1, 1890)

Chapel of St. John the Evangelist   1890*

Thomas and Josselyn Canyon roads, Monterey
Designed 1890; built 1891 on grounds of Del Monte Hotel; moved to present location in 1950s
Extant; altered
(Sources: *PC*, Mar. 1890; Coxhead Papers)

Chapel of St. Mary the Virgin   1890

Filbert Street, between Filmore and Steiner, San Francisco
Project
(Source: *PC*, Jan. 1, 1890)

Chapel of the Holy Innocents   1890

455 Fairoaks Street, San Francisco
Extant; altered
Cost $4,400
(Sources: *AN*, Nov. 1890; *Ch*, July 4, 1890; Oct. 17, 1890)

Church of St. John the Evangelist   1890

15th and Julian streets, San Francisco
Original scheme designed 1889; redesigned 1890; built 1890–1891
Destroyed 1906
Cost $45,000
(Sources: *CABN*, Jan. 1890; *AN*, Dec. 1890; *Ch*, Apr. 27, 1890; Sep. 19, 1890; Sep. 12, 1891; *Ex*, Jan. 16, 1890; Coxhead Papers)

Church of the Messiah   1890?

Tucson, Arizona
Project; exact design date unknown
(Source: *AN*, Dec. 1890)

James Davis house   1890

117 San Mateo Drive, San Mateo
Demolished 1947
(Source: *AN*, Jan. 1891)

"Lynch Gate for a Countrie Church"   1890

Schematic design
(Source: *AN*, Nov. 1890)

St. John's Episcopal Church   1890

5th and C streets, NW corner, Petaluma
Extant

*Work designed from 1890 on was under the firm name of Coxhead & Coxhead.

(Sources: *PC*, May 1, 1891; Coxhead
Papers)

Church of the Advent   1891

11th Street, south of Market, San
Francisco
Designed 1891; built 1891–1893;
spires not executed
Burned 1906
Cost $30,000
(Sources: *PC*, Oct. 15, 1891; *Ch*, Mar. 27,
1891; June 28, 1891; Jan. 24, 1901; *Ex*,
Feb. 5, 1893; Coxhead Papers)

First English Lutheran Church   1891?

16th and J streets, Sacramento
Construction begun ca. 1891; church dedi-
cated 1897
Demolished ca. 1930s
(Source: Coxhead Papers)

David Greenleaf house   1891

1724 Santa Clara Avenue, Alameda
Extant; altered; now used as Boy Scout
center
(Source: attribution based on circumstantial
evidence)

James McGauley house   1891

2423 Green Street, San Francisco
Designed 1891; built 1891–1892
Extant
Cost $3,200
(Source: *CABN*, Nov. 1891)

St. James Episcopal Church   1891

Paso Robles
Project
(Source: *PC*, June 1, 1891)

St. Peter's Episcopal Church   1891

Jefferson and Elm streets, Red Bluff
Extant
(Source: attribution based on circumstantial
evidence)

Trinity Church   1891

1668 Bush Street, San Francisco
Project; competition entry; winning design
by A. Page Brown
(Source: Coxhead Papers)

California Building, World's Columbian
Exposition   1892

Jackson Park, Chicago, Illinois

Project; competition entry; winning design
by A. Page Brown
(Source: *California's Monthly World's Fair
Magazine*, Feb. 1892)

Andrew Carrigan house   1892?

96 Park Drive, San Anselmo
Exact design date unknown
Extant; altered in 1960s
(Source: Coxhead Papers)

E. Wiler Churchill house   1892?

486 Combs Street, Napa
Exact design date unknown; early-twen-
tieth-century additions possibly by
Coxhead
Extant; altered
(Sources: *OM*, Apr. 1902; attribution based
on circumstantial evidence)

Stable for John M. Cunningham   1892

Washington Street, east of Lyon, San
Francisco
No longer standing
(Sources: *CABN*, Sep. 1892; Coxhead
Papers)

David Loring house   1892

Channing Way and Dana Street, SW
corner, Berkeley
Designed 1892; built 1893; moved to SW
corner of Dana and Durant streets for
use as parish house of First Congrega-
tional Church ca. 1923
Demolished ca. 1955
Cost $6,800
(Sources: *CABN*, Jan. 1893; Coxhead
Papers)

Luning Building   1892

Market, Drumm, and California streets,
San Francisco
Designed 1892; built 1892–1893
Burned 1906
Cost $62,000
(Sources: *AABN*, June 9, 1894; *Ex*, May 3,
1892; Coxhead Papers)

Oakland Gas Heat and Lighting Company
Building   1892

13th and Clay streets, Oakland
Two stories added before 1911
Demolished ca. 1950s
(Sources: *AABN*, Feb. 10, 1894; *CABN*,
Sep. 1892)

Speculative building for George Whittell 1892

Park Street, San Francisco
Extant?
Cost $6,400
(Source: *CABN*, Jan. 1893)

George Whittell house   1892

1143 California Street, San Francisco
Designed 1892; built 1892–1895; interiors
   and stables by Townsend & Wyneken
Burned 1906
Cost over $30,000
(Sources: *CABN*, Apr. 1894; *Ch*, May 14,
   1894; May 28, 1894; Nov. 8, 1895; *Ex*,
   Jun. 3, 1894; *Wave*, July 9, 1892; Nov.
   10, 1894; May 4, 1895; Coxhead
   Papers)

Beta Theta Pi fraternity house   1893

2607 Hearst Avenue, Berkeley
Designed 1893; built 1893–1894; addition
   ca. 1900 probably by Coxhead
Extant; altered by Bakewell & Brown early
   1920s; currently owned by University of
   California and used as offices
Cost $12,000
(Sources: *Ch*, Aug. 28, 1893; *Wave*, May
   5, 1894; Coxhead Papers)

Commercial building for Luning Estate 1893

Turk and Larkin Streets, NW corner, San
   Francisco
No longer standing
(Source: *CABN*, May 1893)

Ernest and Almeric Coxhead house   1893

2421 Green Street, San Francisco
Extant; minor alterations probably by
   Coxhead
Cost $5,500
(Sources: *Ch*, May 17, 1893; Coxhead
   Papers)

Ernest and Almeric Coxhead house   1893?

37 East Santa Inez Avenue, San Mateo
Exact design date unknown; minor altera-
   tions probably by Coxhead
Extant
(Source: Coxhead Papers)

William Loy house   1893

2431 Ellsworth Street, Berkeley
Demolished 1960s
Cost $3,600
(Source: *CABN*, Mar. 1893)

Charles Murdock house   1893

2710 Scott Street, San Francisco
Extant; minor alterations
Cost $4,200
(Source: *Ch*, Feb. 22, 1893)

Prayer Book Cross   1893

Golden Gate Park, San Francisco
Extant
(Source: *Call*, Jan. 2, 1894)

St. Mark's Episcopal Church   1893

Bancroft Way and Ellsworth Street,
   SE corner, Berkeley
Project; at least two schemes prepared;
   executed design by William Curlett
Cost $20,000
(Sources: *Call*, Jan. 21, 1894; Coxhead
   Papers)

George Whittell house   1893

1272 Caroline Street, Alameda
Extant; altered and service wing
   demolished
Cost $11,000
(Sources: *CABN*, Mar. 1893; Oct. 1893;
   Coxhead Papers)

Edwin Tobias Earl house   1894?

2425 Wilshire Boulevard, Los Angeles
Exact design date unknown; house burned
   ca. 1894–1895 shortly before completion; house rebuilt according to new
   design by Coxhead
(Source: Coxhead Papers)

Ida and Luella Gillespie house   1894

2940 Jackson Street, San Francisco
Extant
Cost $3,900
(Source: *Ch*, Oct. 22, 1894)

James Brown-Reginald Knight Smith house
                                        1895

2600 Jackson Street, San Francisco
Designed 1894–1895; built 1895
Extant; later addition to rear
Cost $20,000
(Sources: *Ch*, May 31, 1895; Dec. 20,
   1895; *SFNL*, Sep. 30, 1899; Coxhead
   Papers)

Cliff House   1895

1090 Point Lobos Avenue, San Francisco
Schematic design prepared at request of *SF*

Examiner
(Source: *Ex*, Jan. 6, 1895)

Edwin Tobias Earl house   1895?

2425 Wilshire Boulevard, Los Angeles
Exact date of design unknown; built ca.
   1895–1898 on foundations of earlier
   house
Demolished 1957
(Sources: *Craftsman*, Dec. 1910; *LA*
   Times, Aug. 18, 1957; Coxhead Papers)

Bishop William Kip monument, Cypress
   Lawn Cemetery   1895

El Camino Real, Colma
Extant
(Source: *PC*, Nov. 15, 1895)

Alonzo McFarland house   1895

400 Clayton Street, San Francisco
Extant; parapet and dormers altered
Cost $10,000
(Sources: *Ch*, Nov. 13, 1895; Coxhead
   Papers)

Bridge   1896

Kennedy Drive, Golden Gate Park, San
   Francisco
Extant
(Sources: *Ch*, Sep. 4, 1896; *Ex*, Dec. 12,
   1896)

Russell Osborn house   1896

3362 Clay Street, San Francisco
Basement addition by Coxhead 1907
Extant; minor alterations
(Sources: *Ch*, May 15, 1896; June 20,
   1896)

C. L. Perkins house   1896?

157 Elm Street, San Mateo
Exact design date unknown
Demolished ca. 1960s
(Source: Coxhead Papers)

St. Luke's Church   1896?

Van Ness Avenue and Clay Street, SE
   corner, San Francisco
Project; designed 1894–ca. 1896;
   church built 1898 by Albert Sutton
(Sources: *Ch*, Jan. 15, 1897; Feb. 12,
   1898; Coxhead Papers)

John Simpson house   1896

2520 Vallejo Street, San Francisco

No longer standing
Cost $9,000
(Source: *Ch*, July 18, 1896)

James Ferguson house   1897

Baker Street, north of Vallejo, San
   Francisco
Extant
Cost $3,000
(Source: *Ch*, Oct. 23, 1897)

Robert Foute house   1897

1915 Gough Street
No longer standing
Cost $3,400
(Source: *Ch*, Jul. 9, 1897)

Margaret Jones house, alterations   1897

1820 Washington Street, San Francisco
Extensive remodeling of existing residence
No longer standing
(Sources: *Call*, June 22, 1897; Coxhead
   Papers)

Bertha and Mrs. Theodore Lilienthal houses
    1897

California and Gough streets, NW corner,
   San Francisco
Project; houses built 1898 by Edgar
   Mathews
(Source: *Ch*, Mar. 26, 1897)

Apartment house? for Alonzo McFarland
    1897

O'Farrell Street, north side, west of Jones,
   San Francisco
Designed 1897; built 1898
No longer standing; presumably burned
   1906
Cost $6,500
(Source: *CABN*, Jan. 1898)

Julian Sonntag house   1897

2700 Scott Street, San Francisco
Extant; minor alterations
Cost $5,700
(Source: *Ch*, Apr. 24, 1897)

John Tennant Memorial Home for Aged
   People   1897

Pacific Grove
No longer standing
Cost: $10,000
(Sources: *Ch*, June 18, 1898; *PC*, Feb. 15,
   1898)

425

Phoebe A. Hearst Architectural Plan
for the University of California   1898

Berkeley
Project; competition entry
(Sources: *A&E*, Sep. 1912; Coxhead
Papers)

Houses for Florence Ward   1898

Broadway and Laguna streets, SW corner,
San Francisco
Demolished; house on adjacent Laguna
Street property possibly by Coxhead
(Source: *CABN*, July 1898)

Warehouse for Hartland and Herbert Law
1898

Bonita Street, San Francisco
No longer standing
(Source: *CABN*, Mar. 1898)

"A Village Church, Cost Fifty Thousand
Dollars"   1899

Schematic design
(Source: *BB*, July 1899)

Apartment house? for Rudolph Spreckels 1899

2171 Pacific Avenue, San Francisco
No longer standing
Cost $11,000
(Source: *CABN*, July 1899)

Irving Scott house   1899?

Pacific Avenue, north side, west of Divisi-
dero, San Francisco
Project; exact design date unknown;
scheme included several speculative
houses on Pacific Avenue
(Sources: Chicago Architectural Club,
Catalogue, 1900; *Ch*, June 9, 1900;
Coxhead Papers)

Sarah Spooner house   1899

2800 Pacific Avenue, San Francisco
Extant; exterior altered, interior destroyed
Cost $13,000
(Sources: *BB*, Mar. 1902; *Ch*, Mar. 25,
1899; Coxhead Papers)

Apartment house for Irving
Scott   1900

840 Hayes Street, San Francisco
Appears to be extant and heavily
remodeled
Cost $16,000
(Source: *Ch*, Nov. 14, 1900)

Charles Dougherty house   1900

Foothill Road, near Pleasanton
Project
(Source: Coxhead Papers)

Julian Waybur house   1900?

3232 Pacific Avenue, San Francisco
Exact design date unknown
Extant; minor alterations
(Source: Catherine Porter Short)

George Bixby house   1901?

11 La Linda Drive, off Bixby Boulevard,
Long Beach
Exact design date unknown
Extant; minor alterations
(Sources: *PCA*, Dec. 1918; Coxhead
Papers)

Chapel, Church Divinity School of the
Pacific   1901

East Poplar Street and North San Mateo
Drive, NW corner, San Mateo
Scheme included dining hall and dormi-
tory; both buildings probably not
executed. Dean's residence and other
house on grounds (now at 119, 123 East
Poplar) erected before 1898 and probably by Coxhead
Chapel destroyed 1906
(Sources: *PC*, June 15, 1898; Nov. 15,
1901; *Ch*, June 29, 1901)

George Stratton house   1901

2434 Hillside Avenue, Berkeley
No longer standing
Cost $3,000
(Source: *Berkeley Gazette*, Oct. 8, 1901)

WILLIS POLK

Schoolhouse   1882

Hope, Arkansas
Winning competition entry
Extant?
(Source: *Sunset*, Apr. 1922)

David McMechan house   1885*

1307 Penn Street, Kansas City, Missouri
No longer standing
Cost $5,000
(Sources: *IA*, Oct. 1885; May 1886)

John Stone house   1885*

Linwood and Prospect streets, Kansas

*W. W. Polk & Son

City, Missouri
No longer standing
(Source: *IA*, Sep. 1885)

J. H. Banerlin house   1886*

Kansas City, Missouri
Extant?
(Source: *IA*, May 1886)

Manuel Diaz house   1886*

1414 Forest Avenue, Kansas City, Missouri
No longer standing
(Source: *IA*, May 1886)

Speculative row houses for Benjamin Estill
1886*

Kansas City, Missouri
Two groups of six and eight units
Probably no longer standing
(Source: *IA*, Mar. 1886)

Speculative row houses for R. G. Estill 1886*

Kansas City, Missouri
Five units
Probably no longer standing
(Source: *IA*, Mar. 1886)

James Hitshaw house   1886*

2110 Annie Street, Kansas City, Missouri
No longer standing
(Source: *IA*, Mar. 1886)

Double house for B. Leibstader   1886*

Kansas City, Missouri
Probably no longer standing
(Source: *IA*, Mar. 1886)

Lockwood House Hotel   1886*

Merriam, Kansas
No longer standing
(Source: *AABN*, Mar. 12, 1887)

Double house for J. C. Nettleton   1886*

Kansas City, Missouri
Probably no longer standing
(Source: *IA*, Mar. 1886)

Peter Otto house   1886*

Kansas City, Missouri
Probably no longer standing
(Source: *IA*, May 1886)

H. R. Smith house   1886?*

Kansas City, Missouri

Exact design date unknown
No longer standing
(Source: *AABN*, Feb. 4, 1888)

Store for Dr. Bell   1886*

Kansas City, Missouri
Extant?
(Source: *IA*, May 1886)

Store for Henry Lebrecht   1886*

1009 East 12th Street, Kansas City,
Missouri
Extant; vacant
(Source: *IA*, Mar. 1886)

House   1887?

Probably in Kansas City
Exact design date unknown
(Source: Louis Gibson, *Beautiful Houses*)

"An Imaginary Mission Church of the Southern California Type"   1887

Schematic design
(Source: *A&B*, Apr. 12, 1890)

Municipal Buildings, Washington, D.C. 1887

Unsolicited? project
(Source: *AABN*, Feb. 23, 1889)

"Sketch for a City Home"   1887

Kansas City Architectural Sketch Club,
prize-winning design
(Source: *AABN*, Dec. 17, 1887)

"Sketch for a Clock Tower"   1887

Kansas City Architectural Sketch Club,
prize-winning design
(Source: *AABN*, July 2, 1887)

Memorial Library   1888

Lexington, Kentucky
Project
(Source: *AABN*, Mar. 9, 1889)

First Presbyterian Church   1888

138 North Main Street, Liberty, Missouri
Designed 1888; built 1888–1889,
W. W. Polk supervising architect
Extant; recent additions
Cost $6,800
(Sources: *AABN*, Aug. 24, 1889; church
records)

Kittie Beardsley house   1889

Plymouth, Massachusetts
Probably a project
(Source: *AABN*, July 27, 1889)

Fritz Maurice Gamble house   1889

San Francisco
Project
(Source: *A&B*, Feb. 15, 1890)

Frederick Rosenthal house   1889?

Alameda
Probably a project; exact design date
   unknown
(Source: *A&B*, Apr. 12, 1890)

"Un Chateau Imaginaire"   1890†

Schematic design
(Source: *AN*, Nov. 1890)

Craig Hazel, John Dickinson house   1890†

26 Alexander Street, Sausalito
Extant; altered
(Sources: *Sausalito News*, Mar. 21; 1890;
   Chesley Bonestell)

House   1890†

San Francisco
Project
(Source: *AN*, Nov. 1890)

House   1890†

San Francisco
Project
(Source: *AN*, Dec. 1890)

The Nook, Francis Avery house   1890†

77 Buckley Drive, Sausalito
Demolished; gates extant
Cost $10,000
(Source: *AN*, Jan. 1891)

William Boericke house, alterations   1891†

1812 Washington Street, San Francisco
Extensive remodeling of existing residence
Demolished
(Sources: *CABN*, May 1894; *Ch*, Mar. 13,
   1891; Polk Papers)

Mrs. Charles Webb Howard house,
   alterations   1891?†

1206 Alice Street, Oakland
Exact design date unknown; work probably
   limited to interiors
No longer standing
(Sources: *Ex*, Sep. 13, 1891; Polk Papers)

George Howison house   1891?†

2731 Bancroft Way, Berkeley
Exact design date unknown; work probably
   limited to interiors; executed?
No longer standing
(Source: Polk Papers)

Madroño, Mrs. William Bourn (Sr.) house
          1891?†

St. Helena
Project; exact design date unknown
(Source: Polk Papers)

Horatio Livermore house, alterations   1891?†

1045 Vallejo Street, San Francisco
Interior alterations to mid-nineteenth-
   century house owned by Livermore for
   Polk's own use; exact design date
   unknown; extensive alterations and additions ca. 1897 for Livermore's use,
   probably with Polk advising on design
Extant; altered ca. 1950s by Wurster,
   Bernardi & Emmons
(Sources: *Wave;* Dec. 19, 1891; *OM*, May
   1893; George Livermore)

Felicien Paget house   1891†

2727 Dwight Way, Berkeley
Extant; altered by 1902
(Source: *CABN*, Aug. 1891)

Centenary Methodist Episcopal Church 1891

Bush Street, west of Gough, San Francisco
Designed 1891; built 1892; earlier plans by
   W. W. Polk
No longer standing
Cost $20,000
(Sources: *Ch*, Dec. 25, 1891; Feb. 27,
   1892; Feb. 27, 1893; *Pacific Methodist
   Advocate*, Dec. 24, 1891)

Examiner Bear Pit   1891

Golden Gate Park, San Francisco
Project
(Source: *AABN*, Apr. 25, 1896)

Examiner Building   1891

Market Street, San Francisco
Project
(Source: *CABN*, May 1893)

Martin Kellogg house, alterations   1891

Bushnell Place, Berkeley
No longer standing
(Sources: *Wave*, Dec. 19, 1891; ms. by

†Polk & Gamble

Annette Chamberlin, BL)

1900 World's Fair   1891

San Francisco
Schematic design prepared at request of *SF Examiner*
(Source: *Ex*, Dec. 25, 1891)

Owl's Nest Fishing and Hunting Company clubhouse   1891

San Carlos
Project
(Sources: *Ex*, May 15, 1892; *SFNL*, Aug. 15, 1891; *Wave*, Nov. 28, 1891; Dec. 5, 1891; Mar. 5, 1892)

Stage set for "Bluff King Hal"   1891

Grand Opera House, San Francisco
Destroyed
(Sources: *Wave*, Sep. 12, 1891; Nov. 7, 1891)

Joseph Batten house   1892

116 Cherry Street; San Francisco
Extant; minor alterations
Cost $4,500
(Source: *CABN*, July 1892)

Church of Our Saviour   1892

Old Mill and Lovell roads, Mill Valley
Demolished 1956
(Sources: *PC*, Apr. 17, 1894; church records)

Charles Eells house   1892?

111 Upper Road, Ross
Exact design date unknown
Extant; extensively altered
(Source: George Livermore)

G. H. Hellman house   1892

1620 Clinton Avenue, Alameda
Extant; altered
Cost $2,200
(Source: *CABN*, July 1892)

"Study for a Mausoleum"   1892

Schematic design?
(Source: *AABN*, Apr. 25, 1896)

Alfred Wheeler house   1892?

Clear Lake
Exact design date unknown
No longer standing
(Source: *Wave*, Aug. 13, 1892)

Annie Bernard house   1892‡

Hyde Park, Kansas City, Missouri
No longer standing
(Source: *CABN*, June 1892)

Speculative houses for Alfred Moore   1892‡

San Francisco
Project
(Source: *AABN*, Dec. 17, 1892)

Mrs. Thayer house   1892‡

Vacaville
Project?
(Source: *CABN*, Jan. 1893)

Mrs. Virgil Williams-W. W. Polk house 1892‡

1013–1019 Vallejo Street, San Francisco
Built 1892; addition to rear of Williams unit ca. 1897, probably by Polk; Polk unit divided into apartments ca. 1900
Extant; altered
(Sources: Mrs. Max Stern; George Livermore)

Administration Building, California Midwinter International Exposition   1893‡

Golden Gate Park, San Francisco
Competition entry; possibly two designs submitted; winning design by A. Page Brown
(Sources: *Ch*, Aug. 6, 1893; *Call*, Aug. 6, 1893)

Katherine Atkinson house, alterations   1893‡

1032 Broadway, San Francisco
Extensive alterations, mostly on interior, to 1853 house
Extant; altered
(Source: Polk Papers)

Storehouse for Nathaniel Brittan   1893‡

San Carlos
Executed?
(Source: *CABN*, June 1893)

Commercial building   1893?‡

Market Street, San Francisco
Project; exact design date unknown
(Source: *AABN*, July 6, 1895)

Commercial building   1893‡

Sutter Street, San Francisco
Executed?
(Source: *CABN*, Feb. 1894)

‡Polk & Polk

Eugene Davis house   1893‡

Belvedere
No longer standing
(Sources: *Ch*, Oct. 2, 1893; Polk Papers)

Winfield Davis house   1893‡

Lagunitas Road, Ross
No longer standing
(Sources: *Souvenir of Marin County;* Polk
  Papers)

Guatemala Building, California Midwinter
International Exposition   1893‡

Golden Gate Park, San Francisco
Project
(Source: Brown Scrapbooks CHS)

William Joliffe house   1893‡

2015 Pacific Avenue, San Francisco
Designed 1893; built 1894
Extant
Cost $5,200
(Sources: *Ch*, Jan. 5, 1894; Polk Papers)

Gustav Marcus house   1893‡

465 Throckmorton Avenue, Mill Valley
Extant
(Source: Polk Papers)

Alfred Moore house   1893‡

416 Golden Gate Avenue, Belvedere
Extant; extensively altered
(Source: *Wave*, May 13, 1893)

Valentine Rey house   1893‡

428 Golden Gate Avenue, Belvedere
Extant; minor alterations
(Sources: *CABN*, Apr. 1894; *Ch*, Oct. 2,
  1893)

Villa Veneta, John Kilgarif house   1893‡

16 San Carlos Avenue, Sausalito
Extant; alterations ca. 1904 probably by
  Polk; later alterations
(Sources: *Ch*, Oct. 2, 1893; Polk Papers)

Frank Washington house   1893‡

276 Cascade Road, Mill Valley
Extant; altered
(Source: Polk Papers)

William Bourn house   1894‡

St. Helena
Project

(Sources: *Ch*, Sep. 10, 1894; Polk Papers)

Examiner Building   1894‡

Market Street, San Francisco
Project
(Sources: Polk Papers)

George W. Gibbs house   1894‡

2622 Jackson Street, San Francisco
Designed 1894; built 1894–1895
Extant; owned by Music and Arts Institute
  of San Francisco since 1949
Cost: $40,000
(Sources: *Ch*, June 26, 1894; July 16,
  1894; May 11, 1895; *Wave*, Oct. 19,
  1895; Nov. 23, 1895; *Ex*, Aug. 17,
  1894)

Adam Grant house   1894‡

1112 Bush Street, San Francisco
Burned 1906
(Sources: *SFNL*, May 26, 1894; Sketch
  Club of N.Y., *Catalogue*, 1895; Polk
  Papers)

E. J. McCutchen house, additions   1894‡

Lagunitas Road, Ross
Work included hall and living room
Extant; altered
(Source: *Wave*, June 30, 1894)

Press Club   1894‡

Sutter and Kearny streets, SW corner, San
  Francisco
Interiors located in Thurlow Block
Burned 1906
(Sources: *Call*, Dec. 31, 1894; *TT*, Oct. 2,
  1897)

William Boericke house   1895‡

near Garden Valley, El Dorado County
Executed?
Cost $10,000
(Source: *Ch*, Nov. 1, 1895)

William Bourn house   1895‡

2550 Webster Street, San Francisco
Designed 1895; built 1896
Extant
Cost $50,000
(Sources: *AABN*, Aug. 8, 1896; *CABN*,
  Jan. 1896; *Ch*, Mar. 19, 1896; *Wave*,
  Mar. 14, 1896; Polk Papers)

Cliff House   1895‡

‡Polk & Polk

1090 Point Lobos Avenue, San Francisco
Schematic design prepared at request of *SF
Examiner*
(Source: *Ex*, Jan. 6, 1895)

William Dimond house   1895‡

2128 Broadway, San Francisco
Designed 1895; built 1895–1896
Demolished ca. 1971
Cost $20,000
(Sources: *Ch*, Aug. 8, 1895; *Wave*, Mar.
14, 1896)

Isaac Flagg house, interiors   1895‡

Berkeley?
Project; interiors for a house by Frederick
Roehrig; executed design by Maybeck
1900
(Source: Polk Papers)

Admission Day Fountain   1896

Market, Post, and Montgomery streets,
San Francisco
Designed 1896 in collaboration with Doug-
las Tilden; built 1896–1897 at Market,
Turk, and Mason streets; moved to
Golden Gate Park 1948; relocated on
present site 1977
Extant
(Sources: *Ch*, Sep. 12, 1897; *Wave*, Sep.
12, 1896; Oct. 24, 1896; *SF Municipal
Reports*, 1896–1897; Polk Papers;
Tilden Papers)

Stevenson Fountain   1896

Portsmouth Square, San Francisco
Designed 1895–1896 in collaboration with
Bruce Porter and George Piper; built
1897
Extant; setting destroyed and fountain relocated in square.
Cost $2,000
(Sources: *AABN*, Dec. 4, 1897; *Ch*, Apr.
16, 1896; *Ex*, Oct. 18, 1897; *OM*, Nov.
1897; *SF Municipal Reports*, 1896–
1897)

Arch, peristyle, and commercial buildings
1897

Market Street at The Embarcadero, San
Francisco
Unsolicited project
(Sources: *AABN*, Aug. 10, 1901; *A&E*,
July 1910; *Ch*, Mar. 25, 1895; *SFNL*,
Christmas 1900; *Wave*, Mar. 10, 1900;
Polk Papers)

Empire Cottage, William Bourn house   1897

East Empire Street, Grass Valley
Designed 1897, work included house and
offices of the Original Empire Mine Co.;
built 1897–1898; gardens, casino and
other buildings designed by Polk in
1900s
Extant; now owned by the State of
California
(Sources: *Ch*, Apr. 18, 1897; May 2, 1897;
Polk Papers)

Residential development   1897?

Burlingame
Schematic project; exact design date
unknown
(Source: *Wave*, Mar. 20, 1897)

Belmont School   1898

Ralston Avenue and Alameda de las
Pulgas, Belmont
Project
(Source: *AABN*, Dec. 10, 1898)

Otto Greenwald house (alterations)   1898

1812 Van Ness Avenue, San Francisco
Alterations to 1895 design by Brown; in
construction at time of commission
No longer standing, probably burned 1906
(Source: *Ch*, Mar. 27, 1898)

Madroño, Mrs. William Bourn (Sr.) house
1898

St. Helena
Project
(Source: Polk Papers)

Charles Wheeler house   1898

Broadway and Lyon streets, north side,
San Francisco
Project
(Source: *AABN*, May 27, 1898)

The Bend, Charles Wheeler house   1899

near McCloud, Siskiyou County
Extant; extensively altered by Julia Morgan
in 1930s
(Sources: *AABN*, July 15, 1899; *Ch*, Mar.
16, 1899)

Stables and garden for Francis Carolan   1899

Hillsborough
No longer standing
(Source: *Ch*, Mar. 25, 1900)

431

Central Fire Station   1899

Arlington Street and Commercial Row,
  Reno, Nevada
Designed 1899; built 1900
Extant; altered, vacant
Cost $6,000
(Sources: *Ch*, Oct. 21, 1899; *Reno
  Evening Gazette*, Mar. 30, 1901)

William Crocker house   1899

Hillsborough
Project
(Sources: *AABN*, Oct. 5, 1901; *Ch*, Apr.
  22, 1899)

Donohue (Mechanics) Monument   1899

Market and Battery streets, San Francisco
Original design 1898 by Douglas Tilden;
  redesigned in collaboration with Tilden
  1899; built 1900
Extant
(Sources: *Call*, Nov. 15, 1897; *Ch*, June
  17, 1899; *Ex*, Sep. 12, 1897; Jan. 21,
  1898; Tilden Papers)

Reno Wheelman's Club   1899

1st and Arlington streets, NW corner,
  Reno, Nevada
No longer standing
(Source: *Ch*, Oct. 21, 1899)

St. John's Episcopal Church   1899?

Clear Lake Avenue and Forbes street, SE
  corner, Lakeport
Exact design date unknown; dedicated
  1899
Extant
(Source: *PC*, Aug. 1, 1899)

Alexander Young Building   1900§

Bishop Street between King and Hotel,
  Honolulu, Hawaii
Designed 1900; built 1901–1903
Demolished 1981
(Sources: *Ch*, May 30, 1900; *Honolulu
  Advertiser*, Dec. 25, 1900; Polk Papers)

Mrs. Frederico Barreda house, alterations
                                  1900?§

2139–2141 Buchanan Street, San
  Francisco
Alterations to ca. 1870s house to accom-
  modate Polk and family; exact design
  date unknown
Extant

(Sources: Chesley Bonestell; F. Barreda
  Sherman)

Beaulieu, Charles Baldwin house   1900?§

21250 Stevens Creek Boulevard, Cupertino
Work included new house, staff quarters,
  and gardens on existing ranch; exact
  design date unknown
House extant, moved to new location on
  property and altered; staff quarters
  extant; gardens and other buildings
  demolished for development of De
  Anza College campus ca. 1967
(Sources: *H&G*, Dec. 1902; *Ch*, July 27,
  1901)

City Warehouse Company Building   1900§

Battery and Lombard streets, SW corner,
  San Francisco
Designed 1900; built 1901
Extant; altered
(Sources: *Ch*, Dec. 30, 1900; Jan. 4,
  1901)

Commercial building for Harry Bothin 1900§

Mission Street, south side, west of 1st, San
  Francisco
Burned 1906
(Source: *Call*, Apr. 9, 1900)

Commercial building for Mrs. Vrooman
                                  1900§

12th Street, between Washington and Clay,
  Oakland
No longer standing
Cost $19,000
(Source: *Ch*, Apr. 14, 1900)

Commercial building for Frank Woods 1900§

Geary Street, north side, west of Kearny,
  San Francisco
Burned 1906
Cost $65,000
(Sources: *Ch*, Jan. 21, 1900; July 14,
  1900)

De Fermery Building   1900§

Oakland
No longer standing
Cost $60,000
(Source: *Ch*, May 12, 1900)

Hayward Building   1900§

400 Montgomery Street, San Francisco
Designed 1900; built 1900–1901, Henry

§G. W. Percy and Willis Polk

Meyers supervising architect
Extant: minor alterations
Cost $400,000
(Sources: *AABN*, May 11, 1901; *A&E*,
    May 1911; *Ch*, Jan. 14, 1900)

House for William Keith   1900§

3204 Washington Street, San Francisco
Extant; now owned by Church of the New
    Jerusalem
(Sources: *Ch*, July 27, 1901; Polk Papers)

Lisser Hall, Mills College   1900§

Richards Road, Oakland
Designed 1900; built 1901
Extant; altered beyond recognition 1927
(Sources: *Ch*, Nov. 28, 1900; Dec. 15,
    1901; Mills College archives)

Mercantile Trust Company Building   1900§

464 California Street, San Francisco
Project; limited competition entry; winning
    design by Albert Pissis
(Sources: *AABN*, Aug. 3, 1901; *Ch*, Apr.
    7, 1901)

Mutual Savings Bank   1900§

700 Market Street, San Francisco
Project; competition entry; winning design
    by William Curlett
(Sources: *Ch*, Mar. 31, 1900; *Wave*, May
    12, 1900)

Lloyd Osbourne and Mrs. Robert Louis
Stevenson houses   1900§

1100 Lombard Street, 2319–2323 Hyde
    Street, San Francisco
Extant; extensively altered
(Sources: *Ch*, Apr. 21, 1901; Polk Papers)

Tamalpais Tavern, additions   1900§

Mt. Tamalpais, Marin County
Additions to 1896 building
Burned 1923
(Sources: *Ch*, Jan. 6, 1900; Feb. 18, 1900)

Theater   1900§

Hermosillo, Sonora Province, Mexico
Executed?
(Sources: *AABN*, Oct. 5, 1901; *BB*, Jan.
    1908)

Wilson Building   1900§

973–977 Market Street, San Francisco
Designed 1900; built 1901

Extant; minor alterations
Cost $100,000
(Sources: *Ch*, July 15, 1900; Dec. 30,
    1900)

Emile Bruguiere and Charles Rollo Peters
house   1901

Monterey
Probably a project
(Source: *Ch*, July 30, 1901)

Church of St. Francis and the Apostles   1901

San Francisco
Schematic design
(Source: Chicago Architectural Club, *Cata-
    logue*, 1901)

William Crocker house, alterations   1901

1150 California Street, San Francisco
Extensive interior alterations to 1888 house
    by William Curlett
Burned 1906
(Source: *Ch*, July 27, 1901)

Lyceum Theater   1901?

San Francisco
Project; exact design date unknown
(Source: *AABN*, Aug. 31, 1901)

Stables for Walter Martin   1901

San Mateo Avenue, San Mateo
No longer standing
(Source: *Ch*, July 27, 1901)

Frank McCullagh house, alterations   1901

600 Pennsylvania Avenue, Los Gatos
Extensive alterations and additions to
    farmhouse
Extant; altered
(Sources: *H&G*, Aug. 1902; *Ch*, July 30,
    1901)

C.O.G. Miller house   1901

Oakland
Executed?
(Source: Chicago Architectural Club, *Cata-
    logue*, 1901)

Polo field casino for Francis Carolan   1901

Burlingame
No longer standing
(Source: *Ch*, July 27, 1901)

A. PAGE BROWN

"Country Hotel Barn"   1882

    Sketch club competition project
    (Source: *AABN*, July 8, 1882)

The Academy   1884

    McCormick, South Carolina
    Designed 1884; built 1885
    Extant?
    (Sources: Brown Scrapbooks; McCormick
      Papers)

Classroom building, Thornwell Orphanage
                                         1884

    Clinton, South Carolina
    Designed 1884; built 1885
    No longer standing
    (Sources: Brown Scrapbooks; McCormick
      Papers)

Commercial building   1884

    McCormick, South Carolina
    Executed?
    (Source: McCormick Papers)

Cyrus McCormick Hall, Thornwell
   Orphanage   1884

    Clinton, South Carolina
    Designed 1884; built 1885
    Demolished ca. 1960
    (Sources: *Sanitary Engineer,* Nov. 12,
      1887; Brown Scrapbooks; McCormick
      Papers)

House   1884

    McCormick, South Carolina
    Extant?
    (Sources: Brown Scrapbooks; McCormick
      Papers)

McCormick Hall, Tusculum College   1884

    Greenville, Tennessee
    Designed 1884, modifying plans prepared
      by Minneapolis architect W. H. Hayes;
      built 1885
    Extant
    (Sources: Brown Scrapbooks, McCormick
      Papers)

Charles Alexander house, alterations   1885

    37 Ward Avenue, Rumson, New Jersey
    Extant, extensively altered
    (Sources: *BA,* Dec. 6, 1889; Brown Scrap-
      books; McCormick Papers)

William Fitzgerald house, alterations   1885

    Prospect Street, Litchfield, Connecticut
    Extensive remodeling of 1867 house
    Extant; altered beyond recognition 1930
    (Sources: Brown Scrapbooks; McCormick
      Papers)

Joseph Henry Plaque, Princeton University
                                         1885

    Princeton, New Jersey
    Destroyed 1920
    (Sources: Brown Scrapbooks; McCormick
      Papers)

Memorial Hall, Thornwell Orphanage   1885

    Clinton, South Carolina
    Built 1885–1889
    Burned 1904
    (Sources: *A&B,* Apr. 6, 1889; Brown
      Scrapbooks)

Recitation hall, Presbyterian College   1885

    Clinton, South Carolina
    Designed 1885; built 1885–1886
    Burned 1940s
    (Sources: *Sanitary Engineer,* Nov. 12,
      1887; Brown Scrapbooks; McCormick
      Papers)

Fowler Hall, McCormick Theological
   Seminary   1886

    Halsted Street and Fullerton Avenue,
      Chicago, Illinois
    Designed 1886; built 1887
    Demolished 1960s
    (Sources: *Sanitary Engineer,* July 9, 1887;
      IA, Dec. 1890; McCormick Papers)

Yaddo, Spencer Trask house, alterations 1886

    Saratoga Springs, New York
    Designed 1885–1886, extensive remodel-
      ing of existing residence
    Burned 1891; new house 1891–1893 by
      William Halsey Wood
    (Sources: *Sanitary Engineer,* Dec. 11,
      1886; Brown Scrapbooks; McCormick
      Papers)

Bethesda Episcopal Church, alterations 1887

    Washington Street near Broadway, Saratoga
      Springs, New York
    Additions to 1841 church by Richard
      Upjohn
    Extant
    (Sources: *A&B,* Apr. 7, 1888; *AABN,* Apr.
      5, 1890; Brown Scrapbooks; Brown

Scrapbooks CHS; McCormick Papers)

Class of '77 Biological Laboratory, Princeton
University   1887

Princeton, New Jersey
Designed 1887; built 1887–1888
Demolished
Cost: $12,000
(Sources: Brown Scrapbooks; Princeton
   Univ. archives)

Clio and Whig halls, Princeton University
                                              1887

Princeton, New Jersey
Whig Hall designed 1887–1888; plans
   acquired by Clio ca. 1890; both buildings erected 1890–1892, replacing two
   1838 buildings by John Haviland
Extant; Whig Hall burned 1960s, new interior designed by Gwathmey-Seigel
(Sources: Brown Scrapbooks; McCormick
   papers; Princeton Univ. archives)

McCormick Chapel, Park College   1887

Parkville, Missouri
Extensive redesign of design by John
   Oliver Hogg of Kansas City
Demolished 1930
(Sources: Brown Scrapbooks; Park College
   archives)

McCormick mausoleum, Graceland
Cemetery   1887

North Clark Street and Irving Park Road,
   Chicago, Illinois
Project; designed 1885–1887 in collabora-
   tion with Augustus Saint-Gaudens
(Sources: Brown Scrapbooks; McCormick
   Papers)

James McCosh house   1887

391 Nassau Street, Princeton, New Jersey
Designed 1887; built 1887–1888 at 33
   Prospect Street; moved to present loca-
   tion ca. 1913
Extant; altered in condominium conversion
   1980
(Sources: A&B, Apr. 27, 1889; Brown
   Scrapbooks)

Museum of Historic Art, Princeton
University   1887

Princeton, New Jersey
Designed 1886–1887; built 1888–1892,
   only portion of scheme executed
Demolished 1964

Cost: $50,000
(Sources: A&B, Sep. 8, 1888; Brown
   Scrapbooks; McCormick Papers; Prince-
   ton Univ. archives)

St. Peter's Episcopal Church   1887

Astor Avenue between Pontico and Pearl
   streets, Portchester, New York
Winning competition design 1887; built
   1889
Extant
Cost $60,000
(Sources: A&B, Apr. 21, 1888; Brown
   Scrapbooks; Brown Scrapbooks CHS;
   McCormick Papers)

William Berryman Scott house   1887

56 Bayard Lane, Princeton, New Jersey
Designed 1887; built 1887–1888
Extant; divided into two residences
(Sources: Brown Scrapbooks; Princeton
   Univ. archives)

William Brown house   1888?

Great Barrington, Massachusetts
Exact design date unknown
Burned ca. 1930s
(Sources: A&B, Feb. 2, 1889; July 6,
   1889; Brown Scrapbooks)

Clubhouse, Princeton University   1888?

Princeton, New Jersey
Project; exact design date unknown
(Source: A&B, Feb. 16, 1889)

Benevenuto, S. H. Janes house   1888

Avenue Road, Toronto, Ontario
Designed 1888; built 1889–1890; later
   additions
Demolished
(Sources: A&B, Oct. 6, 1888; BA, Dec.
   16, 1889; Toronto World, Oct. 25, 1889;
   Brown Scrapbooks)

Albert Dod Hall, Princeton University   1889

Princeton, New Jersey
Project; designed 1888–1889; executed
   building by John Faxon
(Source: Princeton Univ. archives)

Crocker mausoleum, Mountain View
Cemetery   1889

Oakland
Designed 1889; built 1889–1891
Extant
(Sources: AABN, Dec. 27, 1890; Ch, May

15, 1891; May 17, 1891)

Crocker Old People's Home   1889

2507 Pine Street, San Francisco
Designed 1889; built 1889–1890
Extant; third story and towers removed
Cost: $120,000
(Sources: *A&B*, July 27, 1889; *Ch*, July
14, 1889; Aug. 1, 1890; *Call*, Aug. 23,
1889; *SFNL*, Aug. 9, 1890; Brown
Scrapbooks)

C. F. Crocker tomb, Laurel Hill Cemetery
1889?

Presidio Avenue at Bush Street, San
Francisco
Exact design date unknown
Cemetery destroyed 1940
(Sources: *Ch*, Aug. 17, 1889; Brown
Scrapbooks)

Donohue Building   1889

Market, Golden Gate, and Taylor streets,
San Francisco
Designed 1889; built 1890–1891
Burned 1906
Cost $300,000
(Sources: *AABN*, Nov. 29, 1890; *Ch*, Dec.
15, 1889; May 3, 1891; *SFNL*, Aug. 15,
1891; Brown Scrapbooks)

Grace Episcopal Church, additions   1889

Stockton and California streets, San
Francisco
Designed 1889, additions included
entrance porch and tower to 1860–1862
building by William Patton; built 1890
Burned 1906
Cost $19,000
(Sources: *A&B*, June 25, 1892; *Ch*, Oct.
27, 1889; Apr. 4, 1890)

Hibernia Savings and Loan Society   1889

1 Jones Street, San Francisco
Competition entry; winning design by
Pissis & Moore
(Source: *AABN*, Feb. 7, 1891)

Pryor Memorial Church   1889?

Nottoway Court House, Virginia
Project; exact design date unknown
(Source: *A&B*, Sep. 21, 1889)

**St. Christina Home and School for Educating
Servants**   1889?

Ballston Avenue opposite Finley Avenue,

Saratoga Springs, New York
Exact design date unknown
Burned ca. 1970
(Sources: *A&B*, June 8, 1889; Brown
Scrapbooks; Brown Scrapbooks CHS)

St. Timothy's Church   1889?

Saratoga Springs, New York
Project; exact design date unknown
(Source: *BA*, Dec. 16, 1889)

James Coffin house   1890?

Shady Lane, Ross
Exact design date unknown
Demolished ca. 1940
(Source: Brown Scrapbooks)

The Country Club   1890

Shafter Ranch, Marin County
Probably a project
(Source: Brown Scrapbooks)

Crocker Building   1890

Market, Post, and Montgomery streets,
San Francisco
Designed 1889–1890; built 1890–1892
Demolished 1960s
Cost $1,400,000
(Sources: *AABN*, Aug. 16, 1890; July 22,
1893; *CABN*, Mar. 1893; *Ch*, Jan. 24,
1890; Brown Scrapbooks; Brown Scrap-
books CHS)

Mrs. Peter Donohue house   1890?

720 Broadway, San Francisco
Project; exact design date unknown;
appears to be for same client as house
designed in 1894
(Source: *A&B*, Sep. 6, 1890)

Frederick Ginn house   1890?

660 13th Street, Oakland
Exact design date unknown
Extant
(Source: Brown Scrapbooks; Brown Scrap-
books CHS)

**Speculative double house for Alexander
Hawes**   1890

Buchanan and Washington streets, San
Francisco
Designed 1890; built 1890–1891
No longer standing
Cost: $15,000
(Sources: *CABN*, Oct. 1890; *OM*, May
1893; Brown Scrapbooks)

Robert McLean house   1890

Pacific Avenue and Broderick Street, NE
corner, San Francisco
Designed 1890; built 1890–1891
Demolished ca. 1940s
Cost $30,000
(Sources: *Ch*, Oct. 24, 1890; *Wave*, July
18, 1891; *San Francisco Architecturally*;
Brown Scrapbooks)

W. N. Oothout house   1890?

704 East Butler Avenue, Fresno
Designed ca. 1890; built 1891–1892
according to new plans by Brown
Burned 1941
(Sources: *AABN*, Feb. 15, 1890; *Ch*, Jan.
22, 1892)

Alban Towne house   1890

1101 California Street, San Francisco
Designed 1890; built 1890–1891
Burned 1906; entrance portico salvaged
and re-erected in Golden Gate Park as
the Portals of the Past
Cost $80,000
(Sources: *A&B*, July 5, 1890; *AABN*, Feb.
6, 1892; *Ch*, July 11, 1890; Jan. 28,
1891; Feb. 27, 1891; *SFNL*, May 9,
1891; Brown Scrapbooks)

Alexander Maternity Cottage, Hospital for
Children and Training School for Nurses
                1891

3700 California Street, San Francisco
Designed 1890–1891; built 1891–1892
Demolished ca. 1960s
Cost $15,000
(Sources: *Ch*, Apr. 27, 1892; *Wave*, Dec.
19, 1891; Brown Scrapbooks CHS)

Crocker & Company lemon curer and
warehouse   1891

East Valley Road, Montecito
Extant; altered 1960s
(Sources: *A&B*, Dec. 5, 1891; *Ex*, Oct. 9,
1891; Brown Scrapbooks)

Grand Hotel, additions   1891

Market and New Montgomery streets, SE
corner, San Francisco
Work included rear café
No longer standing, presumably burned
1906
Cost $3,200
(Source: *Ch*, June 26, 1891)

Hahneman Hospital   1891

Lake Street, between 14th and 15th, San
Francisco
Project
Cost $100,000
(Source: Brown Scrapbooks CHS)

Edgar Mills house, additions   1891

California and Octavia streets, San
Francisco
No longer standing
Cost: $3,000
(Source: *Ch*, Oct. 16, 1891)

Palace Hotel, alterations   1891

Market and New Montgomery streets, SW
corner, San Francisco
Interior alterations to 1875 building,
included café and furnishings for reading
and writing room
Burned 1906
(Sources: *Ch*, July 3, 1891; Dec. 18, 1891)

St. John's Episcopal Church   1891

El Dorado and Miner streets, Stockton
Designed 1891; built 1891–1892
Extant
(Source: *A&B*, Nov. 28, 1891)

Sharon Building   1891

Mission and New Montgomery streets, San
Francisco
Designed 1891; built 1891–1892
Burned 1906
(Sources: *AABN*, Apr. 30, 1892; *Ch*, July
3, 1891; Sharon Papers)

Irwin Stump house, alterations   1891

1424 McAllister Street, San Francisco
New plans for unfinished house purchased
by client
No longer standing
(Source: *Ch*, Dec. 4, 1891)

Trinity Church   1891

1668 Bush Street, San Francisco
Winning competition design 1891; built
1892–1894
Extant
Cost: $105,000
(Sources: *AABN*, Nov. 3, 1894; *CABN*,
June 1892; *Ch*, Dec. 19, 1891; *Wave*,
Mar. 17, 1894; Brown Scrapbooks;
Brown Scrapbooks CHS)

University Club   1891

437

Sutter Street between Taylor and Jones,
San Francisco
Extensive alterations and additions to exist-
ing house for use as club; built 1891–
1892
Burned 1906
(Sources: *AABN*, Oct. 28, 1893; *Ch*, Apr.
24, 1891; July 23, 1891; Oct. 12, 1892;
Brown Scrapbooks)

Young Men's Christian Association   1891

Ellis and Mason streets, San Francisco
Designed 1891; built 1893–1894
Burned 1906
Cost $242,000
(Sources: *AABN*, Oct. 24, 1891; Apr. 20,
1895; *Ch*, July 3, 1891; Sep. 10, 1891;
Mar. 1, 1893; YMCA, *Annual Reports*,
1889–1894)

Atkinson Building   1892

Sutter Street, south side, west of Taylor,
San Francisco
Burned 1900
Extensive additions designed by Coxhead
c. 1902
Cost $11,000
(Sources: *AABN*, Sep. 30, 1893; *Ch*, June
15, 1892; *Wave*, Feb. 4, 1893; Brown
Scrapbooks; Coxhead Papers)

Bank of Nevada   1892?

241 Virginia Street, Reno, Nevada
Exact design date unknown
No longer standing
(Source: Gladding McBean Co. records)

California Building, World's Columbian
Exposition   1892

Jackson Park, Chicago, Illinois
Winning competition design 1892; built
1892–1893, P. B. Wight, supervising
architect
Demolished 1894
Cost $96,000
(Sources: *AABN*, July 30, 1892; *Ch*, Feb.
12, 1892; Apr. 20, 1892; Apr. 23, 1893;
Ex, Feb. 12, 1892; *Final Report of the
California World's Fair Commission;*
Brown Scrapbooks CHS)

Golden Gate Park facilities   1892

Golden Gate Park, San Francisco
Work included boat house and bridge on
Stow Lake, merry-go-round, and pump-
ing station
Bridge and merry-go-round extant; others

no longer standing
Cost: merry-go-round $3,500; pumping
station $10,900; bridge $7,000
(Sources: *A&B*, Oct. 1, 1892; *Ch*, Feb.
19, 1892; Feb. 20, 1892; Sep. 4, 1892;
Oct. 9, 1892; Oct. 12, 1892; Oct. 30,
1892; Jan. 4, 1893; Brown Scrapbooks)

Grand Market   1892

Lima, Peru
Executed?
(Sources: *A&B*, Dec. 12, 1892; *Ch*, Aug.
21, 1892; Brown Scrapbooks)

Jelly Palace, Women's Department exhibit,
California Building, World's Columbian
Exposition   1892

Jackson Park, Chicago
Project
Cost $2,400
(Sources: *Ch*, June 23, 1892; *Call*, Jan. 8,
1893)

Pacific Mutual Insurance Company Building
1892?

San Francisco
Project; exact design date unknown
(Source: *AABN*, June 18, 1892)

Palermo Hotel   1892

Palermo
No longer standing
Cost: $20,000
(Sources: *Ch*, Aug. 10, 1892; Oct. 12,
1892; Brown Scrapbooks)

Speculative houses for the Sharon Estate 1892

El Camino Real between Bellevue and
Floribunda avenues, Hillsborough
Designed 1892; built 1893
Three houses extant (50 Kammerer Court,
141 Pepper Hills Road, and 1615 Flori-
bunda Avenue); two houses demolished
Cost $6,000–$8,000 each
(Sources: *Ch*, Apr. 26, 1893; *Wave*, Feb.
1, 1893; Brown Scrapbooks)

Alban Towne house, additions   1892

1101 California Street, San Francisco
Addition to rear of house
Burned 1906
(Source: *Ch*, Nov. 10, 1892)

Burlingame Country Club   1893

Forest View Road, Hillsborough
Designed 1893; built 1893–1894;

purchased for residence 1898 with
subsequent major alterations
Demolished ca. 1945
Cost $16,000
(Sources: *Ch*, Oct. 15, 1898; *Wave*, Nov.
18, 1893; Apr. 7, 1894; Brown Scrapbooks; Brown Scrapbooks CHS)

California Midwinter International
Exposition   1893

Golden Gate Park, San Francisco
Work included: Administration Building,
Manufacturers and Liberal Arts Building
(both winning competition entries);
Agricultural Building, Fine Arts Build-
ing, Mechanical Arts Building (competi-
tion entries); Northern California Build-
ing (project); grandstand, Emergency
Hospital, and Festival Hall
Executed work demolished 1894
Cost: Admin. Bldg. $30,000; Manuf.
Bldg. $105,000; Ag. Bldg. $75,000;
Mech. Bldg. $85,000; Fine Arts Bldg.
$45,000; grandstand $8,800; Emergency
Hospital $1,100; Fest. Hall $17,000
(Sources: *AABN*, Nov. 4, 1893; *CABN*,
Jan. 1894; *OM*, Apr. 1894; *Ch*, Aug. 6,
1893; Aug. 25, 1893; Sep. 2, 1893;
Nov. 28, 1893; Jan. 15, 1894; *Official
History of the California Midwinter
International Exposition*)

California Midwinter International Exposition, master plan   1893

Designed in collaboration with Richard P.
Hammond
Project; executed plan probably by Michael
O'Shaughnessy
(Sources: *Call*, Aug. 16, 1893; *Ch*, Aug.
17, 1893)

Speculative houses for William Crocker 1893

California Street between Jones and Leav-
enworth, San Francisco
Project
(Sources: *Ch*, Mar. 25, 1893; *Wave*, Feb.
4, 1893; Mar. 25, 1893; Brown
Scrapbooks)

Hermann Oelrichs house   1893

Bellevue Avenue, Newport, Rhode Island
Project
(Sources: *Ch*, May 17, 1893; Brown
Scrapbooks)

Palace Hotel, alterations   1893

Market and New Montgomery streets, SW

corner, San Francisco
Work included new billiard room and
staircase
Burned 1906
(Source: *Ch*, Aug. 29, 1893)

Commercial building for the Parrott Estate
1893

835–865 Market Street, San Francisco
Project
Cost $1,000,000
(Sources: *Ch*, Apr. 18, 1893; *Wave*, Apr.
22, 1893)

Sainte Claire Club   1893

65 East St. James Street, San Jose
Designed 1893; built 1893–1894
Extant; minor alterations
Cost $36,500
(Sources: *AABN*, Feb, 1, 1896; *Ch*, Apr.
2, 1893)

Salem Presbyterian Church, Washington
College   1893?

Washington College, Tennessee
Exact design date unknown
Extant
(Source: Brown Scrapbooks)

San Francisco Polyclinic   1893

410 Ellis Street, San Francisco
Designed 1893; built 1894
Burned 1906
Cost $5,000
(Sources: *AABN*, July 21, 1894; *Ch*, Nov.
7, 1893; Feb. 17, 1895; Brown
Scrapbooks)

Southern Pacific Railroad
Station   1893

Burlingame Avenue and California Drive,
Burlingame
Project; several schemes submitted;
executed scheme 1894 by Mathisen &
Howard
(Source: Elliott Evans)

Union Depot and Ferry House   1893

The Embarcadero at Market Street, San
Francisco
Designed 1892–1893; built 1895–1898,
Edward R. Swain, supervising architect;
interior completed 1903; end sections
never executed
Extant; minor alterations
Cost $600,000

(Sources: *AABN*, Apr. 22, 1893; *CABN*,
Sep. 1895; Mar. 1898; *Ch*, Dec. 7,
1892; Jan. 20, 1893; Jan. 11, 1895; Jan.
2, 1898; Brown Scrapbooks; Brown
Scrapbooks CHS)

Book and Snake Society clubhouse   1894

High Street, New Haven, Connecticut
Project; executed building 1900 by R. H.
Robertson
(Sources: *Ch*, Dec. 23, 1901; Brown
Scrapbooks)

Burlingame Country Club stable   1894

Forest View Road, Hillsborough
No longer standing
(Source: *CABN*, Apr. 1894; Brown
Scrapbooks)

Castle Craig Tavern   1894

Dunsmuir
Burned 1900
(Sources: *Ch*, June 18, 1894; July 21,
1900)

California Hotel, alterations   1894

210 Montgomery Street, San Francisco
Work included dining and breakfast rooms,
eighth floor
Burned 1906
(Source: *Ch*, July 2, 1894)

Church of the New Jerusalem   1894

Jackson and Taylor streets, San Francisco
Project; church redesigned for new location
later in year
Cost $7,000
(Sources: *Ch*, Jan. 22, 1894; Feb. 5, 1894)

Church of the New Jerusalem   1894

2107 Lyon Street, San Francisco
Designed 1894; built 1894–1895
Extant
Cost church $4,500; parish house, $4,500
(Sources: *AABN*, Nov. 17, 1894; *SABE*,
Aug. 1899; *Craftsman*, Jun. 1906; *HB*,
Feb. 1901; *Ch*, Aug. 20, 1894; Aug. 27,
1894; Sep. 28, 1894; Apr. 7, 1901; *Call*,
Feb. 10, 1895; Apr. 1, 1896; Brown
Scrapbooks)

Talbot Clifton house   1894

Hillsborough
Project
(Sources: *Wave*, Oct. 20, 1894; Brown
Scrapbooks)

William Crocker house   1894

Forest View Road, Hillsborough
Designed 1894; built 1895
No longer standing
(Sources: *Ch*, Dec. 21, 1894; Mar. 7,
1895)

Speculative houses for William Crocker 1894

2010–2050 Garden Street, Santa Barbara
Five houses; extant
Cost $30,000 total
(Sources: *Ch*, June 18, 1894; Jan. 27,
1895; Brown Scrapbooks)

Michael de Young house, additions   1894

1919 California Street, San Francisco
Work included theater and ballroom
No longer standing, presumably burned
1906
Cost $10,000
(Sources: *CABN*, Feb. 1894; *Ch*, Jan. 22,
1894)

Mrs. Peter Donohue house   1894

720 Broadway, San Francisco
Designed 1894; built 1895–1896
No longer standing
(Sources: *CABN*, Sep. 1895; *IA*, July
1900; *Ch*, Dec. 21, 1894; Brown
Scrapbooks)

Frank Douty house   1894

Elm Avenue, east side between Tilton and
Monte Vista, San Mateo
No longer standing
(Sources: *Ch*, June 18, 1894; Brown
Scrapbooks)

Edward Eyre house   1894?

Menlo Park
Project?; exact design date unknown
(Sources: Brown Scrapbooks; CHS Library
[plans])

Joseph Grant house   1894

Forest View Road, Hillsborough
Designed 1894; built 1894–1895; exten-
sively altered 1899
Burned 1909
(Sources: *AABN*, June 8, 1895; *Wave*, Feb.
23, 1895)

William Randolph Hearst house, alterations
1894

Sausalito

Project; extensive remaking of existing residence
(Sources: *TT*, Apr. 7, 1894; Brown Scrapbooks)

Inn   1894

San Mateo
Project
(Source: Brown Scrapbooks)

Morris Lowenthal house   1894

2226 Sacramento Street, San Francisco
Appears to be extant and greatly altered
Cost $6,800
(Sources: *Ch*, Aug. 20, 1894; Aug. 27, 1894)

Mark Hopkins Institute of Art, alterations
                                                              1894

California and Mason streets, SE corner, San Francisco
Alterations to stable of 1878 house converted to new quarters of San Francisco Art Association 1893
Burned 1906
(Sources: *Ch*, May 28, 1894; July 9, 1894)

Riverside Hotel   1894?

101–105 South Virginia Street, Reno, Nevada
Project; exact design date unknown; hotel erected on site ca. 1898, possibly adaptation of later plans by Brown
(Source: Brown Scrapbooks)

George Roe house   1894?

San Francisco
Project; exact design date unknown
(Source: Brown Scrapbooks)

William Sharon tomb, Laurel Hill Cemetery
                                                              1894

Presidio Avenue at Bush Street, San Francisco
Designed 1894; built 1895
Cemetery destroyed 1940
Cost $1,500
(Sources: *AABN*, July 6, 1895; *Ch*, July 5, 1895)

Commercial building for Mrs. Frank Sullivan
                                                              1894

Grant Avenue and Sutter Street, SW corner, San Francisco
Project
Cost $200,000

(Source: *SF Daily Report*, June 11, 1894)

Alhambra Theater   1895

835 Main Street, Redwood City
Destroyed 1906
Cost $10,000
(Sources: *Ch*, Jan. 21, 1896; *Redwood City Democrat*, July 18, 1895)

A. Page Brown house   1895?

813 Sharon Road, Hillsborough
Designed ca. 1895 for architect's residence, possibly intended for a different site; design executed 1897 for Francis Carolan by Frank Van Trees
Extant; altered
(Source: *Ch*, Jan. 5, 1897)

Builder's Exchange of San Francisco   1895

40 New Montgomery Street
Burned 1906
Cost $6,800
(Sources: *CABN*, Dec. 1895; *Ch*, June 30, 1895; Sep. 27, 1895; *Handbook of Builders' Exchange*, 1895–1896)

California Building   1895

Sutter and Grant streets, San Francisco
Third story added from plans by Brown same year
Burned 1906
Cost $40,000; addition $10,000
(Sources: *CABN*, Aug. 1895; *Ch*, Apr. 7, 1895; Apr. 12, 1895)

Cliff House   1895

1090 Point Lobos Avenue, San Francisco
Schematic design prepared at request of *SF Examiner*
(Source: *Ex*, Jan. 6, 1895)

University Club, ladies' annex   1895

Sutter Street between Taylor and Jones, San Francisco
Burned 1906
Cost $15,000
(Source: *Ch*, June 7, 1895; *Ex*, Nov. 3, 1895)

Otto Greenwald house   1895

1812 Van Ness Avenue, San Francisco
Designed 1895; construction begun 1895–1896; Polk hired to complete house 1898
No longer standing; probably burned 1906
Cost $30,000
(Sources: *CABN*, Jan. 1896; *Ch*, Aug. 30,

1895; Mar. 27, 1898)

Richard Queen house 1895

2212 Sacramento Street, San Francisco
Designed 1895; built 1895–1896
Extant
Cost $35,000
(Sources: *CABN*, July 1895; *Ch*, Aug. 22, 1895; Dec. 4, 1896)

Speculative houses for Chevy Chase Land and Improvement Company 1895?

Chevy Chase, Maryland
Project; exact design date unknown
(Source: Brown Scrapbooks)

A. C. SCHWEINFURTH

Charles Dennison house 1890

Denver, Colorado
No longer standing
Cost $20,000
(Sources: *WABN*, Feb. 1890; *AN*, Jan. 1891; *BB*, July 1894)

Lewis Lemen house 1890

1601 Pennsylvania Street, Denver, Colorado
Demolished 1961
Cost $50,000
(Sources: *WABN*, Feb. 1890; *BB*, Jan. 1906)

E. F. Thomas house 1890

Denver, Colorado
Extant?
Source: *WABN*, Feb. 1890

House 1893

Santa Barbara
Project
(Source: *CABN*, Apr. 1894; Architectural League of New York, *Catalogue*, 1893)

Hotel 1894

near Montalvo
Project
(Source: *CABN*, Apr. 1894)

Hacienda del Pozo de Verona, William Randolph Hearst-Phoebe Apperson Hearst house 1895

Foothill Road, near Sunol, Alameda County

Designed and built 1895 for W.R.H.; additions and minor alterations 1896 for P.A.H.; later additions by Frank Van Trees and Julia Morgan; converted to Castlewood Country Club 1924 with numerous subsequent alterations
Burned 1969
(Sources: *AABN*, May 2, 1896; Dec. 23, 1905; *SABE*, July 1900; *Country Life In America*, Oct. 1904; *Ch*, Feb. 4, 1900; *Wave*, Mar. 13, 1897; Ferree, *American Homes and Gardens;* Garnett, *Stately Homes of California*)

Little Jim Ward, Hospital for Children and Training School for Nurses 1895

Sacramento Street, west of Maple, San Francisco
Cost $17,000
Demolished ca. 1950s
(Sources: *CABN*, Jan. 1896; *Ch*, Apr. 19, 1895; *Call*, Dec. 22, 1895; Hospital for Children, *Annual Report*, 1895)

James Bradford house 1896

2516 Union Street, San Francisco
Extant; extensive alterations 1955 by John Funk
(Source: *Ch*, Oct. 30, 1896)

Examiner Building 1896

691–699 Market Street, San Francisco
Project; extensive alterations and additions to Nucleus Building; plans abandoned 1897 for new building on site
(Sources: *Ch*, Sep. 25, 1896; Jan. 22, 1897)

Eye and Ear Ward, Hospital for Children and Training School for Nurses 1896

Sacramento Street, west of Maple, San Francisco
Designed 1896, scheme similar to Little Jim Ward; built 1896–1897
Demolished ca. 1950s
Cost $19,000
(Sources: *CABN*, Aug. 1896; Hospital for Children, *Annual Reports*, 1897–1898)

Hearst mausoleum, Cypress Lawn Cemetery 1896

El Camino Real, Colma
Designed 1896; uncertain if executed building by A. C. or Julius Schweinfurth
Extant
(Sources: *Call*, Apr. 26, 1896; Phoebe Hearst Papers)

James Ward house   1896

2700 Broadway, San Francisco
Extant; extensive alterations ca. 1920s
Cost $17,000
(Sources: *CABN*, June 1896; *Ex*, July 30,
  1896)

Weltevreden, Volney Moody house   1896

1725 LeRoy Avenue, Berkeley
Designed 1896; built 1896–1897
Extant; extensively altered for fraternity
  house in 1950s by Michael Goodman
(Sources: *SABE*, Oct. 1898; *Ch*, Nov. 6,
  1896)

Examiner Building   1897

691–699 Market Street, San Francisco
Designed 1897; built 1897–1898
Burned 1906
(Sources: *AABN*, Feb. 19, 1898; *Ch*, Feb.

12, 1897)

Nurses' Home, Hospital for Children and
  Training School for Nurses   1897

Sacramento and Maple streets, SW corner,
  San Francisco
Designed 1897; built 1898–1899
Demolished ca. 1950s
Cost $15,500
(Sources: *Ch*, July 9, 1897; Hospital for
  Children, *Annual Report*, 1899)

First Unitarian Church   1898

Bancroft Way and Dana Street, NE corner,
  Berkeley
Extant; owned by Univ. of Calif. and used
  as rehearsal hall
Cost $5,100
(Sources: *Berkeley World-Gazette*, Nov.
  14, 1898; church records)

INDEX

Figure numbers are given in italics following page numbers. Complete references to buildings are given under the name of the building; buildings are cross-referenced under the cities in which they are located.

450

Printed in the United States
47974LVS00002B/5-8

9 780520 214156